RONALD ARONSON was born in Detroit in 1938. He studied at
Wayne State University, Detroit, and at UCLA, and obtained
his doctorate in the History of Ideas from Brandeis University,
where he was a pupil of Herbert Marcuse, in 1968. Professor
of Humanities in the University Studies/Weekend College
Programme at Wayne State, Aronson is author of the study,
Jean-Paul Sartre: Philosophy in the World (Verso, 1980).
He is preparing a study, *Sartre's Second Critique.* He has
received fellowships from the National Endowment for the
Humanities and the American Council of Learned Societies.

Ronald Aronson

Verso

The Dialectics of Disaster

A Preface to Hope

Earlier versions of some chapters of this book appeared in *Socialist Review*, *Social Text* and as *Technological Madness: Towards a Theory of the Impending Nuclear Holocaust*, London 1982.

First published 1983
© Ronald Aronson 1983

Verso Editions
15 Greek Street London W1V 5LF

Filmset in Souvenir by
Comset Graphic Designs

Printed by
The Thetford Press Limited
Thetford, Norfolk

ISBN 0 86091 075 X
          775 4 Pbk

Contents

To the memory of my parents
Saul and Helen Aronson,
for my children
Pamela and Nina,
and for their children
and all the children to come

Preface

Is there reason to hope today? This question was the starting point for a course given to a group of adult workers at Wayne State University's Monteith College in spring 1976. The instructors, Charles Rooney and myself, sought to address our students' cynicism by presenting a historical sketch of this century which would explore some of its worst catastrophes and greatest struggles. Rooney and I decided we had something to say against the prevailing wind and that we would, consequently, write a book about hope today. The first fruits of this collaboration turned out to be a profession of our faith: that social change leading to a better world was still possible. We started back through the manuscript, realizing that we had nowhere directly confronted the despair it implied and opposed. A book about hope today must first address the reasons for cynicism, we realised. But not long afterwards, our collaboration began to feel the consequences of the university's decision to close Monteith College. Leaving the university, Rooney soon after left his active participation in this project. He remained tied to it as co-author of many of its ideas, purposes, lines of study and even words, but it nevertheless became my own study of catastrophe and hope.

I have talked with dozens and dozens of people about the project, and have received nearly universal encouragement and support. The question of hope, as *question*, as *our collective question* today, touches something deep in nearly everyone I have talked with, and invariably leads to discussions which enrich and extend my thinking.

I have also had the opportunity to present many of these analyses more formally, in the Senior Seminar of Wayne State University's Weekend College, as well as at its weekend conferences, at the university's History Department Forum, before the Western Social

x

Science Association, the Radical Philosophers' Association and the International Conference on the Holocaust and Genocide, as well as to the Jewish Parents' Institute of Detroit and New Jewish Agenda. The American Jewish Committee made possible my first trip to Israel and heard my observations on my return. In these presentations I have not always won agreement, but I have always learned from the opportunities to test my ideas.

It has been taxing and difficult, this wrestling with the Devil, and I have more than once despaired that my powers were not equal to the task. But each time I realized that my despair was induced by the events I sought to understand, not by personal weakness. There are indeed so many current reasons for despair. But at crucial moments history intervened: the achievement of majority rule in Zimbabwe, the victory of the Sandinistas in Nicaragua, the eruption of Solidarity, the electoral victories of Mitterand and Papandreou, the massive anti-nuclear demonstrations in Western Europe and the United States, the appearance of the Israeli peace movement. Each event, for all its reversibility, incompleteness and unresolved questions, became another answer to the question I was asking.

Over these years I have been blessed with friends, comrades and colleagues who have not left me alone in the often-difficult and painful search for hope. Collectively, I must say, they have made possible the book that follows.

Accordingly, I have many people to thank. Phyllis Aronson lived with the man obsessed with walking through the Valley of Death for these seven years, and tolerated, encouraged and helped him. Steve Golin read two drafts of the manuscript and gave me his best—an illuminating, committed, loving critique which, as always, helped me to find my voice. Ernst Benjamin talked with me about many of my ideas, often contributing decisively with his penetrating intellect and cogent formulations. Saul Wellman helped me to connect this intellectual project to our common political praxis, and gave me his deeply caring and loyal support. Richard Schmitt read the manuscript and raised a number of penetrating questions which I have done my best to resolve. Dianne Hansen typed the manuscript with her customary speed, accuracy and good cheer. The administration of Weekend College has helped me in large and small ways, in the process of becoming a model institutional home for committed scholarship.

In addition, the following people talked with me, encouraged me, read parts of the manuscript, and were collectively indispensable to what follows: Robert Deneweth, Anson Rabinbach, George Mosse, Christopher Johnson, Israel Charny, Anthony Rudolf, Ronald Santoni, William McBride, Douglas Kellner, Susan Wells, Miriam Jerris, Tony Rothschild, David Herreshoff, Perry Anderson, Kenneth Waltzer, Lenore Goldman, Fred Lessing, Joseph Walsh, Jim Jacobs, Diana Kuper, Helen Samberg, Dian Wilkins, Hillel Schenker, Francis Mulhern, Mark Shapiro, Robert Bailey, David Levey, Nabeel Abraham, Melvin Small, Lisa Blum, Evelyn Millstein.

Wayne State University
Detroit
September 1983

I
Introduction

1
Catastrophe and Hope

Is there reason to hope today? This is an appropriate question for the final years of the twentieth century because the shadow of death hangs over us all, because revolutionary expectations have been so thwarted, because the century has been a charnel house. Over 100 million human beings have been killed in our century: shot, bombed, starved, gassed, destroyed more slowly by the famine and disease that follow mass killing. Our world is characterized by technology, revolution—and death. The nearly absolute silence about the last is as deafening today as the talk about the others.

In an exceptional book, Gil Elliot remarks: 'The scale of man-made death is the central moral as well as material fact of our time.'[1] We have created a veritable world of the dead in the twentieth century that rivals the world of the living in size and meaning.

In the world of the living, asking about hope is appropriate also because so many of us have lived through the destruction of revolutionary expectations, have seen our faith shattered that human beings could create and dwell in the peaceable kingdom. So much love, so much caring, so much revolutionary fervour have been stirred, and then dashed, by the Soviet Union, then China, then Cuba, then Vietnam, as well as by movements gone awry in the advanced industrial world. It is not just that hope for a better life has repeatedly met defeat, but that defeat has again and again become disaster, encouraging committed and courageous millions to let their commitment and courage lapse into cynicism. Certainly the strength and victories of the various powers that be can produce despair; but it is the apparent self-corruption of our inspirations which has led to an even more profound and far-reaching despair among those who might be expected to seek change. What is left to say when good intentions produce great evil? If, for example, Soviet socialism is the meaning of socialism, then why struggle for it? And if not, then what other inspiring models have emerged in the hundred years since Marx died?

Moreover, so much of what has been humanly positive in our century—the struggles of trade unions for workers' dignity in the capitalist West, for example—seems today inseparable from its own negative side. Unions may indeed protect their workers as never before, but many of them have become vast bureaucracies committed to smoothly managing the process of production, have developed their own stake in economic and social waste and irrationality, and relate to their constituency as clients rather than as members. Even where it is most genuine, progress often seems to bring its own regress, offsetting its own achievements.

It is also appropriate to ask about hope because the advanced industrial societies seem to have reached the end of a historic phase of accelerated economic growth, because the poorest and hungriest countries seem to have become locked into their poverty and hunger, and because the whole world is approaching fundamental ecological limits which must redefine 'the good life' that we expect, covet and defend. As the eighties unfold it becomes depressingly clear to what extent hope has been based on the expectation of ever-expanding economies.

Yet in spite of all these reasons for abandoning hope, the question about reason to hope has an odd ring to almost anyone who has been formed within our dominant culture and is thus committed (even in spite of themselves) to see the world in terms of the march of human progress. It has an unaccustomed ring, indeed, even after the recent chorus of doubts. For example, in the 1970s two established scholars with left-wing orientations created sensations by publishing books whose effect was to doubt the very possibility of hope. Robert Heilbroner, author of *The Human Prospect*,[2] and Christopher Lasch, author of *The Culture of Narcissism*,[3] both wrote against their own traditions and argued that basic transformations were creating a dark prospect for the long term. Their books were unusual studies, courageous for thinking against the grain, admirable for following their analyses to pessimistic conclusions, and both were widely read and discussed. Certainly since its beginning there have been profound critics of the modern world who have attacked its 'dark satanic mills'. What distinguished Heilbroner and Lasch from earlier writers like

Blake and Baudelaire, the Symbolist poets and Nietzsche was that they wrote as scholars of the contemporary world and not as poets and philosophers hostile to 'progress' and determined to voice its dark side. What spoke through them was not an older aesthetic sense and spirit of vitality protesting against the industrial order, but the modern world itself, its very spirit of scientific analysis and anticipation of human betterment. Their writing had the effect of being a reflection by the mainstream on itself, informing us about the end of progress.

As it turned out Heilbroner and Lasch were not lone voices but part of the new dominant chorus as it took shape in the 1970s—including 'neoconservatives' and 'new' philosophers—whose doubts and forebodings about the future, for the first time since the Enlightenment, overwhelmed its hopes. 'Disbelief, doubt, disillusionment and despair have taken over', wrote Robert Nisbet in 1980, '—or so it would seem from our literature, art, philosophy, theology, even our scholarship and science.'[4] For this historian of progress, our period is 'almost barren of faith in progress'.[5]

If this 'mood of the 1970s' was the most pessimistic trend of sophisticated opinion in over two centuries, its great notoriety stemmed from the fact that the chorus both voiced a widespread public mood *and* attacked dominant assumptions. But it is notable that this scepticism has not been absorbed and transmuted into a compelling philosophy. Dominant social and characterological structures and values remain officially organized around progress. No matter how widespread, the doubt remains a personal one, never directly challenging the prevailing faith. Today our societies, and whatever oppositions they continue to generate, remain overwhelmingly committed to the old assumptions. For all our doubts we are unable to shed these assumptions easily—whether they are nourished by a continuing commitment to the steady advance of technology, the spread of modernization and enlightenment, the slow victory of democracy or the struggle for socialism. They structure our very perceptions. We possess no equally compelling alternative vision. Yet such rose-coloured lenses make it remarkably difficult to sustain appropriate perspectives for viewing the present, and thus to live in our minds the real life our century has forced us to live in fact.

The Dialectics of Hope

Is there reason to hope? Hope itself is not a given, but an attitude with its own history. As A. O. Lovejoy described it, the hope embodied in the idea of progress sees, 'a tendency inherent in nature or man to pass through a regular sequence of stages of development in the past, the present and the future, the latter stages being—with perhaps occasional retardations or regressions—superior to the earlier.'[6] Nisbet explains 'superior' as meaning improvement in knowledge and in 'man's moral or spiritual condition on earth, his happiness, his freedom from torments of nature and society, and above all his serenity or tranquility.'[7] Today this means that, as Heilbroner points out, industrial societies and all those whose orientation is influenced by them—meaning, today, every society—share the bourgeois or Marxist commitment to a steadily bettering life based on industrialization and modernization. They place their hopes in the growth of the industrial system and the concomitant development of human powers. In the Marxist variant the working class, limited and exploited by the narrow class relations within which the growth of productive and human powers takes place, slowly struggles to consciousness of its vital need to abolish class society. In Ernst Bloch's formulation, humanity becomes the material of hope.

As the foremost philosophy of hope of the industrial era Marxism anticipates both more than the bourgeois hope, and a qualitatively different kind of hope. As Bloch put it: 'Once man has comprehended himself and has established his own domain in real democracy, without depersonalization and alienation, something arises in the world which all men have glimpsed in childhood: a place and a state in which no one has yet been. And the name of this something is home or homeland.'[8]

Marxism takes account of the pain and struggle of the present. It analyses present trends, both positive and negative, and presents a path for action towards future goals. As such, Marxism captured the dialectics of hope for an earlier period both by expressing the age-old human longing for an alternative to a life of pain and suffering, and by showing this alternative to be a realistic tendency issuing from the present. For the first time in history Marxism made the other world of dreams and longings into a project to be struggled for in *this* world.

Yet if Marxism was a philosophy of hope, Marx *a fortiori* never had to inquire about whether there was *reason* to hope. Given his Hegelian, progress-oriented cast of mind and the earth-shaking developments of his time, he simply looked at industrializing Manchester and revolutionary Paris to see the dialectics of hope at work.

To ask, today, about reason to hope is to confess to the crisis of our world and to underscore the inability of the Marxian or any other readily available vision to point the way to hope in the final decades of the twentieth century. To search in theory is to assume an absence in reality. The seemingly short-range detours of history, its many aporias, its catastrophes, its modulations of good into evil, have accumulated to a point beyond being 'accommodated', as new astronomical discoveries once were by the Ptolemaic world-view—i.e. by yet another ingenious effort to 'save the phenomena' and preserve the original construct with another epicycle. Yet the widespread doubts of today undermine hope itself without sweeping away the old reflexes. It is necessary, then, to ask about reasons to hope, meeting all the burdens that the question implies.

A dialectics of hope today must not accept as given the assumptions of an earlier period; it must ask, rather, whether and how far there has been human progress. What positive directions, if any, can we conclude and project, and can these be separated from the negative? The positive and negative tendencies of the present must be placed in an analysis which comprehends them and, where possible, suggests alternative paths. And finally, today's dialectics of hope must suggest lines of possibility as well, in the process exploring the present and future meaning of the major path of hope, socialism. But (this several-volume programme notwithstanding) the dialectics of hope needs to begin above all at the beginning, with the beleaguered tone of the question itself. *Is* there reason to hope today? This implies something so deeply askew, so fundamentally troubling, as to acknowledge how flimsy have become our previous hopeful assumptions. And no wonder. The very first step, the preface to hope, demands coming to terms with the inferno of our century. It must be based on a dialectics of disaster.

Inferno

For 100 million people, perhaps one out of every hundred people who have lived in this century, Doomsday has happened. Death—untimely, violent, human-made death on a scale never before possible—has become one of the keys to our civilization.

Ten million people died in the First World War, with the indecisive battle of Verdun alone costing 700,000 casualties and the Somme a million. The Turks massacred nearly a million Armenians. In the early 1930s the building of socialism in the Soviet Union involved the death of perhaps 10 million peasants; as many as another 10 million died during the Purges, mostly in forced labour camps. The Second World War in Europe killed more than 40 million, including 6 million Jews. The Asian Second World War killed perhaps 20 million in the twenty years from the Japanese invasion of China through to the victory of the Chinese Revolution.[9]

Doomsday has its own history in our century. Most of the dead in the First World War were soldiers at the battlefield: to the degree that *All Quiet on the Western Front* reflects their experience, it describes a turning point in human history. Launched on every side as a noble and heroic cause, the war quickly became a purposeless machine of mass death seemingly beyond the control of those caught up in it. It ground on relentlessly, killing six thousand soldiers a day for four years. The Russian Civil War added two features to the century of mass slaughter. It was an explicitly ideological war: social systems were at stake, not nations or national groups. Not only did both sides shoot prisoners, consequently, but civilians became partisans and victims in vast numbers. If, as Elliot says, 'the foundations of massive military attrition were laid in the First World War', the Russian Civil War did the same for massive civilian attrition, 'and on precisely the same scale'.[10] This included the 'bread war' of 1918, in which the peasants settled old resentments toward many of those who had abused them; starvation caused by the large-scale breakdown of social life during the war; influenza and typhus epidemics; and the famine caused by peasants who reduced by one-half the areas sown with grain. The Soviets, and later the Nazis, introduced a new mass-death instrument: forced-labour camps in which people worked to death on skimpy rations and without adequate clothing or shelter. The Nazis took another step into the inferno by deliberately gassing and shooting millions, creating a world of death as an end in itself. During the war the British and Americans added massive aerial fire-bombing to the twentieth-century techniques of mass killing. The

United States went further by using atomic bombs and later (in Vietnam) by developing and using defoliants and anticivilian weapons such as napalm and CBUs, and by perfecting automated air warfare.

If 100 million people have been killed, more than half of those have died directly at the hands of their adversaries, while the remainder have died by the increase in famine and disease emanating from mass killing (unanticipated at first, now quite predictable). If perhaps one of every hundred people alive in this century has been thus killed, we can only be awestruck by the possible total number who have experienced the inferno: the diseased but not dead, the wounded survivors, the comrades and relatives of the living, the surviving inhabitants of the ghettos, concentration camps, battlefields, and cities under siege. Do the afflicted survivors outnumber the dead by ten, or by twenty-five to one? Whatever the number, an astoundingly high proportion of people have *experienced* Doomsday—not just death, but the destruction of their immediate world and the permanent affliction of their memories.

Achieving this on such a colossal scale has required both human and technical preparation. The First World War began the process of brutalization that would make mass murder humanly thinkable. It is in the decades since that the technical and organizational capability for mass murder has reached its full flowering. Mass murders presuppose a mood of total warfare, a brutalized population which accepts the need to 'save' itself, suitable weaponry, and organizational procedures to rapidly identify, process, and kill enormous numbers of enemy people. And so, today, we are prepared. We hover on the edge of oblivion, waiting—perhaps protesting—as total warfare is brought to perfection. The many Doomsdays point towards an ultimate one as the refinement, production and deployment of nuclear weapons continues and the strategists lay plans for their use in combat.

Inferno and Hope

Can we speak of hope today, then, without allowing these facts into our speech? If not, we lie, our optimism trivialized by denial. Its landscape reminds us that we live in a historical period for which we have not been prepared, where hope itself appears more as an unquestioned reflex than a meaningful anticipation, a period characterized as much by mass murder as by progress, which demands we describe it using terms like *evil* and *madness*. If it is to be authentic today hope can no longer remain an unquestioned term, an assumption. It must rather be restored, if this is indeed possible, by first wrestling with the Devil of the holocausts—the Nazi, the Communist, the bourgeois-democratic[11] and the universal holocaust. The paradox of this study reflects the reality—beleaguered, hope calls for a contemporary statement which cannot even be begun until we have come to grips with our century's disasters. If a preface to hope is possible, its site can only be in the Valley of Death.

Hope is a way of acting. It implies more than faith, need or dream. As action it is objective claim and subjective anticipation: referring always to real possibilities whose roots are planted here, in this ground, even if it be the Valley of Death. In his study of the subjective terrain of hope, Ernst Bloch never permitted himself to unlearn his Marxism: in the deepest sense hope always depends on events.[12] Humans may irrepressibly project a field of images, dreams, desires—but the real-world prospects for realizing them are decisive.

Yet to call our century one of revolution, technology *and death* is to acknowledge the cloud that has stolen over all political analysis and action. That Doomsday cloud casts a shadow of absurdity on our efforts to live, work and struggle as before, as if life could be so easily normalized after the catastrophes. We continue unmindful, ritualistically—seeking out prospects and tendencies for the betterment of life, looking for ways to intervene positively, treating the world as if it were not grotesquely skewed. The same course after the Holocaust as before? Yet what alternative is there (except withdrawal) to continuing as usual, resting on accustomed but petrified premisses, and using accustomed but blunted tools?

The purpose of this study is to begin to construct an alternative. Yet we cannot help but begin rather like Serenus Zeitblom in Thomas Mann's *Doctor Faustus*: a witness of catastrophe, trying to reflect on it even as he shakes and trembles, trying to return the world to its normal categories even as he describes its falling apart. The catastrophe is morally, politically, emotionally and intellectually too much to grasp; yet he wrestles with his own corner of it, driven by a desperate need to tell the story. Indeed, the first lesson of the catastrophes should be to let ourselves be derailed, rather like Serenus. Just let the facts sink in: what seemed to be the world's most advanced country—with its highly

developed capitalism and equally developed working class—under
great stress created the monster-movement of Nazism with its paroxysms of power and degradation; in its isolation the revolution which
was truly the hope of humanity made its people into the enemy of the
people, accordingly killing and enslaving one in every six of them on
its great path to industrial and military progress; and the world's
richest, freest, most powerful postwar society, out of the success of its
normal functioning as a bourgeois democracy, saw fit to virtually
destroy a small, backward Asian society while trying to remake it in its
own image. These catastrophic events demand to be noticed, and
their impact *felt*. Then, their lessons may be learned.

Why?

These three examples—the Holocaust, Stalinism, and the American
war in Vietnam—command the stage of this study. There are, alas,
other candidates but these three have dominated the consciousness of
our century for good reason: one by its colossal barbarity and all-but
unspeakable results; another by its murder of hope along with humanity in a process of construction: and the third because of its David-
Goliath encounter.

A preface to hope which leads us through this Valley of Death must
paint its evil *as* evil. On the twisted trees, the bombed-out buildings,
the heaps of rubble, the piles of bones and teeth, is written everywhere
the question found and scratched all over the Gulag by Old
Bolsheviks: *Zachto*—Why?

Why? is the appropriate question for a humanity caught up in the
ruins without knowing it, dominated by past Doomsdays yet unable to
tear itself away from the path to the next and final one. We must sift in
the ashes and understand why these events happened, because otherwise we will be little wiser about which paths to follow and which to
avoid, which dynamics poison societies and which liberate them.

To ask why means to avoid both the demonizers—who would raise
Doomsday beyond the human—and the trivializers, who would integrate it as one more fact into the network of facts amidst which we
make our way. It is to look for the human beings who are responsible
for these heinous human acts. Again and again in our century, evil has
been a *praxis*—the conscious, deliberate project of human collec-

tivities. Understanding it means studying the social structures and dynamics out of which humans acted to destroy other humans by the millions. What kinds of societies, what social stresses and contradictions, produced mass murder?

This study will ask then, to what extent a shared history, social process, set of attitudes generated all three disasters. I will focus in turn on the striking impotence, the madness, and the choice of evil of those holding state power.

We must return to our starting point: in spite of everything, is there reason to hope? Can anyone any longer retain faith in the progress of democracy, socialism, modernity? In humanity? And if not, what lessons of hope can be drawn from the century? Certainly we may each preserve our own images—of the Kronstadt rebels fighting and dying for the proletarian revolution, say; of Trotsky resisting Stalin until his last breath; of the insurrection at Treblinka which destroyed that death camp; of the stars of David with which Jewish soldiers decorated Hitler's looted and bombed-out retreat at Berchtesgaden; of the Vietnamese fighting from tunnels to withstand B-52 bombings. But do such images stand for any more than a subjective and Sisyphean commitment to keep on, no matter what? Or are they irreducible acts of resistance from which any future hope begins?

Conclusions

One inescapable conclusion is that our century's catastrophes have transformed the field of possibilities. Every positive possibility, every progressive tendency, now has an explicit alternative—the abyss. And the abyss now contains familiar paths and shapes, not merely the ominous, imponderable threat of I-know-not-what. We need not *imagine* or *guess* at the results of nuclear war; as Jonathan Schell has pointed out, we have *information* and *testimony* about it. We know what the worst is like—at Auschwitz, at Hiroshima, at Kolyma, at My Lai.

Another conclusion is that the worst can be done in the name of socialism and democracy as well as in the name of the Master Race, that it can be done, indeed, in the name of survival and revolution as well as of racist oppression. Claiming universal human improvement, Stalinism destroyed differently from Nazism, but on such a colossal scale that it is the destruction and not the difference which stands out.

Events have proved the negative currents of history to be no less real than the positive, and sometimes more so. Jewish ex-Communist survivors on Israeli kibbutzim overlooked by the now-silent bunkers of the Golan Heights speak of the death of internationalism at Auschwitz, of the need to protect 'our own' even if against all of humanity. The main task today may therefore be particular survival rather than universal justice, in a world where barbarism is so palpably real. Isn't this the meaning of a 'Never Again' which, in addition to genuine self-defence, justifies to the continued repression of Palestinians by Jews?

I remain convinced of the force of Rosa Luxemburg's prediction that the future paths of humanity are socialism or barbarism; but alas, our world is not so simple. We cannot avoid the question Luxemburg could only begin to conceive: what if socialism itself develops in ways that are barbaric? Marx articulated perhaps the most sophisticated notion of progress—one which included the sense of contradiction and bitter conflict as the very motor of advancement, the negative as a source of human social growth. But our history shows even this view to be overly sanguine, shows social reality to be more obstinate and explosive than anyone formed in the Enlightenment tradition could ever have imagined.

The Death of Progress

'But in contemplating history as the slaughter-bench at which the happiness of peoples, the wisdom of States, and the virtue of individuals have been sacrificed, a question necessarily arises: To what principle, to what final purpose, have these monstrous sacrifices been offered?'[13] Hegel's answer rested on Progress: 'The events which make up this picture of gloomy emotion and thoughtful reflection are only the means for realizing the essential destiny, the absolute and final purpose, or, what amounts to the same thing, the true result of world history.'[14] Today, the Holocaust has cancelled Progress. It has put human beings in a new situation, one which allows no faith in a transcendent and saving law. Progress was a kind of secular religion, a congenial faith for those who had abandoned God as well as for those who had not.[15] Progress capitalized implies that there are great forces at work improving the world despite our own limited consciousness or our destructive acts, be those forces divine or human in nature. As they eventually draw all of humanity along with them, suffering becomes redeemed as sacrifice en route to a better world.

To capitalize Progress reflects well its reified, hypostatized status, severing it from its human agents and raising it beyond them. Even while claiming to base itself on human beings, Marxism accommodates their relapses, reversions and resistances—all of which ultimately point forward again—but not their mad, wanton destruction. Germany, the Jews and the world did not move 'forward' because of Hitler. The Soviet Union's modernization under Stalin could by no standard be said to 'require' the massacres and brutalization accompanying it. Neither set of events can be described as a temporary regression along the basically positive human path: so great is their scale, their sheer weight on the conscience and consciousness of the survivors, that they must annul forever any laws of human advancement.

Such events demand that we abandon what we now know were the illusions of hope—which made one tendency into the dominant and permanent one, and projected laws and trends as independent of actual human beings. Alongside genuine human improvement, the century forces us to give at least equal weight to human destructiveness. Without the lenses of Progress we can see that the world indeed displays many and contrary tendencies. If any new notions of progress are possible they should be rooted not in reified concepts and passive hopes but in concrete human beings who act in history, and will have to accommodate the full range of their past and potential actions. In some respects humanity and human life may indeed improve over time. But can we any longer deny that both may also *worsen*?

The Reasons of Unreason

We are, it will become clear, pursuing the reasons of unreason. We all know, spontaneously, before turning to reflect on it, that much of life and death in this century has been mad. The intuitive sense—expressed for example in countless daily conversations about the madness of planning for nuclear war—becomes violated and repressed by 'serious' discourse which presumes catastrophic events to be guided by rational and functionally minded political intelligence. Yet Enlightenment categories and their Marxist progeny are mocked by the Valley of Death—where normal sense has been drastically ruptured, mental constructions substituted for attention to the real world, and human reality systematically bent into a caricature of itself.

At the root of our own commitment to Progress has been a sense of history as the steady, if halting and contradictory, realization of Reason and Freedom. The class struggle, the progression from lower to higher forms of social life, the initiation of History as a self-conscious under-taking with the advent of socialism—these Marxist expressions reflect the dominant mood no less than the bourgeois-democratic hope of human advance through 'Enlightenment'—democracy, education and technology. Modern, secular hope has been fundamentally tied to various nuances of belief in the progress of Reason in history.

Perhaps the most unanimous and deeply felt moment of such hope was immediately prior to the First World War when nearly all voices in the West, official and oppositional, spoke as if the advent of a truly ra-tional world was at hand. And indeed the war employed the tools of modernity, of reason and progress, as never before—but to explode its own hopes, in the process sounding the opening chords of the history of unreason in our century. 'Henceforth', wrote Georges Sorel, 'everything is given into disorder; nothing is necessary any longer; no predictions are possible.'[16]

If I avoid capitals for unreason to emphasize that it is not a force beyond human beings, we must also insist that it has *a history* in our century, just as Hegel insisted on speaking of a history of Reason and Marx of a history of class struggle in relation to the development of productive powers. The history of Doomsday is the history of unreason. I avoid 'Unreason' to emphasize that its history is no more, and no less, than the story of human beings who choose, under whatever pressures and within whatever structures, to act madly.

In the chapters that follow I will sketch some key moments of that history in order to trace their logic. I will explore societies that have organized themselves against phantoms, murdered systematically those who threatened no one, and plunged masses of people to their death for no comprehensible purpose. After drawing the conclusions from our meditation on past disasters we will be better able to confront two of the greatest threats of the present—the Israeli-Palestinian con-flict and the growing spectre of nuclear war. With an eye toward avoiding yet greater disasters, we will seek to understand their sources, and their links with the history of unreason.

The history? We shall see not only that the catastrophes have their own internal histories, but also that they absorb, and are generated by, each other. Is there then a movement, a historical progression of humans acting madly in our century? Yes, just as surely as there is a movement of liberation, of class struggle. If so, its human sources, its logic must be traced back into their social roots. *Must* because its unchecked progress leads us towards the final burst of unreason, the flash of ultimate madness in which everything will be destroyed. Of our century's tendencies, possibilities and experiences, this choice of total destruction remains with us today as one of the most present and real.

Such a threat—palpable, present at every moment—gives a special urgency to this study, making a work of the philosophical and historical imagination into a work of politics. No book can save the earth, however. This study, like any other, is *only* a work of thought—action lies elsewhere, beyond the intellectual experience of these pages. Politics is the appropriate response to this history of unreason.

Authentic political analysis today searches for the people who will make it *real*, and such a lack of self-sufficiency puts a hole at its centre. I have mentioned Lasch and Heilbroner—I would fault them for a false objectivism and self-sufficiency, for writing at too great a distance from this search, for ignoring the hole. Neither remembers or anticipates the power of people acting collectively to transform our history. Any reason to hope must lie there, not on the level of reified forces of Progress, Reason, or class struggle, but among concrete human beings who oppose *this* war, demand the end of *that* injustice, or seek to overturn *this* social system and take it into their hands. Lasch wrote in the 1970s as if the 'narcissistic' 1960s had not also witnessed committed mass movements which helped to end the war in Vietnam, to improve the position of blacks in America, and to reopen the space for political opposition. Heilbroner, likewise, ignores the only possible solution to the problems he raises—that human beings have again and again moved to the centre of the historical stage on which he seems inclined to see only their managers, rulers and analysts. Political writing which does not grope for this subject and see itself as lost without it, both arrogates to itself too much importance and condemns itself to melancholy.

This is a political study, then, first because hope is action, and a reason to hope would lead there. Also because this century has made it unthinkable to wait on the relentless unfolding of History—next time the world itself may be destroyed as its people rest secure in its relentless Progress, while its rulers again go insane. And also because, (as we shall see) after Auschwitz, the Gulag and Vietnam, human struggle—politics—is the only possible antidote to social madness. As I shall argue, the mad destructiveness of the last two at least, as well as of the nuclear threat, began in a politics which sought to repress politics. The struggle against such madness begins the very way the American Civil Rights movement began, with human beings saying 'No'—themselves deciding to resist. By way of a philosophical and historical conclusion, after exploring the dialectics of disaster, I shall argue that resistance is one of the fundamental lessons of hope. Today, hope is indeed a different hope, one with a different meaning and focus, from that with which the century began. It is chastened, diminished, without transcendent support, yet nonetheless firm and strengthened by having survived this horrible reality. In this spirit, let me give away the ending before we begin: I will conclude that the last word is action.

II
The Valley of Death

2
Why? Towards a Theory of the Holocaust

'To write poetry after Auschwitz is barbaric.'[1] Poetry, a language of hope, wrestles with the present to give it form and beauty.[2] Carrying out its task must so mock those who died that 'it has become impossible to write poetry today.' Poetry, hope, no longer possible? Poets are certainly writing today, among and around us, even about Auschwitz—every time they take up the pen refuting Adorno's assertion as if it were mere hyperbole, a rhetorical flourish. Just as certainly tens of thousands of survivors have long since created new lives—finding shelter, settling anew, recreating normal worlds, raising families—showing indeed that hope is inextinguishable even after Auschwitz.[3]

Yet the assertion is correct. The survivors know, the poets know, we all know that along with the six million Jews—and with them the tens of thousands of gypsies and millions of Poles and Russians who were gassed, shot and starved to death—something fundamental to all who come after them, perhaps the very premises of poetry and hope, did die in the extermination camps.

The experience of this catastrophe will not vanish: it eventually finds its way into the material and mental structures of the entire world. Whether we comprehend it or not, it undermines our hope, mutes our struggles and expectations—and diminishes our ability to deal with many of the urgent issues facing us.

Adorno certainly knew that poetry would continue no matter what, just as Auschwitz would recede into the past. But whenever it is evoked in the present, the Holocaust crushes hope if it is felt at anything remotely approaching the force with which it lies in wait in the recesses of our consciousness. Until such an encounter, and afterwards, it is possible to hope. But to *see* the extermination camps, even for a moment, withers and paralyzes our usual pre-misses, categories, forms, words and voice. It happened, but it is beyond belief. Nothing in our language, nothing in our range of feel-ing, is prepared to grasp or render the nature of this event. Whatever we say, or even feel, falls short. In fundamental ways it will probably remain forever unspeakable, and hence incomprehensible. Its scale and nature are such to ensure that, as Friedrich Meinecke once said of the entire Nazi period, that understanding its deeper causes 'will still occupy the coming centuries—provided these centuries are in-deed still able and inclined to ponder problems of this kind.'[4] When one has, perhaps only temporarily, lifted oneself beyond the over-whelming hopelessness and rage the Holocaust produces when closely studied, it is only to confront dismaying intellectual obstacles. The courts which tried Adolf Eichmann, acknowledging that the mind can hardly encompass the intentional and systematic murder of six million people, suggested that its understanding was a matter 'for great authors and poets.'[5]

One reason is that the Holocaust permits no stable point of view: language and concepts strain to capture its enormity, yet when con-jured up its *presence* paralyzes language and concepts. Cold, detached description of numbers killed, of body piled upon body fosters stunned outrage, which then in turn gives rise to repression. The importance of daily life vanishes before it, but, sooner or later, it then dissolves back into the normality of daily life. We cannot help but feel impotent and mute before it, and we cannot help also feeling that perhaps we are wrong to ponder it, and try to write about it. Wrong, that is, to try to organize and conceptualize something the essence of which is to remain hideously far beyond our normal range of thoughts and feelings. Indeed, does it not trivialize the Holocaust, and thus defile the memory of the dead, to try to *grasp* it?

Yet as poets continue to write, so we continue to strain to under-stand it, spurred on by the continuing *presence* of the catastrophe a generation later, knowing that to raise it beyond the human, to call it 'demonic' and give up trying to comprehend it is perhaps the final outrage. After all, human beings planned and carried out the 'Final Solution to the Jewish Problem', and did so under specific conditions and for specific reasons. Even if stunned by the result, we know all the same that the facts are human, and thus demand to be understood and their recurrence prevented.[6]

The Nazis set out to eliminate a people who were not even remotely combatants in a war—to eliminate them precisely and only because they existed. This is too horrifying for a 'proper' response... we read it and think it and if we can imagine it our heart grows numb, our mind weak. ... The deliberate murder of an entire people including (of course) its children! But the country-by-country statistics impose their own strange calm as we read about the Final Solution: in Poland, of an estimated Jewish population of 3,300,000, 3,000,000 were killed; in the Soviet Union over a million and a quarter; in the Baltic countries 228,000 died of 253,000; in Austria and Germany 210,000 of the 240,000 who had remained; in the Netherlands 105,000 of 140,000 died; in Hungary, 450,000 of 650,000. ... The total, just short of six million, was over two-thirds of the Jews that had lived in these areas prior to the war, and was perhaps ninety per cent of those within the Nazis' reach.

Remembering the horrifying specifics shatters the numbing calm: the Yellow Star; the forced ghettoization of Poland's Jews; the German efforts to starve Ghetto populations everywhere on a diet of bread and potatoes; the Nazi claims of 'a paradisiac existence' awaiting those Jews who would freely 'relocate'; the accounts of long trains of freight cars packed with people headed for extermination; people denying to the last this unbelievable thing that was happening to them; people struggling to the last to retain even the most pitiful fragments of human dignity; specific catastrophes such as the mass execution of 33,000 people in a single day at the ravine of Babi Yar near Kiev in 1941; the final 'shower' at the gas chambers; the piles of gold teeth extracted from the mouths of the dead, the fingernail marks made on the ceilings of the gas chambers by those who were clawing, animal-like, for the last drop of air. ...

Having been kept in the dark about it until then, the world learned about the Holocaust immediately after the war. A wave of shock and sympathy for the victims was followed by a generational coma. But for a few insistent voices most of the Western world seemed to be in a kind of shock about the Holocaust for a generation. Was the Holocaust too difficult to talk and think about until enough time had passed to give birth not only to new children but also to their children in turn? Does so great a catastrophe numb automatically, ebbing only with time? Today, however, the mood of silence is dissipated and a whole culture is beginning to absorb the Holocaust into its consciousness. Even in the years of shock and silence, a heroic few would not stop telling the story, creating memoirs and fiction, studying the history, writing for those who would listen and for those who felt lost. Recently they have increased so many times over that in our world the Holocaust has become an everyday term. Every best-seller list and every new book shelf seems to contain works on the 'Final Solution of the Jewish Problem', its perpetrators, its survivors, even their children. Several hundred college courses are now given on the topic, and countless others include the Holocaust as part of required discourse and reading. Not long ago it received two sure tokens of public legitimacy in America, a Presidential Commission and a week-long television special. The long period of numb and silent shock has ended.

Some people have been asking why for a generation, at first the *why* that beseeches the heavens in protest, the dumbfounded *why* that refuses to accept, the *why* one of whose meanings is *no*. With the passage of time and the development of distance, that *why* has begun to be refashioned into the *why* spurring reflection and scholarship. Considering how few years have passed, a remarkable amount of indispensable work has been done towards describing the Holocaust and the world that produced it.

To speak of *explaining* the Holocaust, however, is to refer to a level of generality which would grasp its essential features in such a way as to connect it with major lines of human history before and into the twentieth century. I speak, in other words, of a *theory* of the Holocaust.[7]

What are our starting points for a theory of the Holocaust? First, that the 'Final Solution of the Jewish Problem' and the entire camp and murder system was not 'demonic' but a human action. We must begin there, and call for understanding in human terms. On the most simple level this means establishing *what* manner of act was the Final Solution, *who* was responsible for it, and *why* was it done. Even describing the Final Solution turns out to be no simple task. *What*, after all, is it that we are seeking to explain? That so many were killed? Or that they were killed so systematically? Or that they were non-combatants and occupied no defined territory? Or that, like their killers, they were European? What *is* it, if anything, that makes the extermination of European Jewry a unique historical event?

Secondly, the question of who is responsible has already received a number of unsatisfactory answers, from Taylor's condemnation of the German people as the source of Nazism to Golo Mann's opposite emphasis on one evil man, Adolf Hitler.[8] Understanding the Holocaust involves clarifying the relationship of the process of genocide to those who ordered it, those who carried it out or supported it, and those who 'merely' accepted it without protest. The question, after all, points us to ask not only about the 'chain of command' but also about the nature and structures of a society which made the unthinkable into the possible.

And finally, we must ask *why* did it happen? This is perhaps the most taxing and speculative of the questions, not only because explaining any large historical event is so difficult, but also because of the obvious irrationality of Nazi policy. If the Jews were not really the force of evil that the Nazis claimed them to be, then why did they act to exterminate them? What madness, both social and psychological, infected the society that created the Holocaust? As should be obvious, these questions entail significant issues and demand chains of reflection and speculation. They demand combining the psychological and the social dimensions into a single coherent account in order both to insist on the fundamental irrationality of the Final Solution and to explain its deeper logic.

Describing the Holocaust: Its Historical Uniqueness

Is there anything unique about the Holocaust when placed against the century's other mass murders? The Holocaust stands out against the twisted landscape of death in the twentieth century as the one mass murder utterly devoid of instrumental purpose: there is no comprehensible reason for it. Certainly obsessive antagonism towards the Jews was a functional bedrock of Nazism, first uniting the movement, then later providing enormous material benefits to tens of thousands during the dispossessions.[9] But all this was secondary, if not unintended: the Nazi passion against the Jews was just that, a passion. Jews were exterminated not because they stood in the way of Nazi goals—for example either by occupying contested space or offering resistance. Rather, their extermination *was* the goal. All other mass killings of this century have at least a clear, if tenuous, connection with significant political purposes. And in most cases the murders have ended with the conflict which produced them. The Germans, on the contrary, rounded up Jews and shipped them off to be gassed *after* they became masters of a certain area, not *in order* to master it. Extermination of the Jews was an end in itself.

The Final Solution indeed *weakened* the Germans' ability to fight.[10] Nearly the entire Hungarian Jewish community was shipped to Auschwitz in May and June 1944, and gassed there while the Soviets were pushing the Germans out of Eastern Europe and the British and Americans were invading Normandy! Were not the troops and supplies more needed in the battles to keep the Soviets out of eastern Hungary? Were not the 147 trains of thirty cars each more needed for rushing troops to the multiplying fronts?[11] 'More needed'—no such calculus animated German policy because extermination of the Jews was itself so necessary that the approach of the Red Army, and certain defeat, only intensified the work of the ovens. It was as if, after all, *this* was Hitler's purpose, the Nazis' holy mission, their contribution to Western civilization. That work stopped only when, by October 1944, it had become substantially completed: Central Europe had been rendered *judenrein*, free of Jews. Only a handful of survivors still lived in territories which were once home to nine million Jews. One must insist on the diabolical uniqueness of the Final Solution, even in this century of death.

Objectivity and Subjectivity in Describing the Holocaust

Unfortunately, as time passes, the Holocaust even if diabolically unique, becomes a *historical* fact like anything else. It achieves a solidity, a *thereness* which incorporates it all too easily into the rationality of human history. In seeking its causes and meanings we cannot help but endow it with an aura of inevitability which indeed suggests a kind of historical legitimacy. Actions, trends lead *to* it; actions, trends lead *from* it. The Holocaust becomes part of the order of things. Furthermore, when historians try to bracket out their outrage and shock that such a thing has happened, when they approach it dispassionately in the name of scholarly objectivity, the last step may be taken towards making it a rational project of human energy and intentions, merely one possible project among others. The Greek term *Holocaust*, evoking as it does the uncontrolled horror of mass burning by fire, as well as the Jewish determination to remember it forever, are only feeble antidotes to this distorting process of object-ification.[12]

Study might profitably begin with a *subjective* response, one which points towards the structures of the Holocaust by suggesting what it means *to us*. By saying *to us* I have in mind a yet more specific subjectivity, that of the Nazis' actual or intended victims. When words can be found, what indeed does the Holocaust mean to *Jews*? Among the most frequent terms used to describe the Final Solution are *evil* and *mad*. They are used freely, without self-consciousness about their technical appropriateness or objectivity, and they simul-taneously express, judge and describe. To call the Final Solution *evil* is to judge it morally; to call it *mad* is to judge it morally and psycho-logically. Moral judgements, where they are serious, are descriptions of the actions they judge and illuminate their structure. Thus they are key terms for a moral phenomenology of the Final Solution.

To speak of evil may make the reader pause. Claims of good wag-ing war on evil have accompanied every one of the catastrophic events or threats to be treated in this study. Most of the hundred million victims of our century are sacrifices to one or another form of moral Manicheism. Indeed, the Nazis saw their victims as the abso-lute embodiment of evil, and their mission as cleansing the earth of them.[13]

Gil Elliot is not only mistaken but implicitly self-contradictory, when he argues in the *Twentieth Century Book of the Dead* that moral judgements convey and illuminate nothing about the great mass murders. After all, his own book has a deeply moral purpose: to sketch the great *evil* of our age. And implicit in such a project is the goal of better understanding it to avoid repeating it. We cannot dispense with such terms of judgement, because morality is both fundamental to political understanding and a necessary dimension of the structure of every action.

If we are to rescue the word from misuse by religious or political holy warriors we should restrict the application of *evil* to actions, not people. As Peter Phillips argues most convincingly and movingly, we simply perpetuate the moral blindness of the Nazis by considering them a race apart. They differ from us only by degrees.[14]

In evoking this perspective, however, I have replaced the subjective starting point with a call for a certain kind of engaged objectivity. Are the two compatible? I have suggested that we all, non-Jew as well as Jew, begin our encounter with the Holocaust *as Jews*. That is, we can minimize the false objectification as far as possible and begin to glimpse and appreciate *what actually happened*, if we situate ourselves in the victim's place. Then it is crystal-clear what is meant by *extermination*. The shock, the rage, the initial unbelievability give rise to calling the Nazis evil and mad. They were barbarians. But at some point the process of understanding can continue forward only if we shift our perspective to look *behind* the act to try to understand those who did it and why. At this point it may impede understanding to view the Holocaust *as Jews*: rage towards those who carried out the extermination programme may indeed be millennial, and may make all studies of it into thinly veiled acts of revenge. What is needed then is a perspective which can ask *why* such evil and madness *made sense*. Is such understanding possible without sympathy? If we may best begin to grasp the Holocaust *as Jews*, perhaps we may best complete our understanding of it as the Nazis' *fellow human beings*. Then, perhaps we can glimpse why these particular people became demonic. In fact, as I will argue, the Germans who participated in the Final Solution acted in response to the pressures they experienced and the prospects they saw before them: which means that anyone, ourselves included, could under certain circumstances become mass murderers. A perspective appropriate to this fact precludes all righteousness.

Evil and Madness

What makes the Final Solution evil has already been indicated: its purpose was to destroy the Jews of Europe. That was its only purpose. Certainly we may speak of all contemporary societies as being in some sense evil, just as we may comment on all war as evil. Indeed, in systemically inhumane societies such as ours, we may all have to concede our own participation in exploitation, oppression, the stunting of human capacities and wasting of lives. But the age-old systematic practice of harming and even killing of human beings has always been kept within certain limits. One limit has been its economic purpose as with slavery. A certain rudimentary regard for human beings was always built into slavery. Slaves were, after all, valuable chattels. Another kind of limitation, in the case of war, has been set by its military purpose.[15] Above all, humans have been exploited and killed *for a reason*, and those reasons have defined—and restricted—the various evils visited upon humans by humans as means to specific ends. However, rarely if ever in history can we glimpse the spectacle of extermination as a policy, and certainly never on the scale wrought by the Nazis. The building and operation of killing centres whose sole purpose was to exterminate the Jews and other lesser peoples are the most eloquent arguments that the Final Solution deserves to be regarded as unmitigatedly evil in its structure.

It might be argued that because the Nazis believed that they were ridding the world of what they regarded as its source of evil, they, too, killed for a reason. But the very fact that the Nazis believed that the Final Solution would 'cleanse' Europe of the 'vermin' who were the source of its ills marks their undertaking not with moral purpose but with madness. *Mad*: this term of outrage and judgement is also a term of description, and it may have an unsettling effect on the reader. Irrational perhaps, but *mad*? I use this as a term of moral phenomenology with intentions similar to those in speaking of the Final Solution as *evil*. The issue is not whether the individual Nazis were themselves mad: like Arendt's Eichmann, they all may have been quite normal in their environment. Our concern is rather with their outlook and actions.

To be sure, if Freud is right we are all somewhat mad, in the sense that being civilized is a sure token of a rupture with significant dimensions of our own and external reality. To employ madness, as a term of social diagnosis, however, is to suggest a collective inability or refusal to experience that reality, and the substitution for it of something mentally conjured up. Individuals regarded as clinically mad dwell systematically among such wholly subjective conjurings, to the point of ordering their lives around them. They differ from the rest of us, of course, only by degree. Similarly, if there is no completely sane society, at various moments of history it is none the less possible to point to societies which in decisive ways have ruptured with reality and acted out wholly subjective fantasies. To describe the Final Solution as mad is to characterize it as a policy which expresses such a systematic rupture with reality.[16]

The question is unavoidable: was Hitler mad? At the end, of course, he had lost contact with reality, refusing to even hear reports from the fronts. His last words, which blame the war on the Jews, were clearly the rantings of a madman, as was his less widely known decision to destroy Germany.[17] But just as clearly his tactical course between, for example, 1930 and 1933 shows him to be a political genius. His brilliance and extraordinary talents included a fine grasp of the objective situation and how to steer through it, exploit it, and ultimately dominate it.[18] But even if on this tactical level he was consummately rational, on a deeper level Hitler had already broken with reality.

Mein Kampf is a crazy quilt of sense and nonsense, of brilliant perception and mad railing. But it remains an integral whole, a *Weltanschauung*. At its root, as the source of all evil to the German *Volk*, one finds the Jews as international conspirators, controllers of the world's press, carriers of disease, leaders of Bolshevism, financial swindlers, pornographers and procurers. In his study of Hitler's *Weltanschauung* Eberhard Jäckel presents a remarkable catalogue of references to the Jews from the first volume of *Mein Kampf*: 'The Jew is a maggot in a rotting corpse; he is a plague worse than the Black Death of former times; a germ carrier of the worst sort; mankind's eternal germ of disunion; the drone that insinuates its way into the rest of mankind; the spider that slowly sucks the people's blood out of its pores; the pack of rats fighting bloodily among themselves; the parasite in the body of other peoples; the typical parasite; the people's vampire ....'[19]

Madness, like evil, is self-evident to those not sharing in it. What is most remarkable about this particular example is that it became enough of a mass outlook for a movement, and then society as a whole to be organized around it.[20] As Peter Merkl says, speaking of those believing in antisemitic[21] conspiracy theories: 'The movement was literally led by the paranoids.'[22] Hitler and Nazi Germany meant it and acted on it: step by step the Jews were isolated as the non-human carriers of disease, removed from the community, set apart and isolated, and then, appropriately, exterminated.

Most political ideology disfigures reality. In the next chapter we shall see how Marxism, though containing a critique of ideology, succumbed to the same distorting process as liberal and conservative

ideologies, and for the same reasons: to fit a refractory reality to an
outlook which needed to see it differently. The Nazi vision, however,
and the process of implementing it, leaped far beyond even these
political distortions.

Nazi antisemitism is a rupture with reality. I choose this formulation
rather than the overly functionalistic emphasis on the Jews as
scapegoats in order to insist on the element of madness in Nazi
policy.[23] There is indeed a logic to the Final Solution, and I will argue
that its roots lie in the history and structure of German society. But it
is the logic of a movement which has decisively rejected logic, which
has, that is, broken in key respects with the instrumental rationality
we usually assume to govern political thought and action.[24]

The Nazi Party Programme, drafted in 1920 and 'declared to be
unalterable', rejects citizenship for Jews but unlike *Mein Kampf* does
not yet make them the source of all evil. However, the party
manifesto on agriculture, proclaimed ten years later when Nazism
had become a mass movement, reflects the full-scale paranoia we
have seen in Hitler's words. It largely blames the state of German
farming on 'the Jewish world money-market, which actually controls
parliamentary democracy in Germany [and] wishes to destroy German agriculture'; on Jewish domination of wholesale trade; and on
Jewish control of electric power, fertilizer and credit.[25]

One of the essential features of such madness is the abandonment
of the distinction between fantasy and reality. To Nazism destroying
the Jews meant literally destroying the source of the world's evil.
Symptomatic of its delusionary universe was the prominence given
to an organic, magical, and biological language, an antiscientific
language of incantation. For Alfred Rosenberg, in a book which sold
over a million copies by 1942, the Jew's parasitism should be
described 'exactly in the same way in which we speak of parasitic oc-
currences in the life of plants and animals. The sacculina pierces the
rectum of the common crab, and gradually grows into it, sucks away
its vital forces; the same process occurs when the Jew invades society through the open wounds of the people, consuming their creative
forces and hastening the doom of a society.'[26]

Such language served Nazi needs well. It raised their assertions
beyond dispassionate, objective study while imparting to them a
pseudoscientific cast. Detached from the need for verification, such
language evoked the mystified fears of those unable to face reality

directly. Thus detached, it gave license to complete subjectivity, allowing them to combine the most incongruent ideas into a single whole. Thus, in this 1937 statement of Goebbels, the subhuman Jew becomes the superhuman threat: 'Behold, this is the enemy of the world, the destroyer of civilizations, the parasite among the nations, the son of chaos, the incarnation of evil, the materialized demon of mankind's decay.'[27]

Above all, such language had a transforming function. Alex Bein argues that Nazi teachings were so widespread and widely believed that the Jew ceased to appear as a human being to most people. He came to appear 'as some lower animal, like worms and insects, terrible and incomprehensible in their destructive effect and, above all, like the parasitic microbiological creatures invisible to the naked eye, the bacilli and bacteria which one daily heard and read about as carriers of disease and decay.'[28] Hence, the rupture: social problems were successfully pointed away from social causes, evocatively focused on a 'carrier of disease' who, moreover, lacked social power and was susceptible to attack. The Jew was weak but strong, subhuman but superhuman; the image of 'parasite' unifies these contradictory conceptions.

The conception of the Jews that made genocide possible is summed up by an instruction manual for the Nazi leadership. 'The subhuman man, who to all appearances is a biologically homogeneous, natural creation with hands, feet, and some sort of brain, with eyes and a mouth, is all the same a totally different, a terrifying creature; he is endowed with human features—though merely a sketch version of the true human being—mentally, spiritually he stands lower than an animal. Inside this man there rages a violent chaos of wild uninhibited emotions: unspeakable destructiveness, primitive lust, unashamed vileness. Subhuman man—nothing else.... He hates the work of the other [that is, of the true man]. He rails against it, furtively as a thief, openly as a slanderer—as a murderer ... Never has the subhuman man kept the peace, permanent troublemaker that he is. ... He needs for his self-preservation the mire, the hell, but not the sun.—And this underworld of the subhuman man found its leader! The Eternal Jew!'[29]

Even forty years later this language has not lost its power to shock—and yet, how much more shocking that these mad ravings should have become the language of policy! Already in *Mein Kampf*

Hitler had indicated what should have been done to Germany's Jews at the start of and during the First World War: 'twelve or fifteen thousand of these Hebrew corrupters of the people' should have been gassed.[30] In power, this madness moved to its conclusion: the parasites were exterminated.

The Nazi outlook began as a systematic distortion of reality. In power, however, the Nazis were able to reshape reality until it conformed to the distorted fantasy.[31] In this wild sense, the Nazi outlook became true. The blood fellowship of the German *Volk* was *brought into being* in step after deadly step as the Jews were systematically reduced to the status of subhumans: removed from the civil service, disenfranchised, deprived of German citizenship, prohibited from ritual slaughter, their property expropriated, made to wear a special badge. Nazi policy made the Jews over into the vermin Nazism claimed they were from the beginning. Finally, having changed their legal, social, political and economic status into that of living subhumans and having threatened them with extermination should Germany go to war, the final step was carried out: Jews were exterminated. Elimination of humans as vermin was the final break with reality. Madness became policy in the *Einsatzgruppen* and the gas chambers.[32] If this meant that psychopathic insanity became normal character structure in the leaders of the Third Reich,[33] it also meant a systematic corruption of thought and speech patterns.[34] Language militates against the extermination of a people. If *it* could not be said without implying that it was horrifyingly evil, then references to it had to be detached from all conventional associations in order to disguise what was being said. Thought and language themselves underwent a systematic rupture with reality during the Third Reich.

Responsibility for the Final Solution

The issue of responsibility for the Holocaust appeared at Nürnberg in 1945 and has not left us yet. Was Hitler primarily to blame, or was it the Nazis, or the German people as a whole? Was extermination of six million Jews a direct result of the *movement* that brought Hitler to power or in some sense the product of German *society*, or *Hitler's* own project carried out by hundreds of thousands unable or unwilling to resist his authority? If our first question was *what* was the Final

Solution, we must now ask *who* was responsible for it.

It is ironic, but perhaps appropriate, that the most sweeping and powerful argument ever made on behalf of human responsibility, Sartre's *Being and Nothingness*, was being published in Paris as French Jews were being shipped away by a system of evil perfected to minimize anyone's sense of responsibility for it. Only a handful did the actual killing. In a characteristic combination of gangsterism and bureaucracy, the rest either gave the orders without speaking the words or were mere distant accomplices operating this or that corner of the vast machinery under orders. How far can responsiblity for such an operation be extended?

It may help us to think in terms of *circles* of responsibility, moving from the actual perpetrators themselves—both political and technical—to the network of those whose activities supported the extermination, then to those who knew about it and passively acquiesced in and accepted it, and finally to those who perhaps knew nothing about it or even opposed it inwardly but helped to create the conditions in which it became possible.

Certainly in the first circle of responsibility stands Hitler himself, who conceived[35] of the mass murder of the Jews and ordered the Final Solution. And here we must include those closest to him, such as Himmler, who directed its carrying out, and the inner circle of leading Nazis. In the next circle of responsibility are the several hundred who, claiming to act only under Hitler's orders, planned and directed every phase of the Final Solution and who have largely been brought to trial since.[36]

There is no debate about the direct responsibility of the inner circle of perpetrators themselves. And there is compelling reason to include in the outermost circles of passive responsibility those outside Germany who knew of the great secret and kept it secret, doing nothing to stop the Holocaust. I refer especially to the leaders of the countries which remained indifferent to the Jews' fate, such as the United States and Great Britain—not only by restricting immigration but later by refusing to attack the camps or the rail lines leading to them.[37] But the greatest area of controversy concerns all those in between: the obedient operators of the extermination machinery and those who peopled the various layers of the interconnected administrative, mechanical and policing apparatus; the loyal Nazis unconnected to the Final Solution, and non-party members who had helped, or supported, or merely accepted Hitler's rise to power; and loyal Germans elsewhere who knew of the exterminations and did nothing to stop them.

Whose Authority?

In the third circle are the executioners themselves, hardly more than fifty thousand SS members at the camps and in mobile killing teams. Members of this group have occasionally been brought to trial and convicted, often in connection with 'excesses'. What is their responsibility? The problem of establishing responsibility in a hierarchical structure such as Nazi Germany (or indeed America during the Vietnam War) led Stanley Milgram to devise his experiments on obedience to authority. Milgram's starting point is his notion that, while the policies of the Final Solution originated in the mind of Hitler, they were carried out on a massive scale only because a very large number of people abandoned their consciences and obeyed orders to do harm to the innocent.[38]

Milgram's question was: Why did they obey? To answer this he devised the celebrated experiments which tricked people hired as assistants into becoming subjects;[39] these showed an alarmingly high willingness of subjects to obey orders, no matter what. But his 'proof' that a large percentage of individuals will obey an evil authority hinges on distorted notions of both individual and authority.

Milgram's guiding image of the individual is that of an autonomous person who 'merges ... into an organizational structure' and so abandons his own ability to weigh his actions and their consequences morally.[40] Milgram's guiding image of authority is of someone rigorously external to the individual, who seeks to have the individual do his purposes, and easily manipulates and lies to the individual.[41] With these guiding images Milgram constructs for us a model of the moral individual murdering under a chain of command which extends back, in the case of the Final Solution, to Hitler.[42]

However significant his purposes, Milgram asks the wrong question and gives the wrong answer. After all, Milgram's 'subjects', as late twentieth century Americans, believe in the authority of science and share with their manipulator a whole set of implicit and explicit values about the employer-employee contract. Should we not expect individual disobedience to legitimate authority in a smoothly functioning society to develop only slowly and with great difficulty? What, after all, is more striking, that in the master experiment 60 per cent of the 'subjects' *obeyed*, or that 40 per cent of them *refused* to obey?

Milgram's distorted sense of individual autonomy is but the obverse of his distorted sense of authority: he himself acts as a devious manipulator whose goal is to impose radically foreign purposes on his subjects. But was this how Hitler functioned? Contrary to Milgram's assumptions, it is necessary to insist that for the German SS guard, Hitler was his *chosen* authority. Milgram seems not to realize that this was the man who had received 13 million votes for president in 1932; that he was seen as the *Führer*; that his party was hegemonic in German society because of the very ideas found in *Mein Kampf* and Nazi propaganda; that the victory of Nazism was in its essence already a surrender of whatever 'autonomy' had been possible in Weimar society; that joining the SS meant the complete acceptance of Nazi ideas and a determination to carry them out. The SS oath of induction promised: 'I swear to you, Adolf Hitler, as Führer and Chancellor of the German Reich, loyalty and valour. I pledge to you and to the superiors whom you will appoint obedience unto death, so help me God.'[43]

Those who spoke these words murdered six million Jews. They were overwhelmingly not 'ordinary Germans' but members of the Nazi movement. From that movement came the 3,000 executioners of the *Einsatzgruppen*, who shot a million Soviet Jews, this 'determined army of death', in Heinz Höhne's words: 'Wholly dedicated to achievement, hardness and camaraderie, they reached a degree of insensibility surpassed only by those soulless automata, the concentration-camp guards. Here was to be found the elite of that barbaric type of mankind, intoxicated by its own achievements, which Himmler exalted as the SS ideal; it was indeed an Order of the Death's Head, divorced from the world of ordinary mortals and from their moral standards, ready to undertake any mission ordered by its masters, and prisoner of a community claiming the sole right to decide the SS man's social and ethical standards. For years their leaders had drummed into the men now forming the *Einsatzgruppen* that they should yield themselves to the intoxication of power, that they should savour the elite's feeling of superiority and consider themselves a class above the mass of Party members, too superior to conform to their moral standards—they even claimed for themselves the right to turn men into subjects for biological laboratory experiments.'[44]

If anyone thoroughly believed the propaganda of Nazism—and if anyone was selected and trained to embody Nazi ideals—it was members of the SS. From them were chosen first the mobile killing teams, and later the staff of the extermination camps. If it had been central to *Mein Kampf* and Nazi propaganda, the outlook that led to Auschwitz became a standard part of the SS training lectures: 'The Jew is a parasite. Wherever he flourishes, the people die. From the earliest times to our own day the Jew has quite literally killed and exterminated the peoples upon whom he has battened, insofar as he has been able to do so. Elimination of the Jew from our community is to be regarded as an emergency defence measure.'[45] In short, those who actually killed Jews were carrying out a policy for which they were quite prepared and to which they had become personally committed.

Beyond the Camps: Whose Responsibility?

But how deeply into German society, how far beyond those who directed it and those whose hands were bloodied, does responsibility extend for the Final Solution? Certainly some degree of responsibility is borne by all those hundreds of thousands who were part of the complex and far-reaching death machinery—including the soldiers and SS troops who rounded up Jews and shipped them to the camps, countless clerks, construction workers and railroad crews. Beyond these are all those hundreds of thousands of Germans who, years before, dutifully performed the various tasks which led up to the Final Solution, and who have argued since that the open and vigorous antisemitism of the 1930s—disenfranchising and expropriating Jews—was one thing and Hitler's policy of extermination quite another. What kind of responsibility extends to the hundreds of thousands who joined the NSDAP before it achieved power, or to the nineteen million who voted for it in the 1933 election? Or to those who, sensing the evil and madness of this man and his movement, did not devote themselves to blocking the Nazi path to power

by whatever means necessary? To those who were politically para-
lyzed by the rapid Nazi rise to prominence? Does it extend indeed
to German society as a whole?

Or is the truth rather the opposite—namely that Hitler and his barbarian clique elbowed their way into power at a time of crisis and
then, bit by bit, imposed their insane will upon the party, German
society, and Europe, to the point of genocide and suicide? While no
historian denies the relevance of the flourishing German tradition of
antisemitism in the 19th and early 20th centuries, neither is it possible to deny that the Final Solution, as Dawidowicz put it, 'had its
origins in Hitler's mind'.[46] Indeed, even Himmler claimed to have
been astonished when he first heard Hitler's plans for the Final Solution. If the NSDAP and SS leaders directed it with monstrous efficiency, not one of them believed in it sufficiently to stand up for it
and defend it at Nürnberg.

The fact that extermination was hardly ever discussed directly, and
that official policy was to keep it secret, makes it even more difficult
to ascribe it to German society as a whole. Whatever their sense of
divine mission, those who ordered and directed it were equally
aware that it was a crime to be hidden even from the rank-and-file of
the Nazi movement. Nor must we forget that by the beginning of the
war most Jews had already fled Germany, leaving only perhaps
250,000 to be deported from Germany itself; that the killing centres
were located in the newly acquired areas of Poland, not in
Germany,[47] and that the murders were committed in wartime, indeed after the invasion of the USSR opened its bloodiest phase. Moreover the SS was assisted in the extermination programme by native
fascists and antisemites everywhere: Letts, Ukrainians, Lithuanians,
Hungarians, Poles and Rumanians.

Within Germany, it has been emphasized, while many of the votes
that brought Hitler to the anteroom of power may have been antisemitic, many others were votes to destroy Weimar democracy and
entrust the state to a man who would *rule*. Others cast in their lot
with the only party that seemed sufficiently vigorous to be able to end
the depression. And still others because, like Albert Speer's mother,
they liked 'to see clean-cut young men march through the streets, a
sight that promised order in the midst of chaos and exemplified
energy in the midst of despair.'[48]

If bitter antisemitism characterizes many of the Nazi supporters studied by Theodore Abel and Milton Mayer, there was no expectation in the earlier study of the approaching doomsday and no rejoicing in the later one over its achievement. Nearly all of these people leave us with a sense that genocide was *Hitler's* policy, or at most that of the million or so *wildgewordene Spiessbürger*[49] who made up the most committed Nazis. Few among even the most crazed Nazis could have known that the modern nation-state was about to give them the means for translating '*Juda, verrecke*' into reality for the first time in history. Had they known, would they have been so casual in their calls for violence?

Who Was Hitler?

But to point at Hitler and a relatively small group poses another question: who, after all, was this man Hitler, and how did he attain the power to exterminate European Jewry? *Mein Kampf* is emphatically a German, petty-bourgeois document that could have been produced only during Weimar, after defeat, revolution, counter-revolution and disastrous inflation. In Hitler a number of historical currents came together: racism, bourgeois values of law and order, petty-bourgeois resentment, a sentimentalized vision of home and family, nature mysticism, nationalism, and expansionism—plus a 20th century populist determination to realize these ideas politically by activating the German people.[50] No single element was unique to Hitler; rather (in Sartre's formulation), he interiorized a number of decisive historical trends in his developing years, and then re-exteriorized them as his project. However, the essence of the latter was to become *Germany's* project. If the elements which went into the making of Adolf Hitler belong to his class, his nation's experience and his historical moment, it would be contradictory to claim that the resultant project somehow belonged exclusively to Adolf Hitler the individual. To say (as for example Henry Pachter does) that 'Hitler had become Germany's destiny',[51] suggests not only that *he* held power, but that his power and projects all became possible because he had absorbed and lived decisive historical currents.[52] This was the sole basis for his power after 1933: to shape the new incarnation of such trends.

The point, then, is not that fifty thousand Nazis obeyed their

Führer but that, after all, these Nazis became a dominant political force able to take hold of the machinery of the state and make genocide official state policy. Why was Hitler able to become the absolute leader, whose word was law and whose name became the German greeting? Why indeed was he able to attain power quite legally, after receiving one third of the vote? The questions underscore the central point: Hitler and the Nazis were as much created by German society as they were its rulers.

It is beside the point to assert, by way of extenuation, that they took power in a crisis. The spectacular rise of the challenging party, and the absence of sufficiently vital alternatives, were key dimensions of the crisis itself. The ascendant movement *created* the vacuum by paralyzing its enemies politically on the eve of seizing power. The Nazis did this by proclaiming absolute obedience, racism, a cult of violence, aggressive national expansion, and antisemitism: these were not hidden aims imposed *after* Hitler took power, but lay at the very heart of his enormous popular support. However they were understood, outside of the working class a majority of Germans supported the movement that promised them these things.

Antisemitism in Power

Merkl's statistical study of the essays gathered by Theodore Abel in 1934 reveals 'the presence of extraordinary amounts of prejudice and hatred in the respondents, a feature that still has to be fully acknowledged in much of the literature.'[53] Fully 14 per cent of the SS/SA members studied and 11 per cent of the remaining party members reflect full-scale paranoia.[54] In other words, one would expect them to fully believe, constantly espouse, and *act upon*, the Nazi antisemitic madness. 'It is hard to imagine', writes Merkl, 'a reasonably perceptive, mature person who would join the NSDAP without being fully aware of its chief issue.'[55]

What does this tell us about the society in which the enunciators of such madness were able to move from the political gutter into the corridors of power? The point is not to determine what percentage of Germans shared the paranoia of the most rabid Nazis—studies focused on individuals neglect the fact that political parties do not merely reflect, but also crystallize, focus and shape individual feelings. As much as any party can, the Nazis at that moment gained hegemony over German society. At the very least the Nazi ascendancy indicated that there was a widespread acceptance of their racist and paranoid rantings as legitimate political discourse; whether it had majority support or not, an antisemitic course had become acceptable politics. Their enemies' paralysis, their fragmentation and defeat without an all-out struggle, meant their acquiescence before such evil. If before 1933 the paranoiacs dominated the Nazi movement, after 1933 they dominated German society—meaning that their vision of reality and course of action became prevalent. Did the Nazis reflect German society? In politics, such dominance is the ultimate truth.

Thus it is hardly likely that most Germans were surprised when the first government-sanctioned anti-Jewish boycott took place, two months after Hitler became Chancellor. Indeed, Karl A. Schleunes argues persuasively that the boycott, threatening as it did Hitler's precarious *modus vivendi* with Hindenburg and the non-Nazis in his cabinet, was organized as a way of channelling and disciplining powerful grass-roots party pressures.[56] The pressures continued, leading to each further step towards the solution of the 'Jewish Problem': the antisemitic legislation beginning with the expulsion of Jews from the civil service on 7 April 1933, the Nürnberg Laws of 1935, the Aryanizations (expropriations) of 1937–38, and *Kristallnacht* —the nationwide pogrom of 9 November 1938.

From Antisemitism to the Final Solution

Antisemitism, no matter how hegemonic, does not amount to extermination. The stubborn argument for Hitler's primary responsibility in this project recurs in Bullock's conclusion that 'if ever a man exercised absolute power it was Adolf Hitler.'[57] This appraisal is mirrored in the extreme emphasis virtually all Nazi officials associated with the Final Solution have given to 'obeying orders'. And they are right, in one sense: Nazism was Führer-worship. Self-effacement before and unquestioning obedience to Hitler was indeed a cornerstone of the movement. As Rudolf Höss, commandant of Auschwitz, testified: 'I had no second thoughts at the time; I had received an order and had to carry it out. When the Führer himself had ordered the "Final Solution" of the Jewish question, no long-standing National-Socialist could have second thoughts, least of all an SS officer. *"Führer, befehl, wir folgen"*—Führer, command, we follow thee—was for us no empty phrase, no mere slogan. We took it with deadly seriousness.'[58]

What are we to answer to Höss? That to elevate an individual to supreme authority, with such a massive evasion of responsibility, is in itself a deliberate action? Was there not in such subjection a pre-existing acceptance of Hitler's intentions as Höss's own, a pre-cognition of what Hitler would command, a way of muting consciousness of the barbarism that was thereby chosen?

The point is, after all, that process cannot be separated from content. It says a great deal about the Germans who obeyed that they chose obedience. For example, to join the Nazi party, to vote for it, to capitulate before it—each step meant an abandonment of reason. To choose the party and leader who would destroy parliamentary democracy was not like choosing a superior form of workers' democracy that would more fully realize the rationalist and egalitarian promises of parliamentary rule. It was to reject any and all democratic, rationalist, and egalitarian commitments. It meant embracing instead the charismatic leader whose unique, almost mystical powers would direct those who had abandoned reason as a guide.

A choice of unreason, and a choice of evil. After all, the very word of this man, a man of manifestly evil intentions, became the supreme law of German society. In achieving this position, wasn't Hitler giving voice to the malignancy, the irrationality of the social forces that brought him to power? And wasn't his ascendancy a sign of the malignancy and irrationality of a society which could produce no other leading force?

Moreover, it distorts the course of events to describe the locus of the Final Solution as being Hitler. Among Nazis there was general agreement about the 'Jewish Problem': how could it be solved? Schleunes guides us through the prewar period, showing how policies and actions evolved in fits and starts, from a number of centres of action, but were unsuccessful in removing 'the Jew' from German life. Only if we take seriously the Nazi paranoia about the demonic Jewish threat to the Aryan race, can we understand why the need for a solution should have been felt so urgently.

And yet what real solution was there, once total emigration was ruled out because no country was willing to receive the Jews? As

Yehuda Bauer argues, 'the idea of a mass murder of the Jews was the logical consequence of Nazi theories', once emigration became impossible.[59] Logical: each step, from boycott to legislation to Aryanization to ghettoization further separated Jews from Germans, but in the end the Jews' destructive and demonic threat would only be removed if *they* were removed.[60]

As Ernst Nolte suggests, Hitler's lieutenants may well have shrunk back from the consequences of their wishes and wants, because they were not totally without decency. 'They combated the Jews, but they failed to recognize that even a complete emigration, according to the intrinsic meaning of the National Socialist doctrine, could not accomplish any genuinely essential changes. No wonder they became the prey of the more logically consistent mind.'[61] Hitler incarnated, especially in the Final Solution, the utter consistency of the racism around which German society had come to be organized. By achieving absolute power he was able to carry this theology to its logical conclusion.

Who Is Responsible?

How far can we now generalize beyond Hitler, his circle, and the SS troops involved—beyond even the Nazi movement and its supporters—in attributing the Final Solution to German *society* or *Germany*? It is true that no matter how hard we look beyond Hitler we never see more than a relative handful of key actors. But this tells us more about our century's machinery of destruction than about the man Hitler and the German nation-state. Those who could win control over the machinery and organize society around it, needed in the end only a relative handful of obedient servants to operate it. Hitler, we may say, got all the cooperation that was needed.

If genocide can be performed by strikingly few, it is no less striking how many accomplices it requires. Hundreds of thousands were asked only for their complicity, and gave it. Whether or not they desired to exterminate the Jews, they certainly acted, in the only ways that mattered, to bring that end about. Similarly, those who had voted Nazi, whatever reasons they might give, had acted in the ways available to *them* to bring to power a movement incorporating violence, obedience, antisemitism, militarism, and unreason. The two and a half million who joined the Nazis by 1935 more directly endorsed and participated in the movement. All those who became agents and beneficiaries of the antisemitic policies must also be numbered among the accomplices, as must those who knew what was being done to the Jews after 1941 but acquiesced. Even more directly connected are the hundreds of thousands who, though neither directing the Final Solution nor guarding the camps, provided the machinery through which it took place: those disposing of the victims' property, taking inventories of their gold teeth, manufacturing and shipping gas, performing the voluminous paperwork, directing and profiting from the starving labourers. In the end millions acted and assented: those who knew it was happening but let it continue, as well as those who aided and abetted it more directly. They all bear a share of the responsibility for the murder of six million Jews.

Certainly the average German—let us say, the SPD voter who withdrew after 1933 and kept to himself—is no more responsible for the Final Solution than the average American was responsible for the laying waste of Vietnam. Certainly no more, but also no less. Not only all those who participated in one or another phase of the preparation for genocide, or in the Final Solution itself, but also all those who knowingly accepted without opposition their society's actions thereby made those actions *their own*. The Nazis did not demand active involvement; having reduced the population to passivity they needed only complicity. Already in some sense *theirs* in historical origin—just as the technological hubris that destroyed Vietnam is a part of American national identity—the Final Solution further came to belong to tens of millions in Germany and elsewhere by virtue of their silent acquiescence.

To be sure, Nazi Germany was ruled by terror, and opposition meant grave consequences. The concentration camp system had originated as a way of detaining opponents of the regime. There were many who inwardly opposed what was done to the Jews, but went along because they felt they had to.[62] On this level Milgram's experiment is illuminating. The military, for example, was whipped into subservience to Hitler's policy, and many of the millions of military and civilian accomplices must have been decent people who hated Nazism but saw no alternative to obedience to their society's rulers. Nazi Germany, after all, was a society whose policy from the beginning was deliberately and systematically to transform its citizens into passive agents.[63]

One of the most remarkable facts about the Nazi extermination of Jews is that it proceeded virtually without incident or opposition among Germans. Opportunities were certainly available to resist, sabotage, or at least undermine, the Final Solution.[64] It was more than terror, or merely obedience, that caused the exterminations to be carried out so efficiently and be accepted so silently by the citizens of the Third Reich. After all, it was open resistance (culminating in Cardinal Galen's famous sermon), which led the Nazis to abandon their euthanasia programme.

Similarly, even under 'totalitarian' rule most of Germany's seventy million faithful sullenly let die the Nazi pagan 'Faith Movement'. Yet the many and complex steps preparing for and carrying out the Final Solution were taken virtually without incident.[65] Certainly, opposition to the other Nazi projects had developed in peacetime, and they threatened 'Aryans' themselves; while the extermination programme was secret, took place in wartime, and involved 'non-Aryans'. But the overwhelming mood towards the relatively few outcast and then departing Jews seemed to be, if not outright hostility then at least indifference to their fate.[66]

After all, was the Final Solution not rooted in a millennial Christian history of antisemitism, given new focus by recent German history? Did not the Nazis take power on a programme of antisemitism, behind a leader obsessed by it and who gave frequent warning of his intentions? And hadn't the militaristic racists defeated their opponents politically by 1933? And did not their new order proceed, as promised, to organize itself psychologically, socially, economically and culturally for war and expansion and against the Jews? From the start did it not carry out persecution, disenfranchisement, expropriation, and pogrom, and was not this accepted by millions of Germans? And was there not available in the SS—those claiming after all to be the best, the purest Germans in a racial state—a cadre willing to destroy the Jews? And did not this operation proceed with staggering efficiency? Taken together these by-now rhetorical questions point towards another: was not the extermination of the Jews as much an outgrowth of German history and society as the Nazis themselves? If we would understand *why* the Jews were exterminated these reflections point us not towards Hitler's psyche alone, but towards the social soil in which such evil became ascendant.

The Heritage of Defeat

What radical social pathology led to and was expressed in the radical extermination programme? The secret which accompanied Germany into the years of inflation and depression was its history of defeat—not only widely resented defeat at the hands of the Allies in the First World War but that of the peasants three hundred years earlier, that of the bourgeoisie in the nineteenth century, and that of the proletariat after the war.

If one step in this history was the peasants' defeat by the aristocrats in the sixteenth century, another was the later aristocratic reaction to modernization. They squeezed the peasants harder rather than leading a drive for genuine modernization of the kind which, in the case of England, broke the peasantry as a social force and drew the aristocracy and bourgeoisie close together. By 1848 the constellation of forces had become such that no bourgeois–democratic revolution was possible: the latter knew defeat in advance. Paraphrasing Marx, Barrington Moore sketches the resulting bourgeoisie: 'a commercial and industrial class which is too weak and dependent to take power and rule in its own right and which therefore throws itself into the arms of the landed aristocracy and the loyal bureaucracy, exchanging the right to rule for the right to make money.'[67] They were too few, too timid, and too weak; the aristocracy was too strong and, soon, would become the only effective safeguard against the rising proletariat.

To say that the bourgeoisie never triumphed in Germany is to say far more than meets the eye. Moore helps us to see how a mad political outlook had already developed in the late nineteenth century and could become a mass phenomenon in the twentieth because, in 1848, the then-rational one had been defeated. The lower middle class developed the furious will and strength to run amok because, a century earlier, their regressive hopes had not been liquidated by an ascending bourgeoisie. No matter how brutally, he argues, the American, French, and British bourgeoisie contributed to gradualism and democracy by successfully making society over in *their* image. Certainly, they did this to serve their own interest; but they functioned simultaneously as a modernizing, progressive force which, for a time, led and furthered humanity's struggle for freedom and dignity. Their revolution against the feudal world could become 'everyone's' only because it was a *relatively* humanizing, civilizing, and democratizing struggle. The country of the Final Solution was one in which industrialization, the fundamental economic advance, took place without the parallel human, political, social, and cultural advance embodied in constitutional government, an effective parliament, revocation of aristocratic privileges and the victory of new ideas of human dignity and political equality. A decisive revolutionary rupture with the past in the service of the present and future never happened in Germany, even though it industrialized virtually overnight.[68]

Antisemitism and *Völkisch* Thought

The key to German society's 'illness', to its 'distorted social development' was the defeat of the social forces that might have brought progress in human terms—a more democratic government, a more equal society, a more humane and rationalistic outlook—to accompany breakneck technological and economic progress. On the ideological level this defeat left open space for regressive and antirational outlooks to assume a legitimacy and currency unthinkable where successful revolutions had assured the hegemony of values such as reason, equality and progress. At the same time the irresolution and lack of congruence between and within the social, legal, political, economic and educational realms generated tensions which promoted ever more virulent strains of such thought. Regressive outlooks are present in any industrializing society, but in Germany the irrationalist and antisemitic protest against modernity was strong and widespread enough to be a contender for ideological dominance.

We must understand what this means—that prejudice became paranoia. People who hated the coming of the modern world believed what they said when they blamed it on the Jews as the people of the city, of the political and cultural vanguard, of internationalism and commerce.[69] And they were taken seriously, as age-old Christian antisemitism became absorbed and reshaped into this new current of protest.

In 1880 200,000 students signed a petition calling for the exclusion of Jews from government service, public and professional life in Germany. As George L. Mosse points out, antisemitism, antimodernism and *völkisch* (i.e. romantic folkish) thought—generally united in a single outlook—became 'commonplace bourgeois notions' in the late nineteenth century.[70] Espoused by respected thinkers and academicians like the historian Treitschke, this current did more than develop claims to scientific, moral and political legitimacy: 'The fact is that schools dominated by the *völkisch* ideology were so numerous as to constitute the centre rather than the fringe of German education.'[71]

How secure were the Bismarckian reforms, including emancipation of the Jews, in a climate in which the antisemitic *völkisch* outlook 'had permeated much of the nation' even before Hitler came on the scene?[72] Reforms were not won as the fruit of popular struggles, but imposed from above.[73] Not achieved through a real defeat of pre-bourgeois social forces, they rested therefore on shaky soil. This climate of uncertainty, concealed beneath the spectacular rise of German industrial capitalism and of the German socialist movement, is remarkably symbolized in a passage from a letter written in 1917 by Walter Rathenau, then director of General Electric Company, to Mrs von Hindenburg: 'Although myself and my ancestors have served our country as best as we could, I am, as you would presumably know, as a Jew a second-class citizen.'[74]

The Moment of Truth

Nevertheless, it seemed for some time that Germany was the world's most modern and potentially most revolutionary society. It seemed also—among Jews—that assimilation and not antisemitism was the real 'Jewish problem' in Germany.[75] But the real weakness of its progressive forces was revealed. Less in the stampede to war in 1914—which was, after all, universal—than in the defeated revolution and deadlock following the collapse of the Hohenzollern monarchy and discrediting of the feudal aristocracy. The heritage of defeat here reappears in an especially vicious form: the betrayal of a class by its own party leaders.

1918 was the most propitious moment yet for a decisive victory of 'modernity' in Germany. The military was demoralized by the allied victory and the workers had declared a republic. Even if not a socialist republic, a liberal democracy was in the offing which might forever sweep away the pre-bourgeois forces from German life. To achieve this the Social Democratic government would, in Moore's words 'have had to get to work at once to take control of the armed forces, the administrative bureaucracy, and the judiciary, remoulding them as instruments loyal to the Republic. It would have had to adopt an economic policy that included a degree of government control over certain areas of heavy industry, with some concessions to the workers over conditions on the shop floor. In doing all that, the government would have had to be willing to forestall the National Assembly by taking a series of essentially irreversible decisions necessary as the foundation for a liberal and democratic version of capitalism.'[76]

The social basis for this vigorous policy existed in the militant and active revolutionary movement, organized into workers' councils. But the Social Democratic leaders did not seek to change the 'wrong, outdated, anachronistic distribution of power'[77] among the classes of German society. Sebastian Haffner concludes that Fritz Ebert, the SPD leader 'did not want a republic, he wanted to save the monarchy'.[78] Hating the revolution 'like sin', Ebert sought to share power with the bourgeoisie and the aristocracy. His and the SPD's main animus became directed not against the old order, but against the repeated risings of workers.[79] In the end, during the revolutionary wave, the SPD not only failed to push for a liberal democratic programme but accepted, rehabilitated and made common cause with the old bureaucracy and aristocracy *against* the workers themselves.

No wonder that while administering the state apparatus, even at the height of a wave of popularity which gave them eleven million votes in 1919, the SPD made no effort to gain real control of it. Why? Perhaps Moore's description of the bourgeoisie of 1848 can be slightly altered and so made apposite for the SPD of 1918 and after: the party which represented the majority of the working class was too weak and dependent to take power and rule in its own right and therefore threw itself into the arms of the bourgeoisie, the discredited landed aristocracy and the bureaucracy. It exchanged the right to rule and to reshape Germany for the right to further workers' interests under a revived old order.

One can scarcely exaggerate the effect of this failed revolution on subsequent events. Germany was in a constitutional crisis of the deepest sort; yet the one force which could have decisively swept aside pre-bourgeois social classes, institutions and ideology had been defeated. More than defeated: betrayed by its own leaders in collusion with the old order, the working class was now split into two parties. It was in the anomalous position of being formally 'in power' while its leaders continued to call on volunteer soldiers—the *Freikorps*—to put down workers' risings. On the other hand, of course, the old aristocracy and bureaucracy hated the 'Marxist' republic which had been manipulated into negotiating a humiliating peace, while the army remained intact and undefeated. In as much as the *Freikorps* led to the Nazi stormtroopers, the nonrevolutionary SPD republic was saved by those who would soon become its own gravediggers.

If the parties of the working class did not exercise real power after the war, the old order was historically played out, unable now to unite Germany even under a military dictatorship. At the same time, nationalism was intensified by a humiliating and economically draining peace, and by French occupation of the Ruhr. The peace was both too severe and not severe enough,[80] because it humiliated the old order yet allowed the retention of its minions intact—especially the bureaucracy and military. For all its limits, socialism had had a corrosive effect on the old Germany by bringing the masses to the centre of the historical stage, so that in the Republic the old nationalist and aristocratic parties had become irrelevant. The army remained perhaps the most significant force to be reckoned with under Weimar, yet it too was no longer able to rule. Not strong enough to assume hegemony in the nineteenth century, the bourgeoisie was now structurally even less able to take leadership in a society where socialism was already on the agenda. The worsening political stalemate of the Weimar republic thus reflected a social crisis in which no traditional class was capable of asserting hegemony either by itself or in coalition. One could scarcely imagine a more welcoming soil for the *völkisch*, anti-modern, irrationalist outlook to be turned into a mass-based political party.

The Lower Middle Class and National Socialism

The party that emerged owed its origin, nature and phenomenal growth to many things: defeat, failed revolution and constitutional crisis, the deep penetration of the antisemitic and *völkisch* outlook, and the postwar economic crises. In the postwar peace settlement Germany had lost 13 per cent of its prewar territory, 10 per cent of its people, 15 per cent of its arable land, 75 per cent of its iron ore deposits, 44 per cent of its pig iron capacity, 38 per cent of its steel and 26 per cent of its coal capacity. Inflation, tied to the punitive reparations Germany had to pay the Allies, exploded the life savings of many of the hard working and thrifty between 1919 and 1923. After a period of stability the Depression struck, bringing unemployment rates of over 30 per cent by 1932. The Nazis had dropped from 6.5 per cent of the vote in May 1924 to 3.0 per cent that December, and then to 2.6 per cent in 1928. But in the 1930 elections Nazi support skyrocketed to 18.3 per cent, giving them the second largest delegation to the Reichstag.

Barrington Moore confirms that the NSDAP was indeed largely the party of the lower middle class—the 'little men', including teachers, small merchants, white-collar employees and officials, farmers and self-employed craftsmen.[81] Who were these people? The first thing that leaps to the eye, in the studies by Theodore Abel in the 1930s, and Milton Mayer in the 1950s, is that most of their subjects appear quite ordinary and conventional. 'There is little to be found in them', says Peter Merkl of Abel's respondents, 'that seems sinister or ominous. And yet the consequences of their common foibles, errors, and delusions cost an estimated fifty million human lives and untold destruction and misery.'[82]

If there is a direct line of mad rage from *Mein Kampf* through the Nazi movement's tactics and actual behaviour in power to the Final Solution, it is not immediately evident in these people. They are overly sentimental, ardent nationalists respectful of hard work and honesty, authoritarian and antisemitic. As Barrington Moore describes the respondents in Abel's study, their values are those of early competitive capitalism, they are 'petty bourgeois rather than bourgeois . . . with a strong overlay of both bureaucratic and even feudal features.'[83] They are people we can understand and sympathize with, rather than savages from the political gutter.

Hitler himself was patently one of these 'little men'. His jerkiness, exaggerated gestures and insecurity were those of one who lacks the grace and self-confidence learned through operating the levers that reproduce society. His writing reads like that of an autodidact lacking training, culture and polish. He was filled with resentment towards his betters, and indeed towards the whole world. He lacked faith in the future and longed to have been born 'earlier'.

Certainly idealizing the past or one's childhood does not prefigure evil to come, even if it does show desire to withdraw from a traumatic present. The same is true of intense nationalism. But the Nazis absorbed these attitudes into *National Socialism*, which is a definite leap beyond the more ordinary kinds of irrationality. In its deep structure it is a contradiction in terms. The worker who tells his story in Abel's account shows the irreconcilable pressure of idealized family and fatherland on the one side, and his experience and identification as a worker on the other. We can see his 'synthesis' of reactionary sentiment and class struggle in his acceptance of National Socialism. Its inherent inauthenticity was his authentic resolution. Abel's other essays show people living under similar enormous pressures, tensions, blockages and contradictions who chose to 'resolve' their situation by leaping beyond it, either towards the chimera of National Socialism, by faith in the absolute leader, or by fixating upon 'the Jew' supposedly 'polluting' their blood or defiling their race.[84]

As an outlook, National Socialism represents a fantastic joining of two irreconcilables. Nationalism united all classes, socialism sprang from class struggle; nationalism needed a foreign enemy, socialism claimed to be internationalist; nationalism deeply respected existing authority, socialism sought (in people's minds at least) to overthrow it. As a mass movement, Nazism was deeply marked by social-democratic aspirations and the workers' struggles against class society. This philosophy of the 'little man' who wants to leave society as it is begins by articulating enormous resentment against wealth and privilege, only to end by effacing this resentment in the larger community of the fatherland.[85] Its inherent illogic is such that it can be held together as outlook and movement only by three recourses: to an absolute leader, who will mystically cement together the otherwise irreconcilable by force of personality; to aggressive national expansion, as the only way of creating the material means for a 'socialism' providing economic benefits for the workers and poor without disturbing existing economic structures too much; and to virulent antisemitism, as the main defining pole of a Germanic fantasy-community for which class boundaries were irrelevant.[86] As an outlook National Socialism was not only articulated without style or grace, as Neumann pointed out,[87] but it was also contradictory, illogical, and founded on a systematic distortion of reality. Because Nazism *could not be* rational it aggressively promoted the rejection of reason itself, and based itself instead on regression.

Regression was one of the strongest currents of Nazism: its explicit goal was to return to the past. In fact, the movement coalesced around a virulent hatred for modernity. According to Nazi ideology the alienated, depersonalized, faceless twentieth-century world was to be reversed in the pure *Völkisch* state. Medieval virtues, especially of physical prowess, would be given a central place. The peasant, the tiller of the soil rooted in nature, would be honoured once more, and craftsmanship would become socially important again. Irrationalism and obedience to the leader were to replace Enlightenment notions of reason and political democracy. Women would be returned to their role of home-maker, mother and helpmeet for the Aryan warrior.

The very notion of the *Volk*, so central to Nazism, was a deliberate regression from what was seen as the cosmopolitanism and internationalism of the modern world. The Jews were hated primarily as bearers of modernity: an international people, an urban people, adept in the ways of modern capitalism and often proponents of socialism as well. Elemental values common to liberal democracy and socialism—such as equality, civil rights and liberties, the dignity of all people, the importance of rational deliberation and democratic decision-making, rule by law—were violently rejected by Nazi ideology and practice.[88] On the very first page of *Mein Kampf* Hitler introduced a key reversal of both bourgeois and socialist dreams for international peace and respect between nations: through conquest the German *Volk* would increase their daily bread, using swords as ploughshares. Against the panoply of slowly developed civilized values was asserted a brutal vision of Aryan domination: survival of the fittest, subservience to authority, and 'blood purity'.

These analyses take Nazi ideology seriously. We have learned that antisemitism, as the pivot of this ideology, must be taken equally seriously. These key strands of Nazism perpetuated the rejection of modernity and rationalism found in nineteenth-century romantic thought, but they gave it a new active and violent mass character. What was also new in Nazism was its political specificity—it blamed

Versailles and the Jews for the actual suffering of Germans in the late 1920s and early 1930s, it physically attacked Jews, broke up meetings, engaged in violent demonstrations, street fighting and political assassinations. And, as its ideology and actions gathered support, it sought political power. The 'little man' gave Nazism the dynamism, force, and organizational strength to impose its will upon a Germany in crisis, with decisive assistance from the military and large capital. For all other classes it was not the right time: they were either timid, without a popular base, defeated, or obsolescent. The 'little man' alone sought and acquired power.

The 'Little Man' in Power

He did it in a characteristic way, however: by surrendering all power to Adolf Hitler, by abandoning the heart of his social and economic programme, by compromising with his betters and projecting his impotent rage away from *this* situation. Nazism was a 'socialism' which, in power, would not attack the capitalists, which deeply respected authority, and buried class struggle in aggressive expansion and hatred of the Jews. The point is that the profoundly unrevolutionary yet highly explosive character of this 'fools' socialism' reflected the fundamentally impotent structural position of the lower middle class. The years after 1933 verify that the Nazi project—to guarantee the social status of the *Mittelstand* and protect it against both the working class and capital was, as Kühnl has said, 'objectively illusory'. The 'little man's' energies were 'directed towards the restoration of a past historical situation and social structure which has long been superseded by the development of the productive forces.'[89]

In other words, economically and technologically Germany's problems and needs had become those of an advanced capitalist society. Their inherent distance from the real levers of effective social power is expressed in the fact that, by themselves, the social forces of Nazism were incapable of grasping the last rung on the ladder to political power. Without *Reichswehr* and bourgeois acceptance the Nazis would have remained forever suspended between a hopeless putschism on the one hand and their one third of the vote on the other. The fact that Hitler was invited into office by Hindenburg in 1933 is more than symbolic: other classes, in other societies, have had the means and the will to take power *against* their national bourgeoisies and/or military forces. By contrast the very unrevolutionary thrust of 'revolutionary' Nazism suggests, among other things, that its leading group, even if it produced a Hitler and entered the halls of power, could never be genuinely dominant.

Why? The nature of the lower middle class was to depend structurally on large capital—socially, economically and ideologically. Its desires to turn back the clock remained purely subjective. Having no authentic—that is to say, independent and potentially realizable—long-term political, social or economic interests of its own, it was indeed as incapable of actual rule as it was of seizing power on its own.

But after all, did not the Nazis take power in one way or another, bringing tens of thousands of their own into leading positions, and did not Hitler utterly dominate Germany—including, finally, the military, the bureaucracy and the bourgeoisie? We can see this process unfold in Allen's account of Thalberg between 1930 and 1935, and it explains why Mosse uses *revolution* without inverted commas to refer to the Nazi takeover and its aftermath.[90] Indeed, did they not worship power, and exercise it—to promote German recovery, to create a totalitarian society, to expand by the threat of war, to conquer Europe with the most powerful war machine ever developed, and ultimately to assume the power of life and death over whole peoples?

But these were products of an all-powerful *impotence*. The Nazis were structurally incapable of doing the one thing that really mattered to their social class: undoing history. The paradox is vividly demonstrated in the Nazi treatment of department stores, a process that must have puzzled so many of Hitler's loyal supporters.

No capitalist institution had been as prominently attacked along the Nazis' road to power as the largely Jewish-owned department stores—this was in keeping with the necessarily superficial 'anti-capitalism' of a class which would attack its larger, more modern and efficient competitors—especially if they were Jews—but not the very market and property system of which it hoped to remain a respected part. After 30 January 1933, many of the anticipated steps were taken against department stores. Exceptionally high taxes were levied on turnover. Jewish stores were boycotted. Permanent limits were placed on chain and department store expansion. Department stores were excluded from handling certain profitable government and party business, and were boycotted repeatedly by various party groups. The failure rate of their apprentices before local examining boards rose appreciably, and the press and the mails discriminated against their advertising.

But, as the policy of a fundamental non-revolutionary government, these could only be temporary or half measures, taken ambivalently. Rapid economic recovery within the existing order, a vital need of the Nazi regime, depended on encouraging the most efficient—in this case, the largest, most highly developed—economic forms. Corporate capitalist realities undercut petty-bourgeois dreams as the banks, industry and government officials all saw the necessity of keeping the department stores healthy. Already in July 1933, the Reich Minister of Economics decreed for example that two large Jewish chains, which now had huge government investments, could not be allowed to go under. By 1936 turnover at the large stores had risen back to 86 per cent of that of 1932. By 1938 the threats had been removed, if not the formal restrictions. A 1935 official Party statement criticized the inadequacies of small shops, emphasizing that retail outlets where working people could buy cheaply did not deserve discrimination if maintaining the standard of living was the most important economic objective. Thus did the Nazi 'revolution' capitulate to the priorities of modern capitalist society, which it had no serious intention of dismantling.[91]

The vicissitudes of Nazi policy towards department stores reflect the fact that a non-socialist movement of 'little men', even if it held state power, could develop no sensible alternative to furthering the interests of monopoly capitalism.[92] As Poulantzas has argued, this was indeed a secret of fascism: it 'acclerates the consolidation and stabilization of the economic supremacy of big finance capital over the other dominant class and class fractions. But this is by no means to be interpreted as meaning that fascism represents the economic interests of big capital "exclusively". Fascism, rather, operates in the economic sense, as a factor *neutralizing* the contradictions among those classes and fractions, while regulating development to ensure the exclusive domination of the big capital.'[93] This 'exclusive domination' did not give large capitalists a free hand—rather, they had to submit to what Neumann called a 'command economy' in which Hitler's priorities ruled to such an extent that some authors have ridiculed the idea that capitalism was favoured under the Nazis. But to argue the point of whether (Nazi) politics or (bourgeois) economics was in command during the Third Reich is to miss the forest for the trees: a society need not be commanded by big capital to serve the latter's fundamental interests. Even if the logic of his course led him there, serving the interests of big capital was not the main mission of Adolf Hitler.[94] Driven repeatedly into the arms of the bourgeoisie, Nazism continued to dream of going backwards to a more hospitable time but was carried forward by deeper currents than it could ever comprehend. The inevitable 'compromise' between Nazism's original base and military and economic realities was brutally announced on 30 June 1934, on 'The Night of Long Knives' which destroyed the Nazi 'Left'. For all the talk of revolution during the Nazi era and by historians since, basic property relations were not even questioned, the corporate sector became ever more the lynchpin of the economy, and the German capitalism that rose from the ashes after 1945 had stunning continuity with that of Weimar and the Third Reich.

Economically speaking, fascism's hidden historical role may have been to create an alliance between monopoly capital and the 'little men', but this was accomplished only by intensifying the contradictions between them to the disadvantage of the latter.[95] For Adolf Hitler's social class, the Third Reich was a disaster. The Germany of 1939, as David Schoenbaum summarizes its results, confounded all expectations: 'Objective social reality, the measurable statistical consequences of National Socialism, was the very opposite of what Hitler had presumably promised and what the majority of his followers had expected him to fulfil. In 1939, the cities were larger, not smaller; the concentration of capital greater than before; the rural population reduced, not increased; women not at the fireside but in the office and the factory; the inequality of income and property distribution more, not less conspicuous; industry's share of the gross national product up and agriculture's down, while industrial labour had it relatively good and small business increasingly bad.'[96] In the command economy all of this took place deliberately: wages and prices were controlled, large farms and estates were encouraged, migration from country to town and town to city was permitted, women were encouraged to work.[97] In other words, while railing against the modern world, Hitler, like all fascists, was a great modernizer.[98]

Impotence in power

My point is not that fascism served the bourgeoisie, which it did, after all, only by commanding it and by plunging Germany into total war. Nor is it that the 'little man' was swindled during the Third Reich, which he was. But, above all, as Bloch said of the peasant, the petty bourgeois was 'situated in an older place'.[99] The 'swindle' confirmed that as a class, the petty bourgeoisie had no programme. That is, no programme which could be put into effect in the Germany of the 1930s. Its rabid desire to turn back the clock represented a fundamental historical impotence, and thus could only be 'achieved' symbolically through a mad break with that reality.

Impotent? As I have emphasized, one of the most striking characteristics of Nazism was Hitler's power lust. The worship of the Führer already promoted in *Mein Kampf* was central to the conversion of so many to Nazism, and was built into the movement's ethos and electoral appeal. In power, Hitler took every step possible to achieve absolute power. The German state attained unparalleled domination over the Western world. How do these undeniable facts square with my emphasis on the *impotence* of the social class upon which the movement was built?

In the most basic social sense, the Nazi obsession with power only confirmed their *lack* of it. This points us towards the terrible fracture in German society in which the class which sought and then held political power was unable to dispose over the prevailing technical-economic complex to achieve any socially meaningful goal.

The nature of Nazi power is the decisive consideration. Certainly any sophisticated discussion of Nazism has to acknowledge the relative autonomy of the political from the economic apparatus, and recognize that at this decisive moment in history power in one realm did not automatically translate to power in the other.[100] A key but generally unposed question about power is the congruence of an aspiring social force with society's actual level of development.

As Bloch said: 'Not all people exist in the same now.'[101] Those who clamoured for a return to the past rejected, and ultimately took a kind of suicidal vengeance on, the twentieth-century world. They were, in Bloch's term, a 'non-synchronous remainder' living a 'non-synchronous contradiction'. The primary problem was not that the German lower middle class turned to Nazism in droves but that it *existed in the first place* as a particularly regressive social constellation retaining political and ideological legitimacy in the fatal conjuncture of the 1920s and 1930s. Bloch speaks of 'synchronous contradictions' in which the 'impeded future' contained in the Now can be set free by a social class whose being is synchronous with the possibilities of this 'impeded technical benefaction'.[102] No political force, try as it may, can reshape a society *against* its actual historical possibilities. If it can indeed cripple or destroy the society, there is no wishing away the realities of an attained level of historical development. Even the ruler of Germany's totalitarian state was impotent to achieve the illusory aims of his class in the face of its fundamental historical weakness—in the face of the inappropriateness of its goals to the prevailing economic-technical complex and its possibilities. In that society, only a genuinely alternative movement in power could have avoided the economic fate of Nazism, its ultimate acquiescence to the structural limits imposed by German capitalism even as it commanded it. Genuine power is socially effective power: the ability to shape society in accord with its actual possibilities, to move confidently towards the future, to be congruent by orientation and disposition with the demands of *this* society. The Nazis lacked all of these. The ascendancy of this class was the most sinister reflection of a situation in which no other social class was sufficiently strong or sufficiently hegemonic to rule, and the movement able to grab state power was based (in Fritz Stern's words) on a 'wild leap from political reality'.[103]

We have seen that the 'wild leap' had already been taken from the very beginning of Nazism in *Mein Kampf*; indeed it received its shape long before, in the middle of the nineteenth century. If the projection of all of Germany's problems onto the Jews was already built into Nazism this testifies to the incongruence of the 'little men' with the advanced capitalist world. This meant that forces rooted more authentically in that world, like monopoly capital, were bound to triumph when it was a question of hard economic realities, such as ending the depression or preparing for war.

Nevertheless, this virulent outlook had already achieved a certain autonomy from its social sources, was a 'normal' current of German life, and could be reshaped into a legitimate political programme. Their despair about the present, the impossible project of revising history, the redemption of the *Volk*, the turn to unreason, and the fixation on the Jews as the cause of all evil—each step of this wild leap constituted part of the appeal of Nazism. The other part was its determination to *do something* about all of this. Once the Nazis were in power, this determination would meet the limits of reality.

The Final Solution

From the beginning the Nazi *enragés* represented the impossibility of reshaping the twentieth century to the tastes and needs of the *Mittelstand*; they stood for the urge to retreat from a world they hated, and the impossibility of that retreat. They also represented the mad and evil visions of victory which grew out of this feverish, yet sterile soil. After 1933 the Nazis possessed the political power—and military and technological means—with which to try to carry out this retreat imagined as a victory.

Retreat imagined as a victory: this is after all, the meaning of the torchlight parades, the burning of books, the creation of a specifically 'Aryan' culture, the great rallies and celebrations. But none of this could pacify either the pain which had driven the lower middle class onto the political stage—which must only have intensified as their actual social and economic situation worsened—or the antisemitic rage which was its insane product. Given the inevitability of its failure on every other level, Nazism could succeed *only* by addressing and solving 'the Jewish problem'.

This is why the logic of Nazism leads to the Final Solution. It seems clear that no one, even Adolf Hitler, fully and consciously grasped that this is where the rupture with reality by his impotent class would lead. In their first years of power, writes Schleunes, the Nazis 'stumbled' towards a solution. Each step was an improvisation, a response to specific pressures and situations, and each step led to a further impasse. 'They were certain only that a solution was necessary. This commitment carried the Nazi system along the twisted road to Auschwitz.'[104]

The extermination of six million Jews, successfully eliminating Jews from most of Central and Eastern Europe, was the Nazis' one great victory. The Final Solution reflects impotence in power. In radically fulfilling the dream of *völkisch* antisemitism it was the act of those who, having no effective power to shape the social world, still disposed over the political and military might to try to destroy the force allegedly at the source of its evils. This logic, inherent in Nazism from its origin, was finally stated by Hitler in 1939 and put into action by him in 1941 or 1942.[105] As Germany's defeat in the war became at first possible, then likely, then inevitable, the extermination apparatus only intensified its mission. As the prospect of real victory faded, their mad project to save civilization from the Jewish demon only accelerated. By exterminating the people who incarnated it, evil could still be destroyed. Only in this barbaric way could the 'little man' become the master race.

Unfit for the Modern World or Part of It?

In conclusion, what is the source of the impotent and mad rage that led to the Holocaust? Much about Nazism seems to dispute my analyses of it as a lower middle class phenomenon. From the beginning the party proclaimed itself beyond class conflict, seeking to harmonize proletarian and bourgeois in the Aryan state. However deluded, its primary object was the well-being of all Germans, irrespective of class. Moreover, it called itself not only the 'National Socialist' but the 'German Workers' Party'. And in fact, by 1935 over a quarter of its membership were industrial workers—the largest number (662,000) of any occupational category in the 2.5 million member party.[106] This leads us to the root question: was Nazism the response of a 'backward' class resisting integration into the modern world,[107] or did it rather reflect a rage towards that world by those already accustomed and acculturated to it? Was the real root of the problem that Germany, industrializing later than Britain, developed unevenly, its older social layers put into exaggerated tension with its newer ones until an explosion was reached?

For Bloch the central characteristic of Nazism was that it emerged from 'non-synchronous' people—remnants of earlier social forms who persisted into a present for which they were unfit. 'If misery only afflicted synchronous people, even though of different positions, origins, and consciousness, it could not make them march in such different directions, especially so far backwards. They would not have such difficulty "understanding" the Communist language which is quite completely synchronous and precisely oriented to the most advanced economy. Synchronous people could not permit themselves to be so largely brutalized and romanticized, in spite of their mediate position, which keeps them economically stupid, in spite of all the semblance that it has a place there.'[108]

Or is the root of Nazism exactly the opposite, the *successful* progress of the modern world? In *Dialectic of Enlightenment*, Max Horkheimer and Theodor Adorno emphasized that self-denial and renunciation were inherent in the Western programme of the domination of nature, a project not limited to bourgeois society but whose literary record was at least as old as the *Odyssey*. Fascism, and indeed antisemitism, are seen as one pole of the dialectic of Western civilization itself. As domination progressed, so did the mad revolt of brutalized nature, culminating in the antisemitism of twentieth-century totalitarianism—rooted precisely in its most 'synchronous' people.

Its result was not liberation but barbarism: 'the rebellion of suppressed nature against domination, directly useful to domination.'[109] The Frankfurt thinkers saw this barbarism as dialectically linked to the progress of civilization. This is what Herbert Marcuse meant by saying that totalitarian violence 'came from the structure of existing society'.[110] For Marcuse, Adorno and Horkheimer, intensified domination and renunciation make such explosions inevitable. Did Auschwitz express the barbarity chosen by those unwilling or unable to join the modern world, as I have suggested with Bloch, or is its secret the explosion of the repressed side of our long journey away from barbarism and towards civilization? In fact, Auschwitz surely reflects *both*: a consummately civilized barbarism. If they broke through barriers to behaviour long equated with being civilized itself, the Nazis did so under the full weight of domination and renunciation, possible only in advanced civilization, using the technical and organizational sophistication available only in that civilization. The 'return' to the most brutally primitive levels of behaviour was a product of the present using the tools of the present.

In other words, we must turn to modernity itself, as well as the lower middle class rebellion against it, to explain the Holocaust. Or rather, not to 'modernity' as such, but to the fact that after the workers' defeat in 1918 no alternative remained to its most oppressive forms. Defeat was the universal formative experience in Germany. Demoralized, without a way forward, many workers felt such defeat no less than the lower middle class. The ideological and political amalgam they accepted was rooted in a despair which they could see as their own, containing much truth about the destructive side of the modern world. Truth, that is, perceived from the sad position of being unable to create a more humane modern world. If workers moved towards Nazism it was because defeat had made them responsive to the rage of the lower middle class.

Rather then confusing our class analysis, this fact completes it. As during any social crisis, as with any movement, the dominant party was not wholly of a single class. Others joined it for their own reasons, lending their own weight to the movement while accepting its central thrust. In this tragic situation, the impotent rage of the 'little man' without a way forward became generalized beyond the class in which it originated and to whose situation it gave focus. In the years of crisis after the war, more and more Germans became despairing, turned therefore into 'little men', and found their way to the Nazi revolt. Their mixture of fantasy and reality, of impotence and power, of regression and modernity pointed towards total war and extermination of the Jews as its natural outcome.

3
Why? Towards a Theory
of the Soviet Holocaust

In the early morning of the second day of the Bolshevik Revolution, Lenin and Trotsky bedded themselves down on the floor of Smolny Institute. There the momentous All-Russian Congress of Soviets had just adjourned after adopting a 'Peace Declaration of the Peoples of All the Belligerent Countries', and a Land Decree transferring to local Soviets and land committees 'all land-owners' estates and all lands belonging to the Crown, to monasteries, and the Church', as well as constituting itself the new government of Russia.

Thus the Bolsheviks gave stirring proof of their determination to transform the country, and the world, in the direction demanded by the masses of poor and working people in Russia and voiced by Lenin: 'We shall now proceed to construct the Socialist order!' Its first act, the peace proclamation, was addressed not only 'to the Governments and to the peoples of the belligerent countries' but also to the workers of England, France and Germany, whose history of struggle is 'a sure guarantee that the workers of these countries will understand the duty imposed upon them to liberate humanity from the horrors and consequences of war; and that these workers, by decisive, energetic, and continued action, will help us to bring to a successful conclusion the cause of peace—and at the same time, the cause of the liberation of the exploited working masses from all slavery and all exploitation.'[1]

For once in the history of the world the hope was to be acted upon. Certainly the imperialist governments would resist the offer. 'But we hope that revolution will soon break out in all the belligerent countries; that is why we address ourselves to the workers of France, England, and Germany ....'[2] Later in the debate Lenin returned to this point: 'If the German proletariat realizes that we are ready to consider all offers of peace, that will perhaps be the last drop which overflows the bowl—revolution will break out in Germany ....'[3]

The proclamation was accepted unanimously. 'Suddenly, by common impulse', wrote John Reed, 'we found ourselves on our feet, mumbling together into the smooth lifting unison of the *Internationale*. A grizzled old soldier was sobbing like a child. Alexandra Kollontai rapidly winked the tears back. The immense sound rolled through the hall, burst windows and doors and soared into the quiet sky.'[4] 'Did it go altogether into the sky?' asked Trotsky, following upon Reed's description. 'Did it not go also to the autumn trenches, that hatchwork upon unhappy, crucified Europe, to her devastated cities and villages, to her mothers and wives in mourning? *"Arise ye prisoners of starvation! Arise ye wretched of the earth!"* The words of the song were freed of all qualifications. They fused with the decree of the government, and hence resounded with the force of a direct act. Everyone felt greater and more important in that hour. The heart of the revolution enlarged to the width of the whole world. "We will achieve emancipation ...." The spirit of independence, of initiative, of daring, those joyous feelings of which the oppressed in ordinary conditions are deprived—the revolution had brought them now. "... with our own hand!"'[5]

Drifting off to sleep a few hours later, the acknowledged leader of the revolution whispered to the writer of these words, the great organizer of the insurrection: 'Es schwindelt'—'It is dizzying.'[6]

Dizzying, this achievement of proletarian power for the first time in human history.[7] If its provenance was clear in the process by which the October Revolution seized power—relying upon tens of thousands of armed workers—its intentions were broadcast in its first decrees. Together they reflected the fact that, for the first time in human history, the Bolsheviks presided over a state directly resting on and serving the poor and oppressed masses. For the next several years this earth-shaking event reverberated around the world, inspiring revolutionary movements—including those in Germany, Hungary and Italy—and a wave of worker militancy further West—in France, Britain and the United States. Lenin's whispered comment expresses, unconsciously, a key to what would follow. In speaking German at the first moment of release and relaxation, was Lenin not reflexively suggesting Russia's fatal dependence on Germany?

Hitler created Stalin. This simplistic and onesided anachronism points, none the less, to the Bolsheviks' conviction that their revolution was only the opening shot of the worldwide proletarian revolution, and that their own success, indeed survival, hinged on assistance by a victorious proletariat in the West. It suggests that the failure of the German revolution, and its disastrous aftermath, from the beginning turned Russia back on itself to wrestle with the most severe of contradictions: how to build socialism, there, alone. Defeat in Germany was to remove the prospect of proletarian support, and heighten to the breaking point Bolshevik urgency to end Russia's inferiority. Indeed, if defeat in Germany led to Stalin and 'socialism in one country' in Russia, may we not also say that it led to a suicidally introverted foreign and Comintern policy which kept the German proletariat split while Hitler was rising to power? In this sense, perhaps, it is no less true that 'Stalin created Hitler'.

A preface to hope reveals itself most strikingly as a history of unreason when we approach the vicissitudes of this revolution, one of humanity's greatest hopes—and catastrophes—in this century. Even today, the possibility of hope for many continues to turn on how the Bolshevik Revolution is interpreted. Was Stalinism inherent in Leninism—or indeed, in Marxism? Is the Soviet Union a socialist society? Was Russia ripe for a Marxist revolution? Upon such questions seems to rest the very chance of socialism *after* Stalinism and in the light of today's Soviet Union. After all, of all the century's revolutions, only this one erupted in modern industrial cities and was carried through by the industrial working class. As a result the dénouement of the Bolshevik Revolution has done more to stifle hope than any other event in the century, has helped destroy socialism as an ideal worth struggling for in the minds of generations of industrial workers.

The brute fact of the Soviet Union today, no less than under Stalin, makes a mockery of the claims of those who promise that socialism will be more humane than capitalism, more genuinely democratic, more rational, more technologically inventive, and less destructive of the environment. In short, its very existence, no less than its traumatic history, saps the sense that any *alternative* is possible. Why struggle for a revolutionary transformation of our societies if *that* is all that can be hoped for? There are two horrors in the Soviet experience: one is the sheer number of human lives destroyed, the sheer weight of the loss and suffering; another is the defeat of hope.

The second is perhaps the greater barrier for humanity today. After all, even mass death can be somehow absorbed, if it is seen as being en route to a better world; but the defeat and corruption of revolutionary hopes is a moral, intellectual and political loss from which there is no appeal. Humans abandon hope when struggles and sacrifices, accepted in the conviction that they have some meaning and purpose, are seen to lead nowhere.

Achievement and Disaster

The barbarism of Nazi Germany, difficult as it may be to face squarely, nonetheless seems almost easy to comprehend next to the phenomenon of the Soviet Union in the 1930s. The Nazis' madness and evil were apparent in 1933 to anyone who did not share it: war, terror and antisemitism were built into their movement. The great questions about the Holocaust are straightforward, if horrible: why did people choose to commit such staggering evil? But no one contests the complete absence of anything redeeming about the Nazis: no monuments to their purpose are worth preserving except as admonitions. This movement died with its ruler and left everything it touched in ruins.

The Soviet Union is much more taxing to comprehend. Stalin moved to power silently, almost unobtrusively, not at the head of the glorious mass movement of liberation but in the process of the movement's bureaucratization. In power, Stalin's rule made the whole people potential 'enemies of the people' as it created an astounding apparatus of inquisition, forced labor and death. It cost perhaps 20 million lives, one in eight Soviet citizens. Yet in one of history's most spectacular leaps forward it also created overnight a modern industrial society, barely soon enough to repel Hitler's armies at the gates of victory. If it did the work of the Devil, destroying and terrorizing, it also immeasurably enriched and transformed Soviet life, educating, civilizing, spreading medical care, modernizing. If Stalin stands next to Hitler as one of history's great tyrants, he also towers above the leaders of our century as one of history's great builders.

Appreciating the aftermath of October thus means heading simultaneously in two directions, measuring achievement as well as disaster. About both there remains dispute and denial, even thirty years after Stalin's death. The debate is, of course, political—the more Stalinist construction is stressed, as in Nettl's *The Soviet Achievement*, the less is the catastrophe mentioned (it receives there only seven pages);[8] the more the catastrophe is stressed, as in the Menshevik Raphael Abramovitch's *The Soviet Revolution*, the less is the achievement referred to (in this case a single grudging sentence).[9] Avoiding denial means emphasizing *both* colossal facts which the Soviet thirties have left behind—the victory over Nazi Germany, and the destruction of many millions of people—and inquiring into their connection.

Certainly the Soviet victory over Hitler can be discussed in terms of such variables as overall military strategy, leadership and battlefield tactics. Stalin's shocking paralysis during the invasion's first two weeks, for example, had a major effect on Soviet losses. At the nadir of the Great Purge Stalin had stripped the military of competent officers and technical experts: across society the Purge had replaced morale with terror, drastically retarding production, preparedness and skill. On the other hand Hitler's fixation on taking Stalingrad, for example, can also be seen as the turning point.

Nevertheless, in the words of Francis Randall, 'other things being equal, the stronger power wins the war.' The Germans' initial accumulation of armaments and their successful surprise delayed the outcome, 'but Russia's superior strength was never altogether overcome, and eventually won the war.'[10] *Russia's superior strength*: how did this happen, this transformation from the 'weakest link' in the chain of capitalism to a socialist power superior to one of its strongest links and all her satellites put together? In the height of battle, with two-thirds of European Russia occupied or devastated in 1943, the USSR still out-produced Germany in tanks and airplanes. Although his conclusion may be disputed that Russia's production was superior to Germany's in 'every year' of the conflict, Randall points out the Soviet 'miracle' of the Second World War: 'The Germans started the invasion with a larger accumulation of heavy weapons, and destroyed much of what the Russians had in the first five months. But the Russians eventually succeeded in maintaining their superior production—often in quality as well as quantity—and in concentrating their movements (after the first five months) more rapidly and more effectively to achieve superiorities and win key battles.'[11]

It may indeed be that the Soviet Union could accomplish this only by destining 'all for the front', and, in Maurice Dobb's words, 'cutting to the bone the supply of all but the bare essentials for civilian consumers';[12] it may also be that Soviet industrialization had for a dozen years been lopsided towards the heavy industries needed for war production: and it may indeed remain true today that this formidable industrial-technical base has not yet resulted in a bounty of consumer goods. Still, *in spite of every possible qualification*, the undeniable fact remains that the Soviet Union was saved by modernization and industrialization. It might indeed have been carried out more rationally, humanely and efficiently than the breakneck industrialization of the five-year plans. But without an industrial, agricultural, technical and cultural revolution victory would have been inconceivable. *Revolution*: that quantity became quality is attested by the fact that in 1928 production had barely recovered to its pre-First World War level, while by 1940 the basis had been created for a modern industrial state.

The last point is decisive. The immensity of the country, its inexhaustible reserves of population, the vastness of its resources—these became *positive* factors of defence only because they had already been harnessed, developed, organized. This achievement took place in the scant twelve years before Germany attacked. The moving of factories and people eastward as the Germans occupied western Russia, the production of weapons of equal quality to the Germans', the training, equipping and organizing of division after division: all of this testifies to the astounding ability of a country only two generations away from serfdom to function as a modern power in the supreme test of modern powers—total war.[13]

If the achievement is fully half the account, the other half is the holocaust wrought on its people by the state that emerged from the world's first socialist revolution. Stalin was not boasting when he told Winston Churchill that ten million kulaks had to be dealt with during collectivization, most of them being 'wiped out'.[14] Perhaps 5½ million peasants died from hunger and the diseases of hunger in the man-made famine of 1932. Mass starvation was caused not by food shortages, but by steeply increased, calculated government requisition from newly-collectivized peasants. Collectivization itself led to some 16 million peasants being forcibly resettled, some 3½ million being placed in forced labour camps, with perhaps 3½ million ex-

ecuted. 'Liquidation of the kulaks' truly meant the physical extermination of one part of the Russian population. It was followed by
the Great Purge of the 1930s, a gigantic human iceberg of which the
infamous Moscow Trials were only the tiniest tip. Robert Conquest
estimates that perhaps a million people were executed in 1936–38,
that the forced-labour camp population in late 1938 may have been
between 8 and 15 million people, and that during the late 1930s 6½
million people died in the camps, largely as a matter of policy. The
total casualty figure for the Stalin years, 1930–53, is estimated as 20
million dead.[15]

Just as with the Soviet victory over Germany, so should we take
the salient fact of so many deaths as reflecting a much broader reality. That reality takes in all the trappings of a totalitarian state including the cult of personality, the crude bullying of an entire population, the raising of an entire generation on lifeless dogma, and the
return for inspiration to Tsarist models.

In the years of terror, no one was above suspicion. All the other
five men named in Lenin's will were to die at Stalin's hands, as well
as nineteen of the thirty-three Politburo members between 1919 and
1938.[16] As Anton Antonov-Ovseenko describes the years in which
he grew to manhood and saw his father destroyed: 'Fear became a
nutrient medium, part of the atmosphere you breathed. Everyone
and everything was feared. The neighbours in your building, the
caretaker in the building, your own children. People lived in fear of
their co-workers, those above them, those beneath them, and those
on the same level. They feared oversights or mistakes on the job, but
even more, they feared being too successful, standing out. At the top
they also lived in fear. A party or government post was something
like a smoking crater in which someone had just been killed. A newly
appointed minister, Central Committee member, secretary of a pro-
vincial committee, or president of a municipal Soviet executive committee would hunch down and work away in the fresh crater in the
hope that the theory of probability would not let him down: a second
artillery shell shouldn't fall on the same spot.'[17]

These years were epitomized in the situation described by Roy
Medvedev: 'The country had a President [Kalinin] whose wife was
kept in a concentration camp.'[18] Informing became a central social
activity, as every last person was potentially pitted against everyone
else. 'Children denounced their parents, and parents disowned

children arrested for "counterrevolutionary activity." Each denounced the other. Under Stalin the number of informers approached the number of inhabitants able to read and write. Or speak. Only the infants failed to denounce. Even in the kindergartens denouncing was encouraged. Soon every second person in the country was informing.'[19] Under certain circumstances, Jean-Paul Sartre wrote, socialism 'could be synonymous with hell.'[20]

Zachto – Why?

Describing that hell has been the great achievement of Alexander Solzhenitsyn. His *One Day in the Life of Ivan Denisovich* was published in 1962, during the wave of de-Stalinization under Khrushchev. In reading it our question becomes the one prisoners wrote on cell walls, carved into the planks of transit camps and on the sides of prison wagons: *zachto*—why?[21] Why the catastrophe? Is it separable from the achievement, as for example Antonov-Ovseenko and Medvedev claim, or was it necessary, as Sartre insists? Was it a cost of modernization? Or a consequence of Communist revolution? Or of that revolution's isolation? Or of its prematurity, as Rousset argues? Or, more particularly, a result of Lenin's untimely death? Or of Trotsky's defeat? Or of Bukharin's policies being abandoned?

To reply to these questions, we must take issue with even the most lucid Bolshevik self-interpretation. This study will insist that the revolution's deformation was inseparable from its accomplishments —in broad outline the thesis developed so powerfully by Isaac Deutscher. But I intend to reverse his emphasis, by focusing on those respects in which the accomplishments of Stalinism *stemmed from* its irrationality.

To be sure, Deutscher was sensitive to the fundamental irrationality which came to permeate the revolution. Indeed, one of its greatest descriptions is his characterization of the situation in which the Soviet people and their rulers found themselves during the *tours de force* of 1928–33 which transformed industry and agriculture: 'The whole experiment seemed to be a piece of prodigious insanity, in which all rules of logic and principles of economics were turned upside down. It was as if a whole nation had suddenly abandoned and destroyed its houses and huts, which though obsolete and decaying, existed in reality, and moved, lock, stock, and barrel, into some illusory buildings, for which not more than a hint of scaffolding had in reality been prepared; as if that nation had only after this crazy migration set out to make the bricks for the walls of its new dwellings and then found that even the straw for the bricks was lacking; and as if then the whole nation, hungry, dirty, shivering with cold and riddled with disease, had begun a feverish search for the straw, the bricks, the stones, the builders and the masons, so that, by assembling these, they could at last start building homes incomparably more spacious and healthy than were the hastily abandoned slum dwellings of the past. Imagine that that nation numbered 160 million people; and that it was lured, prodded, whipped, and shepherded into that surrealistic enterprise by an ordinary, prosaic, fairly sober man, whose mind had suddenly become possessed by a half-real and half-somnambulistic vision, a man who established himself in the role of super judge and super architect, in the role of a modern super-Pharoah. Such, roughly, was now the strange scene of Russian life, full of torment and hope, full of pathos and of the grotesque; and such was Stalin's place in it; only that the things that he drove the people to build were not useless pyramids.'[22]

This description of the irrationality of 'socialist construction' captures, as do much of Deutscher's *Stalin* and *Trotsky*, the revolution's passage from reason to madness, from good works to evil without ever fully renouncing reason or the good. The strengths of Deutscher's interpretation are the strengths of the Marxist tradition: its rationalism, its understanding of the ways in which situation influences action and action situation, its historical scope, its sense of the interrelation of the political, economic, social and technological planes. But, like that tradition, Deutscher remains uncritical of his own rationalist and progress-oriented premises; he is too confident of 'history', too unquestioningly insistent that the revolution's contradictory outcome *stems from the barbarism of an earlier world*. For example, in describing Stalinism 'as the amalgam of Marxism with Russia's primordial and savage backwardness'[23] he fails to see the utter irrationality of imposing 'enlightenment' on a recalcitrant environment, the irrationality that would become indistinguishable from Marxist rationalism.

Deutscher's lucidity, and its limits, recall and mirror the strengths and weaknesses of Leon Trotsky's appreciation of the revolution's course. Possessing Marxist intellectual tools but not power, Trotsky in opposition and then exile became the lucid self-consciousness of Bolshevism, the one Russian analyst who both shared the revolution's commitments and dared to confront it with the full force of its own betrayal. He alone spoke to it with its own voice, of its own hopes. Like Deutscher after him, he sought the source of the betrayal in the material situation. Thus he produced the most compelling contemporary self-interpretation of Bolshevism: 'Socialism is a structure of a planned production to the end of the best satisfaction of human needs; otherwise it does not deserve the name of socialism. If cows are socialized, but there are too few of them, or they have too meagre udders, then conflicts arise out of the inadequate supply of milk—conflicts between city and country, between collectives and individual peasants, between different strata of the proletariat, between the whole toiling mass and the bureaucracy. It was in fact the socialization of the cows which led to their mass extermination by the peasants. Social conflicts created by want can in their turn lead to a resurrection of "all the old crap" ....'[24]

In Marx's original the German reads *Scheisse*—shit. Meaning classes, exploitation, inequality, the absence of democracy. What else could be expected in a society where the struggle for survival was the dominant feature of life, where the typical citizen was not the literate worker and trade unionist living in cities and producing modern goods with sophisticated equipment, but the illiterate *muzhik*, only a generation away from serfdom? Where by the mid-thirties, while 'the United States consumes twelve pencils a year per inhabitant, the Soviet Union consumes only four, and those four are of such poor quality that their useful work does not exceed that of one good pencil, or at the outside two.'[25]

Seeing the society and most of the population as fatally under-developed, Trotsky sought a way out of the cul-de-sac in which the revolution's own assumptions placed it by describing the Soviet Union as 'a contradictory society halfway between capitalism and socialism.'[26] He might with greater accuracy have insisted that the country was being pushed towards socialism without having first gone through the capitalist advance beyond feudalism. He might have emphasized, according to Marxist assumptions, the absence of a process of *human* development, one which Russia had not yet undergone by itself and to whose fruits it was denied easy access by the failure of revolution in Germany. His theory of uneven and combined development gave a premature happy ending to what would become a tragedy. Writing in the mid 1930s, his vision of the Soviet Union was dominated by his sense of its backwardness—meaning the abysmally low Russian level of education and political development; meaning a general absence of the experience of working in collective, modern industry, of living in cities, of exposure to science and technology. This situation, for Trotsky, explains the growth of bureaucratic rule, increasing inequality, and the cult of Stalin.

Trotsky's extremely penetrating analysis is however hampered by a fundamental blind spot. The weakness of his perspective is perhaps best expressed by the major omission of *The Revolution Betrayed*: Trotsky virtually ignores the fate of the peasantry in the early 1930s. He dismisses talk of induced famine, forced labour camps, mass executions, expropriations and deportations, as simply 'the twaddle of liberals that collectivization as a whole was accomplished by naked force.'[27] But as a whole, it was. While Trotsky accurately describes the mood of civil war in the countryside during these years, he pays more attention to the loss of animals—slaughtered en masse when the peasants were forced to enter collective farms—than to the loss of human life.

Why? While Trotsky emphasizes the goal of the changes in the countryside as being to move from 'barbarism to civilization' he totally passes over the barbaric means employed. The source of this fatal blind spot is that Trotsky, while in some sense perceiving the contradictory situation in which the Bolshevik Revolution found itself, was himself part of that contradiction. Exiled from power—indeed, perhaps only because of this—he could to some extent voice the revolution's humane, egalitarian and democratic aspirations against Stalin's crudeness and brutality. It is Trotsky, after all, whose history of 1917 has been one of the great celebrations of the power of ordinary people. But, as we shall see, when in power himself Trotsky accepted, even promoted and initiated decisive early steps down the road to the police state of the 1930s.

Deutscher, like Trotsky, treats the expropriation, exile and slaughter of tens of millions of peasants with striking callousness. This admittedly 'bloody cataclysm' receives only three pages in *Stalin*, while an entire chapter ('The Gods are Athirst') is devoted to the

Great Purge of 1936–38, treating it primarily as a *party* purge. His *Trotsky* acknowledges, as does his *Stalin*, that 'millions of people [were] dispossessed and condemned to social, and many also to physical, death.'[28] But that is all: where page after page is devoted to the internal manoeuvering under Stalin, to deep and sustained analysis of the causes of the revolution's turns of direction—for example, Deutscher takes seven pages to discuss the consequences of Jacob Blumkin's 1929 visit to Trotsky on Prinkipo—it is little short of astounding that Deutscher does no more than register the event experienced as an unmitigated holocaust by the vast majority of Soviet citizens.

Why does Deutscher's eloquence grow cold when speaking of the destruction of what he regards as the grey, primordial peasantry? To him it seems they scarcely matter, except as obstacles to socialism, as a human mass to be 'civilized'. He seems to regard them with the eyes of a Trotsky, if not a Stalin. Are they not enlightened eyes, Western eyes? His point is that their fate under the Bolsheviks was in a sense foreordained by history. 'In a vast country accustomed to extensive agriculture [the replacement of the unproductive smallholding by the modern large-scale farm] could be achieved either by the energetic fostering of agrarian capitalism or by collectivization —there was no other choice. No Bolshevik government could act as the foster parent of agrarian capitalism—if it had so acted it would have let loose formidable forces hostile to itself and it could have compromised the prospects of planned industrialization. There was thus only one road left, that of collectivization ....' Although the all-important questions of scale, method and tempo had still to be resolved, 'the actual situation of 1929 dictated that Stalin and his followers attacked the opposing forces with mounting fury.'[29]

Deutscher does quote Trotsky's description of the 'liquidation of the kulaks' as a 'monstrosity'. But the 'monstrosity' is not the human catastrophe but the fact that 'collectivization should not outrun the technical means needed for it.'[30] In other words, the surviving collectivized peasants would be unable to produce enough to discover the advantages of social over individual farming! For Deutscher collectivization appears as an inevitable war, against virtually equal opponents, 'a war which the collectivist state waged, under Stalin's supreme command, in order to conquer rural Russia and her stubborn individualism.'[31] Bukharin, reviled by Stalin—and by history

—for his sympathy to the peasants, views this 'war' rather differently in his comparison of 1919 with the period 1930–32: 'In 1919 we were fighting for our lives. We executed people, but we also risked our lives in the process. In the later period, however, we were conducting a mass annihilation of completely defenceless men, together with their wives and children.'[32]

A second blind spot, for all Deutscher's eloquence in rendering the irrational directions taken by the revolution, concerns his unwillingness or inability to comprehend this phenomenon of irrationality. One senses in him no pathos for the millions destroyed; nor even the momentary self-doubt that it might all not have been necessary. For his work is animated by a fervent belief in progress and ultimate rationality. Stalin was driving history *forward*: if the path was catastrophic perhaps this was inevitable. Russian savage backwardness absorbed and transformed the Bolshevik drive to enlighten, modernize, rationalize. Stalin undertook, to quote a famous saying, 'to drive barbarism out of Russia by barbarous means. Because of the nature of the means he employed, much of the barbarism thrown out of Russian life has crept back into it.'[33] It rests with Stalin's heirs to sort out those aspects of the heritage worth keeping from those to be discarded.

One senses that the rationality guiding Deutscher's enterprise and the Marxist project in some sense gilds its subjects: tragedies and irrationality there may be, but they fit within an overall logic of human betterment. However, if the *whole* is indeed becoming insane, may it not be argued that it was not human betterment but 'pyramids of sacrifice' which were being produced?

Deutscher conveys but does not comprehend the break with rationality of a society in which, in Antonov-Ovseenko's words, 'there arose two categories of citizens—those in confinement and those still waiting to be arrested.'[34] This society in which nearly every person became a potential 'enemy of the people' was a society which claimed to be entering into socialism while its children were without milk to drink.

Under Stalin, society underwent a rupture from reality, and proceeded instead by a systematic displacement—by fantasy, by organizing itself around myth, and by a violent and disfiguring assault on reality itself to make it conform to the fantasy and myth. But if the worst features of Stalinism are to be regarded as madness, I will argue that they were neither the revolution's accidental deviation nor its bastard child. They were produced, rather, out of the revolution itself, as were its best features and achievements. Not, as Deutscher argues, as the revenge of Old Russia against her modernizers, but somehow as the product of the modernizers themselves.

The Revolution Against the Workers

For Lenin the event that 'lit up reality better than anything else'[35] was the Kronstadt uprising of March 1921. However the Bolsheviks tried to discount the rebellion at the naval base and surrounding industrial complex—as led by White Guards, anarchists and Social Revolutionaries, as based on new peasant recruits and untried revolutionaries—its locale and character were fated to bring about, as Bukharin said, 'the collapse of our illusions'.[36] Leonard Schapiro's description of it as the 'revolt of the proletariat against the dictatorship of the proletariat'[37] contains more than anti-Communism. Indeed the entire leadership knew quite well that they were using 'violence against the "toiling masses" in the name of the "toiling masses".'[38] First, the sailors of Kronstadt had always been the shock troops of the revolution: the *Aurura*, which had played a major role in the October insurrection, was now up in arms, as was the *Petropavlovsk*, whose crew demanded the overthrow of the Bolsheviks in the name of proletarian democracy. Second, this uprising was undeniably one of workers—in whose name the Bolsheviks claimed to rule Russia. A sympathetic general strike in nearby Petrograd was expected. And indeed the *Petropavlovsk* resolution sought not to return to pre-revolutionary days, but demanded freedoms only for the workers and peasants and their parties, calling for an end to the Bolshevik monopoly.[39] In swiftly and mercilessly repressing the revolt, the party of workers was suppressing what had been one of the main fortresses of the Bolshevik revolution itself, suppressing those who, genuine revolutionaries, now demanded that the revolution live up to its promises. The reversal is captured in the image of Trotsky reviewing the victors of the bloody assault on the pride and glory of the revolution, the Kronstadt that had been his own political base in 1917.

Two simultaneous events confirmed the revolution's direction: the

Tenth Party Congress passed a motion by Lenin to ban organized factions within the party; and this same congress initiated the New Economic Policy. The narrowing of party democracy continued, a process dating back to October 1917. Victorious in the Civil War but frightened by the size of potentially counter-revolutionary forces, the revolution reasserted the Bolshevik political monopoly rather than fulfilling its promise to restore opposition parties. 1920 had seen the debate which led to dismantling the trade unions as autonomous organizations whose purpose was to represent the workers. Deutscher presents the logic of the next step. 'Almost at once it became necessary to suppress opposition in Bolshevik ranks as well. The Workers' Opposition (and up to a point the *Decemists* too) expressed much of the frustration and discontent which had led to the Kronstadt rising. The cleavages tended to become fixed; and the contending groups were inclined to behave like so many parties within the party. It would have been preposterous to establish the rule of a single party and then to allow that party to split into fragments. If Bolshevism were to break up into two or more hostile movements, as the old Social Democratic Party had done, would not one of them—it was asked—become the vehicle of counter-revolution?'[40] But the goal of the Workers' Opposition and the *Decemists* was not to overthrow the revolution, but rather to restore proletarian democracy. The Kronstadt rebels had been slaughtered for demanding one fundamental component of such democracy: free elections to the Soviets. Now the party oppositions were prosecuted for demanding others: workers' control at the factories and over the entire economy. Together these demands had been the Bolsheviks' own in 1917; now they were repressed as actually or potentially counter-revolutionary.

Why had Bolshevik power, which in 1917 meant workers' power, now come to impose itself decisively over the workers, to the point of making their trade unions instruments of factory discipline and of repressing those party members who sought to restore that power to them? Most immediately, this was a time of crisis: the victors ruled over a ruined country. Ten million had died in the Civil War, industry was at a near-total halt, the cities were depopulated, the countryside was providing a fraction of its pre-war produce. By the end of 1921, thirty-six million people were suffering from famine. The working class—in whose name and with whose support the Bolsheviks had made the October Revolution, who had flocked into the party in 1917—had fought and died in the Civil War, had been absorbed into the party and government apparatus, or had fled the towns. The ruling party saw itself as a workers' party, but it also saw as threateningly premature demands for free food, clothing and lodging, as well as medical attention, travelling facilities and education—in a land where the railways were ruined and the factories were producing one-fourth of their pre-war output, a land which was reverting to cannibalism in the countryside.[41]

These urgencies were framed by the momentous fact, already apparent though not finally confirmed until 1923, that no other proletarian revolution had succeeded in the wake of the World War. The Bolsheviks were alone, ruling over a ruined society. Lenin's speeches and writings of the period demonstrate how far the strategic perspective of European revolution had dominated Bolshevik thought. In 1920, on the anniversary of the October Revolution, Lenin insisted that 'ours is an international cause, and until the revolution takes place in all lands, including the richest and most highly civilized ones, our victory will be only a half victory, perhaps still less.'[42] Now that the Civil War seemed won, it was clear that economic development had to precede socialism, and reconstruction to precede development. Lenin did not spell out what was the danger that will continue 'until the revolution is victorious in one or several advanced countries.' But was it not parallel to the bourgeois situation, as Lenin had characterized it: 'however strong it may seem militarily, it is internally impotent'? As time would tell, according to E. H. Carr, 'the Russian proletariat, unaided by the other proletariats [elsewhere] and thrown back on its own resources, was unequal, in numbers, in organization and in experience, to the enormous burdens which the revolution had unexpectedly placed on it.'[43] This weakness is the tragic key to the aftermath of the world's first proletarian revolution.

The solution to the problem was infernal: the weakness of the working class elsewhere and its smallness and dispersion in Russia both allowed and impelled the Party to step into the gap.[44] First, all other parties must be repressed, or allowed to lead only a shadow existence. Then workers' freedom must be repressed: their power to manage, to elect, to voice grievances and expectations. Then, freedom within the party itself must be restricted. Trotsky voiced the implacable if grotesque logic of the process: 'The Workers' Opposition has come out with dangerous slogans. They have made a fetish of democratic principles. They have placed the workers' right to elect representatives above the party, as it were, as if the party were not entitled to assert its dictatorship even if that dictatorship temporarily clashed with the passing moods of the workers' democracy. ... It is necessary to create among us the awareness of the revolutionary historical birthright of the party. The party is obliged to maintain its dictatorship, regardless of temporary wavering in the spontaneous moods of the masses, regardless of the temporary vacillations even in the working class. This awareness is for us the indispensable unifying element. The dictatorship does not base itself at every given moment on the formal principle of a workers' democracy, although the workers' democracy is, of course, the only method by which the masses can be drawn more and more into political life.'[45]

These words betray a striking shift: from the living, breathing workers, with their 'temporary vacillations', to the abstract and now-empty 'principle of a workers' democracy'. The recalcitrant present is appealed to 'the revolutionary historical birthright of the party'. It may be superfluous to comment that the ostensible goal of the entire project—to draw the masses 'more and more into political life'—is rendered quite impossible by a structural orientation intended to override the masses' 'passing moods'.

This exclusive and dictatorial rule of party over class was the result of a successful proletarian revolution *and* of a numb, prostrate and shrunken working class. Victorious, the proletarian leadership had been absorbed into the administrative machinery of party, army and state.[46] This bureaucracy began to become the nerve centre of Soviet Russia and—given the absence of a large and active proletariat in the factories—at the same time substituted itself for the class. As Trotsky's statement eloquently shows, by 1921 they had become *rulers*, concerned first of all with keeping power. Deutscher's and Carr's analyses both suggest that had Russian society been sufficiently developed, the new rulers might have been forced to pull back, to allow a more mature and rooted working class some control over an advanced economic base. But, the interpretation suggests, the situation forced them to become rulers in order to strengthen the state which would create that base. In response to the crisis, they now sought to secure their ability to do just this by expanding their power in every possible direction.

Thus in vital respects they became rulers in the traditional mould: they focused not on restoring power to the people, but on taking it from them and using it to protect their position. They wanted to make certain things happen to and for the people, and 'in their name'. A large, organized, energetic, articulate, and experienced working class in the factories, even one organically tied to the party, would have restricted them. It would have conceded less power to them; it would have made its demands too loud to suppress. For all their references to the proletariat, the Bolsheviks were determined henceforth to function, in Moshe Lewin's words, as 'a dictatorship in the void'.[47]

The void caused by proletarian weakness was only the obverse of Russia's other major demographic fact: the vast majority of its people were peasants. The initiation of the New Economic Policy represented a hand stretched out towards that frightening reality of counter-revolutionary Russia—a remarkable concession to reality by urban and future-oriented revolutionaries who feared being overwhelmed by what Roger Pethybridge calls 'the naked confrontation between Bolshevik aspirations and social backwardness.'[48] Social backwardness, as I have indicated, was *defined* by these aspirations: the vast majority of Russians, living in the countryside, had just received their land, lived on the borderline between modern civilization and starvation, used wooden ploughs often pulled by themselves, and found their solace in religion and vodka or samogon. The Bolsheviks, of necessity, ruled over this mass of illiterates as a conquered province whose every mood needed close watching. Under the NEP, rural Russia, now at peace and relieved of the threat of White restoration, was given the space to develop itself—and feed the country—at its own pace. If the Soviet Union was indeed not ready for socialism, NEP was the most tangible proof of and concession to this. In the face of famine, the government restored the free market and an agricultural system based on individual initiative. It gave its way to the 85 per cent of Russia that had supported the revolution only because it meant achieving an age-old dream—private ownership of land.

As the urban Bolsheviks confronted rural Russia, these activists, who were, in Lewin's words, 'used to deducing the political from the economic and social found themselves in a disturbing situation in which a governing elite devoid of any social basis embodied a kind of "pure political power" and imposed its will on a society whose spontaneous dynamic, under the NEP, tended towards ends that were the opposite of those of the party.'[49] The void in which they found themselves was in fact a "two-storied void", the first being the absence of a proletariat and the second that of an economic infrastructure.'[50] For Lenin this meant not merely that the party must struggle to find ways to build the prerequisites of socialism from the human mass of backward peasants—itself a superhuman undertaking. It meant also the ever-present threat of the party's degeneration: 'Something has happened rather like what we learned in our history lessons when we were children: one people subjugates another. The subjugator is then a conquering people and the subjugated a vanquished people. This is true enough, but what happens to the culture of these two peoples? The answer is not so simple. If the conquering people is more cultured than the vanquished people, the stronger imposes its culture on the weaker. But in the opposite case, the vanquished country may impose its culture on the conqueror. Is this not what happened in the capital of the RSFSR, and were not 4,700 of the best Communists (almost a division) submerged by an alien culture? Is it true that one might have the impression that the culture of the vanquished is of a high level? Not so: it is wretched and insignificant. But it is still superior to ours.'[51]

Ruling over Russia, the Bolsheviks were mortally threatened from without and within. Finding themselves in a void they strove mightily and with vigilance to keep both their power and their purpose alive—by perpetuating that void. Hence the trend in which the revolution was, in Isaac Deutscher's words, 'beginning to escape from its weakness into totalitarianism.'[52] If free elections were potentially counter-revolutionary, and workers' democracy would endanger the dictatorship that had come to be the revolution, then any faction calling for workers' democracy had to be banned. Factions were indeed banned. But from then on the party suspended above the masses had to function with an absolute but unwritten law: no one could take intra-party disputes outside to the masses. As Deutscher points out, a party which can allow no freedom to the society it rules ends up by tolerating no freedom inside itself.

Concessions to individualism and to the anti-socialist character of the peasants worried many of the Bolsheviks: what would become of socialist aspirations? Was NEP itself another step along the path of growing irrationality? But there was nothing inherently irrational in the encouragement of individual farming and the restoration of the market. The point is that the contrary aspects of the NEP period—freedom of enterprise, and the progressive narrowing of political controls—were in truth dialectically linked. Undertaken by Marxists, NEP could not help but be accompanied by grave self-doubts, criticisms, and fear of a complete reversion to capitalism. The very weight of the threat, the extent to which concessions to it violated socialist intentions, intensified the siege mentality in the party and the pressure for greater uniformity. It was felt that the party must rule *over* the peasantry and never permit its own outlook to absorb, however unconsciously, the petty-bourgeois attitudes encouraged by NEP. To this very day Bukharin is criticized for having absorbed and expressed the ideology of the kulaks. *Keeping its distance* from the great mass of the people was thus a fundamental operating principle of the party whose ultimate commitment—and historical and moral claim to superiority over all others—was to be at one with and serve the needs of the great mass of people. Reality itself imposed on the Bolsheviks this rupture with reality.

The Bolshevik Perspective in Perspective

Or so it would seem. This would seem to be the likely self-interpretation of a lucid Bolshevik of the early 1920s. As such, Bolshevism's habits of perception and purposes function like unseen lenses through which all situations are perceived, framing the given through which 'reality' and its 'necessities' are experienced. The self-interpretation of historical actors has always been that their actions are imposed by necessity; the victors among them generalize their lenses as norms through which reality itself seems to be speaking. If nothing else, historical hindsight enables us to see the situation as being one of interaction—composed of events and tendencies which took on their meaning *in relation to* the Bolshevik intentions and modes of perception. If the situation was indeed becoming 'irrational' in 1921 it was so as an interaction between objective and subjective planes of reality, not as an irreducible, irrational given.

Victory made the Bolshevik subjectivity into a dominant objective force, to be sure; but that was not the only possible way of perceiving the situation in which the revolution found itself. Alternative revolutionary projects did exist, and each defined the situation differently. The anarchist Makhnovist movement, to take one example, controlled large areas of the Ukraine until 1921, fighting off Deniken's White Guards in the name of 'the complete liberation of the Working People from every oppression.'[53] The Red Army's victory over it meant the imposition of an authoritarian repressive force, concerned more with party power than workers' or peasants' freedom. The Makhnovists saw the peasants not as the 'huge sack of potatoes'[54] Marxist lenses insisted they were, but rather as a disciplined, creative and revolutionary force capable of achieving 'the egalitarian, stateless community of workers.'[55]

Bolshevik social roots, traditions, prejudices, theory, goals and experience all led them to fear and suspect the peasants on whom the Makhnovists had based their movement, and over whom the Bolsheviks now ruled. Later Marxists, perceiving the peasants and their own situation differently, were to base themselves in the countryside—in successful insurrections in Yugoslavia, China and Vietnam—but no thought could have been further from the Bolshevik mind.

If the suppression of the Makhnovists thus took on the force of necessity to the Bolsheviks, what about the suppression of Kronstadt? Or the integration of trade unions? Or the outlawing of party factions, the proclamation of NEP? In short, were there meaningful alternatives *within* the framework institutionalized by the Civil War? Certainly retrospective lucidity would insist that a more rational policy may be imagined: one capable of halting the dynamic which eventually substituted Stalin for the Soviet proletariat, and moving more deliberately towards socialism. A more rational policy would have allowed for independent trade unions, recognition of all political parties which accepted the revolution and acceptance of factions within Bolshevism, while pushing for a planned economy with stress on building cooperative collective farms. A rational dictatorship of the proletariat would have continued to train and equip workers to rule, and sought to keep alive their power from the shop floor through the party cells to the Soviets. David Rousset, for example, emphasizes that only trade-union democracy could have possibly avoided the organic break 'of the Bolshevik party from the proletariat at the point of production'[56] which he sees as the structural root of the revolution's undoing.

A more rational policy then, might have made fewer accommodations to the non-socialist sector of the economy while drawing less power into Bolshevik hands: the emphasis on tolerance and concession might have shifted from the economic to the political sphere, taking the place of the emphasis on control. This would have meant *sharing power*. Could the party have moved in this direction? If a lucid self-interpretation tends to transform its subject's commitments and modes of perception into unseen givens, retrospective lucidity courts the opposite danger—of imagining a situation that could have been severed from the subjective lenses of its dominant forces. Since the situation consisted of the interaction of 'objective' trends with 'subjective' commitments and presuppositions, we must neither be seduced by the Bolshevik self-interpretation of necessity, as if that gave us *the* situation, nor ignore Bolshevik lenses, as if the situation could have existed independently of them.

One decisive lens of Bolshevism—the very basis for its split with the Mensheviks in 1903—was the idea of the vanguard party. *What Is To Be Done* specifies that, because the spontaneous struggles of workers lead only to trade-union consciousness, revolutionary class consciousness can only 'be brought to them from without'[57] by a 'small, compact core'[58] of professional theoreticians, propagandists, agitators and organizers. 1917 saw a reversal in Bolshevik practice and, with *State and Revolution*, in theory as well; the following years however, brought a reversion to the theory and practice of the original primer of Leninism. There, as Herbert Marcuse has pointed out, 'Lenin aimed beyond the exigencies of the specific Russian situation, at a general international development in Marxism, which in turn reflected the trend of large selections of organized labor toward "class cooperation". As this trend increased, it threatened to vitiate the notion of the proletariat as the revolutionary subject on which the whole Marxist strategy depended. Lenin's formulations intended to save Marxian orthodoxy from the reformist onslaught, but they soon became part of a conception that no longer assumed the historical coincidence between the proletariat and progress which the notion of the "labour aristocracy" still retained. The groundwork was laid for the development of the Leninist party where the true interest and the true consciousness of the proletariat were lodged in a group different from the majority of the proletariat.'[59]

The vanguard party implies that the proletariat's own 'natural' course of development does not coincide with, and may even run counter to, the role Marx assigned it. Such an outlook suggested a sense of the party as more advanced than its class, of its ability to appeal to the truth of a situation as being beyond that situation itself, as well as a sense of bitter hostility to all other parties who might *mislead* the proletariat. As the party more and more becomes the active locus and subject of the revolution the class more and more becomes its raw material and object. But to carry this self-consciously Jacobin idea to its extreme conclusion is to negate the very idea of proletarian revolution. History, of course, decided otherwise.

The revolutions of 1905 and February 1917 flatly contradicted Lenin's sense of the limitations of the spontaneous consciousness of the proletariat—by creating the Soviets and overthrowing the Tsar—and he saw the need to formulate a more revolutionary perspective on its capacities, in order to bring the party in line with both experience and possibility. *State and Revolution*, written in August and September, was '"interrupted" by a political crisis—the eve of the October Revolution of 1917.'[60] In it he threw off the established 'Leninist' lenses he had used since 1902—explicitly criticizing the very Jacobin passages in Kautsky he had leaned on before, and insisting now that under socialism 'for the first time in the history of civilized societies, the *mass* of the population will need to take an *independent* part, not only in voting and elections, *but also in the everyday administration*.'[61] Earlier Lenin had accepted and extended Kautsky's attack on the 'primitive democracy' which absurdly demanded 'that laws should be passed directly by the whole people'[62] and emphasized instead the need for *professional* revolutionaries and officials. Now he defined revolution as 'the proletariat *destroying* the "administrative apparatus" and the *whole* state machine, replacing it with a new one, consisting of the armed worker.'[63]

The old lenses could not have truly seen the new situation, but the revolutionary commitment underlying them prevailed to shape a view more in keeping with the actual behaviour of the Russian proletariat in 1917. The Bolsheviks became a mass party, taking it upon themselves to express the most radical moods of the proletariat, to organize their militia and, ultimately, to direct their seizure of power.

One consequence of the Civil War was that by 1921 the revolution had become a party affair. While theoretically the Bolsheviks had always seen themselves as representing the working class's deepest long-range needs, the actual conjuncture of Bolshevik policy and proletarian self-consciousness in revolutionary practice had turned out to be episodic—only by midsummer 1917 could they be said to have won majority support. As is obvious from parliamentary experience, such support could in the future be withdrawn, and then perhaps returned once again.

Now, by 1921, it became alarmingly clear just how episodic was this conjuncture of party and class. The Bolsheviks could not help but revert to their old lenses, droning on about being the party of the working class even against *these* workers, who after all were now just recruits fresh from the countryside. They knew all too well that in the crisis this actually existing working class was ceasing to follow them and tending to see other groups, whether anarchists or the newly revived Social-Revolutionaries and Mensheviks, as expressing its aspirations and grievances. Moreover, the Bolsheviks could not help but interpret the crisis that led to NEP as confirming both the backwardness and the dominant socio-economic weight of non-proletarian Russia. Ruling over this populace and convinced that it must not have a share in power, the Bolsheviks yet felt the need to grant concessions to its menacing reality. A more socialist-oriented solution than NEP might have had unacceptable political overtones—encouraging, for example, peasant-controlled collective farming. Instead, the political monopoly tightened even as—and because—individual farming was encouraged. The least socialist solution, it was also the one most in keeping with the strengthening of the Bolshevik monopoly.

Would free elections to the Soviets or free trade unions have meant the destruction of the revolution? Certainly the rulers would not have been re-elected. The point is that in the trial by fire since 1917 Bolshevik power had become indistinguishable from the revolution. For them to risk that power after the Civil War was inconceivable—all the more so given the ingrained Leninist conviction that the party reflected the long-range interests of the workers even against their short-range inclinations. Indeed, *had* not their victory in fact been the victory of the proletariat and vice-versa? The victors of the Civil War were above all determined to preserve the revolution, even if against the spontaneous and temporary moods of the working class in whose name and with whose active participation it was achieved. Free elections to the Soviets were therefore unthinkable—especially because in their view an immature working class misled by other parties would have forced the Bolsheviks to share their power.

Whatever it may have meant in the underground struggle against the Tsar or in opposition to reformism, with the Bolsheviks holding state power this vanguard conception now meant that they were fully ready to become usurpers installed over the working class in its name. As this usurpation became possible and seemed necessary, however, it initiated an irreversible process. Using their power against the working class, they leaned heavily on and inflated all those aspects of Bolshevik tradition in which they saw *themselves* as embodying its wisdom over and against it. In the wake of Kronstadt, they would henceforth seek to revive the working class, enlarge it, educate it—while keeping it passive and firmly under control by the party.

This, the great contradiction of the Bolshevik revolution, meant that the party inevitably raised itself high above its class—and Russian society as a whole—and thus ceased being what its Marxism had insisted it must be: the organic expression of the vital modern productive force. The repression of Kronstadt was one decisive step in this detachment, epitomized in the Bolshevik refusal even to negotiate with the rebels. They arrested their representatives, and blamed the workers' and sailors' revolt on White Guards—all acts of a party separating itself from its social base in order to rule over it.

The Need for Mystification

The rupture took place in consciousness as well as in politics. En route to becoming a ruling class, the dominant wing in the party had not only to articulate what was to be done, but also to integrate it into their outlook, to behold it and find it both Marxist and good. The Bolshevik lenses I have described took shape out of a commitment to socialist revolution: in the face of the disjuncture between 'progress and the proletariat' they had sustained a path to the socialist future. But now, in decisive respects, the party itself was veering away from that future. As this happened, the Bolshevik self-conception itself became more and more detached from the reality of Russia in the mid 1920s: Marxism, the great critique of ideology, was itself becoming ideology. And in the process the vision itself absorbed the reality, more and more grotesquely, with ever greater distortion.

Certainly oppositionists continued to voice the socialist promise against this sorry reality, trying to open the party's eyes to the contradiction. At the centre of the party, Lenin himself had emphasized in 1921 the distortion of those who saw themselves as 'representatives of the proletariat' when the proletariat itself was virtually non-existent. In response he was taunted by Shlyapnikov, on behalf of the Workers' Opposition, at the 1922 Eleventh Party Congress: 'Vladimir Ilyich said yesterday that the proletariat as a class, in the Marxian sense, did not exist [in Russia]. Permit me to congratulate you on being the vanguard of a non-existing class.'[64]

An open exchange of such lucid ironies was becoming rare indeed. To see the facts for too long and too clearly was to illegitimize party rule, and worse, to call in question the revolution itself. If I have presented critically the self-interpretation of a lucid Bolshevism, let us be clear that even with its limitations it has been a product of historical retrospect. At the time, only Lenin in the mainstream seemed to approach such lucidity, and even then only for occasional moments. The full force of the contradictions into which Bolshevism had stumbled had become impossible to acknowledge without moving into the opposition, letting go of the levers of power, and risking being cut off from the revolution itself. Instead, the dominant Bolsheviks began to veil and distort their own mode of perception.

The urge to escape the contradictions appears in the enthusiasm for electrification of the early 1920s, as Marxists confronted the still primitive character of the society they had conquered. Roger Pethybridge quotes from a 1921 poster-poem of Mayakovsky which shows the futurist vision confronting the sceptical bourgeois:

At electrification his eyes bulged a bit,
'Utopia,' he said, 'nothing will come of it'.
Just you wait, bourgeoisie.
There'll be New York in Tetushakh
There'll be paradise in Shuee.[65]

The fantasy of what the future would bring to these two remote villages was pathetically contradicted by reality: when a huge map was lit up at the party congress of 1920 to show Russia's future hydroelectric plants, the electric power of most of Moscow had to be cut off to avoid overstraining its power station.

Pethybridge's point is that the fantasy itself was an evasion of Russian reality: 'the existing state of society seemed such a rebuttal of Bolshevik aspirations that it was more comforting to neglect it by looking beyond.'[66] This escape was fatal: 'the tensions between theory and reality in the social sphere eventually contributed to the political climate that led to Stalinism.'[67]

Perhaps the crowning irrationality of the 1920s was the elevation of the party to divine status. We have seen how the situation led to isolating and elevating the party over the workers as well as the rest of Russian society. We have seen this expressed in Trotsky's attack on the Workers' Opposition and Decemists: the party 'is entitled' to reject the 'moods' of the proletariat and exert a dictatorship over the whole of society. Three years later, as he was falling from power and under attack, Trotsky represented and extended this view of the party even as he rejected Zinoviev's call for recantation. As a relatively recent convert to Bolshevism, he may have felt impelled to demonstrate unwavering loyalty in the midst of a fierce struggle; but Trotsky was nevertheless voicing his own and the party's abiding mood, and drew its conclusions with his usual relentless brilliance. 'Nothing could be simpler or easier, morally or politically, than to admit before one's own party that one had erred. ... No great moral heroism is needed for that. ... Comrades, none of us wishes to be or can be right against the party. In the last instance the party is always right, because it is *the only historic instrument which the working class possesses for the solution of its fundamental tasks*. I have said already that nothing would be easier than to say before the party that all these criticisms and all these declarations, warnings, and protests were mistaken from beginning to end. I cannot say so, however, because, comrades, I do not think so. I know that one ought not to be right against the party. One can be right only with the party and through the party because history was not created any other way for the realization of one's rightness. The English have the saying "My country right or wrong." With much greater justification we can say: My party, right or wrong—wrong on certain partial, specific issues or at certain moments. ... It would be ridiculous, perhaps, almost indecent, to make any personal statements here, but I do hope that in case of need I shall not prove the meanest soldier on the meanest of Bolshevik barricades.'[68]

This growing religion of the party originated as a response to the impossible situation. A guardian of historical truth became increasingly necessary in a situation which so violently mocked that truth. Connected to this is the mythology we have seen emerging about the party's relationship to the Soviet working class. Deutscher describes the process of its formation: 'Acting without the normal working class in the background, the Bolshevik from long habit still invoked the will of that class in order to justify whatever he did. But he invoked it only as a theoretical surmise and an ideal standard of behaviour, in short, something of a myth. He began to see in his party the repository not only of the ideal of socialism in the abstract, but also of the desires of the working class in the concrete. When a Bolshevik, from the Politbureau member to the humblest man in a cell, declaimed that "the proletariat insists" or "demands" or "would never agree" to this or that, he meant that his party or its leaders "insisted," "demanded," and "would never agree." Without this half-conscious mystification the Bolshevik mind could not work. The party could not admit even to itself that it had no longer any basis in proletarian democracy.'[69]

If they found themselves in a contradictory situation by 1921, the Bolsheviks lived the contradiction between ideology and reality in part, by losing touch with reality, by distorting it, by lying about it. Only in part, of course: the NEP showed remarkable sensitivity towards reality at a time of crisis. At the Tenth Party Congress Lenin emphasized that 'so long as there is no revolution in other countries, only agreement with the peasantry can save the socialist revolution in Russia. And that is how it must be stated, frankly, at all meetings and in the entire press.'[70] At the Eleventh Party Congress Lenin again emphasized the absolutely central place of the *smychka* with the peasants. 'Then the building of socialism will not be the task of that drop in the ocean, called the Communist Party, but the task of the entire mass of the working people.'[71]

In spite of such moments of clarity the distortion and the lie became, inevitably, a part of Bolshevism's essence, in accordance with—and in proportion to—the narrowing of its circle of power. We will see this paradox intensify to a point of explosion: Russia's lack of maturity in Marxist terms, the Bolsheviks' impotence to achieve the socialism for which they had come to power, led to one of the most powerful state apparatuses in the history of the world; this state apparatus, constructed in a carefully maintained 'void', came to base itself on wholesale distortion and grotesque irrationality.

Already, at Lenin's funeral in 1924, the tendency was explicit in Stalin's medieval prayer to the memory of Lenin: 'On his departure from us, Comrade Lenin commanded us to revere and maintain the purity of the name of the party member. We swear, comrade Lenin, that we will faithfully carry out this command! .... On his departure from us, Comrade Lenin commanded us to safeguard, like the pupil of our eye, the unity of our party. We swear, Comrade Lenin, that we will faithfully carry out this command.'[72]

Stalin Versus Trotsky

On 17 January 1928, GPU agents hustled Leon Trotsky, the leader of the October Revolution, and his family out of Moscow. Exiled to Alma Ata, in Kazakhstan, near the Chinese frontier, Trotsky would never return to Russia or to political power. Kept unnoticed by GPU deception, this momentous departure was both finale and prelude. That the revolution should deport one of its great leaders was given appropriately ironic punctuation by the fact that the commander of the accompanying guards had served in Trotsky's bodyguard during the Civil War. The process and events leading to this event show a further widening of the distance of the leaders of the Soviet Union both from the class in whose name they ruled and the masses over whom they ruled: the dramatic stifling of political life within the Communist Party; the fatal extension of the process of substitution; reliance on ever more grotesque forms of mythmaking; and the development of the characteristic forms of Stalinist legitimation—the quasi-religious cult of Lenin, the rewriting of history, the use of the big lie, the demand for recantation from defeated opponents.

The fundamental differences that emerged between Trotsky and Stalin during the 1920s can be explained by the disintegration of the worldwide revolutionary movement catalyzed by October. Thus, in another example of the lucid self-interpretation of Bolshevism, Jean-Paul Sartre has analyzed the 'monstrous' slogan of the victors' 'socialism in one country', as a response to the impossible situation into which revolutionary Russia awoke in the 1920s. 'Soviet isolation was first and foremost that of a monstrosity: an underdeveloped country moving without any transition from a feudal system to socialist forms of production and property.'[73] For the revolution to succeed in its own terms—to become socialist—required inter-national revolution; for the Soviet Union to survive required turning inward, consolidation, construction. Events had made impossible the unified Bolshevik project—of achieving socialism in Russia as part of a worldwide revolutionary movement—and so it now split into what became seen as mutually antagonistic intentions of radicalizing or surviving. The contradiction became complete as these two irrational fragments of the once unified project proclaimed themselves wholly true when, fundamentally, neither was. On the one hand, 'perma-nent revolution' risked the Soviet Union, where socialism had indeed taken power. On the other, socialism could scarcely be constructed in a single country, least of all a backward and impoverished one: the victorious slogan, while relieving the Soviet Union of the responsibili-ty for promoting world revolution, also claimed that its backward masses could achieve the impossible by themselves. A tragic necessi-ty, isolation, was mythologized into a matter of national pride as well as an excuse for pursuing a cautious and unrevolutionary foreign policy. The 'abstract universalism' of Marxism, preserving the image of worldwide socialist liberation, became Trotskyism, while its real in-carnation in backward Russia became Stalinism. By distorting con-sciousness, the false became true.

The most striking feature of Sartre's discussion is his emphasis on how the false became true in Soviet Russia, in fact as well as con-sciousness. While socialism was impossible in backward Russia, the revolution led by socialists did indeed triumph. Under Stalin's slogan it proceeded to build 'an order based on the fundamental socializa-tion of land and machines, under emergency conditions and through continual sacrifices of everything to the most rapid possible increase in the rate of production.'[74] Certainly socialism in a single country became 'synonymous with hell,' but it also became 'the matrix for the institutionalization of the Russian Revolution.'[75]

In other words, a false idea was the response to an impossible situation. Adopted, it became the guide to accommodating socialism to Russia and to transforming the latter: 'The adaptation of this highly specific reality to the new exigencies was to be long, arduous and embattled. But what was essential had been preserved. The transformations had to be violent but they were no longer required to be revolutionary. In this way, the monstrous slogan acquired a practical truth, because it really was the *idea* of that monstrous but inevitable transformation: of that *distorted* praxis, whose particular distortion was nevertheless the reality (and therefore the truth) of an incarnation which transcended itself in an undertaking which it conditioned at the outset and which remained qualified by it.'[76]

Sartre certainly makes such distortions sound absolutely necessary, if the revolution were to survive. But as Moshe Lewin points out, such necessity also retained a great element of chance at its centre. One leader had seemed capable of calling the monstrosity by its true name; of refusing to give in to ideological distortions which hid the possibilities of the situation: of laying hold of both vision and reality and avoiding the fracture in the party which the revolution's position seemed to impose—in short, of uniting in his person the political stature, moral authority, intellectual acuity, popularity, and devotion to the revolution's goals necessary to keep the original Bolshevik project intact. But Lenin—never mentioned by Sartre —was incapacitated by late 1922 and died in January 1924—an accident of history which certainly undercuts Sartre's necessitarian formulations.

What if Lenin had lived? Lewin argues that it was not inevitable that left-wing dictatorship had to 'degenerate into a personal, despotic and irrational dictatorship.' While only 'daring reforms' could have counteracted the tendencies of the bureaucratic machine that had emerged from the Civil War, Lewin insists that 'there was nothing essentially utopian about Lenin's aim of achieving a rational dictatorial regime, with men of integrity at its head and efficient institutions working consciously to be beyond both underdevelopment and dictatorship.' But such plans could remain only subjective 'wishes' 'in the absence of a capable and undisputed leader.' Lenin's untimely death removed that leader: 'the embalming of his body and the cult of his person helped to dissimulate a type of dictatorship utterly foreign to his plans.'

Lewin does not underestimate the difficulties even Lenin would have had in reversing the situation and reforming the party. But by 1922 this had become his goal, and only illness and death kept him from making a determined effort to remove Stalin. He may have failed, even with his skills, his reputation, and his determination. But if anyone could have prevented what became the Stalinist excesses, it was Lenin. 'As the founder Lenin was not afraid of unmaking and remaking what he had made with his own hands. He was not afraid of organizing the people around him, of plotting, of fighting for the victory of his line and of keeping the situation under control. Trotsky was not such a man. Lenin disappeared and Stalin was assured of victory.'[77]

An Irrational Situation

It is certainly part of the irrationality of the situation that Trotsky became the mythical enemy and Anti-Christ of the revolution only *after* he was defeated. This may have dawned on many of those who encountered 'Trotskyism' first through the eyes of the Comintern, and found out only later that this mighty foe was no more than an insignificant sect. Indeed, Trotsky had already been bested by the time of Lenin's death, so much so that the succession was never in doubt. It was no accident that Trotsky, travelling to a rest cure, should have learnt of Lenin's death by a code message from Stalin which lied to him about the funeral day. Thus Trotsky continued his trip while Stalin made himself the most prominent of the mourners. The result of the momentous contest between Stalin and Trotsky was strictly predetermined by the fact that effective power had been in Stalin's hands since 1922.

Historians tend to present the conflicts of the 1920s as the most articulate protagonists saw them: locked in life-and-death debates about the great policy issues affecting 'the fate of 160 million people; and the destinies of Communism in Europe and Asia.'[78] But two puzzling interrelated features of the Trotsky-Stalin conflict point to the deepening irrationality of the contest. First, the major oppositionists of the 1920s—not only Trotsky, but also Zinoviev and Kamenev, and later Bukharin—remained strikingly obtuse about the real issue, Stalin's accumulation of despotic power. Second, as Deutscher says, 'this great contest took place in a frightful void. On either side only small groups were involved.'[79] The interaction of Marxist blindness and the reality of Bolshevik power doomed any and all oppositions, and intensified the irrational course of the revolution.

So blind to the decisive political process was Trotsky that as late as 1926–27 he was able to proclaim as the paramount principle of the Joint Opposition: 'With Stalin against Bukharin?—Yes. With Bukharin against Stalin?—Never.'[80] In other words, the reigning social and economic considerations dictated a possible alliance with 'centrist' Stalin but never with 'rightist' Bukharin. Bukharin was himself so obtuse to the political process taking place that he contributed to destroying party democracy, without which he himself was destined to be helpless once Stalin decided to change course. When Stalin stole Trotsky's thunder and displaced Bukharin in 1928–29 by his push for rapid industrialization, it should have become clear to both that their Marxist disposition to emphasize social and economic 'substance' over political 'form' had blinded them to the most important changes taking place in the 1920s: the separation of the party from the proletariat and of the leadership from the party apparatus, whose apex of decision-making progressively narrowed until it was wholly dominated by the General Secretary; and the final elimination of all opposition to the latter's domination.[81]

Their Platform, drafted in October 1928, leaves no doubt of the Joint Opposition's primary concern with the social and economic 'base' of Soviet society rather than its political 'superstructure'. In that respect it was on the whole an excellent critique and a plausible programme, projecting a rational Left path towards voluntary cooperatives and greater industrial development and planning, as well as defending the economic rights of workers and poor and middle peasants. In this last sense it would have changed the thrust of the smychka with the peasantry towards those who had most to gain from a more explicitly socialist course. In addition, it rejected—shortly before the Great Depression began—the thesis of capitalist stabilization upon which 'socialism in one country' was based, and sought a more militant International in anticipation of a revival of imperialist aggressiveness and, perhaps, of socialist opportunity.

The programme of the Joint Opposition, in short, projected a course that would have been far more foresighted and humane, as well as effective, than the convulsive 'Great Change' initiated by Stalin two years later. As such, it has for fifty years been the locus of Marxist criticism of Stalinism, achieving the status of *the* rational alternative which, tragically, was not to be followed.

The Platform, like many of those whose sense of subsequent history has been shaped by it, makes a single but decisive mistake: it assumes 'that the situation can be corrected by the party itself.'[82] The circumstances of its drafting, as well as its form, tone and content reflect the Opposition's determination to persuade the party politically to a new course even though, in terms of structure and personnel, it was becoming drastically different from the one that had made the revolution. Certainly the Opposition could count on several thousand supporters among the Old Bolsheviks, perhaps as many as Stalin and Bukharin.[83] But beneath this thin layer was a vast inert mass, members who had joined more recently and who had little commitment to, or experience of, disagreement, debate and democracy. For them the party was the new avenue of advancement, and their relationship to it was structured by the hierarchies and routines of the newly developing system of privilege and power. If Trotsky and his followers still thought and acted in terms of a *party*, most of these party masses were now candidates for the machine: they were not revolutionaries so much as a part of the emerging ruling class. Their adherence to a risky Left deviation was the last thing to be expected.

Manipulated by Stalin, this apparatus had blocked Trotsky at every turn at least since Lenin's death, slowly but inexorably narrowing the ground on which he stood, often with his own cooperation. 'Trotskyism' had already been described as a deviation from Leninism; oppositionists had lost their positions and been deprived of access to other party members, at congresses or in print, and were being hounded from the party. In fact, the Joint Opposition 'offensive' culminating in the Platform may equally be seen as their last gasp, the defensive and impotent response of people fighting for their political lives.

Placed in this context, the Platform reads as an act of uncomprehending blindness, a futile show of intellectual acuity in a situation dominated by a deaf-and-dumb party machine, a test of strength in an internal battle that had already been lost. If anything, the real situation dictated a different kind of struggle for the party, or an appeal beyond it: who could have better sensed this than the tactician of October, the orator of the revolution and organizer of the Red Army? Yet the Platform both presumes an articulate, informed, politicized, enfranchised audience that no longer existed and leaves the life-and-death issue—the stifling of that audience along with party democracy—as one topic among others, even then treating it only briefly.

Following its Introduction, the Platform speaks about the working class and the trade unions (reaffirming the prohibition on strikes in state-owned industries), the 'agrarian question', industrialization and economic planning, the Soviets, and the national question—all before discussing the party. Only as his fifth point under this topic does Trotsky attack the 'systematic abolition of inner-party democracy—in violation of the whole tradition of the Bolshevik Party, in violation of the direct decisions of a series of party congresses.'[84]

Why no frontal attack in these few months before Trotsky's political career would be forcibly ended? Not only did the Opposition face almost overwhelming tactical problems; not only was its great leader blocked from seeing *the party*, 'the fundamental instrument of the proletarian revolution', as almost hopelessly corrupted; but the developments themselves were virtually unintelligible in traditional Marxist terms. Trotsky's fidelity to Marxist categories veiled the situation from him; and so did the reformulation of Marxism in which he had been a leading force.

Marxism as Ideology

Marxism became ideology to the exact extent that all party leaders sought to obscure the structures that had come to dominate Soviet life. They had built into their new society the domination of Russia by a small, beleaguered and disciplined minority. By absorbing into itself most of its own surviving class base—and then deciding, at Kronstadt, to treat as treason challenges from the remaining class base lying outside of itself—the ruling party created the decisive structures of the new Soviet Union. Opposition parties accepted the rules of the new situation, yet still hoped to appeal against the Communist Party to the masses. Because they challenged the very separation from and suppression of the vast majority which had become a central condition of Communist rule, they were inevitably regarded as treasonous and themselves suppressed.

The Bolshevik opposition groups—in a party whose very revolutionary hallmark was its intimate contacts with the masses—implicitly threatened to carry their criticisms and appeals beyond the party. Was this reaching out not implied in the very programme of the Workers' Opposition, which sought workers' control in the factories? But even while some Old Bolsheviks criticized the party for being ruled by a clique, and demanded that the Twelfth Congress (1923) should overrule the 1921 ban on inner-party groups, Zinoviev formulated what Deutscher terms the canon of Bolshevik self-suppression: 'Every criticism of the party line, even a so-called "Left" criticism, is now objectively a Menshevik criticism.'[85] Zinoviev presented the iron logic of the bureaucracy ruling over society as if it were a conquered territory: all criticism is treason. We can also see in this statement a drastic slippage taking place in which revolutionaries who had prided themselves on hardheaded realism seem now, in power, to be losing contact with reality. A lie replaces the truth.

The reason is tied up with the self-interpretation of Bolshevism itself. Minority rule is not necessarily irrational; nor is minority rule of an urban-rooted party over the countryside necessarily irrational. But minority rule *is* irrational if the rulers' claim to legitimacy comes from a mass base that is being suppressed by their rule. Irrational, because such rule embodies a deep conflict between its purposes, outlook, and original bases of support on the one hand, and the real nature of its power and functioning on the other. Since neither side of the contradiction can be abandoned, reason itself abandons the field to unreason, analysis to mythology.

Marxism became ideology—became a weapon of distortion—not in spite of but *because of* its democratic outlook. Unlike Tsarism, it drew its justification from revolutionary origins which *depended* on a mass base. For Bolsheviks their power meant rule by the organized and conscious arm of the proletariat; and in Marxism proletarian rule had always meant the rule of the vast majority. As a twentieth-century movement with a democratic ideology, Lenin's Bolshevism had broken with Tsarism's emphasis on birthright and religion. But whereas Tsarism had no need to convince its subjects that they were a ruling class, Bolshevism emphatically did. The Bolsheviks suffered a deep contradiction between socialism as democratic ideology motivating them and justifying their rule on the one hand, and socialism as the reality of their Jacobin dictatorship over the proletariat and the rest of the population on the other. As their power-base narrowed within the society and the party, there was a greater and greater need for a network of lies and intellectual distortions which would reconcile noble democratic aspirations with the growing monolith. Hence Zinoviev's reference to 'objectivity': the need for myth implies a need for *interpreters*, transferring to the party the power to decide what critics meant, regardless of their intention.

In the same period party critics found guilty of 'errors' began to feel pressure to recant: to disavow their 'mistakes' publicly and praise the correct line. And at the same time we see the first steps in rewriting history. Trotsky's 'literary struggle' ends up with his 'errors' being found as far back as 1903. These grotesque violations of sense have their roots in the flight from the inadmissable Bolshevik contradiction: that the workers' state was becoming a bureaucratic monolith.

Having himself been instrumental in creating this monolith, having challenged none of the steps towards the saddling of Politbureau on party or party on proletariat, Trotsky yet rejected the full force of its irrational and oppressive logic. He demanded a return to inner-party democracy by 1924. But the apparatus, controlled from the top by Stalin, Zinoviev and Kamenev, turned this struggle into a virtual trial of the Opposition at the Thirteenth Party Congress. Trotsky and his allies were found guilty of a 'petty-bourgeois deviation from Leninism.'[86] In non-mythological terms—which were becoming more and more rare in party discussions—Trotsky had tried to open up more space for genuine discussion and debate while accepting all the premisses that had led to their suppression. Indeed, he never rejected the Bolshevik monopoly of power, or demanded freedom for opposition parties.

Now, in 1926 and 1927, he stopped short of the only step which might have given force to his demands and which was a natural one to the great revolutionary orator—appealing to the masses. His defeat was therefore assured. In the end, the only 'mass' protest he attempted was the wretched demonstration by his party followers within the parades celebrating the tenth anniversary of the revolution. And by then it was far too late.

Caught in a trap of his own making, he could only struggle from within as it was sprung, unable to step outside and challenge it properly. He fought, in effect, for a Bolshevik monopoly without its consequences. No wonder he was seen as inconsistent. We have seen Trotsky pay homage to the party. By 1926 the trend had gone so far as to demand worshipful self-abasement from all party members. In-fallibility, recantation, rewriting history, the call for denunciation of those who voiced contrary sentiments, the labelling of all opposition as treason: this was the path into which its objective and subjective reality was urging Bolshevism by 1927.

Trotsky as Anti-Christ

Perhaps the most remarkable fact about the Stalin-Trotsky conflict is the emergence of Trotsky as Anti-Christ of the revolution. By the 1930s he became the Enemy personified, blamed for all that was wrong in the Soviet Union, the evil but somehow inept genius behind the fictional plots found everywhere, the sinister inspiration for most of the millions of poor souls executed or exiled to the Gulag Ar-chipelago, and the prime traitor of the revolution, busy selling out his country to the Western powers. In 1931 Stalin was to give this ap-praisal: 'Some think that Trotskyism is a school of thought within Communism, a faction which has, to be sure, committed mistakes, done not a few silly things, and even behaved at times in an anti-Soviet manner; but that it is all the same a Communist faction. It is hardly necessary to point out that such a view of Trotskyism is pro-foundly mistaken and harmful. Actually, Trotskyism is the spearhead of the counter-revolutionary bourgeoisie, waging the struggle against Communism ....'[87]

Most of this story lies ahead, but for now it is important to see that an increasingly irrational intensity came to surround the protagonists as the battle for different policies became a mortal struggle, as erst-while comrades became deadly enemies. We have seen opposition within the party begin to appear as treason after 1921: already by 1924 'Trotskyism' was becoming named and regarded as a 'devia-tion' from Leninism. Why?

Certainly 'Trotskyism' was a deliberate and cynical invention of the triumvirs—Stalin, Zinoviev and Kamenev—in their battle against the opposition.[88] But the hostility had its own reality, and seems very early to have overflowed any rational intention. The point is that 'the revolution' was becoming a more and more irrational amalgam. And as such it was becoming more and more vulnerable to assertions of its original commitments. By criticizing the loss of inner-party democracy, the abandonment of international revolution and the encouragement of private farming, Trotsky was doing far more than criticizing specific policies: he was judging the revolution by its own repressed yardstick, threatening to puncture the irrational whole and let in the light. This threat of truth gained in force by going hand in hand with proposals to recall the betrayed revolution to its original self. Old Bolsheviks, after all, had withstood exile and Tsarist prisons on behalf of the vision for which Trotsky was beginning to act as spokesman. Trotsky's importance as threat was in exact proportion to the Bolsheviks' need to mythologize: the degree to which reality had to be veiled was the degree to which someone unveiling even a part—and Trotsky never unveiled more than a part of it—would threaten it.

But how threaten? Trotsky was from the beginning outnumbered and outmanoeuvred in a contest for power which he had never waged more than halfheartedly. We can understand the force and fury he evoked only if we treat ideology as *real*, as a decisive component of the new amalgam of fact and myth which the Soviet Union was becoming. Trotsky threatened that amalgam not only by his specific complaints, but by being an oppositional voice of considerable authority. No such voice could be allowed to speak freely where rational discussion had become impossible. The force with which Trotsky was now denounced was the very force with which the Bolsheviks had to deny the real nature of revolutionary Russia and its distance from socialist aspirations. In this sense we may say that Trotsky as Anti-Christ was created by the *praxis* of the revolution itself: *praxis* understood not only as constructive political activity but as the accompanying process of distortion.

If this were not enough to define Trotsky as Enemy, one other fact was calculated to drive his former comrades into a frenzy: implied in Trotskyism, as in every form of opposition in a society whose rulers are usurpers, is the threat to appeal to the masses—first in the party, then in the factories, and finally in the countryside. A great revolutionary orator, Trotsky the oppositionist *might* sooner or later violate the fundamental credo of Bolshevik political life and carry his dissent beyond the party, even if he had no intention of doing so. His exile came, in fact, as a direct consequence of his followers' demonstrating publicly. As inevitably as the dialectic of Bolshevik minority rule in the Soviet Union destroyed inner-party democracy, would not such an effort to restore party democracy destroy Bolshevik minority rule? Thus, the underlying irrationality of the revolution, was the underlying basis for the furious response to Trotsky.[89] The rupture with reality on the one level, paralleled by and causing a similar rupture of ideology from reality, led to the Bolsheviks making into Anti-Christ the one among them who insisted on speaking with their original voice. As such he would be attacked with a progressively more insane frenzy that only grew throughout the 1930s. Whatever he actually said, he always meant *more* to those who attacked him: he stood for all that they betrayed and denied. Thus Bolsheviks *had to* describe Trotsky as *other than* a Leninist—now as a petty bourgeois, now as a semi-Menshevik, now as an agent of the bourgeosie, now as a fascist.

The Great Change

On 27 December 1929, in the midst of the collectivization drive, Stalin declared the 'liquidation of the kulaks as a class'. This mad project beat the countryside into a coma from which it has yet to recover. Breaking with deepest Marxist principles, it was based instead on utopian dreaming, mythology—and brute force. We have already taken several steps towards describing the increasingly irrational universe in which it took shape. 'The Great Change', however, was just that: it crossed the line between mere irrationality and a far more severe rupture with reality. Indeed, the word 'rupture' suggests both subjective and objective act, both withdrawal into a world of the mind peopled by fantasies and a violent attack on the actual world. We can glimpse both sides of the transformation in a famous passage Stalin published just before the assault: 'We are becoming a metal country, a motorized country, a tractorized country. And when we have seated the USSR on an automobile and the peasant on a tractor—let the esteemed capitalists, who boast about their "civilization", try to catch us up then. We will then be able to see which countries can be "classified" among the backward and which among the advanced.'[90]

The historically-based Marxist vision of a confident proletariat battling the haughty capitalist has been replaced by fantasies of a backward Russia catching up with the West. Yet, ominously, this vision contains more than dreaming: Stalin's determination to *make it happen* is evident.

Living according to fantasy—in the sense of trying to bring the impossible into being—became acceptable in these years. Indeed, the term 'vulgar realist' was coined to disparage those who doubted that the Soviet Union could both industrialize and modernize agriculture overnight. The gradualist vision of the 'pessimists' was replaced by the voices of men like S. G. Strumulin, a Stalinist planner: 'We are bound by no laws. There are no fortresses the Bolsheviks cannot storm.'[91] The decisive November 1929 plenum of the Central Committee saw the forced influx of peasants into collective farms as proof 'that the construction of socialism in a country governed by dictatorship of the proletariat can be carried out with a speed never before known in history.'[92]

These visions, of course, were false even when they were uttered. False but used and believed, and because of that effective. Even if some thought it mad, did not 'The Great Change' industrialize the Soviet Union, transform agriculture, and drive out illiteracy: did not the false actually become true? When single individuals depart so far from reality we term it madness. But, Stalin insisted, '[t]he people in the Politbureau and Sovnarkom are sober and calm.'[93] These sober men led an entire society to leap over the customary boundaries of reason, into behaviour whose goal was to transform reality until it came in line with their vision.

The 'madness' of the ruling faction was threefold: a drastic rupture with the world before them; living by fantasies and mythology rather than sense; and a violent—and in their terms successful—transformation of the world to fit the fantasy.

One root of these events was, of course, the Bolsheviks' impotence in genuine Marxist terms: a future-oriented social class presided over a society whose human base was intractably removed from their goals —which was, indeed, barely emerging from its feudal past. Their impotence to carry out socialism had been expressed from 1918 in vacillations of policy towards the vast majority of the country who were peasants. The Bolsheviks' radicalism, their understanding of the dynamics of revolution and their commitment to the poorest and most oppressed strata had originally led them to sanction sharing out land to the peasants in October 1917. In a series of acts described by Medvedev as 'utopian'[94] they sought to impose socialist relations on the countryside and so blundered into creating the conditions for an insurrection. They requisitioned the peasant's grain and conscripted his sons into the Red Army, but still won enough support from the countryside to prevail in the Civil War. Facing famine and renewed peasant wars, they then declared the NEP, which brought social peace and agricultural recovery. After that, amidst the withholding of grain by the peasants in 1927–28 and 1928–29, they returned to a system of forced procurement and confiscation of hidden surpluses. The crisis of 1927–29, refracted through the party's development and adoption of the first Five Year Plan for industrialization, brought to a head its deep anxieties about allowing 'capitalism' to flourish among the food-producing 80 per cent of the Soviet Union. And so, already in late 1927, an 'offensive against the kulaks' was decreed.

Breadlines in the city and a quadrupling of the price of flour—just as the leadership had accepted a plan to become 'a metal country, a motorized country, a tractorized country'—passed the death sentence on Bukharin's evolutionary hope of arriving at 'socialism at a snail's pace'. In a speech before the November Plenum of the Central Committee, which voted for rapid collectivization, Stalin spoke urgently of the need to 'catch up and surpass' the advanced capitalist countries: 'either we achieve this, or they will destroy us.' He spoke approvingly of Peter the Great's 'attempt to leap out of the framework of backwardness'. Had the proletariat taken power in Germany and France, the Soviet Union would be helped by being able to import machinery. But its isolation and encirclement made overtaking them a matter of 'life and death for our development'. Its overwhelming number of backward and small-scale peasants made its socialist industry 'an island in the sea of the Soviet Union'. Agriculture had to be reconstructed on a collective footing, but to do so required industrial development.[95]

This linking of agriculture and industrial development is the key: the Soviet Union which had just launched the first Five Year Plan was fed by twenty-five million primitive small holdings, whose productivity was at the level of fourteenth century England or France.[96] To industrialize depended on an agricultural surplus; that surplus depended on mechanization of agriculture. Under the rule of the pre-revolutionary *mir*, the peasant collective, holdings were divided into strips and cultivated on the three field system. Low productivity was a token of technical backwardness, which was rooted in turn in the fact that Russia's serfs, after all, had only been freed in 1861. Ten years after the revolution more than 50 per cent of the peasants remained completely illiterate, with a goodly proportion only semi-literate.

If, in a significant achievement since the revolution, only 28.5 per cent of the peasants still used wooden ploughs (10 per cent of those sowing grain), three quarters of the 1928 grain crop was still grown by hand, half harvested with scythe and sickle, and 40 per cent threshed by hand.[97] To collectivize this wretched agricultural system made no sense without offering the peasant (and country as a whole) greater efficiency, which depended on mechanization. *Pravda* estimated—at the height of the collectivization drive in January 1930!—that 1½ million tractors were needed for full collectivization.[98] By 1929 only 35 *thousand* were available.[99] But without tractors—and without, by implication, the entry of peasant society into the modern world with the aid of electrification, agronomy, and literacy—collectivization would simply multiply its wretchedness. Thus, as Lewin points out 'the idea that millions of *sokhi* (wooden ploughs) all added together would make an imposing sum had been treated as a joke.'[100]

Stalin's remarks thus reflect the fact that the Soviet Union consisted of what Lewin calls 'almost two nations or two civilizations, profoundly different in modes of production and modalities of organization in *Weltanschauungen* and in religion . . .'[101] He shows the intensifying Bolshevik obsession with backward Russia—haunted by the example of and under mortal pressure from the advanced capitalist West. This fact fuelled Stalin's growing determination to confront, and overcome, the distance between the civilizations.

Party membership figures are a telling index of the distance. Even under conditions of a Bolshevik monopoly of political power only one half of 1 per cent of the rural population had become party members. This number itself (293,000) included non-agricultural workers and officials, and was reduced significantly when only those currently farming were included. By any calculation there was no more than a single party member for each 125 peasant households.[102] As Carr says, '[m]any villages can never have seen a Communist except in the guise of an occasional visiting official.'[103]

Ten years after the revolution the party had established no effective counterweight to the peasant's own *mir*. What this means, of course, is that the Bolsheviks never became part of rural Russia, never understood it, never served it, but rather ruled over it—without the Tsarist aristocracy's time-sanctioned pretension to organic authority, and with the modernizing bureaucracy's arrogance and sense of cultural estrangement. Thus the simple practical task of the Bolsheviks in the late 1920s—*to get more grain* to feed the cities —was undertaken through lenses of incomprehension and hostility. Accompanying Bolshevik rule from the beginning—and one of the very sources of the revolution—the distance between them and the countryside had now to be dealt with.

The Bolsheviks possessed important conceptual tools to deal with this virtually foreign country under the increasingly unstable and demanding conditions caused by industrialization. Marxist realism was best summarized by an oft-quoted statement of Engels disavowing force towards small peasants when socialists came to power: 'Our task in relation to the small peasants will consist first and foremost in converting their private production and private ownership into collective production and ownership—not, however, by forcible means, but by example and by offering social aid for this purpose.'[104] Lenin accordingly insisted on 'the utmost caution and gradualness' in encouraging the middle peasantry to undertake collective agriculture. The transition would take 'generations' and 'decades', though not 'centuries'. In 1925 Trotsky saw a 'gradual' transition awaiting the necessary 'technical base'.[105]

Such remarks had deep roots in an outlook which sees socialism as harnessing, but not creating, productive forces which required long and painful incubation under preceding social systems. The absolute insistence on a voluntary rather than coercive approach reflected three premises: the faith that the superiority of socialism will become self-evident over time to all but the exploiting classes; the conviction that socio-economic change is a long and many-sided process—'organic' would not be inappropriate—whose pace may be encouraged but not forced; and the insistence that this process depends on the mass of working people living through each stage and making their own free decisions about its viability. These premises rested in turn on a profound Marxist democratic commitment—to the well-being of the poor, to their ultimate wisdom, to their progress. Shared by Right and Left Bolsheviks alike, these premises confined the mid-twenties' debates to a surprisingly narrow framework: how far should the transition to collective agriculture be quickened? Not even the Left envisioned a forced collectivization—it ran counter to their deepest Marxist convictions.

In the short run, then, Marxist realism had to be pessimistic: it insisted on remaining rooted in the actual situation and its limits. In Bukharin's words, 'it is not possible to build "present-day" factories with "future bricks".'[106] This attitude, of course is the hallmark of Marxism: its claim to science rests on its insistence on moving with, not against, history; on transforming the political and legal superstructure only insofar as the socio-economic base is ripe for such a transformation; on grasping the contradiction of a given historical moment in order to force the productive forces from the constraints of outmoded forms of production or social relations. This meant that even as dictators, Bolsheviks could not be *tyrants*: the human beings at the root of this process had to be given the space to develop. As Engels had said of the small peasant: 'if he cannot as yet bring himself to this decision [to join the cooperative], we will give him plenty of time to ponder over it on his holding.'[107]

For comparison we must set this emphasis on Marxist tolerance, rationalism and realism—on what Bukharin called 'scientific economic leadership'[108]—next to the words of Stalin's famous 1931 speech. There he passionately restated thoughts we have already heard him voice. He dwelled on Russia's ceaseless past defeats at the hands of the Turks, Mongols, Japanese, Poles, Lithuanians, English and French: 'for military backwardness, for cultural backwardness, for political backwardness, for industrial backwardness, for agricultural backwardness.' And then he rose to the prophetic: 'We are fifty or a hundred years behind the advanced countries. We must make good this lag in ten years. Either we do it or they crush us.'[109]

Stalin was, of course, speaking of the impossible. In our century what backward country of 150 million souls could catch up with the most advanced countries in a scant ten years? This was a mad undertaking, mad precisely owing to its utter rupture with sensible reality, its magical substitution of will for actual possibility. To become policy its absolute prerequisite was the completion of the 'double-storey void' discussed by Lewin: not only had the party to dominate the proletariat, but the party itself had also to become a machine, to be brought to heel under an indomitable will. Not only had all opposition to be removed, but all control by lower levels had to be broken. To carry out such a transformation required that the directing force have freedom of action to impose itself on those being transformed: on the party, on the working class, on the peasantry. The reversal of Marxist sense depended on the reversal of Marxist reality: to transform the base, the Soviet ruling group had to achieve not merely autonomy, but actual control over the base. In the name of science and sanity Bukharin had claimed that it was not possible 'to do as you please'.[110] Will, subjective wishes, had to be limited by objective human and historical reality. But having completed the process of substitution by bringing the party apparatus under his control, Stalin would now use it to try to do the impossible: to transform the reality that had so contradicted Bolshevik aspirations.

The process of rupture we have been tracing was coming to a grotesque climax, a form of social madness. Born out of the Bolsheviks' impotence to achieve their goals, the madness I am describing hinged on their control over state power. The vast extent of their state power, depending as it did on the absence of countervailing social forces, was in Marxist terms fundamentally a reflection of their impotence. Genuine power in such terms—the ability of society to advance towards the socialist future—would have depended on a high degree of industrialization and an organized and enfranchised working-class majority. If the Bolsheviks did not enjoy conditions allowing them to fulfil their project, they could nevertheless use the consequence and surrogate of this impotence, the transforming power of the state. They could use its brute force to try to beat the reality before them into a different shape, one more akin to their goals. I call this *mad* because it is not guided by reality and its own tendencies, but rather by the subjective wishes of the rulers. Madness: systematic enclosure in subjectivity to the point of denying decisive aspects of the objective world. Although the Bolsheviks had long restrained themselves from even thinking the thought, the party ruled by Stalin now decided to *coerce* backward Russia into becoming what they wished.

This was a break with Marxism in order to 'fulfil' it, entailing an assault on the producers themselves. Their property was expropriated by the bureaucracy which, at a stroke, became the ruling class.[111] Rooted in rationalism, Marx had disdained such utopianism and demanded instead that social theory be based on real historical possibilities and tendencies. And yet to do so in Russia meant living with an almost intolerable tension. While celebrating the victory of collectivization at the Seventeenth Party Congress in 1934 Stalin gives a rather telling retrospective voice to this tension: 'Let the Socialist-Revolutionary, Menshevik, and bourgeois-Trotskyist gossips chatter about the peasantry being counter-revolutionary by nature, about its mission to restore capitalism in the USSR, about its inability to serve as the ally of the working class in building socialism in the USSR.'[112] Thus does he reveal the fear that must have haunted the Bolsheviks until the 'Revolution from Above'.

The tension snapped with the push for rapid industrialization and collectivization. The break with sense, the resort to massive violence, was Stalin's way of resolving the contradiction in which the Bolsheviks found themselves caught after 1921.

These general reflections can be brought into specific focus with reference to the literature which accepts the project of forced collectivization in 1929–33, but speaks of Stalin's 'mistakes' in forcing the pace too rapidly and encouraging brutality. Roy Medvedev thus seems to seek retrospectively a rational way of carrying out the process, and criticizes only its cruelties. But to imagine a rational 'dekulakization' is to misunderstand the entire situation: rapid, forced collectivization was intrinsically a mad project. Because it was inherently brutal and *could not help* being so, there was no way on earth to soften its impact. We must avoid the systematic distortions that official terminology contained by 1929: Stalin had declared war on virtually the entire peasant population of the Soviet Union. Since Old Russia would not spontaneously and speedily evolve in the Marxist direction—or, more to the immediate point, would not make available to the state large cheap surpluses of grain to feed and finance the Five Year Plan—Stalin decided to expropriate it. J. P. Nettl unflinchingly characterizes Stalin's project in this 'second revolution' of 1929–30: 'Only by destroying the very basis of the old society and providing a universal infrastructure of literacy, by controlled mobilization into a social environment dominated by crude perspectives of production, could the basis of a new society be built.'[113]

Under Stalin's unopposed rule the time for caution and Marxist respect for reality was over. If Russia was backward, Stalin would modernize it; if it was economically independent, he would collectivize it. If the Plan required grain, even at the risk of creating chaos, he would establish the forms of production which would enable the state to *take* it. Not only was coercion inherent in the process, but so was the extermination or deportation of anyone who resisted: how else could the old society be destroyed? Ironically—and tragically for Soviet productivity—it was the more articulate, enterprising and productive peasants who were killed or forcibly resettled in order to deprive the others of leadership. The property of the largest livestock and land owners was used as an inducement to draw their poorer cousins into the collective farms.[114]

Since the shooting of the Civil War had died down and their isolation in their own country as well as the world had become apparent, the victors had been struggling to square the circle. How does one live in a society so wedded to the past, yet go on to construct the future? The human mind may customarily reject impossibilities as unthinkable: the circle cannot be squared. But unlike the circle, human beings have the power of decision and thus can assume different shapes, directions and actions, or be forced to assume them. If the rulers have will, so do the ruled: they can be *made to* behave differently. State power was now held by transformers who had themselves been twice transformed: into a ruling class, then into a bureaucratic machine. These were the preconditions for state power being used to force the pace of history—by, very simply, insisting that its subjects do what the transformers wished. Unlike the circle vainly waiting to be squared, humans can be threatened and beaten into the desired shape—and those who refuse can be deported or killed. Such a perspective would have seemed mad to the Bolshevik party which took power in 1917. A dozen years later its founder was dead, its entire Left had been expelled, the party had broken with its class base in the process of production, destroyed every last element of internal democracy, and begun systematically to nurture itself on lies and myths. It had become a machine run by a boss who traded privilege, power, and the disposition of state property in return for unqualified support. Expropriation of 25 million smallholdings would vastly enlarge the caste administering state property. Even so, to encourage the army of transformers, the deep-seated Marxist reluctance to use force against a producing class—which explains perhaps why the war was only declared suddenly and without warning or preparation in late 1929—had to be replaced by new layers of mythology.

The Bolsheviks had long veiled the actual pattern of rural social relations—in which village solidarity was very important[115]—to impose a schema of urban class conflict which both made sense of this foreign world and justified their rule. Thus was the proletariat described as 'ruling' in alliance with agricultural workers (*batraks*) and poor peasants (*bednyaks*), but 'supported by' the middle peasants (*serednyaks*), against the 'rich' and 'exploiting' peasants employing more than a single labourer. Most kulaks were themselves workers, along with their families, on pitifully small and unproductive strips of land. But a mad project required lies to justify it. The lie, of necessity, now entered into the heart of Bolshevik policy as it sought to destroy Old Russia: the joke about 'millions of *sokhi*' now became official doctrine: the peasants' resources were 'poor, sometimes downright wretched, but when pooled together, they make an imposing sum.'[116]

Anyone who opposed collectivization became *ipso facto* a kulak or supporter. So compelling was this in a society which was more and more living by myth, that the lie became true enough to motivate masses. We can see the lie and its 'truth' in this striking fictional account cited by Medvedev: 'The door opened and the brigade burst into the house. The OGPU officer in charge of the operation was in front, holding a revolver. "Hands up." Morgunov was barely able to distinguish the frail figure of the class enemy. He was barefoot, wearing white drawers and a dark undershirt; a dishevelled beard stuck out on a face that was long unshaven. His eyes, wide with terror darted from place to place. The lined face flinched, the coarse brown hands were trembling. Hanging from a worn-out cord on his bare chest was a little cross, grown dark with age. "Lord Jesus, save us, have mercy on us." Gusts of freezing air came through the open door into the well-heated little hut. Members of the dekulakization brigade were already standing at each window, their faces stern. Expecting something dreadful to happen, they all were ready to rush into battle for their cause, for soviet power, for socialism. But the kulak-agent Terentyev never thought of resisting. He kept blinking and crossing himself, shifting from one foot to the other, as though he were standing on something hot, and suddenly he began to sob, his whole body shaken by convulsive gasps. He was bending over in a peculiar position, shuddering, and small, glistening tears, one after another, rolled down the coarsened, weather-beaten face. His wife, no longer young, jumped down from the high sleeping bench and began to wail at the top of her voice; the children started to cry; and a calf, apparently rather sick and lying beside the stove, added to the clamour. Morgunov looked around, quite horrified. He saw that the hut contained only the one room and the large Russian stove. In the front corner beneath the icons were two simple wooden benches and a crude table put together from planks. There was no sign of a dresser, or a bed, or a chair. On the shelves there were some simple wooden bowls, worn by years of use, and some old wooden spoons. Some oven forks and buckets of water stood by the stove, and on the left against the wall, a large old-fashioned trunk. The class enemy! The representatives of authority had already informed Terentyev that he was under arrest. He was to be dekulakized and deported straight away. All his possessions would be confiscated. His family would follow shortly, but their destination was not known. He could take with him only the clothes on his back and a change of underwear. Terentyev trembled and wept. "How can you call us kulaks? What for? What have I done?" He got no reply. Roughly breaking the locks, they opened the trunk and the food cupboard and pulled out some sort of footgear, sackcloth, and foodstuffs. "What for? What have I done?" "Nothing. You're a kulak, a kulak-agent. You're against the collective farm. You don't want to join and you're upsetting everything. And that's all there is to it." And they started making a list of all his goods and possessions.'[117]

Perhaps the most striking refutation of the lie of a class-based 'voluntary collectivization' are Stalin's own statistics for livestock production: horses, cattle, and pigs dropped by one half between 1929 and 1933, sheep and goats by two thirds. Rather than surrender their animals to the collective farms, the peasants slaughtered them. Lost in their own myths, a few party members may have dreamed that the peasant, freed from the influence of the kulak, would willingly allow his animals to become state property controlled by a hostile bureaucracy. But when violence so completely effaced the peasant's very deepest nature, he could only respond with his own impotent and self-destructive violence.

Industrialization

Side by side with this process, in the towns and cities forced industrialization was taking place. It too involved a frantic break with sense: in June 1930 Stalin told the Sixteenth Party Congress that the Soviet Union was 'on the eve of transformation from an agrarian to an industrial country', and that in the current year industry had been ordered to raise its output by 47 per cent. Deutscher gives some idea of Stalin's superindustrialist fantasy during the Five Year Plan: 'He was now completely possessed by the idea that he could achieve a miraculous transformation of the whole of Russia by a single *tour de force*. He seemed to live in a half-real and half-dream world of statistical figures and indices, of industrial orders and instructions, a world in which no target and no objective seemed to be beyond his and the party's grasp. He coined the phrase that there were no fortresses which could not be conquered by Bolsheviks, a phrase that was in the course of many years repeated by every writer and orator and displayed on every banner and poster in every corner of the country.'

One illustration of the madness is the quota for pig iron: an industry which had produced 3,500,000 tons in 1928 was commanded to produce 10,000,000 tons by 1933. Then, having already advanced this time limit, Stalin told the Sixteenth Congress that '10,000,000 tons of pig iron ... is not enough ... At all costs we must produce 17,000,000 tons in 1932.'[118] Those sober economists and business managers who doubted the possibility of achieving so high a target were branded as 'right-wing opportunists' and 'wreckers'. By the time of the Nazi attack in 1941, the Soviet output of pig iron was just approaching 10,000,000 tons!

A madness parallel to collectivization, this insane attempt to do the impossible by industrializing overnight was based not only on myth, but also on coercion. Such an effort made workers into appendages of industry, imposed impossible goals on managers, and self-consciously exacted a 'tribute' from starving peasants to feed and finance the process. The spirit of the new situation was epitomized by the building of the Moscow underground—that heroic socialist achievement whose necessity, in a city of few automobiles, was primarily psychological and ideological. It was also epitomized in the fact that 5,000,000 tons of grain were exported in the year of 'Revolution from Above'—1930—initiating a famine process which became devastating in 1932. While millions of the producers were starving, the Soviet Union in 1932–33 exported 1.75 million tons of grain!

Madness and Progress

Such an overnight transformation was both sub- and super-human. It was inherently mad, utopian and brutal at the same time—a fantastic exertion of will, an incredibly successful leap of self-development and an assault on the entire country. The whole project was a violation of human possibility: could its destructive consequences have possibly been distilled out while the constructive were left intact? Or were both sides not 'sides' at all, but hopelessly mixed together in a single process? Is it not a Panglossian illusion to see the 'progressive' results as being the normal and the 'destructive' ones as demanding explanation? Because it is good, it is assumed, it must have been sensible: only the harmful results are seen as aberrant. This is the illusion of Reason and Progress.

As we point to the unmet plan goals, the reduction of grain production, the destruction of most farm animals, the human deaths and deportations, it is certainly possible to imagine a rational non-coercive transformation of Old Russia. We can even read its outline in the Platform of the Joint Opposition. None of the spokesmen for Old Bolshevik rationality—neither Trotsky on the Left nor Bukharin on the Right—conceived of the leap into the void of 1929. The rational Marxist approach always thought in terms of 'decades' and 'generations', as Lenin said. No intelligent analyst of the 1920s would have anticipated as normal and rational the Soviet push to abolish illiteracy or equal the Western supply of physicians overnight. Such progress was itself an aberration.

Yet the deformation of Bolshevism had progressed so far that this headlong and violent rush was experienced by the party members who carried it out as a comprehensible response to an increasingly difficult situation. An indefinite continuation of NEP, based on Bukharin's sober and pessimistic realism, was felt to be unacceptable after 1928. On every front the situation was increasingly threatening, the lenses for perceiving it were becoming increasingly irrational and distorted, and the narrowing of the revolution's social base gave the dictatorship an increasingly free hand. At the summit of the party machine the various factors pointed towards a decisive and shattering break with Old Russia to construct a modern nation strong enough to withstand the threatening world. In retrospect, Stalin's ten years 'or they crush us' remark was uncannily accurate. But of course it was helped to become a self-fulfilling prophecy by Soviet 'third period' foreign policy, which demanded that German Communists treat Social Democrats as the Enemy of enemies. The threat brooded over by Stalin might have been more effectively countered by proletarian politics in the Comintern than by crushing Old Russia. However, Russian and world reality was such that the choice was Stalin's to make. First through successive modulations and then in a sudden leap the choice was made, accompanied by yet another deformation and transformation of original Bolshevik hopes.

False Charges

On 12 March 1938, on trial for his life, Nikolai Bukharin, former editor of *Pravda* and *Izvestia*, ex-president of the Comintern and principal author of the recently-proclaimed Soviet Constitution, admitted 'that I am guilty of treason to the socialist fatherland, the most heinous of possible crimes, of the organization of kulak uprisings, of preparations for terrorist acts and of belonging to an underground anti-Soviet organization. I further admit that I am guilty of organizing a conspiracy for a "palace coup".'[119] Next day he and seven other defendants were sentenced to death, after being found guilty of being members and leaders of the inconceivable 'bloc of Rights and Trotskyites which acted under the direct instructions of the intelligence services of foreign states, carrying on treasonable, espionage, diversive, wrecking and terrorist activities, provoking an armed attack by these states on the USSR with the purpose of bringing about the defeat and dismemberment of the Soviet Union and the severance from it of the Ukraine, Byelorussia, the Central Asiatic republics, Georgia, Armenia, Azerbaijan, and the Maritime Region in the Far East for benefit of foreign states hostile to the USSR, their ultimate aim being the overthrow of the Socialist social and state system existing in the USSR and the restoration of capitalism and of the power of the bourgeoisie in the USSR ....'[120] Within two days, in what is often regarded as the climax of Stalinism, the eighteen were executed.

Beggaring description even fifty years later, the Great Purge was initiated by the murder of Kirov in late 1934, and rolled over the Soviet Union in vast bloody fits and starts until 1939. We have already seen the figures: by late 1938 8 million people are estimated to have been in labour camps for political reasons, and a total of approximately 1 million people were executed in 1937–38. In the process the labour camps became a major part of the Soviet economy. It has been argued that 20 million people entered the camps or were shot between 1936 and 1950—meaning that the Terror fell on perhaps every second family in the country. Bukharin's fate indicates its other dimensions as well: the creation of a vast apparatus for denunciation and fabrication of charges;[121] the most incredible lies entering into Soviet daily life; the insistence that its victims confess their guilt; the turning of the revolution against the whole people; its suicidal devouring of its own leaders.

Bukharin's fate is certainly high tragedy: agreeing to confess to behaviour 'akin to a kulak praetorian fascism' so that his wife and son would be spared, yet marshalling every last drop of intellectual, moral and political strength to outwit his accusers. Perhaps more heartbreaking are the millions of less brilliant stories—for example, the confession, at the same trial, of a respected Old Bolshevik, Isaak Zelenski. A revolutionary since sixteen, Zelenski was first arrested in 1912 at twenty-two. He spent the next several years in and out of jails, in exile, and as a party organizer. Having, since 1917, served as secretary of the Central Committee and of the Moscow Party organization, as well as chairman of Consumer Cooperatives, Zelenski was now required to confess that he had been an agent of the Tsarist *Okhrana* between 1911 and 1917—and that more recently he had been responsible for putting nails and glass in butter![122]

The Terror

Did the revolution need this holocaust? It was insane, destructive and unnecessary. In his 'Secret Speech', Khrushchev, speaking for the bureaucracy which had triumphed with Stalin, emphasized that this terror began only after the revolution had become 'secure': 'It is clear that in the situation of socialist victory there was no basis for mass terror in the country.'[123] After the brutal period of collectivization and the first Five Year Plan had indeed transformed the face of the country—with the assent and active support of the new privileged class of party members—a relaxation now seemed to them desirable and possible. Instead, Stalin moved from what Alec Nove calls the 'situation-determined' terror of 1929–33 to wholly personal and arbitrary measures which brought disaster to the country.[124]

Roy Medvedev focuses on its utter irrationality with a series of questions: 'Stalin was a leader in hard times. He did enjoy the confidence of a majority of the Party and the people. That confidence, that faith of the common people in Stalin, to some degree helped them endure the hardships of economic construction and the war with fascism. But would not the solidarity between the people and the government have been stronger had there been no mass repression? Would not the people have shown the Central Committee more confidence if the best people in the party, government, economic, and military *apparat* had not been destroyed in the mid-thirties? Would not economic and cultural progress have been much greater if Stalin had not destroyed thousands upon thousands of scientists, engineers, teachers, doctors, writers? Would not the war have ended much faster and with fewer losses if our finest officers had not perished before the war and if Stalin had conducted a more sensible foreign and military policy? Would not agriculture have achieved greater progress if Stalin had not grossly and constantly violated Lenin's plan for agricultural cooperatives? And the bureaucracy and rule by fiat, the multitude of mistakes in nationality policy, the inhumanity and wilfulness of Stalinist administration —could all this in any measure strengthen the solidarity of the Soviet people, the friendship among the peoples of the Soviet Union? What then do we have to thank Stalin for? For the fact that his thirty-year rule did not completely ruin the Party, the army, Soviet democracy, agriculture, and industry? For the fact that he did not completely pervert Leninism and the proletarian character of the October Revolution, that he did not destroy all honourable Soviet people, did not bring the country to catastrophe?'[125]

But our discussion of the stages through which Bolshevism has passed leaves us with a somewhat different sense of the Great Purge: it is not so easy to separate the rational from the irrational in the revolution, excess from necessity, the social from the personal. We have traced an intensifying process of irrationalization, of a narrowing power base, of mythologizing, of distorting reality, of a bloody and violent rupture to transform that reality. Many writers want to preserve the good and rational revolution in the face of the bad and irrational.[126] Some still seek to make it all good[127] or make it all bad and irrational.[128] We have rather seen such categories slowly absorb each other.

Stalinism is the grotesque but consistent climax of the processes and tendencies we have been tracing. Murder and deportation of the recalcitrant peasantry became mass murder; imprisonment in concentration camps was now no longer connected with any apparent social struggle and indeed became economically necessary to the new mode of organizing production; control over the party turned into destruction of the party and extermination of virtually all Old Bolsheviks; 'socialism in one country' became in Stephen Cohen's words, 'an almost fascist-like chauvinism';[129] the distortion of the past now became the wholesale rewriting of history; the tendency to mythologize specific areas now became the systematic portrayal of the USSR as a near-utopia; the process of narrowing the locus of power now became an absolute autocracy based on the Hitlerian deification of the ruler; the banning of opposition now became the most feverish witch-hunt in all history; the General Secretary's control over the party apparatus now became his personal control over each and every administrator in the country; party control over culture now became Stalin's personal control over, and direct intervention in, every aspect of cultural life. Appropriately, a certain type of official came into prominence in these years as the original core of the party was destroyed: the half-educated sycophantic bully personally dependent on Stalin. The courageous peasants, workers, and soldiers who electrified the world by overthrowing the old order in 1917 had long since been beaten into a fearful, submissive, passive mass. And, equally appropriately, Marxism became a set of catechistic and magical formulas, losing further its original rationality.

One-Man Rule

The evidence suggests that we can neither exempt Stalin from responsibility nor lay it at the door, say, of the October Revolution. The real history was far more complex. The final steps in its logic now demand to be traced. It is, as we have seen, the logic of illogic—of a process that leads to an absolute dictatorship of one man only because of its increasing irrationality.[130]

Sartre traced the brutal rationality of the revolution as leading to Stalin, and argued that its irrationality was based on his *personal* idiosyncrasies. Stalin's personal sovereignty was demanded by the situation because 'the constructive effort of the USSR implies that this society ... find its unity in the biological indissolubility of one individual.'[131] As such, Stalin as the 'summit of the pyramid, the living suppression of all multiplicity', served the society's need for *maximum* integration. For Sartre, the situation's 'need' for a ruling individual—an individual of specific qualities—entails its domination by the equally deep-rooted eccentricities that go hand in hand with such qualities. *The situation* may have required extraction of a surplus from the population or destruction of the backward peasantry, Sartre argues, and Stalin's character was such as to fit the situation—but his paranoia, having its source in a different place and time, spilled over the demands of the situation and required the purges.

This necessity would explain the remarkable fact that none of the threatened Old Bolsheviks sought to remove Stalin before he destroyed them: their sense was that the fate of the revolution itself lay in the hands of *this* man, no matter how evil or brutal or paranoid. To strike at him, given the seemingly inevitable logic of the revolution fulfilling itself only in his hands, was thus seen as endangering its very fruits and accomplishments.

But Sartre's argument returns us to what I have described as the illusion of Reason and Progress: underlying it is the myth that the Soviet Union's positive accomplishments were *rational* but its disasters were *irrational*. Yet taking grain from the hands of starving peasants to buy machinery which sat and rusted was an excess of overnight modernization which betrays the latter's brutal and quixotic essence. Sartre must be corrected: not only did such an adventure require a ruler who was 'inflexible, without nerves, and without imagination',[132] but a ruler who utterly lacked internal or external restraint. Moreover, the fact that its precondition was the surrender of all political power to a single individual testifies to the radical deformation of Soviet political life whose course we have been tracing.

In the final analysis, the internal process of 'substitutionism' reveals a distorting and distorted response to Russia's situation in the world. Bolshevism's isolation and its vast historical and cultural distance from the bulk of Old Russia mirrors in turn Russia's own vulnerability in relation to the relentless forces of modern Europe. The central role of Stalin's personal brutality, paranoia and obsession with power stems from these larger social logics: the revolution defended itself from its vulnerability and multiple isolation by narrowing and strengthening its locus of power and then by an incredible leap forward. Stalin's own power-madness is only the extension *ab limito* of the revolution's own situation-determined weakness.

Stalin's Responsibility for Stalinism

In 1928 the dominant part of the ruling faction sensed the need for a drastic policy turn, one which required an attack on the countryside: the private sector was to be expropriated by the bureaucratized party, which would then have sufficient control to organize wholesale industrialization. As Nove points out, each step in the years 1929–33 required a more extensive repressive apparatus.[133] Rapid progress in those circumstances can only be progress enforced by a police state against its citizens. Such policies, of course, could not be debated freely—they were imposed by one man on the party, which then imposed them on the society. The consequent repressive apparatus increased his power over society as it furthered (in its own grotesque way) the original Bolshevik goal of industrialization. Thus does the logic of the revolution lead us by twists and turns to the door of one man—Sartre's 'sovereign individual'.

Most commentators focus on Stalin's subjective drives as the single most important force behind the Great Purge of the mid 1930s. Deutscher, a partial exception, explains the Great Purge as the offspring of Hitler's remilitarization of the Rhineland, a product of Stalin's fear of being overthrown in the event of war.[134] Nove, like Sartre, sees the terror as being exclusively Stalin's personal act.[135] Tucker takes us a step further and sees in the Great Purge a coherent delusional system.[136] All are certainly right to focus on the inner obsessions of the individual ruler in a situation where, as absolute ruler, *his* obsessions had come to mean so much.

Worried that allegations of madness might cast doubt on Stalin's competence—and he certainly planned the Purge with consummate skill and self-control—Medvedev insists on Stalin's abiding and conscious *purpose*. The basic motive for his crimes was not 'because he stopped trusting his aides, or because he developed a persecution mania and began to see traitors all around him'—but because of his *'measureless ambition'*.[137] 'A leader's excessive ambition does not automatically lead to mass repression of his opponents and rivals. When considering the personal aspect of the repression in the thirties we must take into account not only the ambition but also the cruelty and viciousness of Stalin. We must also note the contradiction between Stalin's limitless ambition and his limited abilities. It was this very contradiction that drove Stalin into conflict not only with those he saw as his present or future opponents but also with many Old Bolsheviks, who were personally devoted to him, never said anything against him, and carried out all his orders. From his early years Stalin had an inferiority complex. Combined with ambition and vanity, it engendered spiteful envy. Without any serious or systematic education, knowing no foreign languages, he became in 1917 a member of a government that was called, even by its enemies, the best educated in Europe. Surrounded by many brilliant people, Stalin must have felt his inferiority as a political leader, a theorist, and an orator. Hence his envy towards every truly educated Party intellectual. He wanted not only unlimited power but also unlimited glory; no one must upstage him in the historical drama. Thus many people became his enemies not because they were opposed to the regime but because they performed great services for it.'[138] Thus does Medvedev explain the Terror as resulting directly from Stalin's quest for *all power*. The dictator who rules over independent-minded old revolutionary agitators can hardly rest secure; his fear becomes transformed into rule by fear.[139]

To imagine a relaxation, as Khrushchev did retrospectively, was to expect that Stalin might now have laid down the whip and gun, called off the secret police, abandoned the various myths the whole party had been living by—about the working class, party democracy, voluntary collectivization, and the danger of Trotskyism—and allow power to revert back to at least the top layers of the party. It was, further, to suggest that it was then possible to reverse the sense of danger and magic which had propelled the entire project forward—both the obsessive fear of foreign enemies and the mad taking of the will for the deed that had made the Great Change possible. After 1933, however, it would have been impossible to convince a leader who had organized his country's life and structures around it that there was no foreign threat; it would have been equally impossible to convince the ruler of transformed Russia that there were some fortresses the Bolsheviks could not storm; and, above all, it would have been impossible to presume that a country which had accomplished so much through brutality—thus incorporating brutality into its very substance—could now relax its grip over its people.[140]

Instead, Stalin relentlessly continued the process we have traced from 1921 and drove for *all* power. Each step en route seemed to lead logically to the next. Its high point, symbolically, was Molotov's formulation that to be most effective the enemy agent would appear indistinguishable from the loyal Communist—the better able to damage the society at a decisive moment. If so, total vigilance was the only answer. The slightest of counter-revolutionary or anti-Stalin actions, gestures, or thoughts might reveal an enemy of the people to an alert informer. And, fearful of being denounced, tens of millions instead denounced others.

The Social Logic of Stalinism

In this individual logic the reader will no doubt see a social logic. In following at any length the personal dimension suggested by Sartre or Medvedev we rejoin the historical. Not only did Stalin use the revolutionary process for his personal ambition and continue its development beyond what seemed necessary: his own motives parallel those of the revolution itself. To speak of his character traits becoming decisive after 1934—his feeling of inferiority, his boundless ambition, his fear, his appearance of unbounded will and lack of normal moral limits, his aloofness, his insensitivity to people, the 'contradiction between his great ambitions and limited abilities'—is to sound the most striking resonances with the fate of Bolshevism as it unfolded before 1934. Was not the fundamental contradiction of the revolution the same—between 'great ambitions and limited abilities'? And did not the party, and then the leadership of the party, and then the leader, slowly insulate themselves from the threatening reality of a population whose goals and outlook they did not share? And did not the party slowly efface the line between lie and reality, myth and fact, and in so doing make possible the breakdown of its normal political inhibitions? Did it not—under Stalin's leadership—finally overstep its Marxist sensitivity and scruples, and resolve the contradiction by an extraordinary act of will? Did it not do so by trying, like Stalin, 'to force life into a ready-made framework', mangling it and breaking it when necessary, 'chopping limbs off'?[141] Stalin's character, in other words, only paralleled, absorbed—and expressed —key elements of the revolution's twisted path.

If the social logic of Stalinism is indeed inseparable from its individual logic, we must now return to our question: why did Stalin drive the country into the Great Purge? It might seem enough to see the madness of the process of collectivization and industrialization letting loose an even more unrestrained madness: after all, 1936–38 is not very puzzling in the country of 1929–33. Does not one madness lead to another? But I would like to claim an even more direct social logic for this holocaust. We can find our clue by looking first at Stalin's celebration of 'the successful building of socialism', at the Seventeenth Party Congress of 1934.

'During this period, the USSR has become radically transformed and has cast off the aspect of backwardness and medievalism. From an agrarian country it has become an industrial country. From a country of small individual agriculture it has become a country of collective, large-scale mechanized agriculture. From an ignorant, illiterate and uncultured country it has become—or rather it is becoming—a literate and cultured country covered by a vast network of higher, secondary and elementary schools functioning in the languages of the nationalities of the USSR.'[142] Stalin continued, enumerating the industrial accomplishments, the rise in national income, the development of large and populous towns, and the creation of more than 200,000 collective and state farms. His concern throughout was to show how successful was the Soviet Union at creating socialism's *material* basis.

Five years later, at the Eighteenth Party Congress and shortly after the waning of the Terror, Stalin spoke of further progress. 'Whereas capitalist society is torn by irreconcilable antagonisms between workers and capitalists and between peasants and landlords—resulting in its internal instability—Soviet society, liberated from the yoke of exploitation, knows no such antagonisms, is free of class conflicts, and presents a picture of friendly collaboration between workers, peasants and intellectuals. It is this community of interests which has formed the basis for the development of such motive forces as the moral and political unity of Soviet society, the mutual friendship of the nations of the USSR, and Soviet patriotism. It has also been the basis for the Constitution of the USSR adopted in November, 1936, and for the complete democratization of the elections to the supreme organs of the country.'[143]

In the same report Stalin said that the Soviet Union had achieved the most modern industrial system and the most mechanized agriculture in the world, and he set the goal of economically out-stripping the principal capitalist countries.

The contrast is decisive. While the 1934 statement is mostly cor-rect—agriculture had not been mechanized, but the rest of the pic-ture is accurate if a bit rosy—the 1939 statement crosses the border of fantasy. But when we draw both together we discover the key to the Stalinist project: to realize the full goals of the Bolshevik revolu-tion, but to do so through an amalgam of lies, murder, violence, myth and actual achievement. Stalin's madness is the madness whose origin we have been tracing, the original Bolshevik project carried to its limit in an impossible situation. We have seen that to the Bolsheviks in the 1920s, how the situation *should* appear—the ideological dimension—was every bit as important to them as the situation's objective features. This ideological dimension acquires motive force in what Lewin describes as the creation of the base by the superstructure.[144] Obviously, it was absolutely essential that the original Bolshevik outlook, which had played such a decisive role in the process, now absorbed the material changes of 1929–33. Even distorted and mythologized, the ideological plane of Soviet life re-tained its importance—and now presented its demands. If until 1929 reality flatly contradicted aspiration, did not the vast changes since realize the aspiration?

With the Great Purge Stalin took the next, fatal steps in resolving the contradiction between Bolshevik vision and Soviet reality. Achieving absolute power, he destroyed all obstacles to making the vision fit the reality: he constructed the ideal society in fantasy and on the lips of its terrorized people. Those parts of the revolutionary vi-sion which could be carried out in reality were indeed carried out: education, collectivization, improvement of health care, industrializa-tion. In the carrying out, violence was used to create the desired reality—or rather (since *that* was impossible) to create an acceptable approximation of that reality. Those dimensions which were essential to Bolshevism but unrealizable under those conditions, became 'realized' by being embodied in myth, and enshrined in the Constitution: democratic rule by the working class through Soviets. Those parts too threatening to be admitted either into Soviet theory or practice—such ideas as workers' control, economic equality or the withering away of the state—became tabooed and imputed to the Anti-Christ, Trotsky.

If we appreciate the importance of ideology, then it is clear that the new, systematically irrational reality under construction in 1929–33 required 1936–38 as its completion. Even today the latter period is regarded in the Soviet Union as 'the Victory and Consolidation of Socialism'. During it, a recent text on Marxism-Leninism argues, the Soviet electoral system was democratized, democracy developed within the party and its members' rights broadened.[145]

This will help us understand some of the Purge's most striking features: Bukharin's confession, for example, after he had played a major role in writing 'the most democratic constitution in the world'; the insistence that those who were clearly innocent must confess; the attribution of all industrial accidents, all shortages, to 'wreckers'; the use of Vyshinsky, a former Menshevik, to destroy the Bolshevik party; the final steps in the elevation of Trotsky as Anti-Christ of the revolution; the creation of a Soviet dream-world of happy workers and collective farmers; and the resort to systematic mass murder.

It was more than cynical scapegoatism for *Pravda* to declare, in February 1937, that 'not one accident should go unnoticed. We know that assembly lines do not stop by themselves, machines do not break by themselves, boilers do not burst by themselves. Someone's hand is behind every such act. Is it the hand of an enemy? That is the first question we should ask in such cases.'[146] Obviously, a society so abused and terrorized, labouring under such impossible demands, was likely to have more than its share of industrial accidents, unfulfilled quotas, food shortages, etc. What *Pravda* is really reflecting, however, is the mad voluntarism we have seen become central to the party. If the Bolsheviks could storm any fortress, these problems likewise must be products of human *will*. That is, they must result from sabotage. In a country surrounded by enemies in which the class enemy has been defeated and harmony rules, those who sabotage national goals—enemies of the people—can only be in the employ of external enemies of the revolution.

Moreover, were not many former oppositionists and potential oppositionists now in high positions in industry, no doubt carrying on the wrecking that kept people hungry and production inefficient? In reality such people no doubt recalled Marxist teachings and Bolshevik struggles which now had been tabooed; and they might still be able to point out ways in which the revolution failed to live up to its ideals. As a former Menshevik and an obvious opportunist, Vyshinsky, their inquisitor, had no such convictions; he was, therefore the ideal person to pursue them. And pursue them he did. Thus the Society of Old Bolsheviks and the Society of Former Political Prisoners were disbanded. But the entire Party had not only to be purged, but virtually destroyed: even good Stalinists had been revolutionaries, and had memories. It was necessary to kill 110 of the 140 members of the 1934 Central Committee. Only 35 of the 1,827 rank-and-file delegates to the 1934 Party Congress (2 per cent) were present to hear Stalin's 1939 report—1,108 had been arrested as counter-revolutionaries, most of them not surviving.

Building Socialism

Marxism—the patient process of winning people over, using violence only as a 'midwife'—had been superseded by violence *tout court*, as voluntarism, will, and subjectivity led the assault on a terrifyingly recalcitrant reality. Increased resort to violence was accompanied by the enemy-psychology which justified it and in turn needed violence to justify itself. By 1936–38, in the increasingly self-enclosed mental world of Stalinism—now validated by the threat of Hitler and by its own achievements—all actual or potential oppositionists *were* enemies and so had to be eliminated; or, they *had to* be eliminated and so *were* enemies. They were to be replaced by people who would accept the fantasy construction of the 'successful revolution'— people with no revolutionary past or independent minds, people of low culture, people who could obey, people who accepted denouncing potential 'enemies of the people' as a political and personal obligation, people capable of treating the old revolutionaries ruthlessly.

These machinations all culminated in the erection of the spectre of the Anti-Christ of the revolution—Leon Trotsky. Even from this distance of time it is shocking to see tens of millions of people arrested for faked-up connections to an imaginary Rightist-Trotskyist-

Imperialist plot, while its alleged author was fleeing from one exile to another to find safety. But now we can perhaps understand Stalin's obsession. Trotsky was hated by Stalin, in his son's words, as 'the living embodiment of the ideas and traditions of the October revolution.'[147] Both for the revolution at large and his own followers Trotsky had become a mythical figure: the conscience of a revolution that had betrayed itself and deformed its consciousness as it was carried out. We have seen that every deviation from Stalin's Bolshevism, duly noted by Trotsky—who in exile became more and more democratic in outlook—had to be *dealt with*. It had to be disguised, distorted or justified—or else Bolshevism itself had to be altered to accommodate the change. A religious cult of Lenin was combined with the effacement of his living memory by destroying his every heir but Stalin. The other five men mentioned in his Testament (Pyatakov, Bukharin, Zinoviev, Kamenev, and Trotsky) were the main defendants in the three great trials of 1936–38. If these trials make sense from the point of view of removing alternatives to Stalin's personal dictatorship, they also make sense as Stalin's effort to define any independent thought or action—or even its possibility —as treason. And they make sense, above all, as an effort to complete the revolution by making the idea of revolution fit the reality and vice versa.

Reality, Stalin had shown in 1929–33, submits to a design when assaulted. If so, truth could be made falsehood and falsehood truth. This explains the otherwise puzzling insistence on obtaining signed confessions from people who would never even appear at public trial, immediately before they were shot. Days and weeks would be spent interrogating and torturing innocent people when in fact such 'confessions' were wholly faked: why then was there only a handful of prosecutors who simply signed the confessions themselves before having their victims shot? Such lavish expenditure of effort was not at all due to an attachment to legality, when legality was being continuously redefined and only loosely applied. Nor does it seem that the prosecutors could genuinely have believed the confessions to be true. Rather, the explanation must be sought in the nature of the project itself: to *make* the false true and the true false. In the process, these innocent people *became* enemies. And if they themselves withheld assent to this truth, a vital link in the process would remain missing. Thus did the victims, in confessing, themselves contribute to creating the new Soviet 'reality'.

The 'reality' may have been a monstrous structure of lies and distortions as much as of achievements; but by 1939 all eyes, ears and mouths testified that it was the *only* reality. By then the Stalinist construction had been completed: society was harmonious (because terrorized), completely socialist (because the vision had been redefined to mean nationalized production and forced collectivization), industrialized (because of the exertions of the Five Year Plan and the famine), democratic (because any opposition of this grotesque lie had been crushed) and literate (because social energy had been organized to conquer illiteracy). In this utterly mad, deformed, yet palpably real universe Stalin did finally and fully do the impossible: build 'socialism' in backward Russia. Not yet completed in 1934, the task took the Great Purge to accomplish.

The Lack of Resistance

No separate analysis is needed to account for another remarkable feature of this process, the virtual lack of resistance to Stalin. In contrast to the partisans, ghetto fighters and underground networks under Nazi rule, Stalinism generated no opposition worthy of the name. I have mentioned Bukharin's battle for his integrity while trying to save his family—this, one of the great struggles against Stalin, can only appear pathetic alongside the heroic behaviour so often seen against the Nazis. This sorry absence is indeed one of the reasons the Soviet Union has become such a graveyard of hope in our century.

The above analysis has explained why. Not only has good become evil while never wholly renouncing good; it has thereby monopolized the language, values and modes of thought of an entire society. Above all, by representing Reason and Progress, it allowed no space for an independent and contrary sense of morality. We have heard Trotsky on party theory. Trotsky might go on claiming to be right, but he more than anyone knew how abstract were his claims. Stalin, after all, occupied the stage of history. Could one go on believing in the revolution *and* seek to overthrow him? The party's shared assumptions and shared history, its sense of threat and common destiny—indeed, the entire logic we have seen unfold—left little moral, intellectual or psychological space for anyone to be right against Stalin.

Enemies of the People

One startling index of how mad the process became is the fact that on the very eve of war one half of the 70,000 military officers were shot or imprisoned—including 3 of the 5 Marshals, 14 of the 16 Army Commanders Class I and II, all 8 Admirals (Flagmen) Class I and II, 60 of the 67 Corps Commanders, 136 of the 194 Divisional Commanders and 221 of the 397 Brigade Commanders.[148]

While laying waste to his best and most experienced commanders in pursuit of a fantasy–enemy, Trotsky, Stalin was also assuring a military hierarchy loyal to him alone, whose service to the revolution and to socialism would be according to *his* definitions. By doing this, Stalin only crippled his ability to deal with the real enemy, Hitler. In 1941 he also systematically ignored warnings of the impending invasion and kept the Soviet military unprepared until disaster had already struck. With near-fatal consequences Stalin's German policy continued his domestic policy: to take the wish for the deed, to withdraw from the reality before him and deal rather with a 'reality' of his own making.

Another dramatic measure of this disastrous yet cumulative transformation of Bolshevism lies in the use of 'enemy of the people' to describe those many millions of people killed or shipped off to the camps. The substitution of mythology for reality becomes complete in the phrase. Stalin, of course, represented the people and alone spoke in their name. But who was the 'enemy of the people'? If Conquest is right, and the name of virtually every leading official was in NKVD files as a spy by late 1938; if 'the next wave of the purge would have struck at 10 to 15 per cent of the population, and soon after that at 30 to 45 per cent';[149] if every second family was hit by the Purge—the *entire people* had indeed become the enemy of the people. Which meant that the entire people had lost, or was on the brink of losing, the right to be treated like people as the revolution became 'successful'. Conquest reports the effort (which would lead to his death) of one free citizen of the Kolyma camp to obtain better treatment for prisoners: '"These people might die." "What people?" the representative of the camp administration smiled, "these are enemies of the people."'[150]

Enemies all: one wonders whether or when that administrator himself was liquidated by the revolution gone mad. Like Pyatakov, named in Lenin's Testament and the genius behind the successes of the Five Year Plan, he no doubt felt that earlier waves of victims 'have lost the last semblance of humanity. They must be destroyed like carrion which is polluting the pure, bracing air of the land of the Soviets ....' But might he not, like Pyatakov, admit within six months to himself organizing sabotage and terror? And be executed for crimes against the people?[151]

And so, in the bizarre completion of the revolution, we are led to use Vyshinsky's own outraged words for falsely-accused Pyatakov to appraise the progress of the revolution itself: 'This is the abyss of degradation! This is the limit, the last boundary of moral and political decay! This is the diabolical infinitude of crime!'[152]

Or perhaps irony will suffice: the outstanding study of the Stalin Constitution was presided over by none other than Vyshinsky. Thus did the former Menshevik prosecutor stand the revolution completely on its head: the fantasy-constitution which guarantees work, well-being, democracy, and civil liberties is celebrated by the police-state prosecutor who had concluded his fantasy-accusation of the Constitution's guiding spirit, Bukharin, by demanding that he be shot 'like a dirty dog'.

Conclusion: Impotence and Power

On one level this entire discussion has been an essay on power; or rather a continuation of the essay on power begun in the chapter on Nazi Germany. In retrospect, was not Martov right when he foresaw certain disaster if the Bolsheviks seized power in October? Engels understood the problem all too well in another context: 'The worst thing that can befall the leader of an extreme party is to be compelled to take over a government in an epoch when the movement is not yet ripe for the domination of the class which he represents, and for the realization of the measures which the domination implies. ... Thus he necessarily finds himself in an insolvable dilemma. What he *can* do contradicts all his previous actions, principles and immediate interests of his party, and what he *ought* to do cannot be done. ...Whoever is put into this awkward position is irretrievably doomed.'[153]

As one of the fathers of Marxism, Engels is simply insisting on its most basic tenets: authentic social power is a relationship between the 'ripeness' of the situation and the would-be ruling class's many-sided capacity to lead the society. It may be possible to take power politically or to dominate militarily, but these forms of power lack something vital when those who wield them are not ideologically, socially and economically congruent with a significant segment of the society, with its aspirations and historical tendencies. *Impotence* points towards a structural incapacity to realize their goals: Engels's statement of the 'insolvable dilemma' suggests that state power or military force may indeed be employed to *force the issue*; but also that the massive use of force is fundamentally a violation of the human subjects upon whom it is imposed. In this respect rulers who use the greatest violence to compel assent lack the more decisive forms of relational power which stem from a deeper congruence with major classes of their society. Congruence: the society and its rulers must 'fit' each other. Marxists become scientific-minded scholars in order to study the development of the situation, to determine just what is possible, just when, just how: this is what sets off Marxism from utopian socialism, and makes its conception of power so different from an older emphasis on weapons and armies, say, or on the state apparatus. Rulers rooted in and accepted by the dominant social class at a time of its historical ascendancy are those most capable of exercising *effective* power.

While possessing state power, the Bolsheviks remained in this fundamental sense *impotent*: they were structurally unable to create the society they had come to power to preside over. However impotent to solve their 'insolvable dilemmas' and change the agenda of history, ruling groups possess nevertheless the tempting and deadly organs of state power. If these can indeed be used to compel assent, to destroy human lives, can they not be used to transform reality? Can not reality be 'reshaped' out of line with its actual possibilities, in ways seeming to reflect the rulers' intentions? May not their power even command pretence about the ways in which it does not?

If the idea of 'socialism in one country'—in the isolated, unprepared Soviet Union—was, in Sartre's words a 'monstrosity', this was because that society did not 'fit' those aspirations. Thus the reality of 'socialism in one country' would not be less monstrous. The situation became irrational at the moment the Bolsheviks began to use state power to mystify and distort the recalcitrant reality, to repress and transform it physically in ways that contradicted its possibilities and their own original intentions.

In short, Marxist science 'in power', in an epoch such as described by Engels, was indeed 'irretrievably doomed'. This doom took a totally unexpected form, however: holding on to power, this narrowing party cudgelled, terrorized, and destroyed the reality it sought to change.

This essay on power is at the same time, like the previous chapter, an essay on madness as a social phenomenon. At the centre of my essay on madness has been the concept of a rupture with reality. I have said that Marxism is a *gentle* science, concerned above all with tracing the curves of the human world, linking itself with ascendant social forces so as to liberate repressed but decisive social capacities. Again and again its touchstones are demonstrable, visible, experiential: Marxism presents itself as grasping and working to bring about society's future—embodied in living social forces—appealing to and struggling against its encumbered present. In this sense its decisive dimension is the class struggle, whose violence on either side seeks only to retard or to liberate the social forces generated by society itself. Successful violence is thus 'midwifery'. Faithfulness to 'reality' in this complex and dialectical sense is the hallmark of Marxism.

To reject accurate perception—not as a mistake, but as a *modus operandi*—went hand in hand with repressing Kronstadt to hold power. This rupture—perceptual and physical—was accompanied by Bolshevik determination to *theorize* and *institutionalize* it. If *madness* suggests loss of control, lack of capacity to act differently, this took place *after* the initial break, when the new, distorted modes of perception became self-perpetuating and banned the return to original Marxist realism. Perceiving and acting through lies and distortions, first the Bolsheviks and then the Stalinist 'centre' became progressively more removed from authentic perception. The systematic, wholesale, and pathological break came with their action to 'realize' the distorted vision in that society: Stalinist madness thus begins not in 1937 or even in 1934, but in 1929. I have been discussing a complex many-sided process of rupture: on one level by assaulting reality so that it corresponded to aspects of the deformed vision; on another by changing that vision so that its most flagrantly unrealizable aspects were repressed; on still another by changing human thought-processes so that the original vision seemed to have been realized. The resulting whole became an amalgam of sense and non-sense.

'Irretrievably doomed': in our century the fulfilment of this prophecy does not necessarily lead to the loss of state power or death. Again and again, we have seen impotence *in* power—impotence to fulfil the goals to which a certain leadership is tied. The very impotence of the Bolshevik government drove the party to become all-powerful—powerful enough to destroy and create on a scale hitherto unimagined. Not powerful enough to realize Marxian socialism —because for this not brute power but a collective social will was necessary—but powerful enough to extract violently from its people the military strength to defeat Hitler; powerful enough to bludgeon them into the collective farms. The Bolsheviks, alas, were not powerful enough to create a democratic, egalitarian socialism, which presupposed many times the factories and workers Russia had in 1917. But in their Stalinist incarnation they became powerful enough to destroy as 'enemies of the people' most of those who had shaped and been shaped by the struggle for such a socialism.

More than irrational, I am insisting that the resulting amalgam was *mad*. Such judgements, of course, are a question of degree: mad connotes a thorough and systematic rupture with reality, its wholesale transformation in fantasy and distortion—and its transformation in fact as well. It was in speaking about Trotsky's daughter and not about the fate of the revolution that Deutscher captured what was, and remains, at stake: 'it was as if reason itself had discovered in unreason its closest progeny and its double.'[154] The Soviet project to realize reason in history became one of history's great attacks on reason.

Conclusion: History and Chance

Does this aftermath make Martov's prediction correct? Which is to say, how far do the catastrophic events I have discussed stem from the Bolsheviks' 'premature' decision to take power? They must certainly not be seen as utopian in expecting Russian industry to remain intact, its working class to remain their base of support, and to be aided by revolution elsewhere. The first two of these they accepted as premisses, and the third seemed not at all overly optimistic, in the light of their experience of the revolutionary Russian proletariat since the beginning of 1917. From his Finland Station speech of April 1917 onwards Lenin insisted on linking the Russian revolution with the proletariat in Europe: 'The Russian revolution achieved by you has opened a new epoch. Long live the worldwide socialist revolution!'[155] If power was Lenin's first concern, it was because as Marxists the Bolsheviks equated the party's ability to take and hold state power with the social appropriateness of their programme. After all, did not the revolutionary capacity of the proletariat suggest their and the society's maturity for socialism? If we have learned since that state power—control over the governmental apparatus and its means of violence—is not necessarily effective social power, can we fault Lenin for not seeing this in advance of the experience that would demonstrate it so decisively?

Certainly, had the Bolsheviks drawn back and not taken power —or if the Joint Opposition's programme had been carried out, or if Stalin and Bukharin had continued to build 'socialism at a snail's pace' in the 1930s—those millions would not have died *in that way*. A different Comintern and a different foreign policy might have meant that Hitler would have been stopped short of taking power. Or, when in power, he might have encountered a militarily and ideologically well-prepared Soviet Union in 1941, one commanded by its best officers, and capable of responding swiftly and decisively to attack. But—on the other hand—the Nazis might have indeed won the war over a still-primitive, technically backward Russia, exterminated its Bolsheviks and Jews, and ruled over it for generations. In short, our entire history might have been drastically different, in unforeseeable ways, for better or for worse.

Cohen has insisted, rightly, on the alternatives to Stalinism that remained within the grasp of Bolshevism right up to the 'Great Change'. Lewin has indicated the possibility of a vastly different course had Lenin lived. Colletti emphasizes the weight of the defeat of revolutions elsewhere, implying how differently the Bolshevik revolution might have turned out under other conditions. The actors themselves lived with these senses of possibility. None of them could have foreseen the total failure elsewhere of the worldwide revolution, or the emergence of fascism, the recalcitrance of isolated Old Russia to Bolshevik visions. Lenin's untimely death and the blurring of the Bolshevik vision en route to totalitarianism were equally unforeseeable. In 1917, action for the world's first socialist revolution was what political action is always and everywhere: a *chance*. And indeed, not at all a hopeless-seeming chance. The greatest issue for the Bolsheviks at that moment was not the revolution's disastrous corruption-cum-success but whether or not they could actually take and hold on to power. For three years *that* was the life-and-death concern. No one knew, or could possibly have known, that the victorious revolutionaries would end up in such an unthinkable isolation. Or that the isolation would later be reinforced by Stalin's policies. And even had this been foreseen (in 1921, say), should they have abandoned the revolution?

In conclusion, all of this suggests that no matter what we may say today about the ways the Leninist outlook or the Marxist vision of progress distorted the Bolsheviks' perceptions and actions, the subsequent history is not the teleological unfolding of an Aristotelian essence. For example, neither the Leninist party nor the decision to take power created the disaster to follow. We have seen, rather, the rational and irrational human transcending of situations in accord with the biases of an original project, itself subject to deformation and transformation in the process.

Sheer accident, a vast network of unexpected possibilities, and the sedimented results of prior actions all became so many roadblocks to alternative intentions. Complete failure was certainly one prospect open to the October Revolution, as was that of complete success, while a third was any one of several amalgams of disaster and success, the Stalinist version among them. Stalinism hardly 'unfolded' from October as the tree grows from the acorn. If it was the revolution's 'dialectical' result, at the time it was one possibility among many.

4
America's Vietnam

The Vietnam war came to be seen by most of the world as a battle of David against Goliath, the David being a relatively small, poor people seeking to complete its simultaneous social revolution and national liberation, the Goliath being the richest, most powerful country that had ever existed. Vastly superior in tools and techniques, and militarily dominant over much of the world, the Goliath sought to impose on David a peace favourable to his vision of the world and serving the interests of his most powerful countrymen.

'No smith was to be found in all the land of Israel, for the Philistines were afraid that the Hebrews would make swords or spears. So all the Israelites had to go down to the Philistines to have their ploughshares, their mattocks, axes, and coulters sharpened.'[1]

And at first Goliath was not without his own supporters and sources of moral strength, because at home he had given most of his own citizens unmatched wealth and freedom. Emerging supreme from his last war, he now sought to widen his empire. Usually the showing of his unequalled force had been enough to intimidate all who resisted, 'and he was six cubits and a span tall. He had a bronze helmet on his head, and wore a breastplate of scale armour, a bronze breastplate weighing five thousand shekels. He had bronze greaves on his legs, and a bronze javelin [slung] from his shoulders. The shaft of his spear weighed six hundred shekels; and the shield-bearer marched in front of him.

'He stopped and called out to the ranks of Israel and he said to them, "Why should you come out to engage in battle? I am the Philistine [champion], and you are Saul's servants."'[2]

Only a few exceptional peoples dared to defy such might. 'When the men of Israel saw the man, they fled in terror."'[3]

This modern-day Goliath was not a neighbour, but travelled across the world to have his way, seeking his own agents among the most despised of David's people, paying them fabulous sums and offering them power to which they could never otherwise aspire. At Goliath's urging they even claimed the rule of their people for themselves, speaking to their countrymen of the hopelessness of resistance and counselling David especially to accept Goliath's dominance: 'You cannot go to that Philistine and fight him; you are only a boy, and he has been a warrior from his youth!'[4]

But the people resisted nevertheless, led by David. They had already freed the northern half of their country from Goliath's ally and sent him home. At first Goliath, too, might have gone home in the face of great resistance, but instead he proclaimed to the whole world that this battle would be a test of his rule everywhere: 'Choose one of your men and let him come down against me. If he bests me in combat and kills me, we will become your slaves; but if I best him and kill him, you shall be our slaves and serve us.'[5]

David wanted no such arrangement, and certainly had no intention or capacity to impose it on Goliath's country. He fought only to rid his land of Goliath. The battle was prepared, Goliath increased his armies, and he made available to the whole world his magnificent techniques for observing a faraway war, hoping that his rule everywhere would be strengthened by it. At first the battle seemed one-sided and hopeless. Goliath brought all his armour and weaponry. David began to arm himself like Goliath but then changed his mind. 'He took his stick, picked a few smooth stones from the wadi, put them in the pocket of his shepherd's bag and, sling in hand, he went toward the Philistine.'[6]

'The Philistine, meanwhile, was coming closer to David, preceded by his shield-bearer. When the Philistine caught sight of David, he scorned him, for he was but a boy, ruddy and handsome.'[7]

But David, smaller than Goliath and in his own land, knew where to hide as the giant thundered about. He knew, and slowly the people watching began to see, that he had strengths no one had imagined. He was of his people. He lived off the land, hid in tunnels and among his own people, turned to them for soldiers and food, weapons and encouragement, and for information about Goliath's whereabouts. Then, even as Goliath brought in vast numbers of his own soldiers, David was able to rely for reinforcements and weapons on the North, which in turn could rely on its allies. And so Goliath claimed it was a war of himself against David's most powerful allies, of world against world, of God against God. Goliath, it slowly became clear, had faults and weaknesses no one had foreseen. His weapons flailed the land and as more and more of the onlookers became captivated by the battle, Goliath attacked and destroyed the houses. He attacked the North, as he saw he was losing in the South. Behind his words about helping David's countrymen there appeared to all an intention to dominate, and if that failed, to destroy.

David went into the impenetrable mountains and caves and swamps and jungles of his country. Goliath tried to tear the very leaves from the trees to find David and deny him food, and to kill any of David's people who would not come into Goliath's villages. But he had only his wealth, his weapons, and his great physical might. David, on the contrary, organized his people. He taught them to hide, to produce food while in hiding, to set snares for Goliath's men. Goliath tried to teach 'his' Israelites to do the same, but these were the vain and lazy ones who despised the villagers and could learn nothing, no matter how much gold Goliath paid, how much he taught them and how many weapons he gave. David would not surrender because he knew he could not. This was his home. Goliath, however, might one day tire and give up and go away. So he said to Goliath: 'You come against me with sword and spear and javelin; but I come against you in the name of the LORD of Hosts, the God of the ranks of Israel, whom you have defied.'[8]

Who was that God? By the twentieth century that inspiration had become understood as nothing more nor less than the spirit of the weak struggling against the strong, the spirit of David's people and of all people. It had become the spirit of those who insisted on having their own people rule over them in their own homeland, and were willing to fight for as long as it took in order to expel Goliath. By now much of the world was cheering and contributing whatever help they could, telling Goliath's people to bring him home.

The small, poorly armed shepherd and champion of his people was defeating the mightiest force ever known. Even though he was weakened terribly and came more and more to rely on the North, he had only to wait and hold out to win. David's unequal fight had become an inspiration to all who felt oppressed, everywhere in the world. 'You need not submit', it told them. Goliath's destructive persistence had become an embarrassment to his own friends. No one could understand why he stayed; he insisted ever more loudly that those who were helping David and his countrymen in the North were in reality trying to dominate the world and, with the whole world watching, must be taught a lesson. Otherwise his, Goliath's, home thousands of miles away would be in jeopardy.

Finally even many of Goliath's own people could not accept this explanation for the death and destruction, and talked about his coming home and giving up the battle. They said that soon they would no longer give him the weapons to destroy David's land and its people. Without these weapons Goliath would scarcely be able to hold off David's stones and sling. And so he left, leaving 'his' Israelites to fight on with a vast supply of weapons. But the lazy and vain ones had developed nothing, not skill, not courage, not the love of their people. Even after all the death and destruction they endured, David's Israelites still spoke for the land and its people, still had among them the skilled and caring and hardworking ones. And so, the very day Goliath left, David and his comrades vanquished the Israelites who were not Israelites, the helpers of the Philistine. To the whole world, the final battle appeared as a victory over Goliath himself.

'David put his hand into the bag; he took out a stone and slung it. It struck the Philistine in the forehead; the stone sank into his forehead, and he fell face down on the ground. Thus David bested the Philistine with sling and stone; he struck him down and killed him. David had no sword; so, David ran up and stood over the Philistine, grasped his sword and pulled it from its sheath; and with it he dispatched him and cut off his head.'[9]

The Argument

As a parable of the war in Vietnam, the story of David and Goliath helps us to focus on the war's moral lessons, alive today in spite of all revisionism. Goliath represents oppression, David the resistance to it.[10] As such the story of David and Goliath directs us towards a turning point in our study of the century's disasters, and indeed, a possible turning point in human history. An overdeveloped society, using its entire weight of wealth and resources, sought to impose its will on a small underdeveloped people, and lost. Its near-infinite power could transform and destroy, but it could not prevail against a politically organized people who had been fighting for their independence for fifty years.

This was, after all, a war of Vietnamese national liberation against forces of colonialism and imperialism, and was led by the only effective nationalist force in Vietnam, the Communist Party. Achieving authority over Vietnam in 1945, the Communists were denied victory by the French until 1954. Even then, their expected consolidation of victory in the South was held off by the Americans. Close to victory again in 1964, the Vietnamese were held off once more by massive American escalation.

The American goal differed somewhat from that of France, whose colonialist past predisposed it to rule directly over 'its' Vietnam. The US sought, rather, to develop a Vietnamese government congenial to its domination—neither neutralist nor Communist. Given the actual internal constellation of forces, however, an 'independent non-Communist Vietnam' could become only an ineffective, neocolonial client state of the US. Put most simply, American failure lay in the inability of outsiders to create a force both responsive to US interests and genuinely rooted in Vietnamese society. In the end, after fifty years of struggle, the Vietnamese victory over first the French, then the Japanese, then the French again, and finally the Americans, took an unexpected form: the North (and Southern insurgents) defeated the South in a lightning fifty-five-day offensive.[11]

Whatever the policymaker's stated intentions, the manifest American purpose became to transform Vietnam according to American goals. Insofar as the Vietnamese refused this transformation, the Americans began to destroy large areas of Vietnam. However vastly different this project was from those we have studied so far, its parallel dynamic is remarkable: finding themselves impotent to achieve political goals politically, American policymakers ruptured decisively with the reality of the society resisting them and sought its fantasy-transformation and destruction.

They were not driven to this depth of irrationality by the desperation induced by a profound and irresolvable social crisis; they chose it, rather, in the 'arrogance of power'—with remarkable self-assurance about their ability and right to shape the world as they saw fit. In this sense the war claims its own place in relation to the other destructive madnesses I have described, as part of a history of unreason in our century. American arrogance is indeed part of the history of unreason, its material basis arising from the defeat of Nazi Germany and its ideological basis from the American leaders' response to Stalin's Communism. Accordingly, the US became the ruler of the 'Free World'—an amalgam of myth and reality whose core was the assumption and practice of *too much power*.

Its most striking contrast with the Holocaust and Stalinism is that this catastrophic war was waged by the world's richest and most powerful society, functioning at the peak of its wealth and power. It was less an aberration than a natural product of the daily functioning and unquestioned assumptions of American society. Unreason begot unreason, as the American policymakers discovered that all their power was not enough to reach the 'breaking point' of, in Henry Kissinger's words, a 'fourth-rate power like North Vietnam'.[12]

It was a unique kind of madness, one not seen before. One looks in vain in the America of the 1960s for equivalents to the pathological dictator, the paranoid and ruthless builder, for a society in upheaval or a mass movement going mad. No formal death sentence was ever passed on over one million Vietnamese,[13] on their rural society, or on their land itself. The invisible mass murder was carried out on the orders of freely elected officials, during normal times, in keeping with consensually developed and frequently reaffirmed policy. 'The system worked' the entire time, seeking to arrive at a decision after considering alternatives, to reflect the ruling consensus, to avoid extremes and carry out its goal effectively.[14] Its workings were kept in public view by uncensored media, and the war was protested against in an unprecedented wave of opposition which, indeed, played a role in ending it. Yet we must note this as another remarkable contrast with the events we have already surveyed: the Vietnamese won, the United States lost. Although laying waste the country and thus bequeathing it monumental problems which can be expected to dominate it well into the future,[15] the US finally withdrew from Vietnam, failing to accomplish its purpose.

Yet the entire experience raised so few fundamental questions that, in spite of the intense opposition it had generated for almost ten years, its aftermath saw in power and authority the very same officialdom that had planned it, the same intelligentsia that had accepted and justified it, and the same military that had carried it out. Years later one had the memory that Vietnam (as in 'No more Vietnams!') stood for something terrible and divisive, but precisely *what* had never been made clear and was now receding into the past. After all, weren't there the Boat People? And the genocide in Kampuchea, and the North Vietnamese invasion of that country, and reports from the South about how liberation had turned into Northern oppression of the South?

Having failed to make over Vietnam in the image of its policy-makers, the American project there continued retrospectively after the fall of Saigon. Films, articles, books have sought to render the David-Goliath encounter ambiguous, to change a clear conflict between national liberation and neo-colonialism into one of subtle and difficult-to-discern shades of grey.[16] As scholars, political analysts and journalists, building on an unchallenged structure of assumptions, have revised anti-war arguments and retrospectively justified the war, policymakers have undertaken similar involvements elsewhere.[17] Indeed, new acts by American policymakers in our century's history of unreason—such as their effort to make tactical nuclear wars fightable and winnable—may be seen as in large part a response to the American defeat in Vietnam.[18]

Creating the 'Republic of Vietnam'

The destructive yet normal madness began in the American effort to create a Vietnam in its own image after the French had met defeat. From the beginning South Vietnam was less an autonomous reality than an American Cold War creation. Here was a territory and a people, whose government neither sprang from nor reflected the society upon which it was imposed. Diem's installation owed itself to the three years he had spent in the US (during the independence struggle against the French!) rather than to his political successes in Vietnam. As the Vietnamese authors of a Diemist history confess, 'Mr Diem was faced with a difficult situation when he returned to the country in 1954. Few Southerners knew about him. The South, with its feudal rivalries, paid more attention to such local powers as enjoyed by the Cao Dai, Hoa Hao, or Binh Xuyen groups than to the central government; at best people had only vague ideas about the nation's new leader.'[19] Accordingly, the new president returned to

Vietnam in 1954 knowing 'only a restricted circle of old acquaintances from Central Vietnam and admirers from the North.'[20] As Douglas Pike agrees, Diem, favoured by the US because he was both anti-French and anti-communist, 'had no party faithful, no corps of loyal political cadres, no trusted organization.'[21]

In 1954 the only meaningful national force which could claim to govern Vietnam, or indeed any significant portion of it, was the Viet Minh. Besides the Viet Minh in the South were the Vietnamese comprador remnants of French colonialism—an army trained to fight against its own people and civil servants trained to govern them for the foreigners, the military-political-religious sects, and the pro-French and anti-communist Catholic emigres from the North. There were also a variety of small non-communist nationalist groups whom events had bypassed or who had tarnished themselves by allying with the French after 1946. It seemed that their leaders had learned nothing from their years of struggle with the Viet Minh, and 'popular confidence in their talents and prestige was tenuous at best.'[22]

Without foreign intervention there is no doubt that the 'nation-building' process of insurrectionary politics would have completed itself and yielded power throughout the country to the most prestigious and nationally organized anti-colonial force. By stepping in with Diem at the last possible moment the US sought to thwart the process which would have given, according to one observer after the other, a vast electoral majority to the Viet Minh.

Let us look at this more closely: the Viet Minh had become successful because it had succeeded in organizing itself as an alternative government in struggle with the French and in a class struggle within Vietnam.[23] It passed the fundamental test of any revolutionary movement, drawing to it the bulk of the vital, skilled, politically developed elements of Vietnam.[24] In the words of Douglas Pike: 'During the long resistance against the French the more dedicated, enterprising and efficient Vietnamese had joined the Viet Minh, left the country, or become a member of that special class of Vietnamese, the *attentisme*, the permanent bystander. A large number of Southerners had gone North to serve, leaving the less talented or less experienced to man the Southern positions not occupied by the French.'[25]

The implications of this admission by the US government's foremost student of the Viet Cong are remarkable. Assuming a scarcity, in any underdeveloped society, of the talented and skilled administrative and political cadres, what does it mean that the insurrectionaries drew to their cause the bulk of these elements? Very simply, that the first indispensable steps of 'nation-building' had already taken place. Governments do not grow out of the air: those which 'take' express dominant social forces and are adequate to the social constitution and historical situation of a country. As Jeffrey Race emphasized in the case of Long An province, close study of Ai Ngai hamlet 'belies the commonly heard argument that "the Communists only have to destroy, while the government has to build." As Ai Ngai clearly shows, the very ability of the Party to destroy rested on its prior creation of a superior apparatus, and the government's attempts to "build" without first building a superior apparatus were irrelevant.'[26]

With whom could the government build? Of course, an anti-communist and anti-rebel background was a prerequisite for public service at any level.[27] In any case, many Southern Viet Minh villagers had regrouped and gone North.[28] Race emphasizes the nepotism, corruption and cowardice rife among Diemist cadres. It reflects the absence of national mission that abusive officials might be 'exiled' to areas of revolutionary activity for punishment.[29] Moreover, 'the vitality of local government was reduced because qualified people did not wish to hold such posts, as it involved rigging elections and protecting criminal elements within the government.'[30]

Upon whom did Diem rely? A former chief of Long An province gives us the answer. 'Under the Diem regime, the majority of people were employed because of their loyalty to the Ngo family rather than their ability or their willingness to serve their country. If one wanted to have a position, one had to be a member of the Can Lao party, a Catholic, and a central Vietnamese. As a result, in the army as well as the civil administration, the majority of the leading officials were opportunists, bootlickers, and incompetents, and the effectiveness and initiative of the army and the administration were destroyed.'[31]

In the countryside, the installation of Diem meant a counterrevolution: the return of the landlords and officialdom that the Viet Minh had driven out. Although local government now 'had no firmer foundation than a leaf floating on the ocean'[32] it gave the landlords exiled in province capitals and in district towns a chance to return 'to collect nine years of back rents.'[33] In terms of actual composition and the interests it served, the [national] government was a melange of urban middle-class and elite elements, landlords, and mandarin remnants, generally French educated if not actually with French citizenship ....'[34]

The point is that they had met defeat once, on the national level —at Dien Bien Phu. And the Viet Minh, because it had 'built up a strong local organization based on landless or land-poor elements' had been able to dominate the villages and 'had rendered the central government helpless.'[35] Well before the Americans assumed the imperialist mantle the Communists had become rooted in the society and bested the comprador government. If the first phase of 'nation-building' takes place in struggle against colonial rulers, the successful insurrectionaries become the dominant and legitimate force. Certainly former colonial bureaucrats and officers may join them—and be needed by them—but hardly to play a dominant political role. Unless, that is, a new colonial power reasserts and reestablishes its power through the old apparatus. Otherwise, many of the compradors leave, some stay, but they find their appropriate place away from the centre of the historical stage.

Admittedly in 1954 the southern part of Vietnam was not under the uncontested hegemony of the Viet Minh as was the North. Nevertheless, Harrison estimates that they controlled up to 60 per cent of the territory and one third of the population.[36] And even after tens of thousands of Viet Minh and their families went North after the Geneva Agreements, Pike estimates that a sizeable network of 10,000 cadres was left behind.[37] And the South itself possessed no other all-national force with roots in its villages. With the exception of the influx of Northern Catholics, the colonial army, and the remnants of the French administration, Diem's regime could be said to be built on thin air. Is it surprising that Diem's flag was that of the French-imposed Bao Dai regime, as was his national anthem—or that he lived in the former French governor's palace?[38] Constructed from the outside to thwart an authentic Vietnamese force, 'South Vietnam' was understandably expected to melt away by the time reunification elections were held in 1956.

American social science was employed not in order to understand the authentic social forces in Vietnam and to draw the obvious conclusions, but rather to thwart them. Professors and other experts sought the magical way to make an imposed and inauthentic force into the actual government of the territory south of the seventeenth parallel. Americans brought in a land reform policy, made-to-order constitutions, training for the police, military and civil service, advisors to the president, and (above all) money. The US paid for government, army and police, and made up most of the balance of payments deficit. If government agencies ran out of funds they applied directly to the Americans.[39] But the latter could not make their dependents into a genuine government. Diem wanted to return to a long-departed past—reflecting his lack of social ties to *that* territory and *those* people. He used repression to build South Vietnam, relying increasingly on the army and his family.

Discussion of his 'mistakes' and 'correct policy' were so much babble: only a disembodied would-be mandarin turned towards the past would have had the 'credentials' required for investiture by the US in the first place. The remoteness from real Vietnam that made Diem an appropriate candidate of the Americans also guaranteed that he could never become a genuine ruler.

It is remarkable that none of this elementary social science was visible to the Michigan State University team of over fifty professors who came to experiment with 'nation building'.[40] One suspects that they, like most Americans involved from beginning to end, never bothered to see or understand Vietnam, this society they were 'saving'. This is not only because of the great cultural differences between the two societies.[41] The nature of the US commitment dictated a distorted perception: at bottom American observers saw in Vietnam only the drama of Communism versus the Free World.[42] Because he was the alternative to Communism, Diem was said to represent 'independence and democracy' for South Vietnam. No matter that the 1955 referendum gave him 605,025 votes out of a total of 450,000 registered voters in Saigon, or that he was a repressive dictator increasingly alienated from the people year by year.[43]

To be sure, it takes no great political sophistication to see the cynical and rhetorical character of the campaign to sell American-selected Diem back to Americans as the Free World's answer to Ho Chi Minh. The point is, rather, that whatever its conscious intent this was the first step in the creation of an American Vietnam light-years away from the Vietnamese one. Originally an absurd fantasy in the light of Dien Bien Phu, the American creation slowly assumed reality. Not that the US project was successful. However, its realization was attempted through the violent transformation and near-destruction of Vietnam. This did not arise from any understanding or appreciation encouraging the US to change Vietnam in ways congruent both with Vietnamese tendencies and possibilities and American purposes—which would, after all, have been the meaning of success. Rather, the complex of American purposes was imposed from the outside, using obsolescent social groups to reverse the development of a society moving in a revolutionary direction. Instead the society was violently reshaped into a grotesque and totally dependent parody of the United States, the 'society of mercenaries and prostitutes' described by Senator Fulbright. That on the one hand—and a pulverized countryside on the other.

Creation *and* destruction, like Stalin's? Hardly: Stalin's goal of modernization came from the depths of Russia and was a fundamentally progressive one in Russian terms; it was an authentic expression of a vital force in Soviet society. The American goal was foreign from beginning to end. It had virtually nothing to do with Vietnam. From the beginning the American idea of building a government out of keeping with the country's social constitution was stupid and violent *in principle*.

We will see a kind of inevitable logic to the unravelling of the half-fantasy, half-mutant 'Republic of Vietnam' imposed on this social constitution. Certainly in its first two years the victorious revolution in the North made, and later admitted to, drastic mistakes. But, however brutal, these were mistakes of a deeply-rooted and hegemonic social force, not of a 'leaf floating on the ocean' dependent on foreign assistance for its very survival. Are not Diem's 'mistakes' inseparable from his distance from the social struggle that had created and supported the Viet Minh? And is not this distance in turn inseparable from the American election of Diem as ruler? His refusal to abide by the Geneva accords and his repression in the countryside catalyzed the creation of the NLF, which picked up where the Viet Minh left off and virtually controlled the countryside by Diem's death. 'Aside from the NLF', Douglas Pike wrote in 1965, 'there has never been a truly mass-based political party in South Vietnam.'[44] Never before, or never since, as history and scholarship were to show. After such an admission, all the rest is a lie.

Americanized Generals versus Vietnamese Revolutionaries

How could the Communists be combated after years of deterioration under Diem? The wish for 'another pole of influence' was voiced by Philippe Devillers in 1962: 'A change of government in Saigon, with the advent to power of a popular and democratic Nationalist regime resolved to have done, once and for all, with the use of terror as an instrument of government and to follow an advanced economic and social policy would in all probability help toward the relaxation of tension, and would bring about the progressive sterilization of the ground which now acts as a seedbed for Communism and Communist sympathizers.'[45]

It had been too late since Dien Bien Phu: in the Viet Minh and then the NLF, South Vietnam already had its popular Nationalist force prepared 'to follow an advanced economic and social policy'. Accordingly, with Diem gone things got worse, not better: the army, the only national organization besides the NLF, took over. But it was not an authentically Vietnamese institution. The Vietnamese had not created it out of their needs and experience to carry out their own projects. Its origins were less in the defence of Vietnam than in defending the French rulers of Vietnam against its own people. French in orientation, control and financing until 1954, it then became American. If its manpower was Vietnamese it depended on the Americans in every other way. From beginning to end, it was not a Vietnamese national institution but a deformed hybrid, claiming to serve its people only in order to satisfy its real employers. The proof? From 1954 to 1966 only one Vietnamese field-grade officer was wounded in action![46]

We can garner something of the mentality of the officers who became the government after 1963 by examining a rather astonishing document: *Twenty Years and Twenty Days* by Nguyen Cao Ky, onetime Air Marshal, Prime Minister and Vice-President. Ghost-written, this book strikingly parallels that other equally artificial entity, the 'Republic of Vietnam'.[47] Its general atmosphere of unreality only confirms the character of men like Ky as revealed in his story: an essential personal and political emptiness, a fascination and comfort with things American, a drastic separation from Vietnamese aspirations.

Patched together from interviews and speeches, this breezy personal account gives us the *American* Vietnam, a Vietnam that shares US values and prejudices and even speaks to us in American clichés. We never learn what this 'nationalist' originally from the North stands for, never have a sense of any alternative politics or programme to the NLF. The book shows, indeed, virtually no contacts with Vietnamese society—except for a reverence for Ho Chi Minh, these officers could be US-paid mercenaries anywhere in the world whose main purpose was to get 'on with our job of fighting the war' against most of their countrymen.[48]

Ky complains both that the Americans intervened too visibly (they lacked 'subtlety') and that they didn't really make an all-out effort to 'win outright'; he admires the Communists' sense of cause and purpose and complains that the Americans had replaced the French so swiftly that 'we never had the opportunity to learn the art of governing ourselves unaided and uninfluenced.'[49] The muddled intelligence of the book's 'subject' reaches its limits of insight when discussing the problems his 'cause' faced vis-a-vis the Communists: 'While I was preaching the need for freedom, I was not always free myself. True, we were not puppets, yet we never achieved the standing or appearance of an independent, self-governing country. The Americans criticized us for not having a highly developed system of government, but how could we have that when every Vietnamese in Saigon referred to the American Ambassador as "the Governor General"?[50]

'The Americans did not seek this; they were not colonists, but South Vietnam had been a colony until the defeat of the French, and in many ways it remained virtually a colony, though without the restrictions imposed by the French. We still lacked our own identity.

'We never produced a leader to unite the country with its many religious and political factions. The North had one in Ho Chi Minh; rightly or wrongly, the Communists believed in him and fought and died for him. He had a charisma that won many supporters even in the West and not all of them were Communists. Neither Diem, nor Thieu—both backed by the Americans—won the hearts of even the South Vietnamese.

'The Americans controlled the fighting of the war. American aid financed the country; without it we could not survive. Americans selected or influenced the selection of our politicians and leaders, even at the village level, and had a natural tendency to pick the most compliant rather than the most gifted. American culture—its films, television, and advertising—swamped our own.'[51]

This reflection by a leader lacking an identity of his own leads no-where. Should the US never have come in the first place, thus making inconceivable Ky's chance for wealth and power? Singing in his chains, Ky appropriately ends up by attacking the Americans for condescension, and then changes the subject.

How vast is the difference between this chronicle of the absurd and *No Other Road to Take*, a memoir of Madame Nguyn Thi Dinh. Born in Ben Tre province in the South in 1920, Madame Dinh had been active in the revolutionary struggle since 1936. Later to be elected to the Communist Party's Central Committee, she composed this memoir in 1965, while she was Deputy Commander of the National Liberation Front Armed Forces. She was, then, a counter-part to Ky.

Certainly her account must be read no less critically than that of Ky; published in Hanoi in 1968, it is after all a political document in the struggle for the reunification of Vietnam under the North. Its adulation of Uncle Ho's prescience and sensitivity seems a bit forced, and its language often echoes the wooden and ritualized incantations of so much offical Marxist-Leninist writing. Yet the Western reader will feel distant from it for a more basic reason—it is steeped in rural Vietnam, its culture, its concerns, its people.

'Our life was hard but happy. When Tet came, I rowed the sam-pan and ferried the brothers out to catch fish, just like I used to do when I was small: rowing the sampan on the Ba Giong River at night to sell shrimps at the market place. Ten years had passed, but I had not lost my skill at rowing sampans. I always felt terribly sleepy as the night advanced. Sometimes while I moored the boat to let the brothers cast their nets, I went into a deep slumber and once even slumped forwards and fell down in the boat. Every night we splashed around on the river and did not return till three or four in the morning, and then the next night we called out to each other and went fishing again.'[52]

Ky's Americanized playboy vacuity is replaced throughout Madame Dinh's account by a pervasive sense of danger and struggle. Where we never see the Air Marshal in battle, Madame Dinh is one of the Vietnamese leadership for whom mere physical survival was a major task and accomplishment. 'In 1962,' reports Harrison, 'Ho Chi Minh had stated that of the Party's Central Committee (there were then forty-two full members), fourteen had been killed by the French since 1930, and the survivors had spent 222 years in prison, an average of perhaps seven years each!'[53]. Madame Dinh's account describes many narrow escapes; her first husband died in the notorious Poulo Condore prison. Again and again she tells of comrades who died in the struggle.

In response to the danger the revolutionaries built an extensive network of supporters who would shelter, feed and transport them: 'Our survival depended on whether or not we could expand the number of sympathizers. We had often told each other that unless we held on to the people we could not maintain the movement. This was the most critical problem.'[54] With their supporters they created underground hideouts everywhere, developed elaborate disguises and other quick-witted ways of deceiving the enemy, and moved into armed struggle.

The epochal struggle called forth from this peasant woman a sense of conviction, energy, skill, self-reliance and national identity beside which Ky's lament about his dependency on the Americans can be seen for the self-corruption it is. Through the very foreignness of Madame Dinh's account, one cannot avoid the impression that she, like her folk poem, managed to combine being Vietnamese and revolutionary in a way that enhanced the meaning of both:

> The People's hearts are like sunflowers
> Hundreds of thousands of them all turn towards the sun
> Even if everything in nature changes
> They pledge to remain steadfast and
> loyal to the revolution[55]

To read Madame Dinh is to witness the actual process of nation-building at which the American surrogates like Ky failed so dismally. Its ultimate sources were Madame Dinh's repeatedly reaffirmed commitment to the Vietnamese people and her rootedness in rural Vietnam. As Paul Mus and John T. McAlister argued, 'the most essential [reason for Communist success] is the relevancy of their values to the lives villagers must lead.'[56] Unlike Ky, with his penchant for 'the officers' club with its billiard table and bar',[57] Madame Dinh reflects in her national rootedness a *reason* to go on fighting: 'In the face of this enormous and imposing force of the people, I felt very small, but I was full of self-confidence, like a small tree standing in a vast and ancient forest. In struggling against the enemy, I had come to fully realize that we had to have the strength of the whole forest in order to be able to stay the force of the strong winds and storms. As I thought about the protection and support of the people, about the countless comrades and beloved people—some of whom I had mentioned but whose names I could never exhaustively enumerate—I felt more intimately bound, more so than ever before, to the road I had taken and had pledged to follow until my last days. This was the road for which I would sacrifice everything for the future of the revolution and for the interest of the masses. For me there was no other road to take.'[58]

The Turning Point

Reading Madame Dinh and Marshal Ky we understand who won and why. The relative depth of one side and the thinness of the other return us to the distinction between violence as a midwife of a new society and violence as *constitutive* of it. The Communists were hardly gentle, but their purposes were not served by destroying rural Vietnam. Revolutionary bullying, coercion, terror—they employed all of these, but with a substantial social base behind them. The American side, on the contrary, may have hoped for a more plea- sant society, but once their generals took over and failed to stem the tide, destruction of that social base was the only alternative to accept- ing defeat. Violence become a first principle for the Americans after 1964, as the US abandoned its emphasis on political 'counter-insur- gency' and attacked the North, bombing the countryside ferociously and invading en masse. As always, social scientists stood ready to justify this brutality, as in Samuel Huntington's outrageous descrip- tion of 'forced-draft modernization': 'The depopulation of the countryside struck directly at the strength and potential appeal of the Viet Cong. ... For if the "direct application of mechanical and con- ventional power" takes place on such a massive scale as to produce a massive migration from the countryside to city, the basic assumptions underlying the Maoist doctrine of revolutionary war no longer operate. The Maoist-inspired rural revolution is undercut by the

American sponsored urban revolution ....'[59]

If there is any turning point from relative restraint to barbarism, warfare to genocide, relative rationality to madness, it may be found between late 1964 and July 1965. The very notion of *escalation* was framed to make drastic changes appear quantitative only. But the first mass demonstration in Washington in April 1965[60] reflected public awareness that a Rubicon was indeed being crossed.

'Madness', 'barbarism', 'genocide',—no matter how central such terms are for a study of our century, the moderate and bourgeois-democratic character of this specific human disaster demands extreme care in shaping our analysis. The point is not that those in power lost touch with reality and became delusional at this moment. Rather, a group of responsible, sophisticated, self-confident men now chose to transform the conflict into the one they had been falsely claiming it was all along, by bombing the North; substituted for their impossible fantasy-creation the 'Republic of Vietnam' a full-fledged occupation army, which took over fighting the war and created its own dependent economy and society; and they began to destroy the rural society that resisted this project.

Why bomb North Vietnam? By late 1964, George Herring concludes, 'a firm consensus had emerged in the administration that the United States must soon undertake what [Ambassador Maxwell] Taylor described as a "carefully orchestrated bombing attack" against North Vietnam.'[61] A study of the *Pentagon Papers* reveals no shock and little resistance that B-52s should attack this uncontested rear base area, far from the actual fighting. Very little weight seemed to be given to the National Security Council document dated 24 November 1964 which emphasized that '[t]he basic elements of Communist strength in South Vietnam remain indigenous.'[62] The working group that compiled this report had also insisted, while recognizing a substantial North Vietnamese role in the insurgency, that bombing 'would almost certainly not destroy DRV capability to continue supporting the insurrection in the South.'[63]

Then why bomb? Such a significant decision—with its far-reaching consequences for domestic and foreign support for the war—was obviously not taken lightly. And yet it had a decidedly *irrational* quality, in the specific sense that this military step was not undertaken primarily in order to achieve a direct military effect. Despite prevailing anti-communist rhetoric, it was widely known (because American lives depended on it) that the war was essentially a Southern affair, and that enlarging it would have unforeseeable consequences. Indeed, as we read the recommendations accepted by President Lyndon Johnson, there is suprisingly little reference to the specific *military* value of bombing. Ambassador Taylor's principal aim was 'to bring increasing pressure on the DRV to cease its intervention.'[64] Taylor's detailed analysis focuses on three objectives: '(a) The will of Hanoi leaders; (b) GVN or CVN morale; and (c) physical destruction to reduce the DRV ability to support the VC.

'Of these three the first appears to us by far the most important, since our effectiveness in influencing Hanoi leadership will, in the long run, determine the success or failure of our efforts in both North and South Vietnam. Second objective, effect on GVN or CVN morale, is also important, and fortunately the requirements for building morale in the South are roughly the same as those for impressing Hanoi leaders with the rising costs of their support of the VC. In this case, what is bad for Hanoi is generally good for Saigon.

'Effect of the physical destruction of material objects and infliction of casualties will not, in our judgement, have a decisive bearing upon the ability of DRV to support VC. However, degree of damage and number of casualties inflicted gauge the impact of our operations on Hanoi leadership and hence are important as a measure of their discomfort.'[65]

As Leslie Gelb points out, although advisers had earlier opposed bombing as long as 'our base in South Vietnam is insecure and Khanh's army is tied down', they now reversed themselves and urged bombing *in order* to promote stability in the South.[66] Certainly it might have had some value in interdicting the flow southward of men and supplies. But this determinate military goal, the least of Taylor's three reasons, was now eclipsed by the urgency summarized by Herring: 'The possibility of a South Vietnamese collapse appeared to make essential the adoption of a policy American officials had been advocating for more than two months.'[67]

According to McGeorge Bundy its 'immediate and critical targets are in the South—in the minds of the South Vietnamese and in the minds of the Viet Cong cadres.'[68] As Bundy noted, the coup-ridden American Vietnam was expected to collapse 'probably not in a matter of weeks or perhaps even months, but within the next year or so'[69]—unless something decisive was done. Bombing was a tempting action for policymakers who had lost the political war but nevertheless possessed untold destructive force which they had not yet used.

And yet its purpose was less military than psychological. Nguyen Khanh had asked Secretary of State Dean Rusk for action against Laos and North Vietnam in May 1964, emphasizing that if it drove China and North Vietnam to attack the South it would have a 'favourable effect on SVN national unity and faith in victory, and would mobilize [the] usual patriotic reactions in face of [a] more clearcut external threat.'[70] The US had failed politically to create a nation under the rubric of the 'Republic of Vietnam'—as is dramatically shown by Maxwell Taylor's meeting with and angry statement to the South Vietnamese generals in late 1964.[71] In its first decisive step into irrationality, the US sought through bombing to create that nation psychologically. Bombing would show its would-be leaders, its subjects and its enemies the force of American determination. For Bundy such considerations were 'the overriding reason' for 'a policy of sustained reprisal': 'There is one grave weakness in our posture in Vietnam which is within our own power to fix—and that is a widespread belief that we do not have the will and patience and determination to take the necessary action and stay the course.'[72] Bombing would demonstrate this. After ten years of failure on other fronts, at a moment of near collapse, the purpose of bombing ... was nation-building!

The policy was irrational in two of its three goals. First, attacking the 'will' of the North meant operating in a fog of bluff and show where clear calculation of means and ends was impossible. Thus the US sought to convince the North to call off the insurgency and so abandoned understanding both the indigenous roots of the insurgency and the total commitment of the North to reunite Vietnam. The Americans gave their Cold War creation a legitimacy it simply did not possess for most Vietnamese and then miscalculated the depth of Communist determination and popular support for a united Vietnam. More than a mistake, this was an act of wishful thinking, continuing to inscribe American purposes on a social world that had rejected them. To attack the North's 'will' was the obverse of demonstrating American 'will'—both projects were flights from the reasoned analysis which pointed to such gloomy conclusions.

This irrational turn of American policy was made possible by control over the world's most awesome technology of war. Using the technology had a validating function: it enabled US policymakers to ignore the simple fact that Viet Cong success with few weapons was based on local-scale political organizing and struggle.[73] This conceptual failure became entrenched in the American position in Vietnam. Since facing the facts meant withdrawal, the facts were evaded, distorted and transformed. The political incapacity of America's Vietnamese to imitate their enemies' success forced the policymakers to look away from this fact.[74] As in battle conditions where an air strike could be called for to suppress sniper fire, the irrational turn of policy led towards a technological fixation that became the dominant tactical attitude.

Politics was replaced by material plenty and technological wizardry. If this is one characterization of late twentieth century America, it is certainly a description of the progress of the Vietnamese war. By late 1964 the guerrilla war experts had disappeared from the Washington advisory circles as demands increased for the bombing of North Vietnam. As time went by, the reliance upon and experimentation with technology only grew: fantasies of nuclear bombing and of an electronic fence separating North and South Vietnam were only somewhat more outlandish than Operations 'Cedar Falls', or 'Ranch Hand', or the remote control Electronic Air War—all of which *were* put into practice.

At home the decision to bomb had an equally magical and irrational effect: it 'validated' to the American people that North Vietnam was invading South Vietnam. Why else would they be bombed, after all? Yet from this lie developed the cleavage that was to tear apart the country over the next few years. For either American policy was brutal, despicable, 'rational' only in a Poesque way. Or distortions, manipulations, lies were acceptable modes of action and discourse because the ultimate source *had to be* an outside invasion.[75] Without this premiss the emperor, indeed had no clothes: the US was the invader.

Destroying Vietnam

Before the bombing of North Vietnam began US intervention may have been a destructive, arrogant, unsuccessful attempt to conjure up an American Vietnam. But it had not become genocidal or mad. Impending US defeat, and its policymakers' absolute and unquestioning refusal to accept defeat,[76] led to the catastrophic transformation of the war, the land, and the people. What happened when the government of the richest and technologically most powerful country in the world refused to withdraw in the face of defeat because, as its policymakers said, it 'hewed to the belief that if the US be but willing to exercise its power, it could ultimately have its way in world affairs'?[77] What happened to a small Asian country when the US administration, captive of its own Cold-War politics, sought to 'damp down the charges that we did not do all that we could have done'?[78]

In the face of an imminent final collapse of the Saigon government and the assumption of full power by the National Liberation Front, the US indeed chose to 'exercise its power' and make clear that it was doing all it could. It did so in two spectacular steps—the beginning of sustained bombing in February 1965, and the sending of large numbers of American troops, beginning in July 1965. The escalation (appropriately) was accompanied by the absurd farce at Honolulu in which Lyndon Johnson promised a Great Society in Vietnam and Generals Ky and Thieu affirmed the 'social revolution' they were leading. The first fruit of the American decision was, in fact, the further irrationalization of the conflict: the means used no longer bore a meaningful relation to the end sought.[79]

Once the bombing of the DRV began, the situation was out of control. It was impossible henceforth to know what were the terms of success and failure. How was an increase or decrease of 'will' on either side to be measured? The commitment of massive numbers of American troops and the attack on the South Vietnamese countryside, following on the bombing, did succeed in bringing North Vietnam more directly and fully into the war. The propaganda became correct! The bombing had not been undertaken in order to significantly restrict the southward flow of men and supplies or convince the NLF or DRV to call off the insurgency. What level of bombing would have been required to do either? Yet in the minds of policymakers it seemed to take on these impossible goals willy-nilly, their very unattainability leading to ever more intense bombing. Finally, as with all fundamentally irrational, violent enterprises, there was left only a single measure of success, a single purpose: sheer destruction. The climax of this process was reached in the Christmas bombing of

1972.[80] The peace agreement initialed the next month revealed, in Herring's words, 'largely cosmetic changes'[81] from an agreement that had been reached in October but subsequently rejected by the US at Thieu's insistence. What had the bombing achieved? Was not its real purpose to persuade Thieu to accept the treaty?[82]

The bombing of the North was only the most spectacular and visibly irrational change in the war in 1965. The bulldozing, bombing and defoliation of the South also began at this time. Its purpose was far more practical than that suggested by show-concepts like 'will' and 'determination'. Indeed, the decision to grind 'the enemy down by sheer weight and mass',[83] in 'pacification' chief Robert Komer's words, was made so naturally and unreflectively that, as Noam Chomsky pointed out, it never appears in the Pentagon Papers.[84] Its success was first signalled in 1965 by South Vietnam's change from being a rice exporter to becoming a heavy importer.

As Komer described the American response to a successful 'people's war':[85] 'Well, if we can attrit the population base of the Viet Cong, it'll accelerate the process of degrading the VC.' And as General William Westmoreland similarly euphemized the goal of creating refugees and putting them under military occupation: 'If the peasant becomes a refugee, he does get shelter, food, and security, job opportunities and is given a hope to possibly return to his land.'[86] Chomsky contested this description by removing the euphemism: the policy was a 'device for demolishing the society in which a rebellion takes refuge'.[87]

What is the meaning of an intention that, followed logically, even if haltingly, leads to the results we have discussed? The meaning is indeed well-suited to the ends: to deny South Vietnam to the Communists.[88] Yet the means are so savage, so destructive that they carry us beyond any reasonable military-political calculation. The US policymakers said to and about Vietnam what an American officer said in commenting on an air strike he ordered during the Tet offensive against an NLF-held village: 'We had to destroy it in order to save it.'[89] Clearly, if the word has meaning, this is *mad*. Not blundering or blind, because it is conscious; not merely a mistake because it is deliberate; not circumstantial because it is systemic.

To order mass murder, ecological war, the uprooting of an obviously rooted society in order to bring its surviving remnants under control, is evil on a huge scale. To account for it we may expect to find either an absolutely overriding necessity—making it 'necessary evil'—or such a great determination to use destructive violence for the ends of power that 'madness' is the only fitting epithet. When the end became unattainable through normal and customary means, violent destruction itself became the end.

Catastrophe

Let us now try to glimpse the full weight of this destruction. Information was gathered during the war by a number of anti-war groups: the Committee of Concerned Asian Scholars, the Clergy and Laymen Concerned about Vietnam, *Viet Report*, the Russell International War Crimes Tribunal, the Winter Soldier Investigation, and the Air War Study Group. It was reviewed most recently by James Pinckney Harrison.[90] These studies depict 'the greatest use of force on a similar area in the history of warfare'[91] as a calculated and systematic policy. Some basic sense of its scale may be gleaned from its overall cost. To preserve a pro-American regime in South Vietnam, the United States spent approximately 240 thousand million dollars—a sum equal to *ninety* years' income per capita for each man, woman and child in that country! And all this primarily to destroy.

The more than 4,000,000 tons of bombs dropped on South Vietnam, if distributed in five hundred pound bombs—one of the most common types—would equal almost exactly one bomb for each person in the country. More than 90 per cent of these bombs were dropped not for close battle support, but under the elastic category of 'interdiction'— 'to prevent or hinder, by any means, enemy use of an area or route.'[92] To this 'most massive bombing in history'[93] we must add a roughly equal amount of explosives detonated on the ground. And to the explosives detonated on and over South Vietnam we must add a roughly equal amount on and over Laos, Cambodia and North Vietnam. The total was approximately fourteen million tons exploded on a peninsula the size of Texas—seven times the total of bombs dropped by the Allies in all of the Second World War, or 1,269.4 pounds per inhabitant.[94]

Bombing tonnage figures seem necessarily abstract, as are so many ways of measuring destruction in this century of mass death.

Consider that *any* structure or person in enemy-held territory in South Vietnam was regarded as a legitimate target and we will have some sense of the destination of the literally millions of tons of explosives used. Consider that already by 1967 General Earl Wheeler, Chairman of the Joint Chiefs of Staff, had run out of important military targets in North Vietnam, yet the bombing continued. And, finally, consider that the Christmas bombing of Hanoi and Haiphong ordered by Richard Nixon in 1972 dropped an explosive force on the two cities equivalent to the two atomic bombs dropped on Hiroshima and Nagasaki.[95]

Ecological devastation has been extensive, and its effects will continue well into the future. Perhaps 12,000,000 bomb craters were produced in all of Indochina (two thirds of these in South Vietnam) by US bombing, 'covering an area of at least 200,000 acres and excavating about 1.5 thousand million cubic yards of soil.'[96] The typical crater is thirty feet in diameter by fifteen feet deep; it does not fill in naturally. 'A bomb crater destroys the surface organic layer and throws up subsoil; it creates severe local relief and erosion in the soil and may disrupt drainage patterns. Usually it fills with water and becomes very difficult to drain, making heavily bombed areas virtually unsuitable for cultivation.'[97]

In addition herbicides sprayed *one in every seven* acres of South Vietnam—affecting and largely destroying great cultivated areas (560,000 acres), 35 per cent of the country's dense hardwood forest and half of its coastal mangrove forests. Bulldozing destroyed more than a thousand square miles of forests and fields.[98] We have seen that these various high-technology military activities were carried out with a conscious design, as articulated by Huntington: 'forced-draft urbanization and modernization which rapidly brings the country in question out of the phase in which a rural revolutionary movement can hope to generate sufficient strength to come to power.'[99] In other words, the aim was to defeat the Viet Cong insurgency by destroying the peasant society which nurtured it, creating in its place a shantytown and resettlement camp society in which as many as 60 per cent of the people—10,000,000—were refugees![100] Commenting on an earlier estimate of over 1,000,000 casualties and 6,000,000 refugees (April 1971) the Air War Study Group says that 'these figures mean that there is hardly a family in South Vietnam that has not suffered a death, injury or the anguish of abandoning an ancient homestead.'[101] Reflecting on this destruction of Vietnamese society the otherwise rigorously dispassionate authors gave way before its enormity: 'When all the numbers describing deaths, injuries, and refugees have been listed, examined, and absorbed, one has only begun to comprehend the effect of the war on South Vietnam. To many an American the possibility of physical mobility is desirable. To a Vietnamese peasant, the opposite is true. To be removed from his land is not only to be removed from the source of a subsistence crop of rice but also from the site of ancestral graves which must be venerated if he is to fulfil his religious duties. His children may never practice the veneration of ancestors, a rite exemplifying the transmission of culture and shared experience from one generation to the next. More than human life, rice fields, livestock, homes and local institutions of social and political accommodation have been destroyed. Some of the living links to the past are gone.'

The same authors summarized their careful and detached study of the ecological destruction as follows: 'Forests are the first to go. Then the animals—some, like the elephant, are killed deliberately since they could be used to transport supplies; others just happen to be in the wrong place at the wrong time. Finally, the land itself is destroyed: farms, rice paddies, and villages sites in many regions are bomb-pocked and barren.'[102]

Genocide

We are, in short, discussing the wholesale destruction of rural Vietnamese society as policy—a fact now obscured by the victory of its victims. How are we to judge it—indeed, how shall we describe it?

Raphael Lemkin's original definition of 'genocide' in 1943 referred to the peoples held captive by the Germans; he pointed to the Germans' 'synchronized attack on different aspects of life of the captive peoples'—political, social, cultural, economic, biological, physical, religious and moral. While he spoke of genocide as 'extermination of nations and ethnic groups as carried out by invaders' he included in this definition several peoples under Nazi rule. Yehuda Bauer accepts this as genocide: 'their institutions of learning closed, their political leadership decimated, their language and national culture discarded, their churches eliminated from a free exercise of their functions, their wealth despoiled, and subjected to killings of groups and individuals as the Nazis pleased ....'. Beyond this, the Nazis sought the *extermination* of the Jews—the 'wholesale, total murder of every one of the members of a community.'[103]

Did the US intend either the first or the second in Vietnam? The question leads us neither to what policymakers claimed to be doing nor to the unexpected consequences of their policy. In other words, we must set aside both the self-justifying rhetoric of 'helping' and the 'society of prostitutes and mercenaries'[104] which South Vietnam became in spite of proclaimed American intentions.

What were American intentions? Did the US seek to destroy the Vietnamese national identity in the way the Nazis sought to destroy that of the Poles, Slovenes and Russians—or worse, to exterminate the Vietnamese themselves? The American intention seems rather different from either: to allow any and all forms of Vietnamese national existence *as long as* the people did not support the Communist insurgency or a neutralist government. Vietnamese culture, language, schools, politics, religion were not attacked: only the independence movement led by the Communists and its vast human and geographical bases of support. Independence would be encouraged —and indeed was deeply desired—as long as it forswore certain directions in advance.

Vassalage was not the American goal. But, as we shall see, 'our' Vietnamese were inherently incapable of independence. Those who were established to oppose the Communists became the economic, political and military dependents of the US; those who would not, eventually saw their crops destroyed, their forests bulldozed or defoliated, their villages bombed. They became destined for extermination not by race but by politics. All they had to do to escape their fate was to leave their homes and enter refugee camps or US-controlled cities. To assure survival, then, meant giving up the struggle for national self-determination as it had become defined, or abandoning one's ancestral lands and coming under the US-Saigon aegis. Those who could not or would not were marked down for death.

This is certainly a variant of genocide, and perhaps a form of physical extermination—disguised by the fact that its purpose was neither oppression nor extermination as such, but *winning the war*. 'Free fire zones', bulldozing operations like 'Cedar Falls' (which levelled a region of 60 square miles), herbicide operations like

'Ranch Hand', the 'resettlement' programmes, the 'Electronic Air War'—all were systematic policies stemming directly from the effort to defeat a people's war that had developed deep roots in large areas of rural South Vietnam. As Jean-Paul Sartre said in his capacity as president of the Russell War Crimes Tribunal, '[t]he genocidal intent is implicit in the facts. It is not necessarily premeditated.' Is it hyperbole to say with Sartre (speaking of Algeria), that 'the only anti-guerrilla strategy that could work was the destruction of this people, in other words, of civilians, of women and children'?[105]

What is needed is a historicization of the term *genocide* to fit the situation. Destruction of rural Vietnam was indeed willed and carried out by the American war machine. Such destruction was not the primary American goal, however, but resulted from pursuit of military victory in a war that had already been lost politically. In Vietnam it meant making perhaps half of the people refugees, destroying one-seventh of their land, killing one out of every ten people, leaving much of their land looking like a moonscape, malarial and uncultivable. Perhaps then it is no exaggeration to describe the American war as genocidal.

Certainly, there remains 'a world of difference' between Vietnam and Auschwitz. But distinguishing shades of deep grey from black scarcely warrants the delusion that US policy began only with 'blundering efforts to do good', that 'it was not wickedness; it was stupidity', that it was 'more bumbleheaded than evil'. It is as if American commentators, fascinated as we all are by the Nazi standard of absolute evil, are relieved to see no swastikas, no raving dictator, no extermination camps. Relieved, they then conveniently allow themselves to become morally relaxed before what they do see. What they see were not 'foolish' or 'unwise' or 'tragic'[106] decisions, but a practice of evil so hideous that only analogies with Nazism and the Holocaust can make it digestible once again. Its logical result became after all, the destruction of autonomous Vietnamese national life, of Vietnamese rural society, and of a large portion of the Vietnamese people.[107]

My Lai

This is why Robert Jay Lifton regards 'the phenomenon of the body count as the perfect symbol of America's descent into evil.'[108] Day after day the only measure of achievement in such a war became the number of enemy bodies. No victories, no defeats, just death: death as victory. This approach to the Vietnamese produced, in Lifton's words, 'a compelling internal sequence' on the experiential or psychological level in US troops. Policy had to find its way into American military training as well as into the ordinary soldier's attitudes. Lifton concludes that, in training, Charlie Company of the Americal Division received as 'stomach talk' or a 'gut message' the permission to slaughter civilians.[109] In addition, all Americans were schooled in a deep sense of superiority. What else does bombing a whole village to counter a single sniper mean, but the infinite superiority and human worth of one side over another? 'If you can shoot artillery and bombs in there each night', said one of the members of Charlie Company, 'how can the people in there be worth so much?'[110]

This is not merely racism: how else can an army respond which is so technically superior as to see its aeroplanes fly uncontested over the countryside and drop its bombs at will? And what, after all, was the meaning of bombing North Vietnam in order to 'punish' it? As FitzGerald argues, 'a man does not "punish" an equal; he punishes someone over whom he has some legal or moral superiority.'[111] Perhaps we should say that technical superiority allows for the development of the *feeling* of moral or legal superiority. The very disproportion in the casualty figures also conveyed its own message of American superiority.

Permission to kill, superiority—add to this the frustration of not winning, of even being unable to create a decisive confrontation in which the superior force could be used. If on the policy level this led to the sense that the enemy was everywhere and invisible: 'No matter how much effort you put into it, you can't find him. You can't lay your hands on him. And the fact that he also might be anywhere, you know ... as though you were hunting a specific deer and you don't know which one it is and there's a deer herd all over you.'[112] On the American side the ARVN 'gooks' were incompetent, on the other side the enemy simply could not be properly engaged or defeated.

Built into the American presence after 1965 was a hostility towards *all* Vietnamese. 'Don't you realize', a young embassy officer told a startled Frances FitzGerald, 'don't you realize that everything the Americans do in Vietnam is founded on a hatred of the Vietnamese?'[113] He was at one and the same time describing policy and the personal attitudes of individual Americans.

On the policy level this stance towards Vietnam became embodied in the horrible statistics we have discussed. For American soldiers, however, one logical result was the war's most memorable event, the My Lai massacre. At My Lai the American purpose we have been discussing appeared for a moment: distilled, shorn of rhetorical obfuscation, clarified. Feeling pressure to produce a body count, encouraged to kill civilians, aware of their total technical superiority, enraged by losing five comrades, unable to engage the enemy in a battle—the men of Charlie Company stepped from their helicopters on that day and slaughtered the women, children and old people of a village.[114] It is perhaps appropriate that they kneeled or crouched while shooting, as if, in murdering defenceless people, they were really in combat with the enemy.[115] It was *this* event, more than any other, which revealed the meaning of Vietnam that we have been discussing: the initial commitment to 'help'; the incapacity to get to the heart of the problem because *they* were it; the structural inability to do anything but disrupt and destroy.[116] In this sense I take it as representative.

Vietnam Americanized: *the Land of Fifty-five Days*

At the same time the US was pulverizing rural Vietnam it was at last successfully creating in its image its own version of Vietnam. In 1965 American troops entered in force and assumed the main combat role. In their wake the ultimate American version of the 'Republic of Vietnam' was created: a grotesque hybrid of the worst features of both societies, where corruption, drugs and prostitution filled every pore of an economy dedicated to servicing the American presence.

Frances FitzGerald captures well the self-defeating dynamic of American involvement. As we have seem the ultimate ontological fact of this Land of Fifty-Five Days was its dependency on American weapons, manpower, training, administration, commodities, and money. 'Created, financed, and defended by Americans, the Saigon regime was less a government than an act of the American will—an artificial military bureaucracy that since the beginning of the Diem regime had represented no one except, on occasion, the Northern Catholics.'[117]

American 'know-how' intervened furiously to change all this: 'pig experts, rice experts, market and gardening experts, AID administrators, International Voluntary Service Workers, English teachers, city planners, accountants, doctors, police inspectors, welfare workers, handicraft consultants, "psychological warfare" and counterinsurgency experts.'[118] But the underlying logic of the situation—dependency and corruption—was such that every American effort to improve the situation only worsened it. No technical change, no reform, could undo the fact that the Government of Vietnam had its roots in Washington and not in Vietnam! 'The ARVN soldiers fought badly not so much because they were badly trained as because they had nothing to fight for (the proof of this being that they often fought bravely and well when cornered or when defending their own villages).'[119] Built into the 'Republic of Vietnam' from its very inception was one single motivation: individual self-interest. The greater the US presence, the less the GVN officials had to do with the Vietnamese population. 'By 1967 the US presence in Vietnam had reached the critical mass where Vietnamese officials, down to the level of district chief, spent most of their time dealing with Americans.'[120] In effect, they were Washington's native functionaries in Saigon: 'leaders' inherently alienated from their own pretended role.

Structurally, the GVN could not help but be passive, corrupt, self-interested and thus incompetent.[121] FitzGerald describes their stupidity and slowness as acts of resistance, an inverted form of guerrilla struggle against their benefactors. 'Dependent upon the Americans, the GVN was like a parasite attacking its host, engaged in a pure act of self-destruction. The corruption, the endless factional disputes, the civil war of 1966, the bombing and terrorization of the peasantry—all of them were acts of violence against the very population that might have sustained it. They were suicidal acts by a government that had not even the power to kill itself.'[122]

If the government suffered from self-destructiveness and paralysis, what of those over whom it ruled? The bombing, of course, steadily augmented its population base; the 'Free World Forces' totalled 1,300,000 by 1967; the US presence grew to 542,000 by 1969 and demanded great construction projects. The small country of 17,000,000 was saturated with American officials, troops, dollars, projects, aid, commodities, and needs. The millions of refugees, as well as the original residents of the cities, entered the employ of the Americans in one way or another. 'Around the American bases from Ankhe to Nha Trang, Cu Chi and Chu Lai, there had grown up entire towns made of packing cases and waste tin from the canning factories—entire towns advertising Schlitz, Coca-Cola, or Pepsi-Cola a thousand times over. The "food", "shelter", and "job opportunities" that Westmoreland had promised came to this: a series of packing-case towns with exactly three kinds of industry—the taking in of American laundry, the selling of American cold drinks to American soldiers, and prostitution for the benefit of the Americans.'[123]

Certainly the US policymakers did not intend to create this grotesque Land of Fifty-Five Days which, almost a decade after the Communist victory, has still not been reformed into a healthy society. No American intended to paralyze the 'free' South Vietnamese by increasing the number of Saigon opium rooms from 400 to 3,000 between 1967 and 1970. No one sat down to plan the corruption of the cities by enormous quantities of 'luxury goods, including watches, refrigerators, radios, Hondas, television sets, sewing machines, and motorcycles'[124] which remain for sale today in Saigon. Yet, without necessarily foreseeing its exact final shape, the US did insist on the Americanization of Vietnam. Lyndon Johnson's 'escalation' was, after all, a decision to escape defeat by inundating Vietnam with Americans and firepower. If one could say there was a Vietnamese 'will', it had already spoken, as Michael Walzer argued in *Dissent* in 1965.[125] The decision to transform Vietnam against its will, in keeping with *American* purposes, led to this sick society as surely and inevitably as if it had been planned that way.

Overdevelopment

1965 was the year of decisive rupture, when the recalcitrant reality was confronted by those in power and they, in their omnipotence and their impotence, decided to destroy it and transform it violently. I have spoken earlier in this book of madness, of impotence in power, and of a disfiguring transformation of reality through violence—and these themes have recurred in our study of the US war in Vietnam. The resort to massive destruction and transformative violence appears as a way to 'realize' an unrealizable policy; and I have termed *mad* both the accompanying perceptual/cognitive rupture and the destructive/transformative one.

But though the terms developed earlier do fit the bourgeois-democratic holocaust, we must also stress the great difference between both earlier events and post Second World War America: the 'madness' of America's Vietnam issued not from a society in crisis, but from a smoothly functioning society at the peak of its wealth and power. This fact would be anomalous only for an attempt to create some static typology which ignored social dynamics and historical concreteness. It is important to emphasize that this particular catastrophe was characterized by a 'normality' which has let liberal critics limit their criticism of it to this one 'mistaken' policy (and encouraged radical ones to ignore its gross irrationality).[126]

Why, to return to our original question, did apparently sane men and an apparently sane society generate mad policy? Why did a genocidal war issue from one of the freest, richest societies on earth? Just as one looks in vain for a social madness precisely parallel to those of Nazism or Stalinism, so does one look in vain for a social dynamic precisely parallel to that of proletarian power in peasant Russia or German petty-bourgeois impotence in power. We simply do not see the kind of internal unevenness, the constitutional explosiveness, in the United States of the 1960s that we saw in the other situations. Quite the opposite: here a class of the present held supreme sway, uncontested, apparently congruent with its society at every decisive step. It encountered no internal Other resisting its projects, no major class living at a different Now, no conflict between its possession of the instruments of state power and its effective capacity to command society. Internally one can discern no fundamental impotence that drove it forward in flight from reality, or pushed it to use its power to realize fantastically or destroy what it could not realize in the world.

During the war in Vietnam American policymakers felt able to exercise their power unhindered and effectively; they were even able to pursue major domestic programmes to meet rising black expectations simultaneously with their intervention in Vietnam. Indeed, these differences with the other cases bring us face to face with the *overdevelopment* at the core of the catastrophe. The very term suggests a system's unparalleled success, not its collapse or mortal danger; its easy presumption of power, not its urgent need to transform its own reality. Overdeveloped: the war came from a society which at a given historical moment had too much power, too much wealth, commanded and used too great a share of the world's resources. Such a society easily generated a determination to shape the world in its own image, and hence to create its own South Vietnam—an assumption of power and right which was remarkable in the period of decolonization and the rise of the Third World.

The notion of overdevelopment challenges the philosophy of history which has become part and parcel of both the bourgeois and the socialist consciousness—indeed, of today's world consciousness. In a global context it implies some inherent limits to the whole process of Westernization, modernization and industrialization.

Overdevelopment is a relational term: with 5 per cent of the world's population the United States annually produces one-quarter of its goods and services and consumes 30 per cent of world energy output. Overdevelopment is first of all a relationship of drastic and sustained unevenness. Recollecting that unevenness had led to the 'combined development' and the tensions that made possible the Bolshevik Revolution, Trotsky spoke optimistically of uneven development as 'the most general law of the historical process'.[127]

But the twentieth century has seen an immeasurable acceleration of the unevenness between societies. This explosive process reaches back considerably before this century, but today has become so extensive and intensive that the mere notion of uneven development seems scarcely able to convey its force. To put it most generally, what is really distributed unevenly among societies is power—the power to command nature. As it has developed in a world of domination, this power became intertwined with power over other human beings. In an interdependent, conflictual and competitive world system, attaining an edge in such power has placed the ruling classes of Western societies in a position to make quantum leaps beyond others while restricting *their* development.

Too optimistically, Marx and Engels wrote as if the Juggernaut of bourgeois society would ineluctably transform in its own image everything in its path: 'The need of a constantly expanding market for its products chases the bourgeoisie over the whole surface of the globe.

It must nestle everywhere, settle everywhere, establish connections everywhere.

'The bourgeoisie has through its exploitation of the world market given a cosmopolitan character to production and consumption in every country. To the great chagrin of Reactionists, it has drawn from under the feet of industry the national ground on which it stood. All old-established national industries have been destroyed or are daily being destroyed. They are dislodged by new industries, whose introduction becomes a life and death question for all civilized nations, by industries that no longer work up indigenous raw material, but raw material drawn from the remotest zones; industries whose products are consumed, not only at home, but in every quarter of the globe. In place of the old wants, satisfied by the productions of the country, we find new wants, requiring for their satisfaction the products of distant lands and climes. In the place of the old local and national seclusions and self-sufficiency, we have intercourse in every direction, universal inter-dependence of nations. And as in material, so also in intellectual production. The intellectual creations of individual nations become common property. National one-sidedness and narrow-mindedness become more and more impossible, and from the numerous national and local literatures, there arises a world literature.

'The bourgeoisie, by the rapid improvement of all instruments of production, by the immensely facilitated means of communication, draws all, even the most barbarian, nations into civilization. The cheap prices of its commodities are the heavy artillery with which it batters down all Chinese walls, with which it forces the barbarians' intensely obstinate hatred of foreigners to capitulate.'[128]

Marx and Engels could not foresee that the class struggle they perceived as the law of 'all hitherto existing society' would apply as powerfully *between* societies in the twentieth century. They could not anticipate the ways in which the class struggle would come to be projected internationally, at once suspending class struggles internally and creating international relations where certain countries would be frozen into backwardness vis-a-vis those which were overdeveloped.

Consider the specific situation of the American ruling class after the Second World War: its fabulous resources, its self-confidence, its base of support at home, its worldwide hegemony. For a brief time these men lived in a universe where to wish was to command, where they had achieved free rein at home to operate as they wished, where no obstacles to complete hegemony overseas could even be glimpsed except the Soviet Union, and where even the growth of revolutionary Communism could be exploited to solidify control elsewhere in the 'Free World'. They seemed to achieve the impossible as productivity and mobilization allowed the creation at home of a capitalist society without class conflict. Indeed, expansion overseas was intimately tied to the consensus at home, each fuelling and being fuelled by the other, and both deepening any potential opposition's stake in overdevelopment.

Joyce and Gabriel Kolko insist that an 'expansive American capitalism' is 'the central theme of postwar history'.[129] *Power* was seen by the State Department in 1945 as 'the main prize of the victory' over Japan and Germany. It was 'a limited and temporary power to establish the kind of world we want to live in.'[130] Shorn of the qualification 'limited and temporary', this project became US policy throughout the world. Created in a history of successful continental expansion, the only major power to emerge undamaged from the war, the only one to possess the atomic bomb, creditor to the world, the US now sought to implement everywhere an order consonant with its military, economic and technological might. Having accomplished a purge of the Left and labour support for its 'Free World' empire, a bipartisan foreign policy on an awesome technological-scientific base, and the highest standard of living in the history of the world, the American leaders policed the empire from an eventual 275 major military base complexes around the world.

In an international system which shows no signs of peacefully evolving in a different direction, the United States has achieved *too much* accumulation of wealth and power for any one national society. It has too much vis-a-vis the less-developed, poverty-stricken world. This unevenness is less a moral category than an explosive social and political fact which drastically contradicts progress-oriented visions of 'development'. Socially, politically, and ecologically the planet cannot long sustain the systematic impoverishment, subjection and abuse which such overdevelopment requires.

As usually perceived through Western lenses, the explosiveness comes from 'the underdeveloped nations which have "nothing" to lose, [which] will point their nuclear pistols at the heads of the passengers in the first-class coaches who have everything to lose.'[131] The reality in Vietnam, including the nuclear threats, was precisely the opposite of Robert Heilbroner's ethnocentric nightmare. Has not postwar America evolved in such a way as to *depend* structurally on a relative overconsumption of resources? And have not its rulers developed the politics of the 'Free World' in order to extend and maintain it?

The Lenses of Overdevelopment

Although severing it from its connection to their role as leaders of the capitalist system, Leslie Gelb places at the heart of his analysis the policymakers' 'arrogance of power': 'Leaders of the world's first superpower were bound to have a sense of being Prometheus un-chained, able to do anything—or at least to have the right to try to do anything and to meddle. But US leaders went beyond this. They had convinced themselves that meddling was their obligation and respon-sibility.'[132]

'Arrogance' is not quite adequate to capture the subjective lenses through which the leaders of the overdeveloped society perceived their reality and tasks. A better term would be one drawn from a time in history which saw such attitudes as threats to the human com-munity itself. *Hubris* suggests a magical sense of power, a boundless will to dominate cloaked in moral sincerity. Like the hubris of many of the Greek tragic heroes, that of the American leaders was wedded to fear. Under the rubric of anti-communism fear was a natural and necessary part of the outlook shared and propagated by the most powerful rulers in history.

In a world in which colonies were obsolete, anti-communism—the more sincerely fearful and idealistic the more effective—became a vital political and ideological organizing force. The American project of imperial domination voiced by the State Department in 1945 could win only domestic support by being proclaimed as a project of freedom, democracy and self-defence. And so anti-communism was joined with control over local economies and societies, freedom, democracy and self-defence, into a seamless whole—the 'Free World'. In the words of Doris Kearns, Lyndon Johnson believed 'that no problem was insoluble, that Americans could do anything.'[133] Indeed, he acted precisely this way, including his absurd offer 'to turn the Mekong into a Tennessee Valley'[134] while he was busy destroying Vietnam. Nixon's delusions of unlimited power were more purely destructive: 'We have the power to destroy [North Vietnam's] warmaking capacity. The only question is whether we have the *will* to use that power. What distinguishes me from Johnson is that I have the *will* in spades.'[135] From start to finish the Vietnam adventure reeked of its rulers' imperial hubris: the belief that the world's most powerful country should and could govern the world according to its vision.

If historical practice, social structures and ideological bent all predisposed postwar American society to the policies and practices we have traced in Vietnam, anti-communism became its moral, political and ideological cement. The vision was proclaimed in an outlook that, like all ideology, distorted reality, hiding it and yet simultaneously revealing and expressing it. The Red menace justified American imperial intervention, its military-industrial complex, the witch hunts at home, and a bipartisan foreign policy. But it could do all this only insofar as the belief was sincere.

As such, it achieved a force of its own, becoming a quasi-religious creed which ceased to be descriptive of reality and instead became a reality in its own right. It became its own reality because, as ideology its functional essence was to separate itself from being the crass material justification of specific economic interest. When Podhoretz says that the United States went into Vietnam not for the sake of its own direct interests in the ordinary sense but for the sake of an ideal he is voicing an essential aspect of the project. He is not effectively analyzing US policy, but presenting it as it *had to* be presented. He is presenting the noble self-image which the policy makers were constrained to believe. The ideal? 'To say it once again: because we were trying to save the Southern half of the country from the evils of Communism.'[136]

If it could have been framed in terms of 'direct interests', anti-communism might have been a correct, fearful, rational response of the American capitalist class to the spread of socialist revolutions. In the case of Vietnam, the withdrawal of one small country from the capitalist world system and its abrogation of private property relations was no threat to American capitalism, but its *example* certainly was.

Liberal critics tended to dismiss this dimension of the war, falsely seeing the North Vietnamese and NLF only as Vietnamese nationalists.
Their ultimate victory depended on their deep roots in Vietnam, to
be sure, but also on their links to the consolidated anti-capitalist
revolutions in Russia and China. They were indeed part of an international movement, both formal and informal, which stood to be
strengthened by their victory. Capitalist self-assurance and expan-
siveness stood to be weakened by it. However distorted, the notion
of the 'international Communist conspiracy' apprehended this. David
did capture Goliath's sword many times over; but without Chinese,
and above all Soviet military assistance, it is difficult to see how the
Vietnamese could have held out for so long against such odds and
won so dramatically in 1975.

But it was the irrational aspect of this rationally-based class fear
that was decisive. One could not speak of capitalism and socialism
—the true reasons for fighting—but only of 'democracy' and 'dictatorship'. America's Vietnam, however, could not be a democracy
except in the most pathetically formal sense. Under the rubric of anti-
communism the US created a sincere yet self-effacing imperialism
which fought economically useless battles *here* to protect economic
interests *there*; instead of celebrating itself with a Trafalgar Square it
concealed itself in The Departments of State and Defence. The distance of any given society's self-perception from reality has its
degrees and they are measurable historically: how difficult is it to
hold the two together, how much tension between them is there in
fact and in consciousness, and how central does that tension become
to effective functioning? In Vietnam the ideological self-concealment
would not work.

Vietnam was being destroyed 'in order to save it'. But that it was
being 'saved' at all was patent nonsense, compelling only to the most
ideological of anti-communists. Indeed, Podhoretz and Lewy find
themselves compelled to remould the story to make the intervention
look humane and non-destructive. With the reality of Vietnam left
behind, however, few conventional standards remained to measure
what was beneficial and what destructive. An openly economic intervention has at least economic criteria by which it must be measured;
but an ideological war? A war of example which had to be presented
as a noble war? In Vietnam the distance became too great between
the noble way the war *had to be seen* and its ignoble reality.

The Strategy of Overdevelopment

Insofar as overdevelopment and the hubris linked to it were the material reality of postwar America and the lenses through which its leaders saw the world, the challenge of Vietnam was met by a *strategy* of overdevelopment. Most simply, the United States flooded Vietnam with its wealth and power. It was the most lavish such undertaking in human history, squandering on killing and controlling a dollar sum that could easily have doubled the living standard of a generation of Vietnamese. As the American situation there deteriorated, the wealth, military personnel, technology and destructive force only increased: foodstuff, weapons, tractors, all manner of experts, indeed even constitutions. It was as if all this stuff, substituted for the human and properly political struggle which alone could win the war in any meaningful sense, was shipped there in a magical effort to conjure away the real problem. Like Goliath's armour, it failed. This suggests another dimension of overdevelopment: the attempt to subdue the fundamentally political problems of human relations with products, wealth, tools and techniques. Having addressed the political realm and lost, the US could only appeal to the fruits of its higher level of material development—especially its destructive power.

Vietnam thus became a fundamental test of the strategy of overdevelopment, and, I would suggest, of its ultimately genocidal logic. Can productivity, technology and destructive power master social conflict? US policymakers assumed that they possessed an undifferentiated political and moral, as well as technological superiority. They exercised that superiority with a hubris that can only be described as god-like. The debate about restraint is itself revealing of the assumptions and practice of overdevelopment: so many US policymakers and military men pointed to how much they could have destroyed, while claiming to be holding back. And in a sense they were. An indefinite American occupation would have produced a stalemate indefinitely. Nuclear weapons would have mastered Vietnam, and the US did not use them. But the debate missed the point, because this was not a battle of equals, sharing the same assumptions and techniques. This was a battle fought on dramatically different terrains, using different weapons and even different systems of comprehension. The world-historical meaning of the struggle for Vietnam thus takes us beyond the timeless drama of David and Goliath and projects alternative and contending futures. Short of staying indefinitely or using nuclear weapons, the strategy of overdevelopment was bound to be defeated.

Too Little Power

Vietnam demonstrated decisively the inner contradiction of overdevelopment: that American power was not great enough to carry out American aspirations. As the Kolkos argue, American policymakers sought through the war to achieve a goal far beyond even their means. They lacked the ideological, economic, and technological capacity to impose an American order on the world: 'it is an axiomatic piece of political arithmetic that 6 per cent of the population cannot control 100 per cent of the globe. Therefore, the United States is simply, deliberately, and with as much reason and power as it can marshal, attempting to do the impossible. It cannot succeed.'[137] It could not win in Vietnam, for example, without removing the critical material and territorial back-up the Soviet Union and China were able to give Vietnam at crucial moments in the war. But it could not do this without first cancelling the Russian and Chinese revolutions. Nor, short of total destruction, could it root out an insurgency that was able to count on such back-up and which had deep roots in the countryside. Nor was it able to buy, train and equip an alternative leadership. Nor could it fill the deep distance that the whole world noticed between proclaimed goals and actual practice. Vietnam proved that with all its means, the US had *too little power* to control the world: far too little. American domination over the prostrate international order in 1945 encouraged the illusion that the American rulers could indeed create a world in their own image. Vietnam was their moment of truth. Internationally they were to find themselves in a situation analogous to the German lower middle class or the Bolsheviks: impressively powerful, but impotent to carry out the purposes to which they had become bound.

Madness

For the third time in our study, therefore, the dialectic of impotence, and power has led to madness. This madness is far less apparent subjectively than the others, and must be grasped as an objective phenomenon, as an act. Whatever its sources, in Vietnam we have seen a presence so violent, so self-defeatingly destructive, so blind and adamant, that the notion of a systematic rupture with reality is unavoidable. The US attempted violently to transform the society in keeping with a fantasy imposed on it from outside and, ultimately, to obliterate it.

We see American presidents confronted with defeat, believing their own absurd, hubris-infected propaganda, and ever so moderately and self-righteously destroying another society. For Lyndon Johnson, '[n]othing could possibly be worse than the thought of being responsible for America's losing a war to the Communists.'[138] To read Johnson's off-the-record defence of American involvement is to be struck by his systematic absorption of myths and lies. At root was his deep, sincere belief that 'we *are* quarantining aggressors over there just like the smallpox.'[139] The assumptions that ruled his thinking were that the war was a defensive struggle 'against Communist aggression' and that the US had a right to transform Vietnam because it was modernizing and improving it. 'Sure the Vietnamese will never be the same again, but they've had a whole world opened to them. More choices. Freedom from superstition. The freedom of alternative lives.'[140]

In Johnson we see all of the elements of the hubris we have been exploring: the imperial anti-communist outlook, systematic distortion of reality, self-righteousness, fear, deeply-felt belief in American benevolence, and a sense of technological mastery and political domination over the world. And above all, a determination to prevail. Never does this hubris betray a moment of conscious rupture with reality. Its source, after all, was a world which validated it. The madness was composed of a number of projections beyond limits, slight breaks, distortions and irrationalities: the policymakers' magical view of the postwar world; the illusion that technical power could determine and supplant politics; the illusion of limitless wealth; the ideology of anti-communism as the mystification of imperial expansion.

The bourgeois-democratic holocaust of Vietnam cannot be understood apart from the protracted refusal to accept the 'loss' of Vietnam. This posture of an unshakeable determination to prevail no matter what, helps explain the inability of policymakers to make the rational calculations required for a dignified withdrawal. These attitudes received their characteristically concealed expression in the 'domino theory'—the fearful image that the 'loss' of Vietnam would start a chain reaction of defeats by Communism leading to the inevitable collapse of America itself. Defeat there would lead to the fall of Laos and Cambodia (which was likely) and then to the rest of Southeast Asia (which was not); further conceptual elision now foresaw the US itself in peril. The lack of direct, palpable American interest combined with the determination and 'need' to make Vietnam an example[141] excluded for years meaningful negotiations or American goals short of victory. In other words, the 'ideological' character of the American war only intensified the destruction of Vietnam by depriving it of any intrinsic importance. This, combined with a proper appreciation of guerrilla warfare by an antagonist who would not accept defeat led to the project of 'drying up the water'—destroying rural Vietnam. Perfectly rational, yet utterly mad: the logic of a society requiring such practices takes us far beyond reason.

Victory

Yet the story we have traced, for all its destruction, became one not of defeat but of victory. It is a potential turning point for humanity because the madness did not prevail. Their room for manoeuvre narrowed by unyielding resistance in Vietnam, worldwide protest, and unprecedented political opposition at home, the Americans did not complete the destruction of Vietnam; they withdrew and permitted the NLF and North Vietnamese to win. The spectacular American defeat has veiled the considerable success of American military policy. In retrospect Westmoreland and his advisers seem to have been correct: superior American firepower, rapid deployment, refugee-creating tactics, gradually began to dry up the water in which the guerrillas operated. Whereas as late as 1964, 90 per cent of the Viet Cong guerillas were volunteers, after the American large-scale involvement—by 1967—volunteers made up less than half of new recruits.[142] The Viet Cong relations with peasants grew more strained as Thieu's land reform programme went forward, as their confidence in victory waned and regular North Vietnamese military units gradually assumed the preponderant role.[143] By the time of the peace agreement, over three-quarters of the revolutionary forces in the South were Northerners. Indeed, the Communists' central command in the South estimated that their hold over territory had been reduced to 20 per cent of the country, their popular base reduced to about one eighth of that of the South Vietnamese.[144]

Capable of producing a stalemate in the field, the US nonetheless fell victim to the basic asymmetry of the conflict. Succeeding in transforming much of South Vietnam in its own image and destroying much of the Viet Cong military capability only gained the US partial control over one side of a complex situation. First, it appeared capable of achieving only stalemate, but never decisive victory. Although insurgencies may be subject to ebbs and flows in popular enthusiasm and commitment, this one could never be decisively defeated as long as it was backed by a state firmly committed to it. Short of destroying North Vietnam itself the American side could gain only temporary respite.[145] Second, the inner emptiness and decay of 'South Vietnam' continued, promoting little genuine loyalty or commitment. Its course was symbolized most strikingly on 30 April 1975 by the fact that General Nguyen Huu Hanh, who transmitted the ARVN's final cease-fire order, 'was none other than a longtime Communist agent who fed information to Communist units from Saigon's Joint General Staff.'[146]

Finally, the factor least within US policymakers' control was, remarkably enough, the American political situation. The architects of US involvement were forced to accept defeat because of the constraints of American political democracy. Those who see this democracy as a mere facade, behind which imperial domination is exercised, simply miss what really took place. Itself the fruit of past struggles, with all its limitations it exerted a powerful effect on the course of the war.

Although South Vietnam was an American creation, American domestic politics demanded that it be a puppet which danced on its own. Resident Americans could influence the actions of the government they financed, could even intervene directly to force occasional decisions—but they themselves could not govern Vietnam. The history is filled with stories of frustration. The 'advisors' were stuck with corrupt and inept regimes of their own making that they could not force to do their bidding. Again and again the Americans sought reform; again and again they met defiance or incompetence. Their South Vietnamese were unwilling or unable to do as *they*, the Americans, would have wished: to serve the South Vietnamese people responsibly. This service was a vital—and genuine—American goal if only because first the Viet Minh, then the National Liberation Front, were clearly able to accomplish it.

But for all their power, the Americans could neither carry it out themselves nor ordain it: by the 1950s decolonization had proceeded too far for anyone to tolerate direct foreign rule in any part of a country that had already had its Dien Bien Phu. The US project depended on creating a *Vietnamese* government over South Vietnam, and domestic American and international conditions demanded that it be an elected government, in a society with the trappings of parliamentary democracy. The American policymakers' room to manoeuvre was conditioned by the fact that they themselves were elected, and pursuing intervention against Communism in the name of democracy. Thus the bizarre insistence on one meaningless election after another in Saigon for the primary purpose of gaining support for the US war effort *outside* Vietnam and convincing the *American* electorate—the politics of show.

In keeping with a dominant motif of American politics, once Vietnam became an issue, US policymakers were constrained to behave as candidates for office. Witness their early fear of Congressional criticism about 'losing' Vietnam. Witness the efforts of Johnson, then Nixon, to reconcile an unswerving commitment to defeating the insurgents with the domestic demands for peace—including 'peace offensives', 'bombing pauses', a 'war for peace', and even negotiations whose sole intent was to deflate anti-war sentiment. And witness the fact that American elections produced fresh policy teams determined to try their hand, in spite of the fact that the situation's hopelessness had become apparent to the previous administration.[147]

All of these contortions were shaped by the openness of American society and the extent to which, during the war, massive public opposition was possible. Which returns us to the final, decisive fact about America's war in Vietnam: the Vietnamese won. Stalemated militarily until the US withdrew, they won on precisely the political terrain on which they had fought.[148] The unwinnable war became unjustifiable in America, as it was seen and discussed everywhere. From the streets to the television screens to the newspapers to Congress, the opposition went from strength to strength, forcing in turn Johnson's decision to step down, suspensions of bombing over much of North Vietnam, Nixon's gradual withdrawal of American troops—and finally the peace treaty and the Congressional halt to all US military intervention. All of which was anticipated by the Vietnamese.

And here we come upon the crowning bourgeois-democratic feature of this catastrophe. This moderate, sane society which could so naturally and unthinkingly produce such remarkable death and destruction, also generated within itself enormous opposition to its war, perceived the impossibility of winning—and eventually accepted defeat. No suicidal *Götterdämmerung*, no nuclear war was unleashed—sanity prevailed. A world-historical victory took place of humanity over the Machine, of politics over madness. Limits were eventually recognized and acceded to. How striking to read the *New York Times* for 1 May 1975: 'Communists Take over Saigon; US Rescue Fleet Is Picking up Vietnamese Who Fled in Boats'. Inside, on four full pages, is a summary history of the war, obviously prepared well in advance and awaiting this moment. The barely disguised sense of relief bespeaks a society ultimately able to restrain its rulers, in which opposition triumphed and sanity prevailed.

Incomprehension

Let us not forget the damage, whose effects continue to this day. This was, after all, a bourgeois-democratic *holocaust* whose form should not be allowed to eclipse its substance. But the lesson has scarcely been learned. Little has been understood about the society capable of such destruction followed by such minor trauma, about this crime without a criminal. The would-be policymakers of future interventions pursue the elusive secret of Communist success without the remotest understanding of what took place in Vietnam or why. Incomprehension reigns as Vietnam, Laos and Cambodia are themselves blamed for their subsequent disasters, with utter disregard to the ways in which the US destroyed for a generation any possibility of normal life in Indochina.

Francis Ford Coppola's film *Apocalypse Now*, seen by over 25 million Americans, is perhaps the most prominent example of such incomprehension. Critical of the war effort throughout, it yet leaves its audience numb and dumb at the end. It closes with a murky, ambivalent sense of destruction, corruption, evil, and good intentions gone haywire—all somehow connected to 'Charlie', the unseen and utterly ruthless enemy who is at one with the land. They, enemy and land, are at the heart of darkness—or is it called up *by* them, out of us?

The film's protagonist is a Special Forces Major, Walter Kurtz, who has gone off to fight the war on his own. Kurtz makes clear that to defeat 'them' we must become like them—willing to kill without restraint. Kurtz, one of the only two real heroes in the film, follows this path and goes mad. (The other, Willard, is also a professional soldier and sympathizes with him.) Any other conclusions are ambiguous: evil and good can be assigned to no one and indeed merge into each other. War is hell, certainly, but above all Vietnam is hell. The final image of destruction fits this inconclusive and enlightening parable: Kurtz's Montagnard camp is bombed into oblivion by the Air Force. Yet for all the futility of the film's high-technology straining after effect, it succeeds as an evocation of a haunting experience which dare not be understood.

A profounder understanding was already there in *Heart of Darkness*, which managed, in 1902, to connect imperialism with racism, with missionary intentions, with economic exploitation, with the individual lust for power, with moral and psychological debasement masked as grandeur. It is certainly the greatest statement Western culture has yet produced about its domination of non-Western peoples. Yet in the 1970s, when native insurgents had put the whole structure of domination into question, Coppola's understanding is not correspondingly greater than Conrad's but dimmer. Conrad's Kurtz had been able to gain uncontested power among the natives. And then he looked within himself and glimpsed the horror. Respect for reality would have suggested that, seventy-five years later, Coppola's Kurtz be shown as *losing* a neo-colonial war against a movement of national liberation. His presumptions of power were in fact undermined by reality and history—by the native people's successful uprising against the formerly omnipotent colonialists. Acknowledgement of this irreducible political fact would have brought clarity and humility to the story. Another simple insight might also have illuminated the film: Conrad's awareness that the entire enterprise, along with its moral and psychological debasement, began as a foreign invasion to benefit foreigners. Coppola was no more capable of seeing this than were his country's policymakers. Like them, his moral sense dissolved as he tried to dominate the experience through wealth and technology; like them, he lost. And so he misunderstood Conrad just as he misunderstood the war, masking confusion as profundity even while capturing the *feel* of the experience. When Conrad's Kurtz says, 'The horror, the horror!' we understand, and on several levels simultaneously. Brando's Kurtz speaks of the horror, is apparently haunted by it, but cannot convince us that he has seen it. Perhaps 'the horror' is no more than defeat? Kurtz's—and Coppola's—hubris will not even allow the question to be posed.

Coppola's final image shows the only remaining meaning of 'the horror'—the apocalypse of America's destructiveness. The alternate version shows Willard slowly beginning to move back towards civilization, haunted by the voice of the man he has just killed. But the real catastrophe, seventy years after Conrad and in the rice paddies and villages of Vietnam, was not within the all-powerful European: it was visited by the Americans on the Vietnamese. The real ending was American defeat and Vietnamese victory.

Epilogue

For millions of Vietnamese, it has not been a victory. Indeed, 'their' victory over the Americans took the form of a Northern invasion of South Vietnam, a Communist conquest of Saigon, the forced relocation of hundreds of thousands from the cities to the countryside, the destruction of the economic position of over a million Chinese, and the placing of a million South Vietnamese in re-education camps—all of which led to the flight, often the death in flight, of hundreds of thousands of refugees. Other catastrophic events followed on the Communist victories in Indochina—the mass murders in

Kampuchea, the invasion and occupation of Kampuchea by Vietnam, the attack on Vietnam by China. In the words of Truong Nhu Tang, former Minister of Justice in the NLF's Provisional Revolutionary Government, 'the stark lesson of Vietnamese concentration camps and Vietnamese 'Boat People' should wake onetime sympathizers to what has happened. No previous regime in my country brought such numbers of my people to such desperation. Not the military dictators, not the colonialists, not even the ancient Chinese overlords.'[149]

Much of the world came to identify with the Vietnamese David against the American Goliath. With victory, they expected, Indochina would find its way to tranquility. Truong Nhu Tang writes: 'The golden opportunity to harness the energy of 55 million people to rebuild their shattered country came in April 1975 when foreign involvement ended. That was the moment to initiate a policy of national reconciliation without reprisals, to establish a representative government that would include a spectrum of political parties and pursue a foreign policy of nonalignment. That was the moment to foster a spirit of brotherhood and focus the country's attention on the task of national reconstruction.'[150]

One reason why this failed to happen was certainly that Vietnam emerged from victory ravaged by the genocidal war we have described. One in ten people in the South had died. The countryside contained over twenty million bomb craters and hundreds of thousands of tons of unexploded ordnance; 60 per cent of its hamlets were said to have suffered serious damage; and vast tracts of agricultural land and forest had been ruined.[151] In the North, according to United Nations representative Alexander Casella, 'there was not a bridge, not a single industry, unrelated as it might have been to the war effort, that had not been destroyed.'[152]

Another reason was the specific character of the Vietnamese victory, given the American transformation of South Vietnam. By 1975 one in ten people was working for the Americans or their client government, hundreds of thousands more had come to depend on the Americans for economic survival. The crowning success of America's mad design in Vietnam was that the Vietnamese victory over the US took the form of the very Northern conquest of the South the Americans had been warning against for twenty years. In the South the US had created a monster which could not fail to pose enormous problems to Hanoi. The fact of conquest and the reality of two now vastly different cultures, were hardly likely to encourage a 'spirit of brotherhood' even among brothers.

Another obstacle to a happier outcome was American policy itself, developed not to heal and reconcile, but in the words of Assistant Secretary of State for Pacific and East Asian Affairs John Holdridge, to make the Vietnamese 'feel pain' through 'maximum political and economic pressure'.[153] In concert with Chinese anti-Soviet policy —especially the Chinese invasion of 1979—this pressure led to diversion of scarce resources. Together with the Vietnamese invasion of Kampuchea[154] and the stationing there of an occupation army, American and Chinese hostility could not help but have a deforming effect on the Vietnamese revolution. In Chomsky's formulation, the vast destruction and subsequent policy have given 'a partial victory' to American imperial violence, assuring that David's country would remain a sad, ruined place even with Goliath gone.[155]

Yet Goliath is gone. The Vietnamese Communists have held power since 1975. In discussing the Soviet Union I have traced how Bolsheviks themselves deformed Bolshevism. A close study of Vietnam 'after the cataclysm' would show that the Vietnamese too have transformed the pre-1975 'revolution from below' into a 'revolution from above' since liberation.[156] It would reconstruct the most rational and humane courses open to the leadership, exploring the paths that were chosen and why. It would trace the relationships between North and South, between Communists and non-Communists, including such people as Truong Nhu Tang. Such a study, awaiting as it does significant detailed information on the years since the fall of Saigon, will alone make it possible to appreciate the extent to which that liberation has become reality, or remained a myth.

The world that placed its hopes in the liberation of Indochina, the generation shaped by this struggle, have probably been more discouraged by the aftermath than the Left of the 1930s was by Stalinism. The spectacular events after 30 April 1975 certainly stunned much of the worldwide anti-war movement. Did not Pol Pot murder far more Cambodian children than all of Nixon's B-52s? In helping to power that government as well as the one that created the Boat People, had not those opposed to the war been unwitting accomplices to worse evils than those they had opposed?[157]

On the Left in the 1930s only a small fringe rejected the

Comintern's definitions of Trotskyism and Stalinism; no such hege-monic apparatus existed to deny officially and convincingly the catastrophic events of the late 1970s. As a result, a depressive amnesia has settled over all those who once supported David but later came to see him as unable—and perhaps increasingly unwilling —to realize the peaceable kingdom. Alongside his smaller neighbours, he too came to appear as a petty Goliath.

For the whole world, the question remains: who won the war? The Vietnamese Communists? The Vietnamese people? The people of the whole world, because of the inspiration and example of struggle against great odds? The US, even in defeat, by conceding victory under conditions so severe as to validate its worst predictions about Communism? It may be possible to accept any of these answers for the moment, but a final answer must await not merely further study and information but the development of history itself.

I have suggested as much in calling the war a *possible* turning point of human history. Whether this possibility is realized depends on the Vietnamese people and its Communist leadership; but it depends also on American leaders and the American people. Can the US make peace with Vietnam, can Vietnam yet become the kind of society which redeems the destruction it cost to achieve—rather than a pyramid of meaningless sacrifice? Other people, elsewhere, will also decide whether the war becomes a turning point: by gaining the in-spiration and courage to liberate themselves, even against great odds, and by turning their victory into one worth the terrible cost.

In any case, and in spite of its cost, to bequeath all of us this possi-bility remains an epochal result of the Vietnamese struggle. The war remains one in which an overdeveloped society madly sought to trans-form a small, poor country in its own image, fought a genocidal war to do so, lost, and withdrew. Nothing that has happened since can cancel these facts. In spite of everything they stand before us, a possible turn-ing point waiting upon the acknowledgement and action that can alone transform this possibility into actuality.

III
Lessons of the Past

5

Afterword to Catastrophe, Preface to Hope

In spite of everything, is there reason to hope? I have said that hope without illusion is impossible today unless along a path that takes us past the piles of bodies, the bombed-out villages, the crematoria, the concentration camps, and the assorted madnesses that created these monuments. We have lived with them, we have sought the logic of their illogic; now we must draw some conclusions. We will re-establish hope as victims and survivors, as perpetrators and accomplices, as the disillusioned and overwhelmed—or not at all.

Are we now consigned to wrest hope from catastrophe like many a survivor—against all evidence, by exceptional chance and through utter persistence? If so, there is for us no Palestine, no Soviet border or approaching Red Army, no Western world, no North Vietnam or other sanctuary politically barred to US bombers—no refuge we can hope and move towards, whose very existence can sustain us against complete despair. Next time, Doomsday will be too complete to allow even such dreams the space to form. So we are forced to find hope where we are, in this continually mangled and rebuilt world, literally in spite of everything.

Let us be certain of one thing: namely, that if there is an answer to those who have given up hope completely it must be based directly on these analyses, on the chapters above, and not smuggled in or imposed from outside. Do such histories and prospects leave us reasons to hope? Especially in the face of the new threats?

Dangers

First, we must be mindful of the sheer immediacy of danger. I will speak in the final section about the threat of nuclear war, but for now let us acknowledge that no form of society today is exempt from becoming genocidal and, indeed, that *any* contemporary ruling class or national group is capable of using the modern state's weapons for catastrophic purposes. The point is not only that, as I will argue in a moment, we are living in the very midst of social dynamics which promote the urge to turn to genocidal solutions for unsolvable problems. It is also that once humans can commit such acts, we are destined to live with a sense of danger that will not go away. We know it is possible: this is our permanent heritage from Auschwitz. The study of Nazi society reveals no genetically warped race, but people like ourselves, living under social and historical pressures which found their issue in the project of murdering another people. Is it not thinkable that similar kinds of pressures could come to rest on any social group, that we ourselves could be drawn to brutality and evil under similar circumstances?

At moments we may indeed allow ourselves to be terrified by the hard reality of the danger: the existence of weapons designed to destroy us all and aimed at each and every one of us, the persistence of tensions which constantly exacerbate such prospects, the increasing tendency to place leaders in power who have already begun to lose contact with these realities. 'Long live death!'—the Falangist watchword is with us today, insisting that Doomsday can happen again and again, until it is total. There is no point in sustaining the illusion that this is not so, or the illusion that the very leaders moving towards it can be trusted to avert disaster.

Our world has been permanently changed by such events. No landscape, no matter how serene, is free from the instantaneous threat of the mushroom cloud, no carefree moment secure from being broken by the ending of the world. Can we ever again love as fully or freely? Or be totally innocent about other people for more than a moment? Can we avoid living every moment of our lives either with denial blurring our experience or in a desperate reaction to our sense of loss and horror?

And yet what is it that we are doomed to fear in this way until the end of time? Not mysterious, demonic forces, but *other people*. Sartre described it strikingly: 'Nothing—not even wild beasts or microbes—could be more terrifying for man than a species that is intelligent, carnivorous and cruel, which can understand and outwit human intelligence, and whose aim is precisely the destruction of man.'[1] Indeed, our century's great lesson is, as Sartre says elsewhere, that 'hell is other people'. The mushroom cloud is not really a non-human power over humans; it *is* human power, grotesquely disfigured, become evil—but human nevertheless. The evil is not chaos threatening us but we ourselves, trapped in social systems gone mad and in technical powers projected out of our grasp. The bomb is human. Frightening as it always seems, we should never forget that it is neither a force of nature nor a demon—it is human reality which has somehow broken with itself. It terrifies not only because of its violence, but also for its unreachability, its appeal to a logic which has rejected logic.

Conclusions: Power

The guiding principle of this study has been that evil is a praxis, and is therefore intelligible. Its codes can be cracked. But when they are understood, what lessons do they teach? The cases we have studied reflect a fatal dialectic of impotence, power, madness and mass murder. It is a social process: these genocidal undertakings had their sources in fundamental problems whose real solution evaded the comprehension, desire or capacity of the ruling forces—and whose fantasy–solution therefore became state policy. Hopefully each case has shown both its own historical specificity and a common dynamic at work. But if there has indeed been a common dynamic, what does that tell us about our world and its prospects?

It is necessary to return to two essential terms to answer this question: power and madness. I have suggested in several places that this study may in part be read as an essay on power and on madness, the two concepts being fatally linked to each other. Each case we have studied moved towards some kind of ultimate denial of reality: a madness of those holding state power who found themselves impotent to use that power effectively to change reality, and instead sought to destroy it. We have seen such destruction accompanied by the creation of fantasy-states, amalgams of madness and reality —Stalin's socialism, the realm of the Holocaust, and America's Vietnam. In each case mass murder became the denial-solution of an otherwise insoluble situation.

The dialectic of impotence, power, madness and mass murder brings us to the very nature of power itself. Holding *state* power does not assure *effective* power. Controlling the courts, the government apparatus, the army, indeed even the communications media or the economy itself still gives no ruling class the capacity to make over society in its own image. Marx, on the contrary, had spoken of the bourgeoisie as having *effective* power: 'It compels all nations, on pain of extinction, to adopt the bourgeois mode of production; it compels them to introduce what it calls civilization into their midst, *i.e.*, to become bourgeois themselves. In one word, it creates a world after its own image.'[2]

Why was this possible? Not because of any simple control over the instruments of the state and its violence, surely, but because of the bourgeoisie's fundamental congruence with society's major developmental tendencies. The bourgeoisie's control over the decisive means of production meant that the major social processes were becoming *its own*, from laws to values, from technological processes to modes of organization. Attaining such power meant placing people loyal to its definition of reality in key positions throughout the society, gaining effective command in decisive administrative, economic and social arenas, ensuring that hegemonic values were reflected in society's culture, attaining control over the law and the courts. This class holding effective power did not dispense with the violence of the state in getting there—indeed, as Barrington Moore argues, violence was a vital weapon in suppressing the British peasantry en route to establishing bourgeois society[3]—but insofar as it was the ascendant historical force, such violence was used primarily as midwife, as accessory. It was not employed to conjure up a reality without basis in social fact, against an overwhelmingly reluctant populace.

Effective power means the ability to command, stemming from a basic and deep congruence between a class's priorities and existing social tendencies. What the rulers seek to achieve then becomes a meaningful, or let us say a *plausible*, political project: 'a world after its own image'. The history of our century shows how rare has been this congruence, how overly optimistic and even simplistic were the broad strokes and confident sweep of the *Communist Manifesto*. In reality classes have been able to gain political ascendancy *without* holding effective power, a fact which has led to unforeseen and disastrous consequences.

The sense that state power must entail effective power was so native to Marxism that Marx and Engels leave only an occasional worry about development taking some other course.[4] A generation later, Trotsky's theory of uneven and combined development emphasized Russia's fundamental backwardness vis-a-vis the advanced capitalist world.[5] How was the achievement of socialism conceivable, let alone possible, in a country which had just freed its serfs? Under pressure from the West, Russia sought to catch up, making use of 'the privilege of historic backwardness' which permits 'skipping a whole series of intermediate stages. Savages throw away their bows and arrows for rifles all at once, without travelling the road which lay between those two weapons in the past.'[6] In other words, the external pressures leading to combined development could help to solve the lack of congruence between the Russian proletariat and the rest of Russian society. In fact before 1917 this process had already given backward Russia some of the world's largest and most sophisticated factories as well as its boldest and most imaginative working class. But at the same time it gave Russia no other class and leadership capable of meeting the crisis of 1917.[7]

Trotsky, the strategist and historian of the revolution, focused with Lenin on the opportunities afforded by this situation which placed the proletariat in a decisive position, allowing the Bolsheviks to seize state power with their support and in their name. It was scarcely conceivable to them that achieving state power—the burning issue— would not bring effective power. Nevertheless, as the dust settled in the wake of the Civil War and the defeated revolutions elsewhere, it became clear that that class, with that leadership, in that situation, did lack the effective power Marx had described as the privilege of the bourgeoisie. That party, leading that proletariat, found no easy congruence with that society.

In our century this dichotomy has borne catastrophic fruit, and the similarity running through remarkably different social situations leads us to the reasons. A paramount fact of each case we have studied is the effort by the ruling group to turn state power into power to create 'a world after its own image'. Destruction, genocide and defeat have been the result, even where, as in the case of Stalinism, the project of transformation can in some sense be labelled a success.

This will to power, for all its universal and timeless ring, has a peculiarly contemporary cast to it. The decisive twentieth-century fact is not the death of God and his replacement by blasphemous visions of power. Nor is it the 'power complex' or the 'domination of nature' taken by themselves. Nor is it the existence of powerful technology. All of these are elements of a more complex dialectic in which a class's survival or rule seemed dependent on transformations that sane analysis concluded were impossible, in which contemporary societies have thrown up mighty means and ideologies of power alongside structural limits too deep to be overcome by any rational method.

A central tension of our century has been struggles in which social classes have simultaneously too much and too little power. Too much power in the sense of possessing state power, with all that this has come to mean in our century; too little, in the sense that these various tools and weapons not only did not assure effective power, but could function as temptation and as blinkers by encouraging futile efforts to dominate the indomitable.

The deformation and distortion of the process of development envisioned by Marx began at the beginning: since early industrialization, a decisive dimension of every society's internal dynamics has been economic, technical, political and military intervention *from outside*, bringing at the very least an urgent need to catch up. Yet once the industrial revolution occurred, only those major countries were able to escape disaster who were closest to the British in social, economic and political development. Much of the world was subjugated and systematically 'underdeveloped' due to the uneven distribution of effective power between societies. In non-colonial countries whose rulers sought to catch up, such as Germany and Japan, rapid technical and economic development in the nineteenth century foreshortened the social and political process in ways that led straight to the disasters of the twentieth century.

For most of the world, Marx's 1867 prediction of the 'tendencies working with iron necessity towards inevitable results' was to be read later rather as mockery than prophecy: 'The country that is more developed industrially only shows, to the less developed, the image of its own future.'[8] In this line of his thought Marx's infatuation with technical progress lost sight of the deepest meaning of class struggle: the monopolization of the fruits of 'development' by those holding power, the consequent systemic and explosively uneven development. He died too soon to be confronted by the fact that within a world of class societies *all* industrialization and modernization has occurred enmeshed in the process of domination. In our deformed and distorted history, we live with the results. The unevenness is only apparently belied by the fact that the most advanced contemporary technology is freely available to all rulers, and is embodied in the most advanced military and communications technology. Every society has or can hire the Westernized experts trained in its development and use, even if on the outskirts of the capital people move slowly through the ritualized life of thousands of years ago.

Marx once said that '[i]n acquiring new productive forces men change their mode of production, and in changing their mode of production, their way of earning their living, they change all their social relations. The hand-mill gives you society with the feudal lord, the steam-mill society with the industrial capitalist.'9 Simplistic perhaps, but he was suggesting the congruence in any social order (however contradictory in other ways) of its values, its ruling class and its political order with its technology. Once Britain industrialized, the hope of seeing that congruence duplicated widely was lost, perhaps for hundreds of years, and replaced by the explosive situation in which we have been fated to live—where social structures themselves perpetuate the separation between state power and effective power. Nazi Germany and the Soviet Union under Stalin have instructed us on the internal explosiveness of such a situation, the American war in Vietnam on its irrational explosiveness in relations between societies.

Madness

Impotence in Power is not the only rubric under which we have gathered these histories. I have spoken also of *madness*, and this study may be seen as an essay on madness as much as one on power. If there can be hope today, we must take account of the tendencies to madness we have encountered much as we must take account of the distances between state power and effective power. Does the second create the first; does the blocked situation generate the violent urge to break with and transform it against its real possibilities? To paraphrase Sartre, is madness the path social classes invent 'in order to be able to live an unlivable situation'?[10] If there is madness afoot, it is not impulsive, ahistorical and unpremeditated in character, but in each case has its own history and structures. Specific subjectivities go mad as they interact with situations which *they* find unlivable.

Certainly one of the subjective streams is the climate of expectation encouraged by the industrial revolution: 'Subjection of Nature's forces to man, machinery, application of chemistry to industry and agriculture, steam-navigation, railways, electric telegraphs, clearing of whole continents for cultivation, canalization of rivers, whole populations conjured out of the ground—what earlier century had even a presentiment that such productive forces slumbered in the lap of social labour?'[11]

Since Marx's breathtaking vision was written human expectations have grown exponentially along with human power—including mass desires for comfort and dignity hitherto reserved for the most elite of minorities, and a magical sense of technical possibility. While this subjective dimension cannot be fully separated from the technological, political, social and economic history that nurtured it (and which it in turn drove forward), it also moves on its own, into the present.

For it is in turn rooted in still older and deeper layers of the human project, sometimes referred to as a 'Promethean urge' or a 'project of domination' of nature, or the 'dialectic of enlightenment'. Lewis Mumford, to select only one example, speaks of 'the power system' which in the present has been mistakenly identified 'with capitalism, with fascism, with communism, even with the Welfare State. But this multiple identification points to a more important characteristic: the fact that the power complex increasingly underlies *all* these institutional structures; and as it knits more closely together, seizing more power and governing wider areas, it tends to suppress original cultural differences that once, under feebler political institutions, were visible.'[12]

The root of the power complex is the 'imperious will to conquer nature', which means 'to remove all natural barriers and human norms and to substitute artificial, fabricated equivalents for natural processes: to replace the intense variety of resources offered by nature by more uniform, constantly available products spewed forth by the machine.'[13] For Mumford this quest for 'inordinate power and productivity' has borne direct fruit in 'equally inordinate violence and destruction' exemplified by Auschwitz and Hiroshima.[14]

Many others, in surveying the same wreckage, have come to a similar conclusion about the Promethean human effort to achieve *too much* power. In *The Politics of Hysteria*, Edmund Stillman and William Pfaff speak of 'the quest for a total solution in history, for a universalism which will resolve tragedy, [as] the dark besetting sin of the Western political experience; only when the political goals of the West have been most exalted, when we in the West have sought a thousand-year *Reich*, a Marxist, or even liberal, obliteration of evil or conflict, a universal society disciplined to a transcendental creed —Catholic, Protestant, Marxist, Populist—have we committed our unique Western crimes of violence. These have been, in our West, the times of murdering—when murder could be justified as creating precisely that kind of society which the realism which also distinguishes the West would have testified to be in history impossible. There has been no unspeakable crime of the modern West that has not been justified as a cruel but idealistically warranted necessity.'[15]

Even if they blur social issues, such assessments ring true in one vital respect: without the characteristically Western project of mastery there would indeed have been no gas chambers or concentration camps or strategic hamlets. These are all forms of mastery. Yet no single project stands behind and explains the specific contours of our history. If, under certain conditions, the project of mastery goes mad and creates hell itself, under others it so pacifies our world as to suggest heaven on earth. Our tasks are to try to clarify what those specific conditions of catastrophe and madness are. It is too universal, too sweeping to speak with Stillman and Pfaff merely of an excess of optimism, of ideological, missionary zeal: they base their argument on a seemingly irreducible subjective drive springing from nowhere but human nature itself.

If humans are capable of great good and great evil, we must ask *when* and *why*. Trying to answer this, Max Horkheimer argued that 'man's avidity to extend his power in two infinities, the microcosm and the universe, does not arise directly from his own nature, but from the structure of society.' Horkheimer had in mind class society in all of its contemporary forms, tending as they do towards 'monopolistic collectivism' based on the perfection of reason and scientific techniques *as tools of domination*. He insisted that 'the totalitarian attack of the human race on anything that it excludes from itself derives from interhuman relationships rather than innate human qualities. The warfare among men in war and in peace is the key to the insatiability of the species and to its ensuing practical attitudes, as well as to the categories and methods of scientific intelligence in which nature appears increasingly under the aspect of its most effective exploitation.'[16]

Domination, exploitation, social classes: the project of mastery becomes a destructive historical force as it enters into the dynamics of specific socio-historical relationships, which it expresses and which push it to the fore in particularly mad and grotesque forms. As we have seen, those struggles reveal the relentless force of technological progress when carried out under structures of domination, as well as something yet more explosive. Each case has been a story of progress *and* resistance, of the growth of technical and political power *and* its ineffectiveness; and of the response of those holding state power to this ineffectiveness. The conflicts have been not of impersonal forces, but of specific social classes. Class conflict remains at the core of our history: the collision of classes under determinate conditions has been central to the catastrophes we have studied.

How does the project of mastery become mad? Horkheimer, like Ernst Bloch, focuses on the act of *regression* in a situation of increasing 'resentment and repressed fury'.[17] Horkheimer must be criticized for going on to abandon his earlier insistence on social conflict, and instead directly applying psychoanalytic dynamics to the political plane. But even in doing so he gives us further insight into the process of rupturing with reality which I have been discussing as central to our catastrophic century.

As Freud argued, resentment against civilization is inseparable from the process of becoming civilized. But industrial society, by completely transforming 'the world into a world of means rather than ends' destroys those absolute values and truths, the realm of transcendence which had once justified human renunciation. 'Therefore self-renunciation of the individual in industrialist society has no goal transcending industrialist society. ... Since the subjugation of nature, in and outside of man, goes on without a meaningful motive, nature is not really transcended or reconciled but merely repressed.'[18]

Increasingly frustrated by the nihilism of such a world, (human) nature increasingly seeks to express its rage. Lacking any sense of truth or other transcending values, more and more people become unable 'to overcome the tendency to regress to their mimetic and other atavistic urges.'[19] Lacking any basis from which to champion 'truth' over 'reality', most people develop 'a deep-rooted tendency to treat their own "inner nature" brutally and spitefully, to dominate it as they have been dominated by ruthless masters. When they give it rein, their actions are as warped and terrible as the excesses of slaves become tyrants. Power is the one thing they really respect and therefore seek to emulate.'[20]

Their 'revolts' combine submission with rage. 'Hitler appealed to the unconscious in his audience by hinting that he could forge a power in whose name the ban on repressed nature would be lifted.'[21] Thus does Horkheimer formulate what Marcuse was later to call 'the fatal dialectic of civilization': 'Some among the masses seize the opportunity to identify themselves with the official social ego and as such carry out with fury what the personal ego has been unable to achieve—the disciplining of nature, domination over instincts. They fight nature outside instead of inside themselves. The super-ego, impotent in its own house, becomes the hangman in society. These individuals obtain the gratification of feeling themselves as champions of civilization simultaneously with letting loose their repressed desires. Since their fury does not overcome their inner conflict, and since there are always plenty of others on whom to practice, this routine of suppression is repeated over and over again. Thus it tends toward total destruction.'[22]

Bloch had similarly spoken of the 'anachronistic savagery and re-collection' discharged by a crisis in the present. He emphasized that because of their structural incapacity, the urge of the lower middle class 'for past levels of consciousness, transcendence in the past, increases to an orgiastic hatred of reason, to a "chthonism" in which there are beserk people and images of the cross, in which indeed —with a nonsynchronism that verges on extraterritoriality—Negro drums rumble and central Africa rises up.'[23]

Both analyses, the latter in racist overtones, show the world being left behind in a process of regression. The social world is rejected for an inner and past world, for primitive feelings and images, for a powerful but manipulable layer of destructive rage. This other realm becomes expressed by being visited upon *this* world through violence, through a fantasy-driven process of transformation. Thus does the Western project of mastery become mad, a substitute for the effective power of a social class able to create 'a world after its own image'.

For a class to fully perceive its own and the world's reality—and thus to gear fully its activity to real tendencies and possibilities—may still be considered a sign of complete sanity. To rupture with reality, on the other hand—whether in the regression described by Bloch and Horkheimer or in some other form—is not merely to misperceive, but wilfully to deny decisive aspects of the world as given by various codes of objectivity. Words like 'deny' and 'reject' emphasize the active, intentional character of this madness, its roots in a project of rupture which has reached the point of preferring mental images to material reality. This act of rupture yields the political project of substituting *something else* for that reality—structures, relationships, modes of being drawn from a class project which bears little or no correspondence to the actual social modes of being. Madness may differ from other projects of social change 'only' in degree—but with it the degree has become qualitative. It differs by its intensity, its wholesale rejection of reality, its determination to transform without regard for real possibility or tendency. The social world ceases to be subject matter, guide or referent, and instead becomes object. In this sense, therefore, the madnesses we have been describing are extreme versions of the Western project of mastery—mastery as utter violation of what is being mastered, to the point of its systematic destruction.

Usually judgements of sanity and madness are difficult to make, because all projects of transformation are to some extent routinely imposed on a shifting, complex, subtle world where even accurate perception or effective action are achievements. But still, when we hear Hitler rail about the Jews, or Stalin about the 'Trotskyite-rightist-capitalist-imperialist-fascist' plot, or Lyndon Johnson about the Vietnamese Communist 'threat' to America and American 'help' to the people of Vietnam, it remains plain that we are in the presence of a perception and a policy that have decisively broken with reality.

Evil

With the mad destructiveness of those who hold state power but have no effective power we are approaching, in our secular world, the meaning of this force that must apparently remain central to our lives for generations to come—evil. The characteristic of madness we have neglected so far is its *unreachability*: it yields a praxis out of circuit in relation to the world which generates it. Evil is the human out of touch with itself, driven there by extreme circumstances out of its control, finding the power to strike blindly even while unable to strike truly. It is mad, frozen, impotent human praxis, striving to lose touch with its source.

Evil, for example, is not directly reducible to or derivable from prior suffering. It is not just that a given social group has been oppressed or brutalized and subsequently does the same to others in equal degree. The fury, the intensity is in no way explained by what has been undergone. Most striking about Nazism, Stalinism and the war in Vietnam, is that the horrors committed have no good reason—in the logic of this or any other system. What is frightening to confront in such evil is that it is indeed rage, fury, destructiveness; but now organized in such a way as to keep itself out of touch with its origins, and with all ways of being remedied. It is the human become inhuman, the ordinary become demonic.

In the Nazis we saw the remarkable dual quality of their simultaneous omnipotence and impotence. And this element of impotence seems central to so much evil in our century—for indeed, as I have argued, if genuine social power were accessible, what need would there have been to kill false enemies? In other words, the spectre with which we end our journey into the Valley of Death is much like the Wizard of Oz—the thundering, frightful voice imposing itself upon us, and behind the curtain, a small, weak man, creating his fearful effects with mirrors. Barbed wire, machine guns, Cyclon B gas were of course more than mirrors: and so we must say that in effect as well as in image, the Nazis were indeed demonic to the Jews. But underlying their enormous power for evil was the stifled, dead-end fear and rage of an impotent class. '*Wildgewordene Spiessbürger*'—little men gone wild. These demons, more grotesque than any that have ever existed, were just crazy little men who were not stopped.

Evil is not functional, then, except in this mad sense, and so cannot be derived from the usual determinisms. It appears demonic precisely because of its quality of being out of control and madly

purposive, especially when that purposiveness expresses a social system that can only devour its people to keep itself functioning.
Demonic, autonomous, beyond reach—evil is created by us precisely to take on these qualities, above all to be beyond and out of touch
with its source. Evil is a 'natural' product, we might say, of the dialectic of impotence and power. Which is why it is so prevalent in this
century of such great expectations.[24]

The Persistence of Evil

Alas, another lesson of our study must be of the *persistence* of
evil—its startling reality, power and regenerative capacity. After all,
for so long, and in so many ways, Hitler won. He did destroy six
million Jews and pitched the world into a war in which forty million
died. Central Europe is effectively *judenrein* today. Only traces
remain of a thousand-year-old civilization. Similarly, no projection of
some future Soviet 'Solidarity' can disguise the current frozen socialism of a party-controlled society. As David Rousset has argued so
persuasively, the structures created by Stalinism remain dominant today. Existing Soviet life hardly redeems the victims of Stalin: the moment of de-Stalinization has given way to a politically, socially, and
economically arrested society of which cynicism and corruption are
the dominant moral features as well as the political props. And as for
Vietnam, must we not pause when Chomsky emphasizes the
American victory alongside the defeat? Inheriting an impossible
situation, the Vietnamese have for some time been making their own
disasters.

But why speak of evil as if it were an autonomous force? Why suggest a hypostasis, why not speak only of humans doing harm to
other humans for determinate reasons? The Marxist insight which
insists that we speak about relations between humans and not about
the self-movement of things retains its illuminating force. And in each
case we have sought the specific social dynamics at the root of the
catastrophe. Does it not contradict our every effort to turn about now
and speak of 'evil', as if it had a peculiar and frightening power of
self-perpetuation?

The Bolshevik Revolution and (as we shall see) Zionism were efforts to root out specific forms of evil—in the one case, class society,

in the other, the oppression of Jews by non-Jews. In each case one may point to major, unarguable achievements; but in each case, new and unanticipated forms of oppression were visited upon those who did not share the project; their response caused yet further hostility and embitterment, seeping into and determining the very structures of society. Similarly, Vietnamese efforts to drive out the foreigners were successful only as the efforts of a tightly structured, disciplined and violent organization. The struggle for liberation called down such destruction as to create conditions of permanent siege, as well as a massive and perhaps permanently disloyal population in the Southern cities. With the Southern insurgency and its social source largely destroyed, liberation took the form of invasion. Control and reconstruction became harsh and oppressive—and encouraged the imposition of a leadership and structures equal to these brutal tasks.

The specific stories only confirm the sense in which evil itself seems almost autonomous and ineradicable—a 'force' perpetuating itself from one generation to the next. The Holocaust did not generate a form of Zionism that led inescapably to Begin, any more than the Bolshevik Revolution led inescapably to the Great Terror, or the American intervention in Vietnam to Pol Pot or the Boat People. Nevertheless, we cannot fail to be struck by the relative powerlessness of the more conciliatory Zionists and the more humane Bolsheviks, or by the dismantling of the NLF. Our history is tragic to a depth previously sounded only by the greatest conservatives. It ordains that projects of national survival, liberation and social transformation take place under the worst of omens.

To complete these negative conclusions we must emphasize that the dialectic of impotence and power leading to madness and evil is more than a formal structure—it is rather a tendency of our century. We have seen history gone askew, creating in each case a vast gap, in Engels's prophetic words, between what *ought* to be done according to a given social class's 'previous actions, principles and ... immediate interests' and what *could* be done. If historical and political reality would not allow the gap to be filled by effective action, state power made other sorts available, however mad and destructive. And so our subject belongs intimately and uniquely to this century of aggravated social contradiction, revolutionary aspiration and counterrevolutionary technology: the new dialectic of impotence and power.

I have spoken of uneven development, of overdevelopment, and of a Western project of mastery which, in class societies, overflows any possible human benefits it may offer to become catastrophic. It may be that the end of class society, the end of unevenness and overdevelopment, together may allow the project of mastery to find its appropriate terminus ın human well-being and a harmonious human life in nature. However, until such a historic turning point we, our children, and their children can expect to survive only in the greatest danger. In conditions of increasing stress will not these classes holding or able to achieve state power again and again find themselves pushed up against the limits of reality, impotent to realize the purposes for which they came to power? And in such extreme situations (which, if anything, may be expected to increase as resources diminish) will they not be tempted again and again to rupture with reality and use their instruments of power to attempt violent and magical transformations? If so, what reason can there possibly be to hope?

Reason to Hope?

Our question is both one of mood and one of science. Can one, today, still remain disposed towards a positive future? For a long historical moment, Marxist and liberal hopes pointed to the facts of Progress: greater productivity, higher levels of human skills, stronger and broader movements of the working class, the growth of democracy. Do the facts today, as amended by catastrophe, still warrant the conclusion that our history is moving or can move towards the pacification of existence and the amelioration of the human lot? After Auschwitz, is there *reason* to hope—reason visible in trends, in actual possibilities? Now, having lived with mass murder again and again, what can we answer?

First, we must surrender the project of finding *reason* to hope. Auschwitz, the Gulag, the Electronic Air War should induce us to abandon any Enlightenment, Hegelian or Marxist version of the inexorable, if convulsive, unfolding of an improved human world. Progress there may be, but there will also be regress. Indeed, the notion of overdevelopment suggests that much of our contemporary technological progress is humanly regressive. This is not to say that the world is chaos, or has no clear lines of development; but these lines are also fault-lines, contradictory and explosive. Far from being unintelligible, I have argued, our catastrophic history has a complex logic at its centre. A number of trends coexist side by side: the mastery of nature *and* the revolt of nature; technical progress *and* overdevelopment; progress in the struggle for human dignity *and* progress in the ever-more-sophisticated control of humans; the perfection of human skills *and* the perfection of human destructiveness; the infiltration of the modern world into every corner of the globe *and* the furious revolt against modernity.

In many ways societies do indeed move forward; but even as they do they may often explode. Marx's too-hopeful vision focused on only two dominant trends: the growth in the means of production and the growth in class conflict and revolutionary consciousness. Today this must be supplanted by our more complex and negative experience, focusing on the struggles between technology and politics; between class struggle and its deadly and false 'transcendence'; between classes of the past, the present and the future; and among developed, underdeveloped and overdeveloped societies. Not only is there no overarching Progress, in the sense of one force operating behind the backs of human beings and imposing itself on and through them—neither is there any decisive human tendency leading towards the improvement of the human lot. Alas, not even one dialectical tendency liable to intensify the antagonisms which lead to liberation. We have explored examples illustrating this and reasons explaining it, but the fact itself remains sovereign, and sobering. Within Hegel's vision of history as a charnel house of human aspirations lay his saving conviction of the inevitable progress of freedom; if our twentieth-century sense of freedom has indeed grown, so has the charnel house, and out of all proportion to our achievements.

To be sure, in our time the struggle for freedom has gone from strength to strength, and evil has grown partially *in relation to it*—the greater the human threat to privilege and domination, the greater have become the means of maintaining privilege and domination. Massive irrationality and overdevelopment have often been a response to the threat that existence might indeed be improved and pacified.

Our century has taught, however, that the very question about a *reason to hope* is radically beside the point. Any such reason would be out there, beyond us, separate: if not God, then History or Progress. We are no longer privileged to sit back and watch the world unfold before us, secure that its inexorable course is for good. Utopia and genocide are both present and possible, as are socialism and barbarism. The logic of social development oscillates around each term of these pairs, with the deepest tension between them. Today, the philosophy of history must terminate with a question mark.

Resistance

Does this mean the end of hope? The *Why?* accompanying any extended confrontation with the Holocaust, the *Why?* scrawled and scratched throughout the Gulag, has a larger meaning than we have yet explored. To what end are we suffering? To be a martyr is one thing, to be a random victim something else entirely. If the Holocaust was no sacrifice, if it produced no lessons, no countervailing movement, then on an essential level it was—meaningless. If Stalin's victory over Hitler did not require a terrorized Soviet Union, if the Americans might simply have let Vietnam be after 1954 (or after 1964, or 1968, or 1975)—if, in other words, the catastrophes did not *lead* to historical turning points, then *every* loss was a waste. For many, the greatest tragedy was death without hope—to die for nothing.

Tell this to the *Zek* in Kolyma, to the Vietnamese hiding in a tunnel, to the Jew struggling to survive in the shadow of the gas chambers. Tell them that it is all to no purpose, produced by a madness whose defeat will relieve the world only momentarily before the next time. As Viktor Frankl points out, hope for the future, a sense that 'our sacrifice did have a meaning',[25] were among the very conditions for survival in the Nazi camps. But if the inmates had known that 'the terrible secret' was widely known but moved no one to action, if they had known that their sacrifice had no meaning, that other paroxysms would follow this one and even greater ones eventually portend—then how would they have responded?

Frankl gives us our answer, as do the combatants in the Warsaw Ghetto and the insurrectionaries who destroyed Treblinka. They give us a resounding answer even in their death, which thus *did* have a meaning. Even in the most hopeless situation and without illusions, there were those who chose to resist. In the words of a proclamation addressed to the Poles of Warsaw by the Jewish Combat Organization in the midst of the Warsaw Ghetto uprising: 'A battle is being waged for your freedom as well as ours.'[26] Freedom? What they faced rather was certain death. But they chose to die fighting rather than passively: this much freedom was left to them, and this much they asserted. A proclamation drafted earlier that year in Bialystock had explained why: 'Do not go to your death of your own free will! Fight for your lives to your last breath! We have nothing left but our honour—we can lose nothing else.'[27] People resisted, even if without hope and without prospects. In a sense every survivor resisted, struggling dozens of times a day just to remain human in the face of overwhelming pressure to give up. Frankl argues that 'any man can, even under such circumstances, decide what shall become of him—mentally and spiritually. He may retain his human dignity even in a concentration camp.'[28] Indeed, the slave in chains is free to—try to—break them.[29] But those who dispute the Sartrean argument and insist on thinking in terms of effective resistance—based on calculating its chances of success—might perhaps stop a moment and reflect on how hope develops from 'hopeless' situations.

People resist, even when there is no apparent point in doing so. Or rather, its point comes to lie in the act of resistance itself, no matter how desperate. When nothing else is left to us we may die freely, with dignity, in struggle against our enemies' definition of us. And if we are remembered, we may be remembered for having done so. Today a preface to hope that would look beyond the Valley of Death begins with resistance. The final word is action.

Action and Hope

If we continue to hope it is because, in spite of everything, we continue to act. Upon what is this kind of hope based? If an illusion-free analysis of today's world yields no Reason to hope, it also yields the greatest urgency and call to action. As we shall see, it concludes that people must act if the world is to be saved. This is so both because our rulers seem bent on moving towards nuclear war, and because our rulers' weapons and power express an overdevelopment that is the negation of humanity itself. The belief in Progress became a negation, trusting to forces beyond people themselves to shape a pacific human world. We have now sifted through enough facts to suggest how absurd it would be for hope today to wait upon the contours of history unfolding in a benign direction, upon the belief that 'things' will turn out all right, or to think that human betterment is either inevitable, or even likely.

To hope is to approach the Holocaust without blinkers, but to see it from the point of view of the survivors and partisans. We have seen grim facts, so many of them, as well as positive ones. Hope is based not on any final reflective weighing–up which tells us only that the world can be the land of milk and honey or the Valley of Death—but on one particular response to catastrophe. It rests, today, on the determination to keep alive a specific project, in spite of everything: bringing into being a better world, a world which will respect both its source and its ultimate term (people), and will abolish the conditions that led to Auschwitz, the Gulag, Vietnam. This project illuminates theoretical questions, and selects from and redefines the facts. Both philosophically and politically, then, a study that would point towards hope must also point towards collective action to achieve its results.

Today, hope is a specific way of acting. First, to save ourselves from destruction; in so doing, to insist on our human dignity; then to improve the world. To hope is to act towards change, that life may be better in spite of everything. It is an existential posture, not at all a matter of knowledge. Or rather, it is our knowledge which leads us to assume this posture: we seek not to confirm a truth of History, but to assert this historical project, and so make it become the truth.

If the project is a response to the century's history, what does our century's history have to teach it? The scientism of Marxism predicted both much less and much more than really happened, and we must abandon it for a more tentative sense of human tasks and prospects. The devastating course of real events also fills our eyes and ears and memories with the desperate beauty of resistance: its 'truth' is terrifying, and perhaps also exemplary. So Marx must be remembered in this study above all for his second 'Thesis on Feuerbach': 'The question whether human thinking can pretend to objective truth is not a theoretical but a *practical* question. Man has to prove the truth, i.e., the reality and power, the "this-worldliness" of his thinking in practice. The dispute over the reality or non-reality of thinking which is isolated from practice is a purely *scholastic* question.'[30]

The depressing realities we have absorbed are profoundly humbling, yet they ultimately return us to lenses of commitment. Was this century of destruction inevitable? Was it beyond human control? Or was it a human creation, the result of forces that can and *should* be understood and overcome? Do we emphasize the moral dimension, urging humane action, or do we wait until the dialectics of development work themselves out? To be sure, the commitments must have a firm basis in reality. And yet they must not simply *wait on* reality —sometimes projects of hope, beginning with resistance, can themselves alter the facts.

Six million Jews were exterminated by the Nazis. The country-by-country statistics indicate an enormous number of Germans involved in the process, native populations collaborating eagerly, agonized cooperation from Jewish communal institutions, and passivity among the victims. The facts are staggering. In occupied Europe in 1943 the project, even the thought, of resisting the Germans' extermination programme certainly seemed hopeless, and for good reason. The Danes, however, refused to cooperate. And by so refusing they redefined the facts of their situation. The 'invincible' German death machine stopped. Individual German officers began to feel queasy. Orders were not carried out. Virtually the entire Danish-Jewish population was ferried across to neutral Sweden. They were not intercepted. There were no reprisals. The 'facts' were redefined by resistance.[31]

Even in reflecting on the past our commitments can redefine the facts. What stance do we, does our society, adopt towards the American experience in Vietnam? To forget it? To allow it to be remade into an honourable cause, while those who do so continue asserting American hegemony throughout the world? To be morally and politically immobilized by reports from Vietnam? The war in Vietnam means several different things, according to our projects: *our* goal can be to make it a turning point of world history. Action in the present will determine the meaning of the past.

Reasons to Hope

Plunged into action without reason to hope, people *create* their own reasons. Many of them are intertwined with the action itself. There is, as Sartre has pointed out, the implication of universality in every action. The moral decision that *one* should act suggests that *everyone* should, or, at the very least, proves that others can. The most individual act thus has its universal structure. The 'impossibility' of resistance is broken by a single resister: all the world can then see that acquiescence is not inevitable, that heroic risks and sacrifices are possible. The individual decision, however isolated, becomes a reason to hope as soon as it is confirmed by another person's decision to do likewise. Those who resist become a collectivity, however small, confronting the common dangers, having common goals, sharing common values and developing a common ethos. They become comrades. In short, their resistance becomes an objective fact, a force in the world and a potentiality, however slim, for transforming it.

So engaged, any community of resistance can refer back well before Spartacus for antecedents, linking itself with innumerable examples of struggles. Is this *a* single common struggle for survival, freedom and justice—the cause of humanity itself, with which one merges *this* struggle of the moment? But many people have resisted their annihilation and oppression who would scarcely have felt much solidarity for others. For example, a contemporaneous eighteenth century struggle uniting Indians, Negro slaves, and American colonists would have been unthinkable. On the other hand, many momentarily coherent movements such as Solidarity or the Sandinistas are fated to fragment badly once the initial goal is won. Thus one does not join, except in fantasy, with a single self-conscious international movement unfolding through time. The International existed only for moments, as did Progress. To project an ultimate convergence ahead, one single cause of humanity, is likewise an act of faith.

Nevertheless, it is undeniable that the cause of *this* group, here and now, was objectively advanced by the struggle of *that* group, there and then: the Civil Rights movement by the Abolitionists, for example; Vietnam by the Bolshevik and American revolutions; the twentieth century labour movements by those of the nineteenth.

There are many histories, but there is also a world history, among whose decisive events are numbered the rise of Christianity, the Reformation, the Industrial Revolution, the French, American, Russian and Chinese Revolutions. Such world-historical events affect all societies sooner or later, influencing the lives of the most remote peoples. In this sense, whoever may have been our antecedents and whatever is our history, Spartacus and the bourgeois revolutions have become a part of our distant past, and the American black and Civil Rights movement has shaped our present being and possibilities. However abstract these links may appear, we are indeed affected by an interrelated process of human struggle unfolding through, and creating, human history.

Though not a single self-conscious and deliberate movement, it is nevertheless the history of all those who seek a better world. I am speaking objectively of institutions, structures, laws, and relationships which we are born into, which are our givens. I am speaking of an objective layer of our subjectivity as well—of those self-conceptions and expectations which make up our irreducible starting points. We make this history ours even more deeply by assimilating its lessons, consciously absorbing its achievements, and finding inspiration in its examples. It comes to exist as a force on our lives, then, both by its definition of our situation and tasks, and by *our* decision to absorb and respond to it. In this sense, our every action today does continue and extend the 'movement'.

In spite of the supplanting of Progress by Catastrophe I would suggest that the great and remarkable fact of history is the persistence of such struggles, the refusal to capitulate completely, the victories eked out of despair. Specific peoples may be virtually destroyed, may be plunged into a generational coma, may indeed be the victim of successful repression (as the Soviet people have been for two generations). But in the end, in the long run, no people yields definitively, and human beings in general tend to renew their struggles and even gain ground. Resistance may assume the slightest of forms according to the situation, such as arranging one's few remaining belongings in an Auschwitz bunkhouse; or it may assume the broadest and deepest, such as the Vietnamese Revolution. It seems as if it always seeks to fill the available space. In any case, if we may refer to world history and project a single struggle—in spite of our own limited goals and consciousness—then it is undeniable that in spite of everything the specific struggles continue and tend to form a single one.

They continue and *progress*. With the eye of action it is possible to draw out of the charnel house a story of slow gain in freedom and dignity, which we continue to further today, and which will not end until either every last form of unnecessary domination and privilege, or human life itself, has been destroyed. These alternatives are dialectically tied together, to the degree that overdevelopment and the perils it produces function to stabilize existing social orders. Liberation: this is indeed one meaning of a more complex story, an abstraction flowing from a certain stance, and is contradicted mightily by new forms of subjection and threat, as well as by the catastrophes and reversals through which humans have already passed. Nevertheless, projects to extend freedom are major historical forces today, and so their history has considerable strength and significance—even if galvanized by acts of faith.

Protracted struggles against overwhelming odds, as in Vietnam, sometimes have their moments of victory, and not only the Vietnamese but all humanity may be inspired by them. But even the desperate acts of resistance, the hope of hopelessness, *survive* to be drawn upon later for courage and strength. The resistance organization at Treblinka was inspired, as we may all be, by the Warsaw Ghetto uprising: 'Unlike the men, women and children of previous transports these were not broken and defeated. Instead of tears in their eyes they brought grenades and other explosives in their pockets. From them we received some weapons. The leadership thought that this was the proper moment to begin the revolt.'[32]

Next to Auschwitz, Treblinka had been the Nazis' major killing centre. Eight hundred thousand Jews had died there. The rebels, in the words of one of them, 'dreamed of setting fire to the whole camp and exterminating at least the cruellest engines at the price of their own lives.'[33] They succeeded in burning the camp to the ground in May 1943. Only forty of perhaps six hundred who escaped, evaded capture and death until the arrival of the Red Army a year later.[34] Today all of them, living and dead, have achieved far more than they could have imagined: they are an example of resistance against overwhelming odds, of human dignity and power and freedom, which will live forever. We have their story, to tell to each other, to tell to our children, and if the world survives, to tell to their children. Like the Danes, the Treblinka resistance assures us that the struggles will continue as long as there are people. With Vietnamese-like persistence the human race will sustain each struggle against oppression until it is finally won or the race itself is destroyed. And these specific struggles, needing each other, inspiring each other, cannot help but tend towards one struggle. The 'movement' may indeed be propelled heavily by faith, but it is the kind of faith that creates facts. After Auschwitz there is no greater hope possible.

IV
Never Again

6

Zionism and the Palestinians

Now we come out of the recent past, chastened and yet not without hope, to face a threat whose scale instantly dwarfs the devils with which we have been wrestling. The threat of nuclear war might make Stalinism seem a 'mere' bloody episode of construction, the Holocaust a burst of nationalist frenzy traumatic only temporarily and mainly to a single people, the Vietnam war a pyrrhic victory finally granted with wisdom and restraint. If nuclear war happens, it may result from one of the super-powers directly attacking the other, whether by design or mistake. However, its flash point may also be in the Middle East, where the Arab-Israeli conflict poses the most acute danger anywhere of a local war triggering the global, final war.[1]

As we contemplate this large threat and the intractable local conflict which may ignite it we can begin to glimpse the outlines of all the other disasters we have studied. Hidden behind the various protagonists of the present are the demons of the past, not in any direct one-to-one way, but as if inverted, the mad originators of present madness. Repeated Israeli invasions of Arab territories— in 1956 in the Sinai; in 1967 Sinai, Gaza, the Golan Heights and the West Bank; the crossing of the Suez Canal and the further push into the Golan in 1973; and the 1982 invasion of Lebanon—all reflect the absolute Israeli and Jewish determination, produced in response to the Holocaust, never again to be victimized. Indeed, to strike out against even the most posturing and formal threats. 'Never Again!', the Jewish response to catastrophe, is shared in varying ways by the other protagonists. The Palestinian 'Never Again!' is taking shape today, on the West Bank and in Gaza: never again to abandon their homeland. Twenty million lost to Hitler have determined Soviet leaders never again to allow an independent government on its borders, even of Polish workers or Czech Communists. The determination by American leadership to reverse the effect of Vietnam on their world position stands behind the current nuclear escalation on one side, as, on the other, the humiliation of the Cuban missile crisis stands behind Soviet determination to maintain nuclear parity on terms acceptable to it.

Is it any coincidence that all of the currents we have discussed come to bear on the Israeli-Palestinian conflict and on the American-Soviet preparation for nuclear war? The ghost of the Holocaust is alive today among Jews everywhere, motivating action daily, making every Israeli-Arab struggle echo the conflict of David and Goliath. But for the Palestinians it echoes in reverse, pointing to Vietnam, suggesting moral and political lessons for an underdeveloped people struggling in its home against the advanced Westerners who seek to impose their rule. At the same time, the virulent ideological conflict between Nazis and Bolsheviks, between Soviet Communists and all those who surrounded and threatened them, between Americans and Vietnamese, is alive and more menacing than ever as American policymakers become determined to fight it out with nuclear missiles. In short, the madness and evil we have studied are with us today, truly dominating our world.

As we shall see, in this century of unreason even the iron determination of these responses to defeat, humiliation and catastrophe, may only increase the likelihood of new disasters. How to break through the circle next time, in time? How to escape the immersion in catastrophe where unreason seems to give birth again and again to unreason, evil to evil? These reflective questions are also questions of action, and with them we move to our two final studies, analyses of current situations in which total catastrophe threatens, but has not yet struck.

Israelis versus Palestinians: Problems of Perspective

Israel, as a Jewish response to the antisemitism culminating in the Holocaust, would deserve a place in this study even were it not one of today's main protagonists. In its history and present situation intersect all of the currents we have been studying: the Holocaust, a deliberate and self-conscious social-democratic alternative to Communism, a technologically-advanced Western people settling among a non-Western and relatively underdeveloped people and transforming their land, and the American-Soviet struggle carried out through surrogates. Spared, thus far, from the fully developed evil and madness we have observed in previous situations, the Israeli-Palestinian conflict nonetheless permits us to observe their powerful weight on those who live today, as well as the forms in which they persist into the present and threaten the future.

And yet nowhere does even the intent to observe objectively meet with such bewilderment. From the beginning most Jews and Palestinians have exuded a one-sided righteousness which has rendered the actual Other almost invisible. Menachem Begin's every warlike act was presented with a self-righteousness so unflinching and total as to shock the non-Jewish world. But he was not one jot more self-righteous than the Palestinians who have spoken of National Liberation when attacking schoolchildren or aeroplane passengers. Every Jew, whether agreeing with or appalled by Begin, has deeply understood: Who are *they* to lecture us? On the one hand, Jews have been shocked by the worldwide moral condemnation of Israel and formal support of the Palestinians, amidst near-universal silence about, say, Afghanistan. On the other hand, the anger makes sense, and is more than implicit antisemitism. In a post-colonial world committed to national self-determination, how can the whole world watch as the Jews continue to displace the Palestinians and absorb their entire country? Thus both sides argue morality with equal fervour, and thus, taken by itself, does each side's argument seem irresistible.

The bewilderment engendered by trying to understand *both sides* raises the question of perspective in the sharpest way yet. In this study we have faced the issue again and again: in exploring the past I have written about Stalinism from the perspective of a socialist for whom the revolution was both achievement and disaster; about the war in Vietnam as an unrepentant critic of American involvement and a supporter of David against Goliath; about the Holocaust both as a Jew determined to call barbarism by its name and as a human being, committed to shaping a perspective in which the Final Solution might appear as the comprehensible act of other human beings. In each case I have sought objectivity not through neutrality, but through a situated and committed analysis, that renders the situation as comprehensibly as possible.

I have implied a *point of view* on all of these events: that it is better to live than to die; that it is better to live better than to live worse; that every situation makes available specific possibilities for the pacification of existence; that reason can, and should, evaluate how well or how poorly these possibilities are being used. Without these biases, reason has no reason: that is, no function, no purpose worthy of the name. Herbert Marcuse helps us to understand these statements by insisting 'that the very concept of Reason originates in this value judgement, and that the concept of truth cannot be divorced from the value of reason.'[2] In each case my analysis has suggested that a stance of neutrality, no matter how fair-minded in intent, is inadequate to grasp such crimes against humanity and against hope. Reason cannot remain neutral before assaults on reason itself. And so I have argued that we can only understand the catastrophes from a position of engagement. For only if we grasp them *as crimes* can we appreciate what they mean to us, can we become oriented to what we seek to understand. Accordingly I wrote against detachment when studying the Holocaust, I wrote of the dangers of both Bolshevik and retrospective lucidity when studying the origins of Stalinism, and I wrote against revisionism in relation to the Vietnam War. Similarly, I intend to write against neutrality in reflecting on nuclear war, and will explore its dangers from my engagement *as a parent*. Once again, I will argue that only a situated and committed analysis can break through the deadly fog of detachment that pretends to rationality, Now, in dealing with the most divisive issue of the present, I cannot pretend to adequately render both sides. I must write as a Jew, one for whom the Holocaust is a decisive formative experience. But I am also a human being committed to universal social justice: the tension between these two perspectives, bequeathed by this catastrophic century, will inform this analysis and drive it forward.

Confusion

The nearly universal pretension to clarity and righteousness about the Israeli-Palestinian conflict conceals a moral and intellectual confusion almost as universal. To listen to Israeli spokesmen talk about 'protecting the settlements of the Galilee' in the summer of 1982 was to hear a sustained and unchallenged lie: a PLO-Israeli understanding, reached on 28 July 1981, had removed the shelling from Israel's northern border for the subsequent nine months. And yet to speak of the subsequent Israeli invasion as 'genocidal' was an equal distortion. Did the Palestinians actually expect to train and arm a substantial fighting force near Israel's border while Israel sat by passively? And since that force was based in the refugee camps, did they expect to be able to find shelter there from the Israelis' advance?

We are dealing, on both sides, with more than understandable outrage or propaganda. There is a confusion in people's minds which has its source in the facts themselves. It is a fact, and a deeply troubling one, that the state established by victims has imposed itself on the Palestinians as a foreign occupier. It is a fact, after all, that to right this wrong many champions of social justice propose with pitiless rationality the very conclusion most designed to terrify the former victims. It is also a fact that on this issue Left has become Right—as traditional Israeli social-democrats and their socialist supporters elsewhere have justified the dispossession of the Palestinians to make way for Israel; while those allegedly further to their Left have sought to reverse the wrong by supporting formulae whose operational meaning is Israel's destruction.

Such contradictions, entirely understandable in singleminded partisans, crop up in the most unexpected places. Simha Flapan— one of the great forces in Israel for encountering the Palestinians with a commitment to peace, reconciliation and justice—has written a landmark historical study tracing Zionism's 'non-recognition of the existence of a Palestinian entity' which emphasizes its reliance on foreign great powers, its Western arrogance towards the native population, and its emphasis on 'strength' as a prerequisite to security. Yet, he prefaces it with a claim which is brought into question by virtually every other page, emphasizing 'that my belief in the moral justification and historical necessity of Zionism remains unaffected by my critical reappraisal of the Zionist leadership. The history of Zionism demonstrates the extent to which the urge to create a new society, embodying the universal values of democracy and social justice, was inherent in the Zionist movement and responsible for its progress in adverse conditions.'[3] If any book shows that Zionism's 'universal values' and its 'social justice' were corrupted from the outset by the way in which Jews settled in a land containing another people, it is the study which follows this preface.

In Israel the material facts themselves contain the same tension and self-contradiction. Indeed, it seems as if no fact about Israel ever is unequivocal. Carmiel, for example, is a strikingly modern high-rise town in the midst of the apparently scantily populated hills of Galilee. Its main square contains an overly dramatic, but nevertheless striking series of three gigantic sculptures: traditional religious Jews wandering in the Diaspora, defenceless Jews under attack, and the strong *sabra* child being held up to the sky by a vigorous Israeli parent. Carmiel is typical of Israel in many ways: a new town wrested from an underdeveloped land, built using the resources of Jews from all over the world, settled with immigrants. Yet this particular place was settled in order to 'Judaize the Galilee'— to create a Jewish majority in an area which in 1947 was almost wholly Arab (and was thus to be on the Palestinian side of the UN partition lines until the War of Independence decided otherwise). Carmiel is located strategically in the Bet Hakerem valley—approximately halfway between Acre and Safed.

Thirty years after the War of Independence less than one in three residents of Galilee was Jewish. To 'Judaize' it with such development towns is part of asserting the Israeli political claim over an Arab region won in battle.[4] 'The lands expropriated included quarries and orchards from which the bulk of the village's workers made their living. Although the inhabitants suggested that other of their lands in the area be used for the construction of the new town so that they would not be forced to travel to Jewish cities for employment, their requests were refused. Rather, the government indicated that the industries to be built in Carmiel would create jobs for those Arabs left unemployed as a result of the expropriations. The town, begun in 1964, has large numbers of recent immigrants from North America.'[5]

In 1976 the further expropriation of Palestinian land in Galilee led to the famous 'Land Day' demonstrations in which several Palestinians were killed.[6] Carmiel itself was developed *for Jews*: a Druze-Arab stonemason was refused permission to open a business there in the 1970s.[7]

The high rises and statuary set against the timeless hills; American Jews welcomed and indeed subsidized while a twenty-year veteran of the Border Patrol was turned away because his identity card is not marked 'Jew'. In some deeply disturbing sense opposites are *fused together* in these images.

Settler-Colonialism, Shelter, and National Liberation

The moral and intellectual confusion involves focusing on one side only, and speaking only of the 'return' or (on the other side) of the 'settler-colonial' conquest of Palestine. Maxime Rodinson, to select a rigorous Jewish Marxist critic, correctly focuses on Zionism's systematic dependence on foreign imperialism to carry out its goals.[8] But his analysis typically pays no attention to the profound Jewish weakness and need which led to this alliance. The anti-Zionist 'Left' —and I use inverted commas here to emphasize my point that a genuine Left is concerned above all with social justice, and thus would reject the right-wing habit of supporting one national group *over* another —manages not to see that Zionism was from the beginning also a project of shelter.

In *The Jewish State* Herzl did indeed speak of Palestine as 'our unforgettable historic homeland' that offered European civilization 'a wall of defence' against Asian 'barbarism'.[9] But his main emphasis lay elsewhere: on the fact that antisemitism 'increases day by day and hour by hour among the nations; indeed, it is bound to increase, because the causes of its growth continue to increase and are ineradicable.'[10] Which led Herzl to a sigh of hope that Jews might be left in peace. '... But I think we shall not be left in peace.'[11] One after the other the early Zionist writers concluded their analyses of the tenuous position of the Jew in the Diaspora by emphasizing the intractability of antisemitism.[12]

This despair towards the Gentile world became transformed at the same time into hope, as the Zionist project proposed to eliminate the causes of antisemitism and Jewish vulnerability: 'We shall live at last as free men on our own soil, and in our own homes peacefully die.

'The world will be liberated by our freedom, enriched by our wealth, magnified by our greatness.

'And whatever we attempt there for our own benefit will rebound mightily and beneficially to the good of all mankind.'[13]

Hope from despair: Zionism was spurred by the pogroms of 1881–82 in the East and the Dreyfus trial and its aftermath in the West. To be sure, Zionism was inseparable from the fact of the Jewish religious attachment to Jerusalem and the Land of Israel, from the facts of Exile and a continuing—and continuously renewed —small Jewish presence in Palestine. These powerful realities of Jewish life built up irresistible pressure to seek shelter *there* rather than Argentina, which Herzl also suggested, or Uganda, as offered by the British Colonial Secretary, Joseph Chamberlain. Indeed, as Walter Laqueur points out, even after the horrible pogrom at Kishinev in 1903, delegates from this Russian town to the Sixth Zionist Congress joined in opposition to even exploring settling in Uganda.[14] The great emotional power of Zionism lay precisely in the fact that the project of shelter combined the dream of returning home from exile and a project of national renewal.

In his study of its intellectual origins Shlomo Avineri emphasizes that 'Zionism is not just a reaction of a people to persecution. It is the quest for self-determination and liberation under the modern conditions of secularization and liberalism.'[15] The pogroms and the Dreyfus trial notwithstanding, the period from 1815 to 1914 formed 'the most revolutionary century in history for the Jews',[16] bringing them emancipation which gave access to universities, professions, government service and politics. The 'world of growing nationalism' also brought a fundamental new problem of *identity* to emancipated Jews. 'Being Jewish no longer meant a single, sometimes heroic, decision to stand by one's conviction and not succumb through conversion to majority pressure. Rather, it now became a series of innumerable daily decisions, bringing out the difference and distinction *within equality* in hundreds of individual decisions.'[17]

Before 1914 Jews who sought only shelter—and these were the vast majority—emigrated to America. But those few who went to Palestine before America was virtually cut off in 1924 were seeking shelter *and* 'self-determination, identity, liberation'.[18]

A Land without People?

But the Land of Israel was inhabited. Jews spoke, and continue to speak, of how sparsely it was: as in Israel Zangwell's immortal formulation, 'a land without people for a people without land'. Ben–Gurion writes in his *Memoirs* of 'walking through the barren plain' in 1906, 'seeing only an occasional tribe of nomadic Bedouins . . . and a few poverty-stricken Arab villages'. This made him sure 'even then that this land would become entirely Jewish. I knew we had here the ideal opportunity to prove our mettle and ourselves as Jews. There was nothing here. It was literally a forgotten corner of the Turkish Empire and of the globe. Nobody wanted it, certainly not the Palestinian Arabs who were placidly vegetating in their poverty under the Turks.'[19]

No doubt Ben-Gurion would have responded the same way upon seeing the 'barren' hills of Bet Hakerem valley. The fact was that at the turn of the century Palestine had a population of 500,000 Arabs. How ideologically motivated were the people who saw this number as 'sparse' may be gathered by considering that the density of Arab settlement at that time was not equalled in the United States until 1950.

In a visit in 1891 Ahad Ha'am gave a perhaps more accurate picture: 'We tend to believe abroad that Palestine is nowadays almost completely deserted, a noncultivated wilderness, and anyone can come there and buy as much land as his heart desires. But in reality this is not the case. It is difficult to find anywhere in the country Arab land that lies fallow; the only areas that are not cultivated are sand dunes or stony mountains, which can be only planted with trees, and even this only after much labour and capital is invested in clearance and preparation.'[20]

But, on the other hand, why did this perception not *rule out* Jewish settlement? The element of truth contained in Ben-Gurion's perception was that it was *relatively* underpopulated and *relatively* underdeveloped. Ben-Gurion looked at Palestine and saw the thriving Land of Israel that Jews would rebuild there. Its Jewish past and future were more real to him than its Arab present. His was a modern Western vision, even more ambitious than that brought to the American frontier by the generations of settlers who pushed back the Indians. In his eyes there was indeed *nothing* there—nothing of what had once been there, nothing of what he wanted to build, nothing worth preserving, nothing that would oppose his plans.

Colonialism or Socialism?

Ben-Gurion's were Western eyes—this is the point made by Edward Said in his account of how Palestinians experienced the Zionist 'project of detail'.[21] Yet Said does not see how weak were these people he regards as having such aggressive strength, and, paradoxically, how morally and politically developed at the same time. First, they had no state supporting them. This weakness dictated their dependency on one imperial power after another. And it also, along with their commitment to socialism, immeasurably softened and simultaneously exacerbated their relations with the natives. No conquering army first subjugated the Palestinians to clear the land for the Jews and put them in the seats of power and authority. Instead, all land had to be bought and settled 'dunam for dunam, goat for goat'. Not controlling the Mandate government, the settlers had to create the Jewish Agency as a state within a state.

Even if some Zionists dreamed of transferring the Palestinians elsewhere,[22] they had no means to do so. Neither displacement nor an outright colonial conquest was physically possible. Indeed, as a project of shelter Zionism was never intended to be like the more customary practices of colonial domination and exploitation. It was also inhibited from that by demographic and ideological realities intimately connected with this people and its project: their need to liberate and normalize Jewish life, to create space for large-scale immigration, and (especially after the Second Aliyah began in 1905) to carry out settlement according to socialist principles. These facts dictated that Jews work the land themselves, that they seek to create on it their own new society alongside the existing one.[23]

Why did not socialist Zionism, in connection with the Jewish universalist tradition, sensitize the settlers to the ways in which they might inevitably harm the Arabs?[24] First, the dominant position among the settlers was held by those who chose to build socialism in Zion rather than engage in class struggle in the Diaspora. They sought to assert their national identity and their socialism at the same time. But in rejecting both Social Democracy and the Bund, they had inevitably entered into alliance with those forces in the Zionist movement they considered bourgeois and—with those forces—became dependent on great powers, tied to large Jewish capitalists, and dependent on fund-raising in the Diaspora.

Did this mean they placed national reconstruction ahead of socialism? To be sure, one of the main goals of Zionism—and one did not have to be a Marxist to believe this—was the social and economic normalization of the Jewish people by turning themselves into workers and farmers. In this task of settling people in Palestine and finding them work, socialism became a vital tool. For Herzl as well as Borochov, the founder of Marxist Zionism, the project of national renewal depended in practice on Jews becoming workers and farmers, and this was carried out by those committed to an ideology of labour and willing to train people as workers and farmers. It was as socialists then, that they were fulfilling their hopes of renewal and liberation as Jews.[25]

Such people had not the least intention to steal the country from its inhabitants. In rebutting 'the myth of Zionist "original sin"' Joseph Neyer summarizes their experience: 'The Jewish socialist pioneers drained the swampland and marshes, eliminated malaria, and irrigated the rocky soil that nobody had been able to live on for many years. The land was purchased from the Arabs at high prices with money collected mainly from the impoverished people of East Europe, who were looking for an escape from the ghettos and for an opportunity to recreate themselves through communal labour.'[26]

The people who carried out such a project did not seek to exploit a native people. 'They came prepared', as Marie Syrkin has argued, 'with agricultural studies and demographic charts demonstrating that soil reclamation in Palestine would make room for more Arabs as well as Jews and would provide a better life for both.'[27] Indeed, Zionists have claimed, this is precisely what happened: the Arab population of Palestine doubled between 1922 and 1947, and literacy levels and wages leaped as Jewish settlement increased and land purchases brought new capital into the Arab sector.

Yet consider the working class of the *Yishuv* more closely. These socialists were not, in Palestine, a modern industrial proletariat united with their fellow workers in struggle against the capitalist class. Indeed, their ideology aside, they enjoyed few of the anticipated conditions for developing *class* consciousness that brought them to Palestine. Their organized struggle to expand the *Jewish* economy pitted them against Arab labourers employed by Jews, rather than joining them with Arabs against capitalists. Not an industrial proletariat, they were in fact pre-industrial workers infused with advanced industrial ideology—and so able to organize themselves as collective farmers, cooperative road-builders and construction workers. Changing their class, these builders of the *kibbutzim* and the other undertakings of 'constructive socialism' were utopian socialists whose very utopianism was vital to the Jewish project.[28]

If all of this made a class alliance with the Arabs unthinkable, so did the relative underdevelopment of Arab society. 'The Palestinian Arabs', writes Palestinian historian A.W. Kayyali, 'formed an under-developed rural society with meagre resources and minimal effective organization, while the Zionists constituted a highly organized, well-financed movement led by a highly intelligent and determined leadership.'[29] According to many observers, Jewish leftism, one of the effects of this relative advancement, was the catalyst for the riots beginning on May Day 1921.[30] Although, as Kayyali points out, the atmosphere was already inflamed, his account confirms this: 'On the evening of 30 April, Communist pamphlets and leaflets in Hebrew, Yiddish and Arabic were distributed calling for a May Day cessation of work, a proletarian rising against the British and the establishment of a Soviet Palestine.

'On the morning of 1 May an authorized Zionist socialist (Poale Zion) demonstration clashed with an unauthorized demonstration by some fifty Communists carrying a red flag in Tel-Aviv, the Jewish quarter of Jaffa. The Communists (Bolsheviks) were eventually forced out of Tel-Aviv into the mixed Muslim and Jewish quarter of Menshiah. When the police attempted to disperse the Bolsheviks, the Muslims became involved and a general disturbance occurred, which soon spread to the other parts of the town. Wild rumours of Jewish attacks enraged the Arabs.'[31]

Arabs continued to speak of the 'Communist peril' in the 1920s and 1930s. Under such conditions of cultural distance and mutual incomprehension, the fantasy of a joint 'working-class' struggle against class oppression was bound to remain just that—a fantasy.[32]

Right against Right?

Taken together, these various features of Zionism as a project of shelter and national liberation relying on socialism, had the ironic effect of generating *greater* resistance from the native population than other colonial projects. Unlike other settlers, the Jews lacked the means to definitively suppress this resistance. From beginning to end, the national weakness which gave rise to a settler-colonial project of shelter in the first place determined some of that project's key features: the need to create a deeper and more extensive presence than other colonial settlers, coupled with an inability to establish this decisively at the outset.

Its weakness in combination with its strengths radically distinguished Zionism from every other case of national liberation and settler-colonialism. What other national liberation movement took place on *someone else's* land? What other colonial state on its day of independence proclaimed 'full and equal citizenship and due representation in all its bodies' for its natives?

Does this mean that Weizmann's famous moral assessment is correct which argues that 'the conflict between us and the Arabs is not one of right against wrong, but a conflict between two rights'? There we have presented two givens, Palestinian and Jewish, both equal, locked in struggle. How did the Jews attain equal rights to Palestine? The moral complexity of the goal of obtaining shelter appears more directly in Weizmann's qualification: 'Jewish right has precedence over Arab right because a Jewish homeland in Palestine is a question of life and death for the Jewish people, while the loss of less than one per cent of their territory is not decisive for the future of the Arabs.'[33]

A.B. Yehoshua has recently reopened the question within Israel by elaborating on this theme of a 'right to survival'. He argues that neither the moral nor the historical case has yet been made decisively 'because the country was not empty and because the residents were not eliminated or exiled.'[34] 'The question is: By what right did the Jewish people come to this country at the beginning of the century, when the Jews were an insignificant minority within the population (in 1900 there were 50,000 Jews in Eṛetz Israel and about 550,000 Arabs), and say to its inhabitants, "Your land is actually my land!"'[35]

Yehoshua rejects every appeal to either religion or distant or recent history. In the end he follows Weizmann: '*A nation without a homeland has the right to take, even by force, part of the homeland of another nation, and to establish its sovereignty there.*'[36]

But the Palestinians were not sovereign over their own homeland in the first place: they had no self-government, no army, no way of resettling those of their people who were displaced from the part of their homeland taken by the Jews. And if they had their own state, they would in all likelihood have blocked the Jewish project—for example, by restricting the flow of immigration. And so this description is also a distortive abstraction, like 'the Arabs' as used by Weizmann. Casting aside such abstractions, Flapan focuses on those hundreds of thousands of people who actually lived on the land which became a Jewish state. His corrective comment on Weizmann will serve also to clarify the weakness of Yehoshua's argument; in justifying the loss of so little territory as 'not decisive for the future of the Arabs' Weizmann 'ignored the fact that for those [Arabs] who lived in Palestine it *was* decisive.'[37]

The central moral theme thus cannot be 'a conflict between two rights' or 'one right and another'. These formulations ignore the *wrong* done to the Palestinians.

The Wrong

What indeed was the wrong? It was carried out in a thousand little non-violent details, each performed with scrupulous attention to law—from land purchases to the campaign for Jewish labour, to obtaining the Balfour Declaration, to creating the various institutions of Zionism including the Jewish Agency and the Jewish National Fund, to prevailing upon the British not to allow independence as long as the Arabs were the vast majority. In the end, violence needed to be used only to *defend* the *Yishuv* being created on the Palestinian homeland.

Since 1948 'the wrong' has come to include the displacement of Palestinians that resulted from the War of Independence, as I have indicated; but no such dispossession occurred under the British Mandate. Indeed, had the Arabs accepted partition there would have been no war and no displacement. Certainly cultivated land was purchased from landlords in Beirut and Damascus, and tenants were expelled to make way for Jewish settlers; but at least as often the pioneers built on unsettled land. 'Ideology aside', argues Syrkin, 'no Israeli of the pioneer generation will take seriously charges that his coming displaced the Arabs. His personal experience in the process of rebuilding the country testifies otherwise.'[38] Whether they intended to exploit or to rebuild, their wrong was to come in the first place with the intention of remaking Palestine into a *Jewish* land. It is certainly no greater wrong than that carried out by millions of colonists throughout the Western Hemisphere, Australia or Africa. And in the socialist and pioneering ways mentioned above—and in its determination to leave the native communities to continue their own life—Zionism was certainly far less of a wrong.

Nevertheless it was a wrong. Just as the free labour contract in capitalist society conceals more than it expresses, so did the high-minded and entirely legal dimensions of the Zionist project conceal the goal of creating *our* society on *their* land. The impossibility of an advanced Jewish society coexisting harmoniously alongside a traditionalist Arab society was rarely confronted. The Zionists determined that they would bring benefits to the Palestinians—meaning that the harm they would do would be offset by benefits of their choosing. But the key point is that the Palestinians did not determine this. Indeed, *their* collective desires and wishes were ignored from first to last, and this fact was hidden by solicitude. The Balfour Declaration assured Palestinian 'rights', but the Palestinians were not asked. All the benefits in the world, the intended gentleness of Zionism, cannot erase the fact that the transformation of Palestine was imposed on the Palestinians. Little by little, their land became a Jewish land. And the more they resisted, the more of it they lost.

In the world of mass murder in which we live, this was not an exceptional crime; all the less so considering the tens of millions of refugees that have been resettled in our century, and that even *after* 1948 Palestinians who lost their village still had the possibility of returning to another part of their homeland. It was softened by Jewish weakness and by Jewish universalism and socialism, yet only those whose daily life and historical experience has diminished their moral sensitivity would deny the wrong.

One can see the intent, the wrong, in, the very purchase of land by that remarkable agency of a homeless people, the Jewish National Fund. Land purchased was to be henceforth inalienable, owned in perpetuity by the Jewish people as a whole. The free market was used to withdraw land forever from the free market. In the deepest sense it mattered little whether it was fertile land or swamp that was to be drained, or rocky hillside, because what was being acquired in such purchases was the future claim to sovereignty. In other words, in relation to the Palestinians Zionism was a practical, systematic programme each detail of which contributed to the fact summarized so baldly by Yehoshua: 'Your land is actually my land!'

The Right

If Yehoshua's or Weizmann's moral claim is inadequate, is the project fundamentally unjustifiable? At this point it seems necessary to gain some guidance by exploring the tensions within my own identification with Israel. As a thinker and a political actor, I have absorbed the conflict, situated myself within it, made it my own until it has become the stuff of my own daily thought and action.

As a Jew I believe the creation of Israel to have been an absolute necessity. As a person committed to the liberation of all humans and opposing all forms of oppression—as a *human being*—I am convinced that the creation of Israel is a cruel act of the incredibly cruel twentieth century. 'As a Jew', 'as a human being'—such moral and philosophical double-shuffling is not the way one would prefer to talk. But the desired consistency of a single voice eludes me if I write and speak honestly today. My split consciousness, like any contradiction, can provoke reflection on its opposing terms. I do so now in order to understand better the moral, political and historical dilemma posed by the creation of Israel in Palestine.

Said's *The Question of Palestine* forcefully states one of the opposing terms of my own consciousness. He presents a restrained but moving account of the process of the creation of Israel from the Palestinian point of view. The book's wide reception reflects the same process whereby the Palestinians have finally emerged on the world stage as a *people*. Becoming a political subject they have simultaneously become a moral subject, and their homeless presence has become the most basic indictment of Israel. Said indicates some of the key features of the outlook whereby Jews have sought to legitimate the creation of Israel, from excoriating the original Arab inhabitants for refusing to tolerate them as neighbours, to emphasizing the evident fact that the Israelis have long since developed the land in *their own* image and made it *their* home.

His main purpose is to give voice to the *Palestinian* experience, to insist on the actuality of this people, originally on that land, 'with lives being led, small histories endured, aspirations felt.'[39] In doing this

Said challenges in writing the curtain of invisibility with which the West, following the Jews, has draped his people. That it has not succeeded definitively is due to the militant and continued presence of the Palestinians. By their very existence as Palestinians, a fact whose weight increases with each passing day, they constitute an irrefutable moral claim to the very land which Israeli Jews have so desperately tried to make fully and finally their own. The Palestinian refusal to go away and, on the contrary, their self-affirmation as a political entity, challenges even the most righteous Israeli logic.

What Israeli claim has equivalent moral stature to the mere presence of the Palestinians? History suggests its own answer. By 1922, five years after the Balfour Declaration and Allenby's entry into Jerusalem, the *Yishuv* numbered 85,000 Jews, perhaps 12 per cent of the total population. Later events have brought their own sense of necessity and inevitability to reflections on the growth of the Jewish project, but at this point in its history its chances of success looked highly doubtful. It was then that a nationalist antisemitic government took power in Poland, to be followed by the success elsewhere of fascism and Nazism and, ultimately, the Nazi attack on the Jews that culminated in the Holocaust. Furthermore, during these fateful years the United States virtually closed itself to immigration. Without these facts it is inconceivable that 280,000 Jews would have migrated to Palestine between 1920 and 1936, increasing the Jewish population in Palestine to 200,000 by 1933 and 500,000 by 1939. In the early 1920s only one in ten Jews was affiliated with Zionist organizations, and anti-Zionism had a legitimacy in Jewish communities that it is difficult to conceive today. During the first and second *Aliyot* (1882–1914) for example, only one per cent of the 3,000,000 Jews leaving Russia chose Palestine! In short, only antisemitism, culminating in the Holocaust, drove sufficient people to the shores of Palestine to make a Jewish state possible.

In *The Jewish Return to History*, Emil Fackenheim seeks to develop the moral claim implied by such facts. Like Yehoshua, he emphasizes neither the Biblical nor the 3000-year historical claim, neither the Balfour Declaration, nor Jewish land acquisition under the Mandate.[40] Nor does he emphasize that a generation of native-born Israelis since 1948 live by *their* hands and work in *their* factories and fields.[41] Fackenheim's argument rather reflects the tenor of my own identification with Israel by insisting that a very different fact gives most of its moral weight to the Israeli claim to Palestine. For him the key to the Jewish drive to make a home in Palestine and its fundamental moral justification, is the Holocaust.

The Holocaust imposes a dreadful choice on all Jews: to raise their children as Jews, in full knowledge of what this might mean for them or their children; or to give Hitler a second victory by ceasing to be Jews. After the Holocaust, Fackenheim argues, Israel *is* the survival of the Jewish people: the witness that the Jewish people live and will continue to live tomorrow.[42] The very existence of Israel fosters new possibilities of Jewish life and consciousness everywhere in the world, a new assertion of the right to be Jewish in a world in which this was once a fatal sin. Fackenheim draws a striking conclusion: 'At the heart of every *authentic* response to the Holocaust—religious and secularist, Jewish and non-Jewish—is a commitment to the autonomy and security of the state of Israel.'[43]

It is indeed a history of antisemitism culminating in the Holocaust that lies behind the moral and political tension leading me to think, feel, live 'as a Jew' *and* 'as a human being'. These are the missing terms in Said's analysis and, I would suggest, the reason why both Fackenheim's essays and Yehoshua's argument seem so startlingly insensitive to the very existence of the Palestinian Arabs as a people. At the same time the Holocaust is indeed the confirmation of *Israel as shelter*, not merely as image, but as reality for the Jews of the world, myself included. Even if we are unsafe there, our fate is ours.

How does it become the *moral* justification for Israel? Neither Fackenheim nor Yehoshua spells out the real argument but I know it deeply as a Jew: 'The world being what it is, we have had to go ahead to create our own state, with *our own* government and army. We have suffered too much and have received too little help to do otherwise. Hitler liberated us from the illusion that human rights would gradually extend to everyone as the world progressed, that we might place our hopes for security in the gradual growth of tolerance and decency. Out of the jungle created by the Nazis there is nothing left to do but protect *our own*. No country offered to receive Jewish victims of Nazism in the 1930s; no country tried to stop the exterminations in the early 1940s; and no country offered to receive the remnant after the war. To the wandering refugee ships of the 1930s, what other Jewish answer could there be but breaking the British blockade of Palestine? To the Holocaust, what other Jewish answer could there be but our own state? What was needed was, first, a place that would receive Jews and, second, one that would protect them. In the world after 1933, the only way for Jews to find such a place was to *take it* and *create it*. Yes, as fairly and honestly as possible. ... But building a place for our people's safety and survival took precedence over everything, even if it was at someone else's expense. Even if it led to uprooting another people. And we insist on this: any people who *had to* act as we did and *could* do so—would do the same.'

Right Was Wrong

This argument reveals a rudimentary national survival claim that is certainly the equal of any in the world today. Yet, especially in its last sentences, right becomes wrong as it states the fundamental irony of Israel: what was regarded as *national survival* for the decimated Jews was *dispossession* for the Palestinian Arabs. National liberation for one people meant, in practice, subjection and homelessness for another.

While the argument claims no more and no less than any people claim—and thus has an undeniable universal ring to it—it is regressive to the degree that its claim for national survival is made *at the expense of* another people. Right was wrong. It is perhaps better to face this than to try to simplify the moral issue, dispel the tension, ease in thought and on paper the contradiction that exists in reality. For reality has, at least since 1933, made it difficult, if not impossible, for Jews to adhere to their own universal moral values.

Did right *have to* become wrong? Laqueur cites the lonely voice of the farsighted Yitzhak Epstein, who in 1905 sought a way to deal with 'the hidden question' and further the aspirations of both of 'those two old semitic peoples'.[44] Why were not Jews able to coexist with the native Arabs, ultimately to create the bi-national state advocated by Martin Buber, Judah Magnes and, until 1948, by Hashomer Hatzair? First, the mere settling of large numbers of Jews in Palestine created an impossible situation for Arab natives, who saw themselves inevitably falling under Jewish domination, and thus for Jewish-Arab relations. Second, the very fact that Zionism was a response to antisemitism and a form of nationalism ensured that most Jews would be unwilling to accept a homeland which was not a Jewish-dominated state. The Holocaust only confirmed and deepened this. I have spoken of Zionism transforming despair with the Gentile world into hope—but could this conceivably have been a hope for the kind of mutual respect and tolerance life in the Diaspora had proven to be a cruel illusion? Could people fleeing the powerful and brutal Gentiles *there* have been expected to be gentle and sensitive to the less powerful and developed Gentiles *here*? Especially when the Jews were opposed by them, and when they had to scratch and dig just to survive? There could be no question, especially after 1933, that Jews would insist that one of the basic principles of their state would be a Law of Return. And yet unlimited immigration, which offered Jews anywhere immediate entry and protection, was fought by the Arabs out of an understandable fear of domination.

These structural tendencies mean that Laqueur's own conclusion on this point is more persuasive than all the voices and proposals for reconciliation that he cites: 'The Arab-Jewish conflict was inevitable, given the fact that Zionism wanted to build more than a cultural centre in Palestine. Nor is it certain that a cultural centre would not have encountered Arab resistance. Zionism, the transplantation of hundreds of thousands of Jews, was bound to effect a radical change in Palestine, as a result of which the Palestinian Arabs were bound to suffer.'[45]

In short, right was wrong. Creating a Jewish shelter in the world of the Holocaust meant doing a profound injury. The Holocaust consolidated the impulse to create a Jewish state at all costs, and without regard to whoever had to bear those costs as long as they weren't Jews. Survival in the world of Auschwitz: this defines the Jewish national project, and suggests the dual moral universe of victim and oppressor in which it takes place. I insist on these formulations over Weizmann's and Yehoshua's attempts to see right pitted against right, because their language seeks to mitigate the tragedy, contradiction and historical reversal at the centre of the situation. Since it has not been mitigated in reality, theory should reflect this contradiction.

Right was wrong: Israel's mode of creation and existence has effectively reversed the age-old moral universalism of the Jewish people and placed us instead in the unaccustomed role of colonial oppressor. In today's world, ironically, that universalism is embodied in the homeless Palestinian people. *Universalism* refers to what people claim *as human beings*. All oppressed peoples make their demands as human beings, asserting for themselves only what any other human being has a right to. All oppressors obfuscate such claims in order to assert special privileges over others. In the moral universe created by Auschwitz, Jews did the latter in Palestine—by demanding and creating a Jewish state which would rule over Palestinian Arabs—while firmly believing and winning support for the conviction that they were doing the first.

Right was wrong—the subtle transforming power of suffering can be seen in the moving dedication at Yad Va'ashem:

To the martyrs of the Holocaust
To the rebels of the ghettos
To the partisans of the forests
To the insurgents of the camps
To the combatants of the Resistance
To the soldiers of the allied forces
To those who saved the brethren in peril
To those valiant ones of the clandestine immigration
For eternity

Yes, heroes of the oppressed, all. We are left with no doubt of this after reading I. F. Stone's *Underground to Palestine*.[46] But for the Palestinians 'the valiant ones' brought those who displaced them. Up to what point do we condone oppression in the name of the oppressed? Surely we must accept the *Haganah*. But what about Begin's *Irgun* terrorists, committed as they too were to their people's liberation? And those who, after 1948, destroyed Arab villages in order to build Jewish villages in their place? And if so, then also the troops today occupying the West Bank? Those who invaded Lebanon and bombed the Palestinian camps? It is clear that we must draw the line. But where? Or is it a line that simply cannot be drawn?

Those who try to draw it in 1967 are distorting the past, much as are those who blame Menachem Begin. But for an understandable reason: the Jewish conscience, no different from that of other people, prefers not to face the fact of doing injustice. This is especially true because its fruits have never been finally acknowledged and legitimated.

Once again we can see the effects of historic Jewish weakness. As

Yehoshua points out, if the project had taken place early enough or decisively enough to be universally accepted, '[a]"socially conscious" film director might make a moving film about the cruelty of the Jews, just as Americans have recently been making films about the extermination of the Indians in their country.'[47] Then, in retrospect and before the few remaining victims, pangs of conscience would be possible. But the issue is very much a living one, today. Who can admit guilt under seige, in the present?

A Project of Denial

How did these abstract questions of morality enter into the concrete situation in which Zionists found themselves in Palestine? Out of their situation came a certain project; the field before them became defined by this project as so many obstacles, helps, neutral factors, possibilities and priorities. Consciousness then had to render this reading of the practical field in terms that were positive and moral. Jews have always been a people who developed and appealed to notions of universal human rights against racial, national and class rights which would threaten their own well-being or survival. This has been one of the most creative and important products of Jewish weakness. Zionism, like other revolutions and national liberation movements, has been unable to acknowledge itself as the oppressive but necessary survival project of a desperate people. The truth would violate both Jewish ethics and the demands of international support. Rather, as in Moses Hess's formulation, it must be seen as a project to advance Arabs as well as Jews.[48]

Moreover, Jews who have suffered so much and acted out of that suffering, continue to find their project under attack. He who attacks this moral project is easily seen in league with Hitler himself. Victims, especially those who are accustomed to universalizing from their particular situation, easily believe themselves to be right in any and all situations. Hence the Israeli-Jewish blindness about the Palestinians, the tendency to become righteous, and to translate the full contradictory story into a more unitary and glorious one, that of a national renaissance which advances civilization. We are presented today with the image of a democratic, innovative state, indeed a socialist state, being won from a sliver of the desert against reactionary resistance by native rulers and against the stubborn, manipulated refusal of Arab masses to *let them live*. Such an account is also necessary in a court of world opinion dominated by questions of justice.

Politically, morally, psychologically, a project of shelter undertaken by such a people under such conditions not only had to wrong another people; it had alternately to render them invisible and to hide the wrong. Lucidity became impossible, the victims' self-righteousness filled in the gaps in consciousness caused by the repression. A fundamental blind spot could not fail to accompany this particular project of national liberation. The project of shelter and national revival became at the same time a project of political, intellectual and psychological denial.

Shlomo Avineri insists that it is historically 'an utterly false claim' that 'Zionism overlooked the existence of the Arabs in what it considered to be the Jewish homeland.'[49] Yet aside from mentioning Ahad Ha'am's realistic fears, Hess's and Herzl's fantasies and Jabotinsky's racism, his own study of Zionist intellectual history is remarkably silent on 'the hidden question' that dominates Israeli life today. Avineri's journalistic comments on the debate over the West Bank within Zionism in the wake of the invasion of Lebanon are perhaps more reflective of the Israeli temperament. A major political discussion is carried on about the society's life-and-death issue— whether or not to swallow the remaining bit of Mandate Palestine— without a hint of a concern for justice, either on Avineri's part or anyone else's. The sole issue under debate '*within* Zionism, between two schools of Zionist thought' is whether asserting Israel's historic right to Gaza, 'Judea and Samaria' can be accomplished without destroying the Jewish nature of Israel by annexing over a million more Palestinians. Avineri portrays the 'sociological school of Zionism' as worried above all that annexation would 'vitiate the ideas of Zionism about a Jewish society, *avoda ivrit* [Jewish labour], and self-reliance.' He is indeed correct to emphasize 'that this is a debate within the legitimate boundaries of Zionism.'[50] The Palestinians are seen to exist, to be sure, but not as a *people*. The residents of Palestine are merely foreign elements in the Jewish state!

The 'legitimate boundaries of Zionism', it turns out, are lined with self-absorption, national egoism and callousness. They always have been. Such obfuscation of morality is a direct, necessary complement and product of the settler-colonial aspect of Zionism. And yet what else might we realistically expect? Could a Jewish state have been created if sensitivity, universalism and social justice had been the dominant principles? Had the farsighted Yitzhak Epstein prevailed, one can only wonder what refuge half a million refugees from antisemitism and Nazism would have found.

Morality and History

Today we in the non-colonial world, even Jews, can seek an understanding of these bitter facts which removes blinkers and does justice to all aspects of the project, past and present. But the blindness I speak of was shared virtually everywhere outside the Arab world until well into the 1960s. Right certainly seemed to be on the Israeli-Jewish side in the wake of the Holocaust and as long as the Palestinians were not yet speaking about their homeland with their own voice.

Certainly, as Said points out, the Palestinians have suffered and resisted from the beginning. But near-unanimous Western and Communist blindness to the existence of the Palestinian Arabs in the late 1940s was due not only to racism and imperialism, or to horror at the Holocaust coupled with a refusal to give shelter elsewhere to its survivors. Beyond these reasons, the blindness stemmed also from the fact that the Palestinians had not yet come into self-consciousness and autonomous existence *as Palestinians*. As long as the Third World had not yet created itself as a political and thus a moral force, world history remained the property of the West. The lesson is the twofold one that Marx absorbed from Hegel but which his failure to observe consistently lent such an exclusively Western cast to his writing: all oppression is *per se* evil, but it only emerges as such *historically* and not through the judgements of moralists. That is, we may register the oppression by humans of other humans, but we must also understand that this becomes an historical issue only in relation to attained levels of morality as well as the self-consciousness and deliberate struggles of the oppressed.

Casting questions of morality in historical terms may help to explain a feature of the situation which cannot but trouble Israelis. As we have seen, Yehoshua suggests that, virtually alone among colonial settlers, they have been unable to leave their crime behind in triumph, to be accounted for by later generations. The only peace Israel has ever known has been a truce imposed by its own arms. And now, the Jewish claim to a right of survival seems to pale each day further from the Holocaust, while the Palestinian right grows with each rise in their and Third World self-consciousness. Indeed, it grows with each Israeli attack on it, as the war in Lebanon showed. Designed to destroy the organized Palestinian national movement, the invasion only *increased* the visibility and the moral presence of the Palestinians. Attacking their refugee camps in southern Lebanon only made their plight more urgent for all to see. Once more we are face to face with the fundamental *weakness* of the Jewish people: undertaking our national liberation project *too late* to triumph decisively, are we not denied the luxury of remorse for the past by being so widely reviled in the present?

Seen by Jews as the state of shelter built by our own hands, Israel is now seen by most people in the world as a settler-colonial state practicing racism towards the original natives of Palestine. As such, it receives constant criticism, treatment in the United Nations not accorded any other country, and persistent 'Left' questioning of whether there *should be* a Jewish state at all. All this concern for the Palestinians reflects a strange myopia towards the traditionally universalist people who in the face of disaster dared to assert *their* national particularity. Was not the Holocaust real, after all? Have not the Jews been an oppressed people lacking a homeland for most of their national life? Is their right to a state any less legitimate than the Palestinians'? Is not this worldwide hostility just the most recent expression of age-old antisemitism?

If settling Palestine required a Jewish blind spot towards its native inhabitants, the prevailing attitude towards Israel reflects a no less significant blind spot. It points us towards another, more definitive Israeli claim to right. Israel exists. In Palestine today there exists a vital, flourishing, complex, troubled, contradictory Jewish society of nearly four million people. Children are being raised, food is being grown, goods are being produced. Alienation, strikes, exploitation exist: it *is* a society. Unlike South Africa, its citizens' well being does not (yet) depend on the colonial exploitation of *another* people. With astounding tenacity, courage and skill, this people has created shelter and built its own home on the land, and in doing so has inevitably transformed its own moral position. Very simply, they are no longer victims. The war in Lebanon confirmed how far from the present is the reality of the Holocaust, of the impotent, oppressed Jew.

Living in the Holocaust

This returns us to questions of political praxis. Is it not now time for Israel's existence to be accepted by the rest of the world, for Israelis to recognize the wrong done to another people in a time of desperation and to begin the process of accommodation and restitution? If history were only that simple! Jewish support for the war in Lebanon confirmed also how alive in the present are the ghosts of the Holocaust and of the impotent, oppressed Jew. The past cannot easily be laid to rest because it has become part of the present, a decisive dimension of Israel's material identity as a society and its relations with those Palestinians under its rule and within its reach.

On one level the Holocaust, remembered and kept alive in a thousand daily ways, is in the very fabric of Israeli life. How else was it possible to launch a war which was patently one of aggression, its real target less Beirut, Tyre and Sidon than East Jerusalem, Ramallah and Nablus, its real goal less military than political? Yet, as ever in Israel, no fact permits a single reading: what ratiocination can refute the large quantities of captured Palestinian arms, duly shipped back to Israel and put on display there? Did they not represent a threat and, as such, the direct continuation of the Arab rejection of any Jewish state from its very first day? And what country with the means to act can be expected to tolerate political hegemony and military training just over its border by a mass organization whose covenant demands its destruction?

The same ambivalence explains why the Israeli public was so willing to disregard the truce along the northern border that had been operative after July 1981 and accept the first forty kilometres of the invasion. We have seen Flapan's unusual insistence that 'the Arabs' be localized to refer to these specific people, the Palestinians directly affected by Zionism, and also the purpose of the obfuscation—to deny the wrong being done. Yet the formulation has taken on another purpose: 'the Arabs' as a whole did indeed attack the Jewish State again and again, and have remained at war with it for all these years. Could the state seeking shelter from antisemitism and the Holocaust *not see* them as the heirs of the Nazis? Never at peace, can such a state ever hope not to confuse its current enemies with its past ones? And the problem has another dimension. The hostility of the Arabs has given yet a third purpose to the formulation 'the Arabs': to legitimize Israeli expansionism and refusal to acknowledge the legitimate rights of the Palestinian people.

Taken together, these layers of meaning suggest that in some important sense the Holocaust is not over, that it has been kept alive as continuing fear and provides the moral and psychological cement for the Jabotinskyite project in the West Bank and Gaza. It has enabled Jews to reverse their basic ethical stance by demanding for themselves what they are unwilling to grant to others. In other words, the situation explains the ascendancy of Menachem Begin.

Begin's role in Israeli and Jewish life simply cannot be understood apart from his 'determination to free our people of its chief affliction —fear.' He wrote this in 1948, but his actions asserted it no less forcefully in 1982 when the situation had changed so much. 'How could we continue to live in this hostile world in which the Jew was attacked because he was a Jew—how could we go on living without arms, without a homeland, without elementary means of defence?'[51] One cannot neatly separate the writer of these words from either the prior history of Zionism or the fate of the Jewish state since 1948. As Avineri's respectful treatment of his Prime Minister reveals, Revisionism is a wholly legitimate pole of the Zionist consensus, no less valid than the other, more conciliatory pole in its passion for occupying the whole of the Land of Israel in gross violation of the rights of a million Palestinians.

Still, how is it that Begin did not disappear into the ultranationalist backwaters for which he was qualified by his terrorist past, glorification of strength, chauvinist roots, moral myopia and ideological fixation? Why did this man, and not some moderate, flexible and humane leader, become Zionism's most dominant figure since Ben-Gurion? Why has the country with the world's most effective army not found its way to peace? How has the state created to shelter victims become an aggressive occupier of other people? The Israeli conventional wisdom has it that the early bi-nationalists sought justice in relation to the Palestinians, the moderate socialists justice and strength, and the Revisionists strength; by what cruel logic of history does Jabotinskyism become dominant precisely when least needed, at Israel's time of strength, the most favourable moment for reconciliation?

For thirty years the survivor state was threatened by surrounding Arab states. And, as Israelis are fond of saying, *they* have no adjacent territory in which to become refugees: they have no place to go but the sea. Has it not been Arab intention to *exterminate* the state of Israel and its inhabitants? It is surely obvious that political energies in much of the Arab world have for a generation been diverted from social change to organizing against Israel, that ruling elites have developed a material interest in keeping alive the struggle, that the dispute between Israeli and Palestinian has become hidden in and engulfed by a far larger Arab war with this Western-sponsored and Jewish state. Issuing from the world of the Holocaust, Israel has understandably kept the Holocaust before it not only as memory and motivation, but as organizing principle and threat of annihilation by the Arab world.

Did not the new situation itself confirm Jabotinsky's vision of bitter struggle, of the need for a decisive victory of arms? If the original project of shelter became inseparable from settler-colonialism, so does the current and far more ideological project of Greater Israel draw upon Zionism's and Israel's lifelong state of siege, upon their inherent aggressiveness towards the Palestinian and their reversal of Diaspora history, in order to cultivate strength.

The stunning victory in 1967 created a new situation, one in which almost all of historic 'Eretz Israel' was in Israeli hands. Did this prompt a sense of security, a policy of peace, a reversal of the past? On the contrary, those in Israel who seek annexation have a continuing material stake in the society's *not* becoming free of the Holocaust, in not recognizing it as ended. Tempted by power, drawing on a traumatic past, they have deliberately sought a peace of occupation, not of equals. With stunning congruence and irony Begin made the Holocaust into his own moral property, defending his intransigence with the fervour of a victim still unable to find security, even today, after so much suffering. We can see why for so many Jews outside Israel their identification with the survivors continues, a generation later, to override their sense of common humanity with the Palestinians, why their key image is that of the embattled Jewish people who again and again must be defended—why, blind to their own cruelty, they even célebrate its new aggression as being long over-due. The invasion was presented as necessary to destroy the mortal threat of the PLO and protect the West Bank settlements: does not that policy draw its inspiration and justification from the original set-tlement policy? And was not *that* policy a holy one, aiming at the sur-vival of the Jewish people?

Weakness, Power, Blindness: Dialectics of Disaster?

If the original Zionist project became a settler-colonial one in order to achieve shelter and Jewish national liberation, how are we to describe Israeli aggression and intransigence now, when the Jewish state has been achieved? For Jews today, the web of Holocaust ghosts ties together what still seems to be and feels like the original project; but in fact it has changed radically in intent and meaning. The policy of non-recognition of a Palestinian national entity (which Flapan has demonstrated as central to Zionism) has become the policy of domination central to Revisionist Zionism. Given the reality of Israel, *nothing at all* can justify Greater Israel. In hearing first 'self-defence' and then 'Eretz Israel' piously and sincerely invoked to justify continued dispossession of the Palestinians are we, once more, facing one of those madnesses which have beset our century? In the West Bank what we encounter is an evil policy befitting a few reckless racists on the fringe, but scarcely appropriate for a would-be stable and democratic society. A consensus that does not see the evil has profoundly dissociated itself from moral and human realities.

At first, to consider it more precisely, we may speak of *blindness*. Even as a Jew tied to Israel and committed to its flourishing, I have sketched the systematic blindness built into the Zionist project. Without it there would have been no Israel, I have suggested. I have traced its sources and its logic. American slaveholders had a struc-tural need to see their chattels as humans who were less than human; American colonists and settlers the same need to see the Indians as barbarians. All colonial settlers, slaveholders and members of other dominating classes undertake a similar corruption of con-sciousness, and their praxis tries to make it *true*. To assert dominance, the humanity of the other must be diminished. Zionists did this, I have suggested, both to a lesser degree than and differently from others. Not only was their project undertaken out of a national survival need and out of a desire to create their own homeland by their own labour, but they asked of the Palestinians only the space to create a Jewish society alongside theirs. The accompanying Zionist blindness has thus insisted on how *few* Palestinians there were; on their *not* being Palestinians but rather on their belonging to the greater Arab nation; on their lack of significant ties to Palestine as evidenced by the fact that they failed to develop the land as the Jews would.

I have emphasized the partial success of this project: because the Palestinians had not yet developed sufficiently politically, culturally and economically to make their resistance effective, the Jews prevailed and were able to remake a portion of Palestine *according to* their blind spot. Partition, the War of Independence and Palestinian flight led in 1948 to a Jewish state with a Jewish population of 650,000 and a Palestinian population of 150,000 on 80 per cent of Mandate Palestine. This success was partial, and must remain so for as long as it is contested by the Palestinians. And they will indeed go on contesting it until Palestine exists alongside Israel.

Because it has been thus contested, Jews have paid more attention to Hitler's ghost and their profound sense of fear than to the true historical reversal represented by Israel. Yet the need, the desperation that led to Israel's creation are no longer there; we have our homeland, our place to immigrate, our army. One final piece of business remains undone—the matter of a Palestinian homeland. Blindness, imposed by necessity, shades into madness as Israel asserts a 'historic' claim to the whole of Mandate Palestine without a vital need for it, at a time when no one can any longer deny the existence of a fully conscious Palestinian national movement. 'Return' now becomes not merely the necessary emotional basis and ideological prop for a project of shelter, but a totally irrational notion in a Palestine whose people's national survival is attacked by the concept itself. I have criticized the concept of 'right against right' as being regressive for concealing the wrong done to these people; in the face of the emerging madness, however, it appears as humane.

Madness: systematic rupture with reality in areas decisive for societal functioning. To be mad in the terms we have discussed is to guide a society according to a fantasy, and to seek the violent transformation of reality in accordance with that fantasy. The 'sociological' pole of the debate described by Avineri, for all its callousness, at least respects reality. They know that 'such a state would, by necessity, remain a garrison state, in constant tension not only with its neighbours, but with 40 per cent of its own population; such a state would not be able, in the long run, to be democratic, in short it would transform the Zionist dream into a nightmare.'[52] In response, the 'territorial' pole may well fantasize another Palestinian flight, or a Jewish South Africa. In any case, it simply ignores the fundamental, underlying demographic reality by which any small society must ultimately be governed.

They do so out of hubris. They believe themselves to be too strong, stronger than anyone has a right to be, but above all stronger than they really are. Israel's army has developed into the world's best, for example; but only because it has been defending the country. The tremendous upheaval following the invasion of Lebanon reflected the newfound understanding that this was an offensive war. David had become Goliath. In our century, David may maintain high morale for long periods, but never Goliath.

Imperialist wars fought by democratic armies inevitably provoke the most subversive question: Why? Dominating the West Bank and Gaza, increasing settlements there, attempting to impose a new order on Lebanon, retaliating to provocations by a magnitude of ten, bombing the Iraqi nuclear reactor—in all these ways Israel has acted with a hubris that will only deepen the long-term and fatal resentment of its neighbours. Like the United States in Vietnam, Israel will not get its way by greater and greater escalations. Whoever is in power, Israel will remain unstable until the root Palestinian problem is resolved, not on the terrain of conquest, but of mutual respect. Having got this far by force, the Right wing certainly intends that force will make the problem go away once and for all. Yet the insoluble *existence* of the Palestinians is the remaining and the fundamental Israeli weakness. In response, like the United States in Vietnam, Israel has sought to use its advancement, its technology, its power for violence, to resolve what is and always was an irreducibly political problem. In this sense, the mad fantasies of total domination being carried out in the West Bank are rooted in weakness. The project can only create greater resistance which will require yet greater violence to suppress.

Such a dialectic of impotence and power unfolded in the spring and summer of 1982 in Lebanon: like the bombing of North Vietnam in order to change political conditions in the South, enemies were attacked in Lebanon in order to better impose domination in the West Bank and Gaza. Necessarily out of touch with its political *raison d'être*, such a policy is a recipe for ever-bloodier escalation. Israel's dazzling military power was employed with the hubris of a technologically advanced society attacking a backward and unprotected people—like the Americans in Vietnam, the Israelis controlled both sea and sky, rolled over the countryside almost at will. As in Vietnam, the real target of the assault was glimpsed only briefly, at a moment of massacre. Israel's dazzling military prowess could not spare it casualties proportionate to the worst *year* of American losses in Vietnam in only three weeks of active fighting in Lebanon.

Before and since, carrying out the policy has meant crippling the West Bank economy, harassing its universities, jailing its children, intimidating its people and encouraging them to migrate. Yet each success only leads to further problems, as the history of Zionism has shown, and continues to expose Israel's fundamental weakness in a situation of long-term conflict. From the first, creating Israel was attempting the impossible—building a Jewish state on land already populated by Arabs, in the general era of decolonization. Visiting Jews see it as a 'miracle' because it does seem as if their kin have done the impossible. Sooner or later the bill must come due, from the displaced Palestinians. In the long run, the demographics are simply overwhelming. Moreover, Israel simply does not possess the economic means for such a policy: much of its wealth is begged and borrowed. The American pipeline cannot last forever, in Amos Kenan's striking image, to sustain an Israel 'shooting with both hands while kneeling like a beggar.'[53]

Within Israel itself the bill will come due. All the devices of control[54] will only postpone the eventual Civil Rights movement that will emerge from the one-sixth of Israeli citizens whose identity cards are marked 'Arab' and who will challenge their de facto second-class citizenship. When that movement emerges both 'Israeli Arabs' and Israeli Jews can only hope general peace has already been achieved, or a bloodbath is inevitable at home. There, as on the West Bank, Israelis will have to come face to face with the Palestinian people —people dominated in their own home cannot be permanently subdued. They will rise up, generation after generation, until they are free. Repression may be effective, but not forever.

It is, in the end, a policy of impotence. Kenan's remark about the shooting beggar was anticipated by Avineri's insightful analysis of Jabotinsky's 'illusion of power'. Jabotinsky 'demanded a Jewish state in the name of strength and power, but ultimately he found himself begging for it.'[55] Pathetic weakness and an illusion of power—the real world so contradicted his fantasies as to send Jabotinsky begging to the British for a Jewish state. Power is, ultimately, social and political. And, we may add, môral. A genuine social basis does not exist for the permanent suppression of the Palestinians. Indeed, annexation without emigration and current development policies will eventually transform them into a landless proletariat, perhaps even a majority within the Jewish state.

We, the Jews, are the proof of the staying power of a beleaguered people. Why should we expect any less of the Palestinians? We are ourselves proof that even genocide, carried out, cannot finally accomplish its goal. Short of using the Bomb—where, on whom?—Israel can never definitively dominate the Palestinians. And, as Israelis know, they need only lose once and they are lost. This is their weakness.

But let us suppose for a moment that the future continues present trends. The Jewish state will prevail militarily without righting the original wrong and by committing yet further wrongs. Stalinism, we must not forget, *did* the impossible—it 'succeeded' in creating 'socialism in one country'. But it did so by creating a deformed society, maintained by heroic effort, violence, lies, the corruption of language and thought. Its apologists were everywhere, singing its praises, denying its crimes, defending it as a besieged society against its enemies overseas even as half its own people were becoming enemies. Will Israel too 'succeed' by 'creating facts', prevailing over all external and internal enemies while itself becoming deformed as Avineri warns, by becoming unworthy of the history of the Jewish people? If this happens—and so many trends point in this direction—the bill will come due internally, unnoticed. A universalist people of victims converted into a warrior society using its most traumatic memories to justify dominating a less developed people? Hitler's ghost will have the last laugh.

Recognition

How can a single effective step be taken away from this grim prospect and towards an alternative? Israelis themselves have dramatically advanced that process since the invasion of Lebanon. First, by the unprecedented act of creating a mass anti-war movement in only three weeks, with the front only forty miles away—in a country with a citizen army for whom every previous war had been experienced as one of national self-defence. Second, by organizing, after continuing such agitation all summer, what must be proportionally the largest protest demonstration ever to take place anywhere—perhaps one in every ten people in the country—after the massacre of Palestinians in West Beirut. To those who sensed the Israelis as caught in an iron logic of rightward regression, these massive protests taught an opposite lesson—a Jewish rejection of aggression and oppression, a reaffirmation of universalist morality over narrow nationalism. It brought back to life within Zionism, within Israeli history, the many alternative voices who have sought mutual respect, who understood the original wrong.

However, it will take a historic breakthrough to genuinely reverse the catastrophic course I have just sketched. This breakthrough would be immeasurably advanced by a single, simple step: mutual recognition of each other by the Palestinians and Israel.

This political step is resisted on both sides not just tactically, but because it would utterly transform the conflict and its terms. It would break the seemingly iron logic I have sketched. It would amount to a fundamental moral and intellectual shift. For Palestinians it would mean acknowledging that Israel exists, and so has a right to exist. For Israel it would mean an end to denial: acknowledging, for the first time, the reality of the Palestinian people, *as a people*, and thus accepting the legitimacy of their claims to a state of their own in Eretz Israel. Each recognition would amount to a drastic epistemological shift, redefining not only 'Palestine' and 'Eretz Israel' but the way each people sees the land. It could no longer be *ours* lived on or claimed by *them*, but would perforce have to become *both of ours*. Which means the reality of the present would replace the loss and trauma of the past and the fantasies of the future.

Mutual recognition, followed through to the end, would end up by transforming both parties. Israelis would be admitting a wrong done to another people in pursuing their survival right. A different Israel, less egocentric, less self-righteous, would slowly emerge from such a recognition. Self-absorption with Jewish suffering would give way before the *present* of Palestinian suffering. The Palestinians on their side would become a different people, more conciliatory and more realistic about the shape of a final settlement.

Is this an 'epistemological politics' divorced from the material struggle? Not at all. Indeed, confronting material reality—knowing what it is, living with it—is the first premiss of any effective politics of liberation. In this case, both sides have become deluded by ghosts, ideology, fantasy. It is becoming a mad situation, moving towards a series of breaks with reality which must be reversed for catastrophe to be avoided as well as justice to be done. For Israelis the motive is the long-term security of their society; for the Palestinians their urgent need for a homeland before it is too late.

Political praxis can and should work towards these goals. Within Israel this means, among other tasks, reversing the separation of Jews and Arabs and enlarging the slender strands of dialogue and cooperation that have begun. Elsewhere, it also means dialogue, dialogue, and more dialogue: two communities searching for a common language. Simply coming together face to face subverts the growing climate of madness.

Just as I have written this *as a Jew*, these steps should proceed with absolute clarity about the respective roles of Jews and Palestinians, who cannot help but be antagonists in such encounters. Jews who sympathize with the suffering of Palestinians today to the point of losing touch with their own history of suffering are not authentic candidates for dialogue. Their universalism has itself become a form of denial. Clarity about the role of outsiders is also necessary. For a non-Jewish or non-Arab group to be one-sidedly 'pro-Israel' or 'pro-Palestinian' is to court sycophancy rather than justice. In this situation the tradition of social conscience usually appreciated and advanced by the Left can only lead to a course which respects *both* peoples and *both* of their rights to national self-determination, and understands the pressing need for each to recognize the other. The authentic role for the Left is as intermediary—vital, and almost never performed.

For Jews, I am speaking of tearing apart the web of Holocaust ghosts in which we have become trapped. Can we not accept the fact that *we have survived*, and that Nazism has been defeated? The

Holocaust has *happened*, it is over, and Israel and the Jewish people are in no danger of re-experiencing it today. Antisemitism is real and everywhere, but in most places it is a marginal hostility, not serious danger. Can Jews not be disliked and slurred as Jews without instantly invoking Hitler? If so, the Jewish Doomsday vision could possibly give way to an intelligent policy which assesses the short-and long-range strengths and weaknesses of the Israeli position in the Middle East, and of the Jewish position elsewhere.

The Holocaust teaches that evil is done by ordinary human beings trapped in extreme situations. It is always accompanied by great claims of righteousness. For any of us, whoever we are, to accept as a lesson of this study that *we* can commit such evil should be a bit humbling. For Jews, to truly admit what has been and is being done in our name to the Palestinian people should give real pause for reflection.

If it is giving pause, inside Israel, it is because the attack on Lebanon has amply demonstrated that the righteous quest for any security not founded on mutual respect is an impotent one. The ultimate irony is that each violent step by Israelis only underscores this impotence. And so, in the Jewish mind, the Holocaust continues —and must in one sense genuinely continue until the breakthrough which assures Israel's genuine long-term safety. In the meantime, the Palestinians will not go away. Whether in Nazareth or Ramallah, they are promising themselves that *this* time they will not flee or be driven or frightened off, that the primary element in their strategy is to remain where they are, in Palestine or near its borders. It is an important sign that the massive exodus that followed the massacre at Deir Yassin did not repeat itself a generation later, after the massacre in West Beirut.

In relation to Israel, then, our final hope is a political *praxis* so directed that Israelis and Jews may finally and fully comprehend that this other people *exists*. The danger is that Israel may already have become so wedded to the Holocaust, as continuing trauma and moral justification, as to be unable to notice that its major enemy today is only a suffering, displaced people demanding shelter—like the Jews who came to Palestine.

7
Technological Madness

'Long live death!' Nuclear holocaust, our century's ultimate evil and madness, is its decisive revocation of Reason and Progress. Pervasive yet invisible, it hovers over the earth at every moment. How remarkable that, compared with the secrecy and denial surrounding the great catastrophes we have studied, at this very instant every one of us is *aware* of being targets of nuclear weapons. 'Even the Nazis', writes Richard Falk, 'felt the necessity to keep the "Final Solution" hidden from their citizenry.'[1] Every one of us is conceived, born, and raised to adulthood at the brink, fated to make sense of our life within this state of terror. We know with certainty that 'the machinery of destruction is completed, poised on a hair trigger, waiting for the "button" to be "pushed" by some misguided or deranged human being or some faulty computer chip to send out the instruction to fire.'[2]

And yet we refuse to know this. As the effect of the Vietnam anti-war movement demonstrates, ruling policies are crippled where significantly large numbers of people fully and directly face such knowledge. And, manifestly, this has not yet happened anywhere with regard to nuclear war. We do not and cannot know, without some undoing, without a special effort of intellect, imagination and feeling. Because it is so politically and psychologically shattering to know, great forces within and around us conspire to hide it. Yet if the problem is psychological and political, it is also epistemological and ontological.

The threat remains hidden because of its very nature. The threat is indeed possibility, not fact; it is threat, not reality. In this sense we live at the brink, but we *live* there, leaning for our daily functioning on all that is solid and stable, necessarily repressing the danger.

We dance on the edge of a cliff. Jonathan Schell has, hopefully, dispelled all denial about what lies on the other side. 'Bearing in mind that the possible consequences of the detonations of thousands of megatons of nuclear explosives include the blinding of insects, birds, and beasts all over the world; the extinction of many ocean species, among them some at the base of the food chain; the temporary or permanent alteration of the climate of the globe, with the outside chance of "dramatic" and "major" alterations in the structure of the atmosphere; the blinding in ten minutes of unprotected people who go out into the sunlight; a significant decrease in photosynthesis in plants around the world; the scalding and killing of many crops; the increase in rates of cancer and mutation around the world, but especially in the targeted zones, and the attendant risk of global epidemics; the possible poisoning of all vertebrates by sharply increased levels of Vitamin D in their skin as a result of increased ultraviolet light; and the outright slaughter on all targeted continents of most human beings and other living things by the initial nuclear radiation, the fireballs, the thermal pulses, the blast waves, the mass fires, and the fallout from the explosions; and considering that these consequences will all be added to as our knowledge of the earth increases, one must conclude that a full scale nuclear holocaust could lead to the extinction of mankind.'[3]

This is the worst threat. Yet as Edward Thompson has warned, such war might take place so as to 'not necessarily extinguish all mammalian life, unless the globe's ozone layer was irreparably punctured. What this would destroy would be Northern civilization and its economic and societal life-support systems. The survivors (one might suppose) would then be exposed to waves of plague and famine; great cities would be abandoned to rats and to rattish genetic mutants. People would scatter to un-contaminated lands, attempting to reinvent a sparse economy of subsistence, carrying with them a heavy inheritance of genetic damage. There would be banditry: fortified farmsteads, fortified monasteries, fortified communes; and a proliferation of strange cults. Eventually there might be the re-emergence of petty city states, nudging toward new trade and new wars. Or this scenario could be all wrong. Advanced economies might survive, relatively undamaged, in the Southern hemisphere: Australia, Argentina, South Africa. After an interval for stench and plague to die down, these might come back, with their muskets, to colonize European tribes: perhaps to fight over the spoils; perhaps to establish one superpower's world dominion.'[4]

Whichever scenario we choose, the brutal fact is that we *live at the brink*. This is a radically disorienting state of being, making it impossible to hold a consistent point of view towards the threat or the world that is threatened. Nuclear war is, after all, *beyond* this brink, in the future. Unlike economic crisis or oppression, it can be encountered, understood and resisted only *before* it happens. Yet on the brink everything seems solid and stable, as it has always been. When we have struggled our way to a sense of normality about it, those who sound the alarm can easily seem disruptive and hysterical to us. Beyond such ontological equivocation, built into being-on-the-brink, we find it literally impossible to conceive of the nothingness that might follow an all-out nuclear war. When we seek to reflect on the extinction of the human context in which alone all things have meaning, writes Schell, we are in 'a predicament that exists not because of a psychological failing or the inadequacy of the human mind but because of the actual nature of the thing that we are trying to think about.'[5] This issue is not only our death, difficult enough to imagine, but also a 'second death' in which *nothing continues*.

By themselves these epistemological, ontological and psychological problems of comprehension make it difficult enough to face the nuclear threat. Yet politicians, military leaders and theoreticians do not illuminate the situation, but further becloud it by a sustained project of denial. They plunge themselves and their citizens into a fog: sowing illusions, corrupting language, manipulating the threat from the Enemy, and banishing the most subversive force, normal human feeling, from political discussion.

The Fog of Denial

Nuclear policy rests on the illusions described by Robert Jay Lifton: of foreknowledge, of preparation, of protection, of stoic behaviour under nuclear attack, of recovery, of rationality.[6] Without these articles of faith the nuclear establishments would be unthinkable—yet they are nothing more than self-deceptions. As Lifton has pointed out, the nuclear world is also a world of linguistic amelioration, whose strategists speak of a 'deterrent' rather than of the threat of unacceptable destruction, of a 'window of vulnerability' rather than an alleged Soviet advantage in one single area of the overall mutually catastrophic arsenals. Its thought is further corrupted by terms like 'civil defence', 'superiority' and 'inferiority', 'nuclear exchange', 'escalation', 'nuclear yield, 'counterforce', 'megatons'. 'Quite simply', writes Lifton, 'these words provide a way of talking about nuclear weapons without really talking about them.'[7]

Denial is a prerequisite for entering into this universe and its accompanying style of thought. Its stupefying effect is evident on a tour through earlier strategic logic, for example the writings of Herman Kahn. Presented neatly, with great regard for precision and clarity, his analysis is in fact premissed on a strictly paranoid view of the Soviet Union's relentless drive for world conquest.[8] On the other hand, Kahn never presents American purposes as anything but peaceful or defensive, even though he speaks with telling American hubris about avoiding pursuing 'an *undue* superiority in our overall strategic posture.'[9] He minimizes the consequences of nuclear war,[10] noting dismissively that nuclear weapons were used at Hiroshima and Nagasaki 'on a relatively minor scale at the end of the Second World War'.[11] From such premises Kahn *reasons* about nuclear war. We may disgree with his assumptions and seek to read his work critically, but to enter into his argument is little by little to become confused and beclouded by it.

To study nuclear war theory is to risk radically losing one's way in a process of reasoning which is impermissably abstract. Certainly all systematic thought must proceed by abstracting from a complex and shifting reality those aspects of it deemed decisive for explaining the area under study. But *this* abstraction breaks with the very human concerns which the theory claims to be protecting. Medical abstraction, for instance, returns again and again to its assigned task—to heal, to cure. Wherever they allegedly begin, the scenarios of nuclear abstraction terminate again and again not in plans for protection or disarmament but in visions and plans—or just threats—of overwhelmingly massive destruction. Thinking of our own potential annihilation is possible only by leaving behind our normal human concerns and losing ourselves in the ultimate neutral 'objectivity'. This 'objectivity' is central to the logic of exterminism. It is a deformed objectivity, one so total, that we—fearing, feeling, caring—cease to stand behind or shape it. The 'objectivity' which contemplates our destruction has suspended its ties with its subject.

Kahn's many tables and charts reflect reason cut off from reality. His analysis is convincing in its portrayal of a series of remote, abstract possibilities only because it has separated itself from concrete history, policy, purposes, politics and people. Adrift in a relentlessly logical world without the usual moorings, benumbed and confused by its appearance of rigour and science, some readers will sooner or later succumb, for example helplessly granting logic to Kahn's inherently absurd statement: 'We preserve the peace today by the threat of war.'[12]

To accept this as rational discourse is to surrender to the fog. And yet, as a voice of policy, it commands the capacity to recreate the fog as quickly as it can be dispelled, to generate passivity and deference, if not assent. For Kahn's writings are *real*: they refer to a world that exists, the world of nuclear weapons and projected nuclear war. Within that world one can argue how much is enough, whether Mutually Assured Destruction is stable or whether a first-strike capacity is needed, whether new bombers or missiles are truly necessary. Under Reagan, for example, policymakers have spoken and acted with renewed commitment to the fact that Japan 'not only survived but flourished after the nuclear attack',[13] to the idea that the greatest danger to the US is not nuclear war but American vulnerability to 'the Soviet drive for dominance',[14] and above all, to the idea of surviving and winning a nuclear war. But their premises were largely shared by their most articulate opponents among former policymakers, such as Robert MacNamara and Cyrus Vance, who questioned not the threat in general—to which they themselves had made contributions—but only its intensification under Reagan. Such a debate does not challenge the premises themselves of the *need* for nuclear weapons, of the Soviet threat, or of the stability of a world with 50,000 warheads. Its 'doves' themselves sustain the fog, largely unable to express authentic fears and needs for security, incapable of penetrating the usual absurd arguments about security that pass for intelligent discourse, lacking a clear conceptual basis from which to challenge nuclearism itself.[15]

As a Father: The Only Possible Objectivity

Where do we find such a basis if denial befogs seemingly every level?

Stultified and immobilized, where are we to locate firm conceptual moorings from which to address it effectively? The answer begins as an existential one: to leave the suffocating plane of abstraction and to address the threat from where we *stand* —not as neutral minds, ceding power to the unanswerable logic of strategists' obsessions, but as living, breathing people, concerned for survival. Just as clarity demanded that I approach the question of Israel and the Palestinians as a Jew and as a human being committed to social justice, so do I approach the threat of nuclear destruction similarly engaged—this time as a father.

To think of my daughters, even for a moment, dispels the fog. No illusions, no impermissibly abstracted reasoning, no language of denial, can resist my love for them, my urge to raise them to become healthy, happy human beings, to provide for them a world in which they can flourish. This, my primary engagement in life, returns me to the clarity I tend to lose amidst the logic of exterminism. I love, I feel, I care, I desire—I live. And all of this commits me, commits my mind and heart. When I face the nuclear threat it fills me with pain: the pain of impotence and terror and rage. The point is not just that the world may end and we may end; that in a stroke, without warning, everything we do or see or feel can be shattered. Neither is it that the 'second death' would simultaneously remove the entire surrounding 'web of institutions and arrangements necessary to the function of any human group.'[16] These contemplated horrors lie ahead, beyond the brink. Other horrors mark the *present*, whether or not the bomb is dropped. Lifton speaks of 'the ubiquitous presence of the bomb at some level of people's minds.'[17] The bomb is with us today, every day. As a father, I cannot *be* a father, because my girls are not safe and I cannot make them safe. Lifton speaks tellingly of 'the radical new situation between parent and child. Undermined now in that relationship is the fundamental parental relationship: that of "family security", seeing the child safely into some form of functional adulthood. The parent must now doubt his or her capability of doing just that.'[18]

To feel one's pain as a parent is difficult if only because of the structures of denial which pervade our world. But not to feel it for any longer than called for by the needs of daily functioning and psychic balance is to risk living in a permanent state of repressed rage, impotence, and passivity. It is to allow no expression and discharge of the pain, permitting both it and our love for our children to be surrounded and contaminated by futility and resignation.

If, as an 'objective-minded' citizen I am likely to be lost in the fog, as a father I can *see*. Why? because as a father I am committed first to life, and then to the betterment of life. My point of view reveals reality *in a certain light*, but it is the light which gives me the basis for judging the nuclear threat. Such *biased* objectivity is the only possible meaning of historical objectivity. As Herbert Marcuse argued, authentic thought begins with a *value judgement*: a commitment first to human survival, and second, to the pacification of existence. Without such commitment there is little point in talking. Lenin said, following Napoleon: 'First you commit yourself, and then you *see*.'

If our starting point is therefore an existential stand, that is in turn made possible by political praxis. The anti-nuclear movement draws upon such feelings and commitments, but it also gives them definition. My feelings as father must remain private and personal—*subjective*—until enough people have acted publicly and politically to make them objective. What I feel privately, receiving political legitimation, thus receives its philosophical legitimation. Feelings find their voice, make their claims, assert their truth.

Madness

And what I say as a parent is that the nuclear strategists and theorists, as well as the system of exterminism they live by, are mad. For some time now it been clear that every 'advance' on one side will be, must be, met and even exceeded by the other, that planning on each side already anticipates this race, that proliferation is proceeding apace, that the drive for such 'security' only increases the general insecurity by multiplying the threat of destruction. In this world of over 50,000 nuclear warheads, a random accident could begin the process that destroys civilization. To continue to produce and develop such weapons in such a situation is madness. To seek to fight and win a nuclear war is madness. To justify, rationalize, and accept the situation is to become lost in the web of that madness. To do anything but assert a contrary direction is to live by, and perhaps to die by, this madness.[19]

Madness? One can seek the evidence in the intention of mutual

total destruction, in the preparation for it, in the widespread acceptance, calmly and without protest, of a situation which makes us all
hostages. Certainly madness is afoot in a civilizational project one of
whose main goals, and whose tendency, is to destroy civilization
itself. Thompson's category of 'exterminism' takes us beyond questions of means and ends, of cost and effectiveness—to the brutal fact
that for a long time now human life itself has been put in question by
the people and technology who ostensibly serve it. Ours is the first
generation to live in such terror. As we face it we can describe only as
mad the undeniable fact that, as time goes by, the preparations only
increase to destroy civilization itself.

Looking at America from the outside, Thompson concludes a discussion of immediately pre-Reagan American pronouncements on
preparing to fight limited nuclear wars with the comment: 'If all this
sounds crazy, then I can only agree that crazy is exactly what it is.'[20]
And what of the Reagan project to fight and win an all-out nuclear
war? Could we look in at our planet from elsewhere, free from the
fog of denial, we would surely judge the situation as one in which the
human race itself has gone mad.

Arguments for Normality

Even if we temporarily dispel the fog of denial, a number of factors
mitigate, and even undermine, our use of such a term as 'madness'.
It is elusive, this madness, difficult to glimpse for more than shifting
moments because so normal, so intrinsic to our world. We are accustomed to living amidst awesome technology, forces beyond
human control, in an absurd world which supports and prepares
war, which accepts class and race violence, poverty in the midst of
plenty, and an unrelenting and ferocious assault on the planet. Is not
the threat of nuclear war just one more normal absurdity? Also, we
are accustomed to sober rational leadership—surrounded by
scientific-minded advisors responsive to the slightest shift in the
public mood. Some of them may indeed be slightly unhinged; but
mad enough to use nuclear weapons? As astute politicians, even the
most obsessive ideologues among them—such as Reagan, Begin, or
Thatcher—show themselves aware of limits beyond which they may
not tread. The absolute power and patent madness of a Hitler or a

Stalin still seems to belong to a different historical conjuncture. Lyndon Johnson, for example, restrained American involvement in Vietnam even as he presided over its escalation; indeed, he showed enough political realism to withdraw personally from political life rather than seek victory where that had become impossible.

Moreover, ours is a civilization of undreamed-of technical power. Who could imagine that in a given day a single individual could rise and prepare for the day helped by an array of mechanical servants; could use the power of hundreds of horses simply to go to work; could there engage in technical tasks commanding or operating forces that would boggle the minds of all previous generations? Not to mention the ability to step into a mighty machine that would cross the ocean almost instantly. Directly and indirectly the ordinary citizen of advanced societies today commands more power than the mightiest kings of old—and scarcely knows it. Is the power to destroy civilization, and the living threat to do so, an aberration in a world of such power?

At the same time technological society itself holds its individuals at a remarkable psychological, physical and political distance from the use of this power. We 'push buttons'—this is the meaning of much of our power. Nuclear war 'may be conducted in a sterile atmosphere of computers, consoles, and dimly lit launch-control facilities, far from its intended victims, whose suffering cannot be perceived.'[21] Then too the situation is normalized by the fact of historical drift: the atomic bomb was originally developed in response to what was a potential mortal threat to the Allies, and was used after that threat had passed only to end the world's bloodiest war. There followed a step by step development towards the present danger, which is itself unthinkable outside the context of American-Soviet hostility. Each side perfects its ability to destroy not civilization, but *the other side*. In the Hobbesian world of relations between states real danger begets a dangerous response, in a terrifying but understandable spiral.

Objective Madness

And yet, no matter how much the cumulative logic of our history may mitigate and normalize it, the situation is indeed mad. This may appear with complete clarity only when it is too late, at the moment when the bomb goes off. Then, in that instant left as Doomsday sweeps over us, we will speak without qualifications. Some of us will say as our last words, the earth's last words: 'They're mad!' Precision will no longer matter, but for precision's sake it would be better to say: 'They *were* mad!' Since an accident of miscalculation or technical malfunction is as likely to produce the fatal blast as human rage or calculated policy decision, the correction appropriately refers us from that future instant to the web of actions and structures of the present. For it is *this* situation, the system of exterminism, which rests the entire fate of the earth on something as absurd as radar misreading a flight of geese for an incoming missile attack.

Much of the debate against current policy uses the concept of madness again and again. And not merely in hyperbolic statements by impassioned peace movement leaders: Robert Scheer's interviews with such erstwhile former pillars of the nuclear war establishment as Cyrus Vance, Paul Warnke, Herbert York, Robert Mac-Namara and Hans Bethe reveal a pervasive and explicit emphasis on the madness of recent American nuclear planning. Terms like 'crazy', 'insane', 'mad', 'demented' and 'deranged' abound in intelligent discourse.

Scheer's interviews suggest that such men use the concept of madness on the level of casual speech, as moral judgement and political indictment, but then discard it when moving on to sustained and serious political analysis. We have seen, however, that used seriously and carefully, 'madness' is indeed one of the primary categories for understanding the twentieth century. We have also seen that when speaking of the functioning of societies 'madness' has staying power as a technical term. Its main intent, after all, is the imputation of radical irrationality, and social behaviour is generally, if implicitly, understood as *rational behaviour*. 'Serious' discourse usually predetermines the range of its results by excluding from analysis of politics and society any such decisive concepts which might threaten to illuminate its grotesque underside.

This study has gone against the various mainstreams by not discarding 'madness' after its initial use and insisting instead that such use contains significant insights which must be mined. If the term *irrational* is woefully inadequate to describe such phenomena as the Holocaust, Stalinism, and the American war in Vietnam, the same holds true for the universe of nuclear weapons. As before, we require a more extreme term than 'irrational', one that conveys something qualitatively different from being simply contrary to reason, more than a lack of realism about goals or a deep discrepancy between goals, means employed and results obtained. As before, we need the very term which indicates behaviour or a tendency towards behaviour exhibiting systematic rupture with reality in decisive ways. And as before, we find that the term recurs in casual discourse about the phenomenon for good reason. Madness *is* afoot in the development of the nuclear world: how else to describe a project of our civilization one of whose main goals is to exterminate that civilization itself?

To speak of it as mad is not to focus primarily on the mental health of those operating the system. However obsessed, they generally demonstrate (as I have already suggested) political intelligence, technical and strategic awareness, and a sense of limits. Scheer argues that the American neo-hawks in the Reagan administration 'are not lunatics who want to destroy the world. They are neither stupid nor insensitive and they know what nuclear war would do to the people they care about.'[22] But in using 'madness' to describe the Holocaust, Stalinism and the American war in Vietnam we focused less on psychology than on policy. The notion of a systematic rupture with reality was used to understand political purpose and practice. I have argued there that madness characterizes our century as an *objective social process*. Therefore to understand the structures of our nuclear predicament we should begin with, as Lifton says, 'its objective social madness, its insanity of consequences.'[23]

The system of exterminism deserves this description because, as Thompson argues, the economy, polity and ideology of each nuclear society 'thrust it in a direction whose outcome must be the extermination of multitudes but this will not happen accidentally (even if the final trigger is "accidental") but is the direct consequence of prior acts of policy, of the accumulation and perfection of the means of extermination, and of the structuring of whole societies so that these are directed towards that end.'[24]

As we explore the continuum of sanity and madness we may argue over how to evaluate various aspects of the project to create and explode the bombs that decimated Hiroshima and Nagasaki; we may debate whether the pursuit of nuclear power itself oversteps fundamental limits of sanity; and we may explore whether or not the creation of any single nuclear warhead can be termed mad. Thompson, however, is correctly concerned with the system of exterminism as a whole, as it threatens us today, 'whose institutional base is the weapons-system, and the entire economic, scientific, political and ideological support-system to that weapons-system—the social system which researches it, "chooses" it, produces it, polices it, justifies it, and maintains it in being.'[25] It is the system that is mad because it is deliberately organized to court death on a total scale. It is mad because it breaks with the basic premiss of all human life, namely survival itself. All other fears, hopes and needs—no matter how crazy—take place on the prior ground of survival. To jeopardize life on any scale without compelling reason, and to do this while denying that one is doing it, is mad. Yet this is the terrain on which the development of the nuclear world takes place.

Let me emphasize that I am speaking once again of a drastic and systematic rupture with reality. In this case the reality being ruptured with is life itself. Or perhaps I should say reality itself. The rupture is one which replaces it with nothing else—neither an Aryan-centred extermination camp universe; nor an amalgam of terror, forced labour and achievement labelled 'socialism'; nor an artificial fantasy-republic of South Vietnam. Each of these 'at least' projected some form of success as its goal, no matter how genocidally mad. Preparation for nuclear war is indeed the ultimate act of madness—the intention to destroy civilization. Those who guide the world towards it make plans and develop the means to break with the world in the most decisive, most fundamental way. Yet it is the simplest way: to destroy.

Self-Defence?

But each side's missiles are manifestly aimed, as I have said, at *each other*. Isn't the heart of the system of exterminism the terrifying fact that each side develops and deploys its missiles to intimidate the other but not to use them? What is the meaning of this incredible instrumental logic that claims to build weapons for a purpose other than their use? Doesn't each side augment its arms in conflict, out of a genuine fear of the other? In asking the questions we must stress that there is a real threat on both sides. Indeed, unlike the bombing of Hiroshima and Nagasaki or the American motivation for founding the Strategic Air Command, the Soviet-American nuclear confrontation seems to drive each side to respond to the other. Can one ignore that there is genuine fear in the voice of the nuclear planners on each side of the system of exterminism? The Hobbesian universe between states is, after all, one without recognized international authorities and rules to which nations submit. Therefore a threatened society has no appeal but to its own physical force. Has not such a situation, given the very existence of nuclear weapons, set off an arms race in which fear gets the better of enlightened national interest?

Perhaps. But such an analysis ignores first of all the decision-making which has created the nuclear world at every step.[26] As Alan Wolfe points out, far from being a genuine response to an actual Soviet threat, obsessive American anti-communism has carried the day politically for *domestic* reasons.[27] The 'missile gap' of 1960 was no more genuine than the 'window of vulnerability' of 1980. As we shall see, it is not the *actual* Soviet threat that prompts American policymakers to seek to fight and win a nuclear war, but a process generated within American society. And the endemic American inability to think of the Soviets as equals[28] stems less from fear than from a continuation of the hubris that marks postwar America. Moreover, to speak of exterminism is to suggest a *single* system: the nuclear establishments on each side, for all their antagonism, depend above all on each other for their own justification. Rudolf Bahro goes so far as to speak of a *conspiracy* between the two sides, who 'mutually condition, reinforce and stabilize each other.'[29] Today this means, paradoxically, that American and Soviet nuclear warriors are each other's own strongest allies, and, as the anti-war movement has begun to understand, they are aligned together against the people they hold hostage in every country. Thompson concedes that the accident, the chance irrationality which would explode their weapons certainly depends on a collision. 'But such collision cannot be ascribed to accident if it has long been foreseen, and if both agents have, by deliberate policy, directed themselves upon an accelerating collision course.'[30] If it happens, the Third World War will have been *intended* because planned for and undertaken for years with full fore-knowledge of the consequences.

Above all, we must remember, as Daniel Ellsberg points out, that 'again and again, generally in secret from the American public, US nuclear weapons have been used . . .'[31] Not detonated as at Hiroshima and Nagasaki, but 'in the precise way that a gun is used when you point it at someone's head in a direct confrontation, whether or not the trigger is pulled.' Ellsberg documents no fewer than twelve separate occasions from 1945 to 1982 in which American leaders directly threatened potential or actual antagonists with nuclear war. In each case it was done for reasons of policy, from a position of nuclear superiority. Thus American nuclear policy is not merely a fearful response to the Soviet threat: Americans *use* the bomb as the ultimate threat, as Carter did in 1980 to carry out state policy in the Middle East.

So used, nuclear holocaust is present and thriving in our world — 'Long live death!' — and not merely kept guarded on the shelf, a remote possibility in the event of a Soviet attack or a mistake. With what did Truman threaten the Soviets by instituting the Strategic Air Command in 1946, or Eisenhower threaten the Chinese in 1953, or Kennedy and Khrushchev threaten each other and the whole world in 1962, or Nixon and Kissinger threaten the North Vietnamese between 1969 and 1972?[32] And why, after all, will not Washington abandon the ultimate threat and foreswear first use of nuclear weapons? Aggressive policy is at stake, not mortal fear. In such a situation talk of fear, of self-defence, of a Hobbesian universe, functions to disguise active planners as helpless agents.

Postscript to Madness: Nuclear Power

The development of nuclear power represents perhaps a different point along the continuum of sanity and madness. But by now its threats are well known: of accident, of volatile wastes, of environmental and human danger. The fierce determination to go forward after Three Mile Island demonstrated that accidents *can* happen reflects at the very least a dangerous dissociation from the threats. And once again, an intentional one, chosen under the veil of 'necessity' because of the lenses through which reality appears to those who choose. In their voices as they reassure us, we can hear their distance from flesh and blood, from concerns about human health, their health, their children's health: a litany of 'safety' which convinces no one but those who are already indifferent to elemental well being. This indifference is central to the pathology. Is 'madness' hyperbole when describing these people and their passion—their frightening combination of blandness and desperation, their fixation on yet more domineering and complex technology as the only answer, their willingness to subordinate everything, even life itself, to productivity? Perhaps, if we cannot see their madness, it is only because we share so many of its assumptions ourselves. And how could we not? Their world is ours as well.

The Madness of Victims

Both policy and the system's drift point towards the explosion that is planned for, prepared, expected, politically justified but has not yet occurred. Faced with it, no wonder that as potential victims we follow our politicians and strategists into the fog. We choose to dissociate ourselves from this reality and our fears about it in order to meet the demands of daily life. We choose the fog of dissociation, abstraction and illusion as an alternative to facing and feeling the actual terror in which we live. As Lifton points out, psychic numbing blocks out the feelings we have about such a threat, and yet such hiding from our fears further endangers us. 'The degree of numbing of everyday life necessary for individual comfort is at odds with the degree of tension, or even anxiety, that must accompany the nuclear awareness necessary for collective survival.'[33]

Indeed, in the words of another psychiatrist, the sickness it occasions 'borders on the insane'. These maladaptive responses include the radical denial of danger; living within fantasies/illusions that more weapons can possibly enhance security; the fight/withdrawal into a condition of deep apathy. In addition, the threat engenders a split between ideation and affect, as when strategists discuss 'acceptable' levels of mega-death; displacement of worry from human life and civilization itself to endangered species; and splitting that casts all evil on the other side and imputes only worthy motives to our own. In these and other responses, we regress to extremely primitive mechanisms of response which slowly, but fatally, rupture with the threatening reality rather than confronting and dealing with it.[34]

The Nuclear Warriors

Thus does the madness of the system react back on and madden its potential victims. Similarly, their hideously abstract language, their illusions, their radical denial, are pathologies imposed by the system on those who operate it. 'For potential perpetrators simply cannot afford to imagine what really happens to people at the other end of the weapons.'[35] However sane and normal they appear in Scheer's account, however rational and even loving, it may help to place the nuclear planners in our mind's eye next to the extermination camp administrators who also loved their families, Beethoven and flowers. Yet unlike those who survived the Nazis, if our policymakers succumb fully to it we will be unable to evaluate their pathological madness afterwards. Their radical dissociation from the world and the human web of feeling surrounding it will appear clearly only when it is already too late, at the moment when bombs go off.

Does this imply that John F. Kennedy behaved madly at the time of the Cuban missile crisis? His brother's account of the crisis depicts him as forcefully carrying out, in Dean Acheson's words, his 'responsibility for the security of the people of the United States and of the whole free world'.[36] But Robert Kennedy was also aware that the crisis 'brought the world to the abyss of nuclear destruction and the end of mankind',[37] and while nowhere criticizing his brother, had planned before his death to add a discussion of the ethical question: 'What, if any, circumstance or justification gives this government or any government the right to bring its people and possibly all people under the shadow of nuclear destruction?'[38]

What indeed? During the crisis the president had confided the following thoughts to his brother, who made them famous: 'War is rarely intentional. The Russians don't wish to fight any more than we do. They do not want to war with us nor we with them. And yet if events continue as they have in the last several days, that struggle—which no one wishes, which will accomplish nothing—will engulf and destroy all mankind.'

Robert Kennedy continues: 'He wanted to make sure that he had done everything in his power, everything conceivable, to prevent such a catastrophe. Every opportunity was to be given to the Russians to find a peaceful settlement which would not diminish their national security or be a public humiliation. It was not only for

Americans that he was concerned, or primarily the older generation of any land. The thought that disturbed him the most, and that made the prospect of war much more fearful than it would otherwise have been, was the spectre of the death of the children of this country and all the world—the young people who had no role, who had no say, who knew nothing even of the confrontation, but whose lives would be snuffed out like everyone else's. They would never have a chance to make a decision, to vote in an election, to run for office, to lead a revolution, to determine their own destinies.'[39]

His brother's account shows Kennedy, and Khrushchev as well, as being keenly aware of the dangers and as remaining restrained in the face of them. Both sides spoke of the 'madness' of initiating all-out war or even the first step in a chain of events that could lead to it. And at the drama's climax sanity did prevail: no war at all occurred, the missiles were removed, and the US promised not to invade Cuba. We cannot help but be impressed by the lucidity of both leaders, their sensitivity to each other's position, and the fact they both actively worked to *avoid* nuclear war.

Yet we cannot help but be struck that each side was also *threatening* nuclear war. Kennedy's strangely abstract concern for the world's children only underscores the fact that he was indeed threatening them with death if Khrushchev did not capitulate. We may speculate whether thinking about children restrained Kennedy from an even more menacing stance, but we may also speculate about whether Kennedy would have been able to push as far as he did if he had thought about *his* children. He rejected removing 'antiquated and useless' missiles from Turkey (which he originally assumed had been removed long ago) in order not to appear to be knuckling under to Soviet pressure. And all of Khrushchev's pained awareness that 'armaments bring only disasters'[40] cannot veil the fact that he ordered the missiles to Cuba in the first place.

Why did Kennedy knowingly threaten Khrushchev and his own people with a war that would 'engulf and destroy all mankind'? Why did he reject the trade of Turkish and Cuban missiles which *he himself* seemed to see as 'a very fair suggestion'?[41] Why did he reject granting the Soviet Union an equality with the United States which would have permitted the Soviets to do in Cuba as the United States did on Russian borders?

The Kennedys' self-interpretation resembles the lucid Bolshevik self-interpretation discussed earlier. '"I just don't think there was any choice," Robert told John, "and not only that, if you hadn't acted, you would have been impeached." The President thought for a moment and said, "That's what I think—I would have been impeached."'[42] The *necessity*, it turns out, was imposed not by the Cuban missiles or Khrushchev, but by the premisses of American political life. Foremost was the belief that the Soviet Union must be denied equality and mutual respect, for reasons of both American dominance and anti-communism. Kennedy also acted as the ruler of a state easily able to give priority to 'national interests' based on a logic of 'power' and 'security' which could be utterly dissociated from the security of millions of Americans. As Richard Falk argues, the 'confrontation revealed clearly that both leaders of the superpowers were prepared to seriously risk nuclear war in order to achieve their geopolitical goals, that is goals related to image and position rather than to such ultimate issues of security as the defence of national territory, vital allies, or even critical resources.'[43]

John Somerville's play *The Crisis* better captures the deeper meaning of the encounter than Robert Kennedy's memoir. One of Somerville's characters naively reacts as follows to the Russian offer of the missile trade: 'But even if the Russians weren't willing to do that, even if the Russians were entirely in the wrong, like robbers who break into a house in the night and say, give me your money or we'll kill the whole family, only a madman would say it's better to have the whole family killed off. Even the police tell you it's better to let them take the money. Don't these men understand that life is the most precious thing?'[44]

No, indeed, they did not and they do not. Perhaps most remarkable of all in the crisis is that Kennedy *expected war*. He *hoped* that Khrushchev would back down: 'It was a hope not an expectation. The expectation was a military confrontation ....'[45] And still he acted, and still he threatened. Another of Somerville's characters is appropriately unrelieved when Khrushchev backs down: 'They'll certainly try it again. Good God! The crisis is *not* over. The *crisis* has just begun.'[46]

The System Creates Its Madness

It is interesting to speculate whether a clinical test could be devised

which could determine Kennedy or Khrushchev to be sane or insane. But in the non-clinical terms we have been discussing certainly
each of them was almost mad. Or perhaps each was mad, fully, for a
moment.

In the end this question is less important than the fact that they ruled over systems of exterminism and managed them according to
premises which allowed all of humanity to be threatened. The
Cuban Missile Crisis demonstrates that individuals achieving power
within the logic of those systems are expected to accede to the
systems' demands, to be devoted to strengthening such systems, to
be willing to use nuclear bluff to promote their own country's perceived national interest. In other words, to *use* the weapons at their
disposal, not to seek to abolish them. Such systemic roles necessarily
demand considerable—although in 1962 not yet fatal—dissociation
from concerns of human pain and survival. Such roles encourage
behaviour that is mad.

Once freed from their systemic role such individuals might indeed
be expected to revive more fully human concerns—as did
Eisenhower in his Farewell Address, warning about the dangers of
the military-industrial complex, as did Carter in his parting reflection
on the threat of nuclear war, as did Rickover in his similar sounding
of the alarm after retirement. In a sense, each of these major con-
tributors to the system was now lamenting that very system's
madness.

The problem is of course that within the system the madness continues and perhaps intensifies, as 'credible leaders are recruited from
among those who believe in the illusions of winnable nuclear wars
and the like, and who might act on such beliefs if pushed in a crisis.'[47]
Falk is suggesting that if policy has created the system, now the
system chooses and creates its policymakers. In this profound sense
it is out of control because, as Thompson argues, the policy *decisions*
which led to the Cold War 'passed long ago into a self-generating
condition of Cold War-ism (exterminism), in which the originating
drives, reactions and intentions are still at play, but within a general
inertial condition. It is this condition (but I am now asking a question
which will, I hope, be refuted) which appears to have become irreversible as a direction.'[48] Jean-Paul Sartre's great insight into
history will, alas, confirm Thompson's fear rather than refute it,
namely that human action creates an 'enveloping totalization' of

human praxis become process which not only shapes subsequent human action, but also deviates consciousness itself.[49] No longer controllable by the humans who originated it, frozen human praxis remakes the human world in its own image. No wonder then, as Falk worries, 'no mainstream political formation has yet dared bring into question the main postulates of nuclearism.'[50]

The system drives itself, and all of us. Thompson suggests how choice becomes inertial, as the system wins a kind of autonomy: 'Superpowers which have been locked, for thirty years, in the postures of military confrontation increasingly adopt militaristic characteristics in their economies, their polity and their culture. What may have originated in reaction becomes direction. What is justified as rational self-interest by one power or the other becomes, in the collision of the two, irrational. We are confronting an accumulating logic of process.'[51]

The Logic of Madness

The whole of this study may be read as an essay on reason in relation to politics. Throughout this essay I have argued that to be rational today still means to be free from drastic illusions, to use logic in the service of life, and to overcome dissociation between thought and the world being thought about—with all its terrors, its obstacles, its limitations. The hallmark of reason, today, is respect for reality.

Nuclear logic not only is but *must be* supremely irrational. We have seen Kahn talk of preserving peace 'by the threat of war'. This is the kind of inescapable contradiction that permeates and vitiates the very logic of nuclear deterrence. Schell describes the 'fantastic intellectual construct—the body of strategic theory built up over more than thirty years—in which ratiocination, unrestrained either by moral feelings or by facts, has been permitted to run wild in a riot of pure theory.'[52] Its classic formulation is Churchill's confident and barbaric proclamation about the nuclear age: 'Safety will be the sturdy child of terror, and survival the twin brother of annihilation.' Schell emphasizes the utter contradiction between the terms: 'We cannot both threaten ourselves with something and hope to avoid the same thing by making the threat ....'[53] Unmindful of such delicacy, the mad situation brings us to its self-description—that for the sake of our survival we must 'cultivate annihilation'.

Looking more closely at the logic, Schell points out that the first strike is supposedly deterred by a massive second strike capacity; but if so 'what reason would remain to launch the retaliation once the first strike had actually arrived?' Everyone concedes that nuclear victory is unattainable, and so 'the logic of the deterrence strategy is dissolved by the very event—the first strike—that it is meant to prevent.' Under the rubric of 'deterrence' the *logos* of a mad situation has illogic at its core, for 'the doctrine is based on a monumental logical mistake: one cannot credibly deter a first strike with a second strike whose *raison d'être* dissolves the moment the first strike arrives.'[54]

Where does this deformed logic lead? Such an astute strategist as Herman Kahn admits that an important component of his logic lies not in logic but psychology.[55] Kahn seeks to fill the logical gaps in deterrence theory by recommending that our leaders cultivate the *'appearance* of irrationally inexorable commitment.' Believing that a madman is in the White House, no enemy will dare to strike first. Yet this leaves a further logical gap: this policy of the rationality of irrationality will not be effective if the enemy senses that the leader is only pretending. Therefore one must take the next fatal step: go beyond pretence and *'really intend to do it'*.[56] 'Reasoned insanity': articulated with enough consistency, thus does theory follow the curves of reality. And so the madness of the weapons is transferred back to the thought of the human beings who seek to manage them.

Dialectics of Doomsday

If it happens by accident it will be no accident. If the system thus selects its people and shapes their boundaries of thought, exterminism appears as a frozen, alienated praxis-process which has lost touch with its original intentionality and now moves with its own momentum. Thompson uses the analogy of imperialism to suggest an original 'rational', systemic-intentional basis which now moves on its own, creating its own functions and structures. But even if we grant its *semi*-autonomy we must not ignore the *current* human intentionality of this mad system. It is more than a frozen and alienated praxis-process in which the past dominates the present: the nuclear world also reflects a continuing and renewed societal purpose. The final flash may well be an accident or mistake of 'the system', but we must now explore the intentionality of the edifice which makes this possible. We must return our gaze from the systemic inertia gone out of control to the people who create it and, even today, inscribe their purposes in it.

First, we must remember that the nuclear world is part of a history of unreason in our century. Indeed, much of that history turns on the encounter between Communism and capitalism, and would make no sense without it. The First World War caused social collapse which led to both the Bolshevik and Nazi victories, even as the emergence of each force deeply affected the shape of the other. Nazism was defeated, and the Second World War won by a resurgent capitalist society moving to the centre of the world stage and by a consolidated Communist society asserting, for the first time, a role as a major world power. The Cold War between the two became deeply structured into an American society which had economic, imperial and internal political reasons for organizing itself against an Enemy, and a Soviet society already wholly shaped by its struggle against both real and supposed enemies.

Intersecting in the war in Vietnam was simultaneously a movement of national liberation from the capitalist orbit, an effort to make American might prevail, and a surrogate struggle between the two antagonists (especially on the part of the US). The American humiliation, at a potential turning point in the history of human liberation, may indicate the objective limits of American power; but it may also lead to the fatal turn in the history of Doomsday. By the mid 1970s, America's 'loss of control over the course of history'[57] seemed to be acknowledged by an appropriately hesitant and cautious leadership. But, as Falk points out, the American course changed after the climax of 1978, which saw victorious revolutions in Nicaragua and Iran, followed the next year by the taking of hostages in Teheran and the Soviet invasion of Afghanistan.

Subject to a revival of the domestic pressures that historically have led to periodic renewals of anti-communist militarism, American policymakers also faced a new storm about the loss of American 'resolve' and the 'decline of American power'.[58] Responding through the same, unrevised lenses that earlier led them into Vietnam, they resorted to what Falk correctly regards as 'sheer mystification' by equating 'American decline either with the insufficiency of military power or with Soviet aggressiveness'.[59] Never dispelled, what had earlier led to the madness of Vietnam took hold again along a yet more dangerous tack—the limited nuclear war option was revived in Presidential Directive 59 in 1980.[60] Loss of control over events, due in reality to a number of factors including national revolution in the Third World and the decline of the American economy—and in its own way affecting the Soviet Union no less than the US—was ascribed to the Soviet military threat! In the words of strategist Colin Gray, 'the most pressing, dangerous, and potentially fatal fact of the real world—[is] that we are at the mid-stage of a shift in relative power and influence to the Soviet Union that is of historic proportions, and which promises, unless arrested severely, to have enduring significance. ... The rise in Soviet standing in the world, which may be traced almost exclusively to the increase in relative Soviet military capabilities, both dwarfs other concerns in its immediacy and seriousness, and renders other problems far less tractable.'[61]

This logic is demented because, dissociated from the actual historical process of American decline, it projects a fantasy-'solution' which threatens war. It is, alas, the logic of policy. Ideologically blind to events and trends, US policymakers are further blind to their causes. Doubly trapped in a world-view which has ruptured with reality, they have sought, as Falk says, 'an intensified commitment of resources to the nuclear arms race in the hope of somehow gaining the upper hand.'[62] We must speak of madness: the lenses of over-development, hubris and anti-communism lead policymakers to respond to American decline by asserting 'the continuous resolve of the United States Government to defend national interests by relying, as necessary, on nuclear weapons threats.'[63]

This response to the American defeat in Vietnam and its aftermath has drastically ruptured with reality in decisive ways, and substituted mental images for an appreciation of reality—multiplying missiles in the hope of once more getting decisively 'ahead' of the Soviet Union, and thus somehow regaining a lost ascendancy. The product of a logic which has broken with logic, its shred of functional rationality lies in its domestic political and economic purpose and in its Doomsday message to Third World independence. The Carter Doctrine showed American 'national resolve to safeguard control over the Persian Gulf oil-producing region by a readiness to use *whatever* military means might prove necessary.'[64]

I am suggesting that this show of power once more puts us face to face with the dialectics of disaster. Lifton penetratingly analyzes the psychological impossibility of achieving security in a situation of objective insecurity, when simply to be alive is to be vulnerable. Building more weapons is politically acceptable because it creates the *feeling* of security. Yet to do so is to *increase* the objective insecurity. In one of the most drastic ruptures of mind with reality, psychological security is purchased by actually *increasing* the threat of extinction.

The attempt to affirm the 'credibility of American power' which nearly destroyed Vietnam ended by demonstrating the absence of effective American power. Carter attempted 'to reassert the "credibility" of that power by retaining the nuclear option, together with the illusion of limit and control. Here the unacceptable actuality that had to be denied at all cost was the self-image of the United States as the "pitiful, helpless giant" so bitterly articulated by President Nixon.'[65] For all his power, the contradictions of his situation 'create in any American president an anxious sense of executive impotence.'[66] The lack of effective power, madness, the possession of state power with all of its instruments of control and destruction—these are the elements of the dialectics of Doomsday.

In the nuclear arena, as Falk points out, these tensions have so far yielded tactics of bluff and the 'fanaticism of the worst kind'[67] which seeks nuclear advantage. Their inability to translate their enormous military power into diplomatic or military victories has led American leaders, and continues to lead them, to try to translate their military power into effective power by planning to fight, survive and win a nuclear war. In a world of fifty thousand nuclear warheads, the penultimate madness is to seek nuclear superiority by increasing one's nuclear arsenal. It is obvious to those not lost in the dialectics of Doomsday that the idea of superiority in such a situation is mad. But those who control the system of exterminism and are absorbed in its logic simply cannot see this. In power without effective power, they steer the world towards its moment of ultimate madness.

Technology and Domination

What kind of civilization produces this madness—and renders it so seemingly normal, so difficult to penetrate, even while making it so public and widely discussed? Since nuclear weapons are the ultimate neg' tive product of industrial civilization, it is perhaps natural that efforts to get to the root of our plight should focus on what Bahro calls this 'misdirected civilization, which is aggressive in its innermost being, based on the principles of expansion and explosion.'[68] It is especially striking, however, that Bahro, a thinker shaped in the Marxist tradition, calls 'into question that traditional historical optimism for which the very essence of the human species points towards socialism, and not to barbarism, let alone a premature self-destruction.' For Bahro 'it cannot be accidental that our civilization should generate a tendency towards the self-destruction of its subject as a defining trait of its most recent stage.' He sees exterminism not only in the nuclear world, but also as 'the quintessence of the whole complex of tools and machines operative on humanity and the planet.'[69] Aggressive and destructive practices, exterminist practices, have been dominant in the industrial world from its beginning, practices which 'break up and destroy natural conditions, degrade energy potentials, suffocate the Earth's surface and isolate human beings from spontaneous energy cycles. The result is inevitably a distortion of both body and mind, whose consequences range from cancer to crime.'[70]

Bahro's provocative sketch calls for a *fundamental* critique of human nature itself' and for 'a practical critique of the industrial system and its military spearhead.'[71] The opening question of any such critique concerns technology itself: is the source of the problem the human drive for mastery of nature—technology and industry —or its embodiment in the societies and cultures of domination in which industrialization has taken place?

As David F. Noble argues, 'a stock device of recent social analysis is to view modern technology as though it had a life of its own, an internal dynamic which feeds upon the society that has unleashed it. Propelled according to its own immanent logic and operating through witting and unwitting human agency, it ultimately outstrips the conscious activities which gave birth to it, creating a society in which people are but functional parts of the mechanism.'[72] The falsity of this view is demonstrated by Noble's study of the role of science and technology in the rise of American corporate capitalism. Specifically he studies the role of *people*—the corporate engineers shaping technology to fit the contours of their social order. 'In stand-ardizing science and industry, reforming the patent system, routiniz-ing research, transforming education, and developing modern management, the corporate engineers of science-based industry strove at once to push forward and to stay their revolution, to reap its immediate benefits and yet forestall the coming of that new day which it seemed to portend.'[73] Under the banner of science—and thus universality—'modern technology became a class-bound phenomenon, the racing heart of corporate capitalism.'[74]

Noble cites Marcuse's reflections on the 'technological veil' which through a pretence of science and universality 'conceals the reproduction of inequality and enslavement.'[75] Blind to the expan-sion of specific forms of class domination, we see the overwhelming, imponderable force of modern technology—cut off from its human source, it seems to move on its own, and holds us in its grip. Yet con-crete human relations shape even its deepest and most fundamental levels. Marcuse argues that science, '*by virtue of its own method* and concepts, has projected and promoted a universe in which the domination of nature has remained linked to the domination of man—a link which tends to be fatal to this universe as a whole. Nature, scientifically comprehended and mastered, reappears in the technical apparatus of production and destruction which sustains and improves the life of the individuals while subordinating them to the masters of the apparatus.'[76] Following Marcuse's insights, Noble's study describes how 'the creators of the new scientific mode of pro-duction, the self-proclaimed revolutionaries who unlocked the forces of nature and heralded the coming of a new day for mankind',[77] did so at every level in strict service to the requirements of corporate capitalism.

Technology, Domination and Nuclear War

We must return from the machines, even the Doomsday machines, to the people who design and control them. If Bahro is right and 'the impulse to obliteration, to the self-extinction of humanity, lies in the very foundations of our industrial civilization and pervades every structure of its economy, science and technology, its political apparatus and its sociology and psychology',[78] every structure *also* contains human domination *and* the struggles to sustain and to over-come it. Insofar as science and technology successfully neutralize this conflict and promote a social consensus, they achieve a consensus forging ahead in repressive unity and (at least in intention) away from its conflictual roots. Like many who focus on the destructiveness of industrial civilization, Bahro cautions against seeing 'class struggle as the key to the contemporary crisis'.[79] Aided by Noble and Marcuse, however, we can see that alienated and technologically veiled domination returns, however repressed, precisely as 'the key' to nuclear war.

Earlier I spoke of the strategy of overdevelopment. This strategy, especially as embodied in nuclear weapons, gives us our clue to their civilizational meaning and function. Writing at a time when the means for such a strategy did not exist, Clausewitz emphasized the political nature of all wars. 'War Is an Act of Human Intercourse' is the title of one of his sections.[80] Elsewhere he emphasized that war 'does not suspend political intercourse or change it into something entirely different.'[81] Break the link with policy, as for example in a war of pure destruction, 'and we are left with something pointless and devoid of sense.'[82]

As Schell astutely points out, nuclear war both completes and con-tradicts Clausewitz's theory of war.[83] It completes it because it is the application of, or threat of, overwhelming physical force to coerce the enemy into doing your will. As such it seems to be but a logical step in the history of force, in which the mightier side wins. Para-doxically, however, on this plane only the *threat* of nuclear war fits Clausewitz's discussion: the actual war would lead to such massive and universal destruction as to destroy all sides along with any original political purpose. Already at Hiroshima it was clear that the drastic new point and purpose of nuclear weapons is not to destroy the enemy's armed forces in combat,[84] but to murder the enemy civilian population in such a horrifying way and to such an extent that the enemy surrenders. Terror is their purpose, and failing that, total annihilation.

For the first time in history weapons are available that are too powerful to be used within the inherent limits assigned to 'battlefield weapons'. Their only purpose must be massive, not selective, destruction—a massive attack on civilian society itself. This redefini-tion of war remained unilateral for only as long as a single country possessed the bomb. Since 1949 terror has become first mutual, then universal, until today, as Churchill proclaimed, terror has become *normal*. The nature of nuclear weapons today gives automatic and immediate access to those who control them. Everything is, and must be, constantly ready. Thus, just as the distinction has been obliterated between military and civilian targets, so can the world at peace be scarcely distinguished from the world at war.

More important than this irony, however, is the redefinition of war accompanying the new normality. Clausewitz was concerned with the age-old struggle of human groups against each other using their skills, productive capacity, experience, organizing ability, morale, and tactical genius. In his view, the human dimension of skills and experience would always be decisive. In this sense, it should be emphasized that Clausewitz presupposed the act of war to be as political as its goal. Total war, involving the societies' entire productive base and millions of civilians, was unknown to him, as was technological war. How could his analysis have accommodated the bombing of a non-military target like Hiroshima to terrorize the Japanese government into surrender? Even if we accept the argument that this fateful act saved American lives by obviating an invasion, it remains clear that invasion is a uniquely appropriate form of warfare if absolute surrender is the goal. Dropping atomic bombs to avoid it was to break decisively with the traditional practice of war, to turn to the genie in escape from the human-to-human combat that Clausewitz had regarded as a variant of commerce and politics.

It may have been difficult, in the spring of 1945, to resist racing ahead with a weapons technology that held out promise of conquering Japan without further combat. Nevertheless, a very specific hubris lay behind the dropping of those two bombs. Overdevelopment: the essentially political project of combat was transformed into a technical one, as war itself was redefined.

A Technology of Madness

I would suggest that nuclear weapons represent *a technology of madness* in a very precise sense. In the terms developed in this study this means a technology forged to carry out properly political tasks, and solve properly political problems—the root of the technology being a rupture with the real nature of these tasks and problems and the determination to dissolve them in a scientific fantasy-universe which stabilizes existing social relations. We know, alas, that a fantasy-universe can become *real*, as real as the 'Jewish subhuman' became in the Nazi camps. In each case the divorce from reality is not contradicted but only confirmed by the human ability seemingly to make over the world according to our own wishes. The 'technological veil' hides the domination at the root of this process of wizardry. *Wizardry* is the ever-more-progressive substitution of technical solutions for political ones—in order to contain and hide the prevailing social and political tensions.

The Vietnam war called upon wizardry all too frequently: American policymakers nearly succumbed to a fatal hubris that believed destructive and constructive technology can control anything. Against this, the victory of the Vietnamese in Vietnam was a victory of the human spirit, of human scale, of human control, over the madness of a power which can, in the end, destroy but not triumph.

The nuclear universe is the outstanding contemporary example of the wizardry which, while accepting systemic problems as structurally irresolvable, seeks to transcend them by erecting uncontrollable giants. It is by now all too clear that the proponents of nuclear power would tamper with the universe and call it down upon us all rather than face more threatening—and fundamentally political—issues of energy distribution and waste. The energy crisis is a *political* problem—it is rooted everywhere in a consensus veiling a system of domination which justifies itself only as long as it increases productivity. The energy crisis is produced on the basis of a social contract which confirms prevailing class structures and the prevailing inequality of wealth and power—but pursues an expanding 'good life' defined to protect and perpetuate the social system.[85] Thus, the consensus of 'growth' is invoked, and energy sources are projected which are vast in size, centralized and require enormous capital investment. The creation of such technology, fitting *by design* the priorities of capitalist and Communist societies, is far less a technical than a political matter.

As William Leiss points out, the programme was foreshadowed at least as far back as Baron Georges de Cuvier's 'Reflections on the Present State of the Sciences and on Their Relations to Society' in

1816. 'Cuvier referred to the "universal opposition of rich and poor", to the jealousy among nations that resulted in wars, and then declared that "industry and the science which produces it are the natural mediators" among these conflicts: "They equalize the nations in overcoming climatic obstacles; they draw together men's fortunes in making enjoyments more easily attainable" ....'[86]

Needless to say, they prevent revolutions and stabilize the existing social, economic and political structures. Which is what Leiss means when he speaks of our current forms of technology as being 'the source of false consciousness—a vital means of masking continuing injustice and class antagonism ....'[87] The masters of society use technology to further the 'mastery of social change'.[88] Ecologist William Ophuls similarly emphasizes that economic growth, based on the unrestrained attack on nature, has until now successfully transmuted political problems.[89]

However hidden, mystified and successfully evaded, at the heart of the nuclear world remains the conflict between man and man. Our great ·danger, of course, is precisely that it is repressed, kept dissociated from what this world *seems* to be about and thus develops not by 'its own' logic but by a mad one. Cut off from this source by design—and thus inherently irrational and without stabilizing roots in human needs—wizardry cannot but become based on and responsive to free-floating fears and dissociated fantasies, power without reason.

The American Bomb Is Aimed at Us

On the deepest level, then, what is the secret of the bomb? Manifestly the American bombs aim to destroy Soviet military and civilian targets in such mass as to annihilate the entire Soviet Union. As American policymakers say, they are deployed only as a threat to the Soviets, that is, in self-defence. The same is undoubtedly true of the Soviet bombs. But if we understand the conditions of the Cold War under which atomic weapons developed, it should be clear that the Soviet people as enemy *represent* something else, however irrationally so. In a most veiled form they represent the 'class threat' to the rulers of American society. The Cold War unified each society against its alternative. In each case those with the greatest stake in such unity and such combat were those seeking to repel the alternative—and they succeeded in uniting all classes against the externalized threat. In however distorted a form, for Americans the Soviet Union represents socialism, including its humane features most lacking in American society. Projected out in a frozen and externalized form, socialism can be hated, attacked, and perhaps destroyed. The Soviet Union's universal employment, guaranteed access to medical facilities, 'cradle to grave' care for its citizens, social and economic planning—all can thus be successfully repelled. For the Soviet rulers, the threatening alternative is likewise not the negative side of corporate capitalism, but democratic and decentralized institutions, a spirit of social and personal freedom, civil rights and civil liberties, and independent oppositional organizations such as trade unions.

In the Cold War each ruling class has successfully repelled not only the *other* society's most appealing features, but any movement to achieve them internally. The internal class enemy was stifled, as was the demand for basic social change, by the defensive-offensive projection of the external threat. This is why we may speak of each ruling class being in *collusion* with the other, and speak of a system of exterminism embracing both societies. When together they unite against the common threat, they reveal the secret intentionality of exterminism.

For each party to the Cold War the threatening alternative may be stated more simply: liberation. As we have seen Bloch say in Chapter One, the ultimate goal of all social struggle, arising when we have established real democracy free from depersonalization and alienation, is 'a place and a state in which no one has yet been': home. Marcuse described it as a state of civilization in which surplus-repression[90] would be removed and it would be possible, in Adorno's phrase, 'to live without anxiety'.[91] 'A new basic experience of being would change the human existence in its entirety.'[92]

The alternative to the violence pervading our world is suggested in Walter Benjamin's formulation of a more appropriate relationship of humans, technology and nature. Leiss cites him as arguing that the essence of human technique should be not the ability to dominate nature, but rather 'the mastery of the relationship between nature and humanity.' Rather than assaulting nature, the goal should be to 'do justice to the subtle interplay of internal and external nature.'[93] Benjamin hoped to combine a sense of mastery with a sense of harmonic interaction. Midwifery? Certainly if the distinction between effective and impotent power has any meaning, the project of assault and violent rupture we have discussed becomes unnecessary once humanity has achieved collective power, effective power.

Our entire analysis of overdevelopment and the technology of madness—and indeed the at once chastened and hopeful conclusions we have drawn from studying this catastrophic century—point us towards the social meaning of a non-repressive civilization. At its root would have to be human relationships of democracy and equality: the traditional meaning of a classless society. Human beings would gain control over their world for the first time in its history. 'Liberation' means a civilization without domination. It would be a civilization without the endless institutional structures, forms and practices of repression and mystification ever more madly heaped upon each other, all needed to perpetuate domination.

Is it merely by chance that the material and technical preconditions for liberation were achieved in the West *at the very time* nuclear weapons were developed? We have seen Horkheimer and Marcuse both emphasize the increased pain and rage occasioned by the absurdity of continuing a life of instinctual renunciation beyond the point of its technological necessity. And so it may be possible to speculate on the *psychological* link between the threat of total destruction and the threat of liberation. Certainly there is also an internal scientific-technological connection between the human capacity to pacify existence and to destroy civilization. But I would rather speculate on a *political* connection: that the bomb is the rulers' response to the threat of liberation. Where liberation is possible, where it has become irrational to live in toil and subjection, the Cold War and the Soviet 'danger' cancel the threat, first by leaving no alternative to continued renunciation, and then—above all—by threatening humanity with total annihilation.

'Military technology', writes Raymond Williams, 'has often, perhaps always, been a significant factor in the constitution of a social order. It also directly affects the struggles of classes. If the characteristic effective weapon is within the reach or use of peasants and workers there is a different ultimate balance of class forces from those periods in which effective weapons depend on control of major industrial plants or advanced scientific research.'[94]

Who then is the real target of the American bombs in this system gone mad? Manifestly the Soviet people, and more directly the threatening aspects of the Soviet system. But the real target of this system of terror out of touch with itself is none other than the people at home. The American bombs are meant for the American people; the Soviet bombs for the Soviet people! On each side, they guard us against their very power being used *for* humanity. They stifle those who, given an unfrozen dynamic, might seek to transform their society against its rulers.

Williams echoes Thompson in asking: 'If "the hand-mill gives you society with the feudal lord; the steam-mill society with the industrial capitalist", what are we given by those Satanic mills which are now at work, grinding out the means of human extermination?'[95] It is now possible to answer the question. We are given a society in which humans, in flight from both their real conflicts and real possibilities, worship machines of destruction. We are given an overdeveloped society, which sustains its system of domination by a total threat which is both dissociated from its source and deviated from its target. Its Satanic mills successfully stifle *politics*—meaningful class strug-gle—by creating a consensus against the Enemy's Satanic mills. In this way energy for social change is frozen or terrorized or turned into war. Yet necessarily divorced from and out of touch with its source, the alienated and mystified intention of the rulers of each side carries us to what is their ultimate and implicit threat: To destroy the world 'in order to save it'.

In 1848 Marx and Engels foresaw a time when 'society can no longer live under this bourgeoisie, in other words its existence is no longer compatible with society.'[96] The nuclear establishment has fulfilled this prophecy by reversing it: Society's existence is being placed in question, rather than that of its rulers. The slowly-dawning realization that most cancer is human created testifies to the mad scientists' relationship to the natural and social world which threatens to destroy us all. The madness and evil once expressed in Nazism has been newly incarnated in an unlikely form—in our technological fantasy-world itself. The human world has become so totally split off from its own power that it can only alternately worship and cower before it.

The nuclear threat is thus political in its essence. The bomb is *human* power, alienated from and turned back on its source. This mad sovereignty over the world suggests that we are nearing a historical watershed. Impotent, threatened, ruling classes threatening to blow up the world and themselves—this suggests that the real choice given by nuclear weapons, however successfully deviated and hidden, is the end of such domination—or of the world itself. Contained and out of touch with itself, therefore mad, is this where the history of class conflict has taken us?

These speculations gain weight when we realize that the prospect of a nuclear holocaust will not be conjured away until the *political* development and power of concrete human beings becomes sufficiently great and generalized for technological fantasy-solutions and wizardry to become impossible and unnecessary. In short, until human power acknowledges itself as it never hitherto has, and displaces the weapons from the centre of our world. Effective democracy would so transform the nature and meaning of power that nuclear weapons will be unthinkable.

In other words, what is the ultimate source of the nuclear threat, on a global scale? Not the impotence of an enraged petty-bourgeoisie; nor of a party elite acting in the name of a dispersed and decimated working class; nor of a nationally satisfied bourgeoisie trying to police a globally uncontrollable environment; but rather the generalized impotence of 'concrete human beings' to create—so far—any *truly democratic society* in which ordinary people really do exercise collective popular control over their lives, and so (of course) over their technology. The successfully veiled meaning of being willing to destroy the world 'in order to save it'—Better dead than Red!—is the determination to maintain domination to the death.

The path to a solution is, of course, implied in this description of the menace: a political-intellectual-emotional praxis of returning to the feeling source, the human source. A series of acts, requiring all that humans can bring to bear, to undo what has been done, to unveil what has been veiled, to deconstruct this deformed, hideous, menacing reality that makes us live in resignation and futility. What awes and overwhelms us in this world, after all, is *only* our own power, deviated, mystified, turned into weapons of annihilation and pointed at us. To seek to return the world to its human source is to struggle for a world not dedicated to the maintenance of domination at any cost. At some point the effort at deconstruction would see open, direct class struggles re-emerge. This would already clarify our life and create a much simpler world, a world which, much later, could possibly return the genie to its bottle.

As always, there have been those who insist on sanity and a return to scale—as during the Vietnam War. They are demanding today a technology that is not inherently uncontrollable and terroristic, and so a world fit to raise children in. They have struggled to break through and, thanks first to the near-disaster at Three Mile Island and then to the US-Soviet nuclear escalation, they have grown in strength and numbers. They will win, eventually, unless we are all destroyed. Perhaps there is hope, then, that civilization may awaken from its delusion, as the Nazis never did, to attack the social structures responsible for the impending disaster. And, perhaps, in becoming a humanity strong enough to control the apparatus we may begin the political work necessary to create an apparatus appropriate to human needs.

8
Lessons of the Present:
Hope and Action Today

What can be the last word of this preface to hope? Evil, in this period, certainly appears ascendant over the oppositional forces of sanity and humanity it continues to generate. Sustained by no deeply committed government or quasi-government, these wholly voluntary movements are fated to wax and wane, gain heart to lose it again, now win victories and now grow cynical with defeat. The powers that be mobilize all their formidable resources in defence of their madnesses. Indeed, freely elected, they reflect prevailing sentiments even as they shape them. Dispassionate analysis disheartens and overwhelms when it locates so few and such slight resistances to increasingly mad mainstreams.

Is a genuinely positive final note possible? Or is it a goal we pursue doggedly, without spirit, out of ideological obligation but no inner necessity? After all, isn't it disheartening to discover the evil of the last two chapters as being, in the one case, inextricably mingled with a response to even greater evil, in both cases, imbedded in societies' normal daily functioning, concepts and values? In the end, does our engaged objectivity lead us not only to clarity, to an illusion-free sense of our limits, tasks and prospects—but also, and as a result, to the verge of despondency? Think of the concluding notes of reflections on our century by earlier writers. Are we left to hope, as Marcuse quoted Walter Benjamin in 1964, only for the sake of those who have no hope?[1] Thus ends *One-Dimensional Man*. Near the end of Doctor Faustus, published in 1947, Thomas Mann expressed unforgettably the pain of that generation and the stubborn persistence of its hope in the face of the German catastrophe. Mann's Serenus Zeitblom describes the final notes of Adrian Leverkühn's 'revocation' of Beethoven's Ninth Symphony, his *Lamentation of*

Dr. Faustus: 'Here, towards the end, I find that the uttermost accents of mourning are reached, the final despair achieves a voice, and—I will not say it, it would mean to disparage the uncompromising character of the work, its irremediable anguish to say that it affords, down to its very last note, any other consolation than what lies in voicing it, in simply giving sorrow words; in the fact, that is, that a voice is given the creature for its woe. No, this dark tone-poem permits up to the very end no consolation, appeasement, transfiguration. But take our artist paradox: grant that expressiveness—expression as lament—is the issue of the whole construction: then may we not parallel with it another, a religious one, and say too (though only in the lowest whisper) that out of the sheerly irremediable hope might germinate. It would be but a hope beyond hopelessness, the transcendence of despair—not betrayal to her, but the miracle that passes belief. For listen to the end, listen with me: one group of instruments after another retires, and what remains, as the work fades on the air, is the high G of a cello, the last word, the last fainting sound, slowly dying in a pianissimo-fermata. Then nothing more: silence, and night. But that tone which vibrates in the silence, which is no longer there, to which only the spirit hearkens, and which was the voice of mourning, is so no more. It changes its meaning; it abides as a light in the night.'[2]

Although equally grounded in pain, a different sort of hope has been the driving impulse of these pages, seeking as they have done the human, social source of our century's actual and potential catastrophes. Not the Great Refusal, a defiant hope which is the last refuge of an overwhelmed and besieged humanity, but the more concrete hopes animating and generated by millennia of movements and the fruits of their struggles.[3] Our appeal to praxis, to political action, has been based on the conviction that, however deviant from its origins and cut off from self-consciousness, Evil is always a human project. It can be understood and combated as intentional human action. And it *will* be combated. As long as people live, some of them will fight for sanity and justice and survival.

But those in the grip of madness put themselves beyond reach, they rupture with authentic discourse and alienate themselves from their reason. In power, they both reflect and create majorities behind them. The more developed their madness, the more terrifying it is. Out of touch, speaking of peace and self-defence, expressing and shaping significant social forces, they threaten to commit their greatest crimes—today, tomorrow.

So, when all is said and done, how can our concluding note be distinguished from the all-but-despondent last words of *One-Dimensional Man*, or from the final high G of Adrian Leverkühn's last composition? I spoke earlier of the impossibility of sustaining a consistent attitude towards the threat of nuclear holocaust. Today, life seems if anything more prone to disaster, to horrible reversals, to the slaughter and betrayal of hope, than in 1947 or 1964—and so to responses that alternate bouts of intense commitment with periods of bitter exhaustion. As the nuclear threat grows, above all, life seems very frail. ... When we remember how committed are the madmen to their madness, and how sustained in it by social dynamics, when we remind ourselves of the stark reality of past histories of genocide and national suicide, can we avoid being immobilized by fears humanity has never had to live with before? At the moment are we not balancing precariously on a margin of hope even narrower than that allowed by Mann in 1947 or Marcuse in 1964?[4]

Yet in the end what is it that seems so overwhelming? Not only that in spite of many inspiring victories we still find ourselves having to fear and fight for our very survival. Not only that those controlling the weapons appear to be beyond our reach by any conventional political process. There is yet a further reason why we are reduced to passivity by, for example, the failure of the great anti-nuclear demonstrations throughout the West of the early 1980s to soften the US government's plans for nuclear escalation, or by Thatcher's overwhelming triumph in 1983. This is that defeats return us to a passive stance, one in which evils appear as autonomous forces, beyond our reach or intervention. We are forced back to a stance in which we disengage and observe.

The end of Progress can teach two opposed lessons—one of cynicism and quietism, and the other more fitting response of active determination to *bring about* survival, peace and well being. Many times the sole difference between hope and cynicism is the decision to act, the shift from contemplating the world's evils to resisting them. Much of this manuscript has been written on the reverse side of old political leaflets, the leftovers of political events in which the author has participated: commemorating the Sandinistas' victory, for example, protesting against the invasion of Lebanon, calling for an end to American involvement in El Salvador, remembering the *desaparecidos* of Chile, honouring Wayne State University's volunteers in the International Brigades in Spain. All of these are reminders of the thought, developed in Chapter Five, that we are left today with one fundamental principle of hope: action.

Our analysis of evil is, after all, only analysis. Our meditation on societal madness is only meditation. No matter how committed, each of the last two chapters is a reflection on a situation and, as such, requires a reflective stance which imposes its own demands—for clarity, objectivity and balance. Commitment may motivate each analysis, but each must stand on its own as a coherent, persuasive rendition of its situation. Each seeks in short, to convey the problem *as it is*, making the situation and not our commitment its decisive touchstone of validity.

Reflection therefore imposes a certain loosening of our links to the issues we seek to illuminate, a determination not to let conviction becloud our understanding. In seeking its logic we seek to view the nuclear threat as a human phenomenon independent of our will to dismantle it, as a danger quite separate from the ups and downs of movements to lessen it.

But we must now in conclusion insist that a complete perspective on the dangers facing us requires a constant and radical shift from reflection to action. The field before us must become redefined as our practical one. Inserting ourselves in its midst as actors, we see that overwhelming problems appeared as such partly because they were comprehended objectively, and thus placed for the moment beyond our intervention. In acting we see ourselves linked with situations we had separated ourselves from at an earlier stage of comprehension, or as a result of defeat. Each evil loses its apparent autonomy and becomes, once again, *our enemy*. Even if we never stopped regarding it as a concrete evil produced by concrete human actions and intentions, it now becomes in addition a *target*. While not abandoning the goal of understanding it, we now primarily seek to vanquish it. The complex historical and social field we have sought to understand once more becomes a series of guides, helps and obstacles.

As I said in the Introduction, then, hope lies outside of these pages, in action. But instead of *encountering* hope there, we *create* it each time we transform ourselves into activists seeking to change this or that practice, these or those trends, this or that social system. Today, hope *is* political practice. To shift from reflection to action is to leave behind a contemplative—and to that degree demobilized and overwhelmed—posture which emphasized observing events unfolding before us. Because it redefines the field before us precisely as *our* practical field, action has an energizing effect and so is often accompanied by newfound feelings of power. Indeed, even if undertaken in desperation it is a kind of self-empowerment in the face of a hostile reality. However doomed they were, in the Warsaw Ghetto uprising combatants redefined their relationship to their own fate. Action replaces the primacy of the threat with the primacy of our project to combat it.

We may recall the great reluctance Plato expected from his philosophers upon shifting from contemplation to action: for him it was a drastically inferior mode of activity and a lesser way of relating to reality. For our purposes, what counts is the radical shift Plato sees between contemplation and action.[5] Certainly, his decision to compel the philosophers to govern reflects the tension between Plato's sense of the greater purity and clarity of the world of ideas and his commitment to this world of our daily life. But it also reflects the wrenching distance he perceived between them. Plato did not and could not see that across that divide lies a superior sense of reality. Marxist epistemology suggests that without action the world cannot help but appear falsely, as a finished product separate from and imposed on us. This reified, 'normally' alienated world seems to move on its own, independently of human decision and action. The philosophical child of the strand of rationalism which tended to see the world as a human creation, Marxism seeks to undo reification by seeing the human labour behind the finished world. Today, more than ever, Marxism's further demand for political practice becomes necessary to our very efforts to understand this reality. The world has grown so threateningly out of control that only an active, *political* mode of apprehending it can restore a sense of it as fluid, unfinished, and capable of redirection. Its human source disguises itself until the moment we find and seek to lay hold of its levers for change. Sartre said that 'there is no non-human situation.'[6] Today, as 'technology' shapes our world and exterminism moves as if on its own, Sartre's full meaning appears only through the political action which challenges and dissolves the non-human facade surrounding us on all sides. For example, the course of events unfolding in the Middle East since the invasion of Lebanon may seem so dismal as to encourage passivity. Israel's great upheaval of 1982 and early 1983 left the government unshaken and the architect of the Lebanon invasion in the cabinet. As intelligent observers predicted at the outset of the war, Israel's grip on the West Bank and Gaza has only tightened. The poisons of our century seem to penetrate so deeply and extend so far that its greatest victims, and their victims, cannot—*will* not, it seems—find a way to share their common home.

Returning to an activist posture, however, recasts the situation. However slim at any given moment, certain possibilities remain open for action, some of these opened up by earlier actions, and dependent on yet earlier ones. In the apparently hopeless days of June 1982, a few organizers gathered several hundred signatures on a statement denouncing the war, and with them the money to publish it in the Israeli daily press. In a country whose every previous war had been seen as defensive, where the front was only a car ride from the northern borders, where each and every military death is mourned as a national tragedy, this courageous opposition tapped and legitimized deeper, unexpected currents of resistance. Within a month of the invasion, an anti-war movement appeared which was as active and proportionally as large as the American anti-Vietnam war movement at its peak. It did not end the invasion and, even after being joined by Labour Alignment for a brief moment after the massacres at Sabra and Chatilla, did not seriously challenge a ruler who needed no consensus to carry out his plans. Discouragement at Begin's persistence and strength or at the failure of the Palestinians to hit upon a genuinely creative and challenging response—or simply sheer exhaustion—could encourage the view that, after months of upheaval, nothing had changed or would change. After all, the dominant trends remained dominant, even after the remarkable Kahan Commission Report criticized virtually the entire leadership for the massacre and recommended that Sharon be dropped. And, worse, in the wake of the destruction of its semi-autonomous territorial base the PLO fragmented and largely became a captive of Syria. A year later, the hope generated in all those who acted had been frustrated. Did not the exhilarating sense of acting expose its utterly subjective roots, its episodic character? Did not the hand grenade that killed Emil Grunzweig at a Peace Now demonstration symbolize the profound resistance to change within Israel, the fatal power of the dominant trends? And did not the assassination of Issam Sartawi suggest the same sorry dominance of the worst trends among the Palestinians?

But 'trends' finally embody human beings, and if some have been moving further towards madness others have been struggling their way to sanity. A vitally important current of criticism among American Jews appeared in the aftermath of the invasion, reaching all the way into the leadership of mainstream organizations; the World Zionist Congress criticized the settlement policy, even if this was suppressed by leadership manoeuvres; in Israel, Begin lost personal strength and resigned. Looking for the decisive breakthrough, we correctly see these trends as subordinate, and may as a result lose heart. But in terms of a commitment to action we can see them rather differently, looking for ways to combat the negative trends, to enlarge and strengthen the peace camp. For example, it continues to promote dialogue between Jews and Palestinians after the deaths of Sartawi and Grunzweig. We continue to study the map of the situation, seeking the promising paths, watching for new weaknesses to develop on the other side, planning to exploit them.

No, by the autumn of 1983, nothing had changed decisively—but beneath the surface the ground had been continuing to shift in large ways and small. How drastically no one knows yet—and in any case only future action will be able to tell. The wave of feeling with which Israelis responded to Sadat's trip to Jerusalem in 1977 revealed their tremendous longing for peace—under what conditions will it surface again? Certainly an enormous, perhaps impassable gulf separates the reality of the Lebanon invasion from the visionary hope of Arafat's reconciliation trip. But the depths of the gulf are not set out in advance: they are human, the product of specific actions, and will be gauged, and changed, only by other actions.

Still, to return to our question, is not any action today fated to return to despair when we reach its limits and fail to achieve its goals? To drive us to the edge of despondency once again when we analyse situations anew and see just how mad they are, how far from a humane solution? In the Nuclear Freeze Campaign for example, the American anti-nuclear movement has been brilliantly successful in formulating the issue, organizing local and national campaigns, and gaining popular support for its position. It grew so remarkably in a short time that the massive demonstration of 12 June 1982 expressed not a dissident minority, but the national majority sentiment. The movement forced Reagan into the Orwellian doublespeak of declaring peace as the purpose of his nuclear escalation. But it could not block the development of the MX missile, or the deployment of the Cruise missiles. The high hopes aroused everywhere in the West by the great efforts of the early 1980s remain frustrated as I write this. At the end of this disastrous century are we fated to waver between energy, hope and action on the one hand and sober analysis, exhaustion and disillusionment on the other? In these concluding words I want to point beyond the endless alternation.

Living the Tension

If hope is action it is action guided, as I said in Chapter Five, by a sense of what is possible at any given moment. Is it now bearing witness, or now preparing for massive social transformation? We dream of a breakthrough, but it will happen only when the ground has been prepared. The preparation takes place in countless series of single steps, any one of which may be seen to further the cause of humanity. *Any single step*: those in struggle exhaust themselves by fixating on their largest goals and becoming unable to appreciate the historical importance of the small victories they do achieve.[7] To make an effective contribution to the cause of humanity is an achievement, anywhere, at any time—and the limits of that achievement are set not by our own strength or weakness but by history itself. There is, no doubt, an inevitable tension between our deep longing for peace and freedom and justice and our mature calculation of what can be achieved here, by this action. The longing seems mocked by compromise, its great dignity trivialized by the smallness of these steps forward. To be sure, all partial results are hollow until Palestine and Israel live side by side in peace, creating the condition for peace in the entire region. If we do not get *there*, it seems, we have got nowhere. Just as all partial successes of the anti-nuclear movement have hardly any meaning so long as the bomb still exists and threatens us. Yet our inspiration and goal must not become our fetish; our sense of limits may become rather a source of strength, not the measure of our impotence. Allowing the interplay between vision and action, theory and practice means that hope is, finally, situated in the tension between the terms. This suggests an answer to the endless alternation of reflection and action sealed off from each other, with little learning passing back and forth. Political energy, fuelled by groundless faith, need not give way again and again to the exhausted understanding of how little we have been able to do.

It need not if we function with a realistic sense of possibility, if we gauge the limits of what can be done in any situation; if we move purposively to achieve what is possible. At the same time, if we experience, and are inspired by, its connection with the deepest human dreams; if we rejoin the movement as we struggle, incarnating it anew while connecting ourselves with its millennia. Does not any moment of success, or even hope, allow us a glimpse of the heroes that have preceded us, and of our living and renewed links with them? It is a tragedy, a cause for lamentation, that wholeness—in the specific sense of being able to sustain a living link between hope and possibility—is impossible today. It is our goal, but we must accept living within the tension it generates by being both so unreachable and so real. Every authentic collective political action, fully felt, revives the entire dream of the race, of peace and freedom, of milk and honey. It must, and yet its hope will be disappointed.

Alternating bouts of energy and exhaustion are certainly inevitable today, but their severity and mutual incomprehension can be tempered by living in the tension generated by hope, engaging in a far more complex dialogue between two quite real planes, of reflection and action, despair and hope. We know that our enemies are real, perhaps gaining in strength, and that the struggles against them cannot even glimpse their turning points. But hope is real also, a force in our lives. Indeed it is our lives, in the sense of being our intention, our project. For example, at dusk on 26 June 1982, Israelis began to fill Kings of Israel Square in Tel Aviv to demonstrate against the war in Lebanon. They came from all over the country, tentatively, unsure how many of them there would be, some even afraid that right-wing thugs would outnumber them and violently disrupt their demonstration. It was a risk, but the risk dissolved when they looked across the square as it filled, seeing how many they were.[8] Speaking to the 20,000 were parents of soldiers killed in Lebanon, Israeli and Palestinian leaders, artists, poets, actresses, students, professors. The following Saturday, four weeks after the invasion began, 40,000 persons were expected at a second demonstration, and 100,000 came—this time to hear returning soldiers denounce the war they had been fighting. As their placards said they hoped to stop the war, to remove Begin and Sharon, to begin the process of reconciliation with the Palestinians. They failed.

But they did break the national consensus, legitimize Jewish criticism of Israeli policies, and show the world and themselves that significant numbers of Israelis stand ready to move towards peace. For a moment, among those people, peace was possible. To tens of thousands an Arafat trip to Jerusalem was not inconceivable.This Jewish community of peace has dissolved and recreated itself dozens of times since the late 1970s, grown and shrunk and grown again, but it remains real, today, on any today when it is remembered and recreated.

With it in mind we return, one final time, to the question that has dominated this Conclusion: how is it possible to retain hope in this mad world when we know so well that the community of peace fails, is frustrated, is defeated, and disperses once again? The question can be formulated more precisely from the perspective of action: when the movement recreates itself, as in New York on 12 June 1982, how can it do so with such joy knowing what it knows about its own fragility and the limits of its effectiveness?

Certainly all action, no matter how desperate its roots, must have hope as one of its structuring elements to the degree that it seeks to transform the situation in which it takes shape. The redefinitions indicated above—of evil into enemy, of autonomous objectivities into fluid situations, are achievements in themselves. Memories of earlier effectiveness, even if of elsewhere, of another time, of other people, expand the horizon of even the most desperate. And then the very fact of acting against evil instead of submitting to it, of doing the right thing, lends a positive tone to actions with only the narrowest prospects of success.

Yet it is the slim prospect of success today, one conclusion from our analysis of social madness in our century, that has forced us to question the very meaning of hope again and again in this chapter. If it is so largely 'subjective', how does our hope differ from Mann's or Benjamin's? In our very last note we must extend our conclusions about the energizing and redefining effects of political action to the limit and emphasize a feature not explored thus far—its collective character.

Acting collectively not only redefines the situation: it does so in ways that transform the participants themselves, creating and allowing the experience of a totally different reality. Such a new reality was produced on 12 June 1982 by the nearly one million people who streamed into New York from all over the United States to demand an end to the threat of nuclear war. As I have already suggested, by coming together they created new possibilities of perception. In addition to the modes discussed earlier, their assemblage made possible the collective sharing of a collective problem: *we* are being threatened. Normally the isolated individual cannot experience this. Collective perception, the possibility of collective experience, reveals our world as *ours* in a way usually inaccessible to separate atoms, no matter how politicized. Those who filled Central Park that day, awed by their sheer numbers, were able to give voice and hearing to those layers of their experience and reality which normally remain closed, lacking appropriate categories of thought and feeling. These collective modes of experience and perception point to the peculiar reality created by our assemblage: *we*, a *collective* subject.[9]

We is the final note of this preface to hope, the subjective-objective force in the world which not only restructures habits of perception and experience, but which changes the world itself. Participants on 12 June could not fail to be struck the moment they arrived by the superb self-organization of the demonstration, down to the slightest detail. One's bus arrived at a pre-designated location, marshals stood at the subways to tell people which way to go. It was, indeed, a self-organization aided by local officials, who seemingly had no choice but to assist the planners so that the hundreds of thousands could enter and leave the city smoothly. One had the sense that much of the business of New York came to a halt that day, allowing the demonstration to 'take over'. Could the awareness of their own collective power be missed by the participants? Certainly this was one reason for their great good cheer, connected as it was with their perception of how many and how diverse they were. On this level it was entirely appropriate that the sense of collectivity may have eclipsed their motivation for being there, and that for many the mere warmth of community was the strongest impression they carried home. The warmth with which strangers greeted each other—moving towards the demonstration, in restaurants around the city afterwards—was not just that of people sharing a goal. It was the warmth of a self-activating *we*; aware of their numbers and potential power, above all of a *we* sharing a specific goal: the peaceable kingdom. The widespread sense of joy no doubt sprang from this, the momentary appearance, among, between and through the demonstrations, of the peaceable kingdom.

Certainly it was only a demonstration, and equally certainly it failed in its avowed purpose. The later frustration, the defeat, even the tragedy cannot revoke the force of this momentary incarnation of the peaceable kingdom. *We* may be co-opted, but we are also intransigent; we may be defeated, but we are also defiant; we may be fooled, but these moments of our self-creation give us an irrefutable touchstone of truth. Certainly we have seen humans again and again choose evil—and madness—in response to desperate situations. We have seen our century grow madder—the progress of unreason. In the end, our reason to hope is that *we* have always existed and—until the end of the earth—will always recreate ourselves. Calling for sanity or social justice, peace or freedom, equality or democracy—or any combination or all of these—we will first seek to realize them simply by voicing our hope. Co-opted, fooled, defeated, we will return to protracted struggle and relearn its terrain.

Our Achievements

A second reason to hope is that we have accomplished so much. Our saltiest realism must acknowledge that the 12 June demonstration so awakened public consciousness and increased the pressure on the Reagan administration that every subsequent effort at escalation has become a major political struggle. And, self-consciously international in outlook, it effectively picked up the baton from the great European movements and brought it to the American side of the Atlantic.

The real historical advances in human social morality have occurred through such struggles. Slavery has been abolished, democratic rights won, certain elements of dignity and equality promised and achieved, wars ended, other wars forestalled—only because we have acted. Projected now desperately, now with confidence, in collective visions by movement after movement, sacrificed for, agitated for, partially achieved, then legitimized by law and custom, social progress has been *made true* each step of the way. Demonstrations, movements, revolutions in each case entail a transformation of subjective awareness into objective force: a collective subject growing conscious of its power, cumulatively creating a new reality. In spite of all qualifications, and even today under the mushroom cloud, the struggle continues. It seeks to extend, to expand this reality-in-the-making: men and women capable of creating and living in a world fit for human beings.

Learning from our Disasters

But can this hope be sustained against the other fact we have seen, that the apparently collective *we* led by the Bolsheviks degenerated into an apparatus attacking the whole people as enemies of the people. Or, more recently, against the Kampuchean disaster, or against the Vietnamese failure/inability to realize the peaceable kingdom. Another lesson: discouraged, defeated, betrayed by our own deformation, dissolving again and again, we must relax the urge to compensate by burying our heads and acting ever more mindlessly and ritualistically—or, alternatively, by withdrawing into cynicism—when our situation rather calls upon us to persist while learning from our own history.

Our capacity for evil is one such lesson. Another, our final one, is that the disasters traced in this book *need not be repeated* if they are recognized, comprehended, and our awareness of them allowed to guide action in the future. I have, after all emphasized the vital role played by human subjectivity—the perceptual lenses, expectations and even ghosts that guide our actions. Can our subjectivities be educated by studying our history? Can we learn to shape our own history without succumbing to the disastrous madnesses so common to our century? Can we learn Marxism's lessons about remaining faithful to reality even as we seek to transform it? Such a hope has motivated every line of this study.

More than an article of faith, this hope derives its material reality from the way in which *we* have responded to the terrible events of the century. Even if it is not yet disentangled from the settler-colonialism and reliance upon imperialism in which it took shape, the Jewish 'Never Again!' has produced an epochal transformation of the Jewish people into collective subjects of their own history. At the same time, many of those Israelis who demonstrated against the invasion of Lebanon, in rejecting the killing done in their name, rose above distortions of the lessons of the Holocaust by refusing to identify themselves with actions many of them saw as Nazi-like.

A similarly ambiguous process has developed in response to Stalinism. Even the catastrophe in Kampuchea, Stalin's partial rehabilitation in the Soviet Union, and the failure of that society to really confront and undo its past cannot nullify the force Stalinism has acquired as a negative object lesson for other revolutionary parties and states. No longer is the Party, as hegemonic force, as authoritarian structure, a self-evident norm freely accepted by a significant proportion of those who seek social change. The New Left everywhere was characterized by new modes of organizing, of conducting meetings, of creating coalitions—of formulating theory and practice—once more, in an effort to avoid recreating the disasters of the past, in a commitment to keep democracy at the heart of the movement and of any society it might build. The libertarian lessons that Daniel Cohn-Bendit drew from his study of the Bolshevik revolution[10] have yet to become victorious anywhere for more than a moment, but ideas of pluralism, of decentralization, of workers' control inspire and guide the new waves of activism.

The Vietnamese war bequeaths some of the same, as well as some very different lessons. Once again, it has reminded us of the error of equating one's own movement, here, given its peculiarities and priorities, with movements elsewhere, given their particular conditions of existence. The *we* is in-the-making but never complete; the movement is never a given, is always changing. Our wholehearted commitment to Vietnamese national liberation did not commit us to those forms, to that party. The era of the Comintern has passed, and one of its lessons has been to make us wary of heavens on earth. Our task, rather, is to learn the moral, political and intellectual meanings of critical support; or indeed, how to oppose one side of struggle without thereby identifying with its antagonist. Another lesson of the Vietnam war concerns the success of the fluid, if chaotic power of an anti-war movement that had no single centre. Its democratic lessons of local self-organization, pluralism and genuine coalition-building have been bequeathed to, and flourish in, the anti-nuclear movement today. Finally, and above all, the victory has taught the Vietnamese, and the whole world, that human beings may just possibly be more powerful than most of their machines. Next time, for survival's sake, the task may well be to combine victory with the triumph of a human order. Difficult as that sounds, will it be any more conceivable, say, than was the Vietnamese victory?

Taken together, these diverse lessons—others can be drawn, will be drawn—suggest that we, acting in the present, may indeed learn from the past to create a different future. In the process, aware of it or not, *we* become little by little the cumulative conscience of humanity, our victories part of its acquired social structures and moral sense.

If our final victory is not foreordained, neither is our defeat. And so *we* fight on, sometimes grimly but sometimes joyously. There are, after all, many reasons for joy. Our own self-empowerment, our learning to appreciate each half-step of victory, our experiencing the richness and depth of the *we*—these are some of the joys of struggle. We wish it were not so, but today the commitment to sanity, to truth, to humanity, to survival, means doing battle. Accordingly, we must learn to cultivate the pleasures of collective action.

Notes

(pp. 3-22)

1. Catastrophe and Hope

[1]Gil Elliot, *The Twentieth Century Book of the Dead*, New York 1972, p.6.
[2]Robert Heilbroner, *An Inquiry into the Human Prospect*, New York 1974.
[3]Christopher Lasch, *The Culture of Narcissism: American Life in an Age of Diminishing Expectations*, New York 1979.
[4]Robert Nisbet, *History of the Idea of Progress*, New York 1980, p.318.
[5]Ibid.,p.353.
[6]Quoted in ibid., p.5.
[7]Ibid.
[8]Ernst Bloch, *On Karl Marx*, New York 1981, pp. 44–45.
[9]Except for the World War I casualties these are Elliot's figures.
[10]Ibid., p. 29.
[11]'Bourgeois-democratic' is likely to irritate most readers, but consider the alternatives. 'Capitalist' focuses wholly on economic structures and ignores both political culture and class as central dimensions of the life of the society; 'democracy' obfuscates the social and economic reality, just as 'bourgeois' suppresses vital positive political features.
[12]The only parts of Bloch's monumental *Das Prinzip Hoffnung*, Frankfurt 1959, to be translated into English appear in *Man On His Own*, New York 1970, and *On Karl Marx*.
[13]Georg Wilhelm Friedrich Hegel, *Reason in History: A General Introduction to the Philosophy of History*, Indianapolis 1953, p. 27.
[14]Ibid.
[15]Nisbet emphasizes the religious basis of the idea of Progress, treating secularists like Marx as exceptions. See esp. pp. 352–53.
[16]Georges Sorel,*The Illusions of Progress*, Berkeley 1969, p. 210.

2. Why? Towards a Theory of the Holocaust

[1]Theodor W. Adorno, *Prisms*, London 1967, p. 34.
[2]See Herbert Marcuse, *The Aesthetic Dimension: Toward a Critique of Marxist Aesthetics*, Boston 1977.
[3]See Dorothy Rabinowitz, *New Lives: Survivors of the Holocaust Living in America*, New York 1976.
[4]Fredrich Meinecke, *The German Catastrophe*, Boston 1963, p. 1.
[5]Horst von Maltitz, *The Evolution of Hitler's Germany*, New York 1973, p. 291.
[6]See above all Thomas Mann's *Doctor Faustus* for a sustained exploration of the 'demonic' and its temptations. Meinecke himself refers to 'demon chance' as aiding Hitler's rise to power (p. 61). On the other hand, for a discussion of the question of

understanding Nazism in human terms see Reinhard Kühnl's outstanding sketch of the key issues and approaches, 'Problems of a Theory of German Fascism: A Critique of the Dominant Interpretations', *New German Critique*, No. 4, Winter 1975, pp. 42-44.

⁷Such theories of fascism have been sketched by Theodor W. Adorno and Max Horkheimer in *Dialectics of Enlightenment*, Horkheimer himself in *Eclipse of Reason* (see below, ch. 5), as well as by Ernst Bloch and Herbert Marcuse. They have been developed more painstakingly and at greater length by Nicos Poulantzas in *Fascism and Dictatorship* and Ernst Nolte in *Three Faces of Fascism*. A theory of the Holocaust itself has been proposed by Richard Rubenstein in *The Cunning of History*. All of these works will be referred to or discussed in the course of this attempt to contribute to such a theory.

⁸See A. J. P. Taylor's 1961 preface to *The Course of German History*, London 1961; and Golo Mann, *The History of Germany Since 1789*, New York 1968, pp. 410-91. Mann speaks of post-1933 German history as the 'adventure of a villain who forced his will on Germany and through Germany on a large part of the world' (p. 418).

⁹The expropriations are discussed in Raul Hilberg's monumental *The Destruction of European Jews*, New York 1961, ch. v.

¹⁰Hilberg describes the considerable drain on the war economy of the cost of destroying Jews. See ibid., pp. 643-66.

¹¹The figures are from Hannah Arendt, *Eichmann in Jerusalem*, New York 1965, p. 125. The problem is discussed by Sebastian Haffner, *The Meaning of Hitler*, New York 1979, p. 144.

¹²In *The Cunning of History* (New York 1978), Richard Rubenstein succumbs to this distorting process even while courageously attempting to account for the Holocaust. We should not, he says at the outset, allow our feelings about it into our reflections, because 'they can add to our difficulties at arriving at an understanding of what took place. In order to understand the Holocaust, it is necessary to adopt a mental attitude that excludes all feelings of sympathy or hostility towards both the victims and the perpetrators' (p.2). He is right insofar as uncontrolled feelings might threaten to flood over us and distort objectivity. Yet he confuses objectivity with neutrality, and so excludes from his work the personal outrage which motivates it and might indeed help him into confronting the barbaric character of the Final Solution. Perhaps this is why his effort to explain it is finally unconvincing. He speaks persuasively and correctly about the bureaucratic 'culture of modernity' which is so capable of abstracting from living and breathing human beings, of defining them as surplus population, rationally developing systems of exploiting them unto death, and finally efficiently disposing of them. But the picture he presents is all too rational and external. Missing from his account is a recognition of the Nazis' savage intentionality, the insane hatred for the Jews which impelled them to cross hitherto impassable moral barriers. The death system did indeed become bureaucratic and rationalized, but its mundane techniques should not be confused with its thoroughly evil goals. And these goals can be better appreciated if we begin by respecting our subjective response to them.

¹³In a remarkable effort to present a historical account integrated with personal experience, Peter Phillips, a former camp inmate, insists on overcoming the 'mental apartheid' which led to the Final Solution and on seeing the Nazis as human beings like ourselves. His point is that the Nazis succumbed to a moral disease in which they lost all sense 'that those who they were convinced were enemies of Nazism were human beings like themselves' (*The Tragedy of Nazi Germany*, New York 1969, p. 168). His anti-communism turns on the fact that in practice Marxism has adopted the same 'mental apartheid'. While championing human dignity the Left has often suc-

cumbed to the same self-righteousness and thus in power has all too easily doomed its opponents to slaughter, (pp. 27-31).

[14]Ibid., pp. 204-205.

[15]Michael Walzer has reopened the argument over the need for rules of war. See *Just and Unjust Wars*, New York 1977.

[16]Is it possible to devise reasonably objective tests to determine whether an individual or society is mad? Might not a Nazi, an American policymaker at the time of Vietnam (or today), a defender of Stalin—all be as justified as I am in regarding their antagonists as mad? At stake here is a willingness to base our judgements on a certain conception of objective reality. Although we have become more subtle in describing and verifying this ever more complex and shifting reality, the notions of relative sanity and madness retain their moral and psychological normative force. Historical, cultural, class, and social dimensions affect our perspective on the 'objective' world before us; yet within all possible qualifications it remains possible to point to patterns of *rupture* in which one functions as if the world or a decisive area of it were drastically different from what it actually is. Rather than specify such norms in advance, this study intends to contribute to the problem by an analysis of specific madnesses.

[17]See Haffner, pp. 147-65.

[18]See Alan Bullock, *Hitler, A Study in Tyranny*, New York 1964, pp. 159-250.

[19]Eberhard Jäckel, *Hitler's Weltanschauung: A Blueprint for Power*, Middletown, Conn. 1972, pp. 58-9.

[20]Certainly antisemitism was if anything more widespread in Austria and Eastern Europe, and led to disastrous results in Rumania and elsewhere. Moreover Poles, Ukrainians and Lithuanians participated in the German Final Solution. In acknowledging this Mosse has argued, however, that non-Germanic antisemitism lacks the racial emphasis of the Nazi version and further, has more continuity with the earlier Christian versions. See George L. Mosse, *Toward the Final Solution*, New York 1978.

[21]I follow Yehuda Bauer's spelling. See *The Holocaust in Historical Perspective*, Seattle 1978, p. 8.

[22]Peter Merkl, *The Making of a Stormtrooper*, Princeton 1980, p. 225.

[23]See George L. Mosse, *The Crisis of German Ideology: Intellectual Origins of the Third Reich*, New York 1964, for the outstanding study of the 'rupture with reality' at the heart of *völkisch* thought. Mosse calls it a 'revolution of attitudes and feeling' (from Hitler) and, more tellingly, a 'displaced' revolution.

[24]Marxist studies tend to presume such functional rationality. A recent outstanding Marxist study on the inner logic of Nazism, Poulantzas's *Fascism and Dictatorship* (London 1974), is mute before the Nazi murder of the Jews. Similarly, Franz Neumann's *Behemoth: The Structure and Practice of National Socialism* (New York 1944), the classic dissection of the socio-economic purposefulness of Nazi structures and policies, leaves no place for a passion, however systematically implemented, which comes from another source. His discussion of Nazi antisemitism, completed by mid 1941, rests on the threefold functionalism of the Reich's Jewish policy: as substitute for class struggle, as justification for Eastern expansion, and as expressing Nazi rejection of Christian morality. Both studies tend to be undermined by the fact that one of the Nazi war's primary aims, announced by Hitler early in 1939, was the supremely irrational one of killing all the Jews, and by the fact (available to Neumann as he was preparing his 1944 revision) that this goal was being pursued in determined indifference to and even counter to the war effort. For a critique of Poulantzas which emphasizes his instrumentalism see Anson Rabinbach, 'Poulantzas and the Problem of Fascism', *New German Critique*, No. 8, Spring 1976.

[25]'Official Party Manifesto on the Position of the NSDAP With Regard to the Farming Population and Agriculture' in Gottfried Feder, *Hitler's Official Programme and its*

Fundamental Ideas, New York 1971, p. 31.

26Quoted from *Der Mythus des 20. Jahrhunderts* in Alex Bein, 'The Jewish Parasite', *Leo Baeck Year Book* IX, London 1964, p. 22.

27Ibid., p. 24.

28Ibid., pp. 26-7.

29Ibid., pp. 27-8.

30Adolf Hitler, *Mein Kampf*, Boston 1943, p. 678.

31See Mosse, *Toward the Final Solution*, pp. 222-4; see also his *Nazism: A Historical and Comparative Analysis of National Socialism*, An interview with Michael A. Ledeen, New Brunswick 1978, p. 20.

32In addition to Hilberg's work, see Lucy S.Dawidowicz, *The War Against the Jews 1933-1945*, New York 1975.

33See Florence R. Miale and Michael Selzer, *The Nuremburg Mind: The Psychology of the Nazi Leaders*, New York 1975.

34See Hannah Arendt's discussion of 'language rules' in *Eichmann in Jerusalem*, pp. 80-82; and George Steiner, 'The Hollow Miracle', in *Language and Silence*, New York 1967.

35Dawidowicz, *The War Against the Jews*, ch. 8, 'A Retrospective View'.

36The figure are from Hilberg,p. 576 and Heinz Höhne, *The Order of the Death's Head: The Story of Hitler's SS*, New York 1970, p. 358.

37See Walter Laqueur, *The Terrible Secret: Suppression of the Truth about Hitler's 'Final Solution'*, New York 1980.

38Stanley Milgram, *Obedience to Authority: An Experimental View*, New York 1974, p. 13.

39Subjects were instructed to administer electric shocks to 'learners' who made mistakes. What they supposed was an experiment about the relationship of punishment to learning in others became, in reality, an effort to test the limits of their own willingness to obey authority when commanded to harm another human being.

The 'learner' was strapped to what resembled an electric chair. He received no actual shock, but was an actor who expressed a carefully rehearsed series of responses. When the 'learner' was placed in a separate room and could not be seen or heard, but pounded on the walls, 26 of 40 subjects moved step to step to administer what they had been told was the maximum shock of 450 volts. When voice feedback came through the walls, 25 of 40 obeyed to the end. When the victim was placed in the same room, 16 of 40 administered the maximum shock; when the subjects themselves had to force the victim's hand onto a shock plate, only 12 of 40 continued to the end. In each case, the rest defied the experimenter and broke off at some point.

Milgram concludes that when in modern industrial society, 'an independently functioning unit becomes part of a system, his conscience, which regulates impulsive aggressive action, is per force diminished at the point of entering a hierarchical structure' (p. 133). In this 'agentic' state the usual inhibitions imposed by one's conscience are out of play: instead of seeing himself as acting out of his *own* purposes, the individual regards himself as the agent who executes the wishes of another person. He becomes responsible to the authority directing him but not responsible for the content of the actions required by the authority.

40Milgram's findings have been widely taken as illuminating the dissociation from responsibility and subsequent extension of violence characteristic of the twentieth century. See for example, Barrington Moore *Injustice: The Social Bases of Obedience and Revolt*, White Plains, N.Y. 1978, p. 329. Also pp. 94-100.

41I refer here to the sense of authority Milgram seems to presuppose, as well as to how he himself operates as authority in conducting the experiment. Milgram's view, and his method of operation, seem to leave no room for a responsible, honest, benign authority who is in tune with his subjects. How else can we view an experiment in ..nich people hired to assist are unwittingly transformed into subjects?

[42]Ibid., p. 133.

[43]Dawidowicz, *The War Against the Jews*, p. 98.

[44]Höhne, *The Order of the Death's Head*, pp. 363-4.

[45]Ibid., p. 327.

[46]Dawidowicz, *The War Against the Jews*, p. 201.

[47]Even so, the evidence compiled by Laqueur means that by late 1942 'millions in Germany knew' that Jews were being killed (p. 32).

[48]Quoted in Mosse, *Toward the Final Solution*, p. 207

[49]'Little men gone wild'. See Milton Mayer, *They Thought They Were Free*, Chicago 1955 (p. 51), referring to T. Abel (1934), mentioned below (p.58) in note 84.

[50]See Mosse, *Nazism*, pp. 61-2.

[51]Henry Pachter, *Modern Germany: A Social, Cultural, and Political History*, Boulder 1978, p. 240.

[52]See J.P. Stern, *Hitler: The Führer and the People*, Berkeley 1975, pp. 9-22.

[53]Merkl, p.223.

[54]For Merkl's discussion of the levels of intensity of antisemitism and of the especially dangerous character of the paranoia see his *Political Violence under the Swastika*, Princeton 1975, pp. 498-501.

[55]*Merkl, The Making of a Stormtrooper*, p. 224.

[56]Karl A. Schleunes, *The Twisted Road to Auschwitz: Nazi Policy Toward German Jews 1933-1939*, Urbana, Illinois 1970, ch. III.

[57]Bullock, *Hitler*, p. 381.

[58]Quoted from G. M. Gilbert, *Psychology of Dictatorship*, New York 1950, p. 255; in Höhne, *The Order of the Death's Head*, pp. 388-9.

[59]Yehuda Bauer, 'Genocide: was it the Nazis' Original Plan?' *Annals of the American Association of Political and Social Science*, No. 450, July 1980, p. 45.

[60]I suspect it is primarily this logic that has led Lucy Dawidowicz to argue that extermination was Hitler's fixed and abiding purpose from late 1918 (see p.208). Schleune's study indicates otherwise; therefore I find convincing the refutations of Dawidowicz by Bauer and Henry L. Feingold (*Jewish Social Studies*, no. 38, Winter 1976, pp. 82-5).

[61]Ernst Nolte, *Three Faces of Fascism: Action Française, Italian Fascism, National Socialism*, New York 1966, p. 401.

[62]Peter Phillips places great emphasis on the system of terror and conditioning. See *The Tragedy of Nazi Germany*, ch. 4.

[63]This is well described in William Sheridan Allen's account of the first months of Nazism in power in Thälberg. See *The Nazi Seizure of Power: The Experience of a Single German Town 1930-1935*, Chicago 1965, Part Two.

[64]See Höhne, *The Order of the Death's Head*, pp. 370-3, 397-400.

[65]See Ibid., pp. 394-6.

[66]See Richard Grunberger, *The 12-Year Reich: A Social History of Nazi Germany 1933-1945*, New York 1971, pp. 460-6.

[67]J. Barrington Moore Jr., *The Social Origins of Dictatorship and Democracy: Lord and Peasant in the Making of the Modern World*, Boston 1966, p. 437.

[68]Ibid., pp. 413-508.

[69]In addition to George L. Mosse's writings cited above, see his *Germans and Jews: The Right, the Left, and the Search for a 'Third Force' in pre-Nazi Germany*, New York 1970, ch. 2 and 3.

[70]Mosse, *The Crisis of German Ideology*, p. 151.

[71]Ibid., p. 154.

[72]Ibid., p. 301.

[73]Moore, *Social Origins*, p. 291.

[74]Quoted in Ralf Dahrendorf, *Society and Democracy in Germany*, Garden City 1969, p. 67.

[75]Schleunes, ch. 1.

[76]Moore, *Injustice*, p. 329.

[77]Sebastian Haffner, *Failure of a Revolution: Germany 1918-19*, London 1973, p. 14.

[78]Ibid., p. 77. See also pp. 81-2.

[79]For the prehistory of this fratricide see Carl E. Schorske, *German Social Democracy 1905-1917: The Development of the Great Schism*, Cambridge, Mass. 1955, Part v.

[80]Pachter, p. 104.

[81]Moore, *Injustice* pp. 398-411; see Kühnl, 'Problems of a Theory of German Fasicsm,' pp. 28-31.

[82]Merkl, *Political Violence under the Swastika*, p. x.

[83]Moore, *Injustice*, pp. 412-13.

[84]Theodore Abel, *Why Hitler Came into Power*, New York 1938.

[85]Nolte, pp. 312-23.

[86]Nazi ideology is studied by Jäckel as well as by Horst von Maltitz, *The Evolution of Hitler's Germany* (New York 1973). Although they have both rightly insisted on the theoreticians of 'opportunism') and on the internal coherence of the Nazi world view, both stop short of doing for the Nazi period what Mosse does for the pre-Nazi-period—namely, of showing the internal logic of völkisch thought.

[87]Neumann, p. 37.

[88]*Mein Kampf*, pp. 442-51.

[89]Moore, *Injustice*, p. 32.

[90]See for example, *The Crisis of German Ideology*, ch. 17, and *Nazism*, pp. 120-22.

[91]See David Schoenbaum, *Hitler's Social Revolution: Class and Status in Nazi Germany 1933-39*, Garden City 1967 pp. 132-43.

[92]Poulantzas, pp. 237-64.

[93]Ibid., p. 98.

[94]For a discussion of recent Marxist thinking on this question see Anson Rabinbach, 'Toward a Marxist Theory of Fascism and National Socialism', *New German Critique*, no. 11, Spring 1977, p. 138.

[95]Poulantzas, pp. 71-113.

[96]Schoenbaum, *Hitler's Social Revolution*, p. 285.

[97]See Karl Hardach, *The Political Economy of Germany in the Twentieth Century*, Berkeley 1980, pp. 64-9.

[98]George Lichtheim, *The Concept of Ideology and Other Essays*, New York 1967 p. 227.

[99]Ernst Bloch, 'Nonsynchronism and the Obligation to its Dialectics', New German Critique, no. 11, p. 35.

[100]See Rabinbach, pp. 137-8.

[101]Bloch, p. 22.

[102]Ibid., p. 35.

[103]Fritz Stern, *The Politics of Cultural Despair: A Study in the Rise of the Germanic Ideology*, Garden City 1965, p. 361.

[104]Schleunes, p. viii.

[105]See Bauer, 'Genocide', pp. 41-2.

[106]Moore, *Injustice*, pp. 403-9.

[107]Barrington Moore's works form perhaps the most sophisticated argument for this

position. In addition to *Injustice* see *Social Origins*, where the democracy and gradualism of liberal capitalist society are compared with fascism and Communism.

[108]Bloch, p. 28.

[109]Max Horkheimer and Theodor W. Adorno, *Dialectic of Enlightenment*, New York 1982, p. 185.

[110]Herbert Marcuse, Foreward to *Negations: Essays in Critical Theory*, Boston 1968, p. xii.

3. Why? Towards a Theory of The Soviet Holocaust

[1]Reported by John Reed, *Ten Days that Shook the World*, London 1977, p. 131.

[2]Ibid., p. 132.

[3]Ibid., p. 133.

[4]Ibid.

[5]Leon Trotsky, *The History of the Russian Revolution*, London 1967, vol. III, p. 304.

[6]Leon Trotsky, *My Life*, New York 1970, p 337.

[7]No doubt, as David Rousset admits, 'it was only one part of the proletariat which constituted the political corps of the state.' But, he argues, 'it is never more than a fraction of the bourgeoisie which administers the bourgeois state. It is therefore legitimate and necessary to characterize the state produced by the revolution as a workers' state.' See *The Legacy of The Bolshevik Revolution*, London 1982, p. 17.

[8]See J. P. Nettl, *The Soviet Achievement*, New York 1967, ch. IV.

[9]See Raphael R. Abramovitch, *The Soviet Revolution 1917-1939*, New York 1962, p. 356. David Rousset, in an analysis of Stalinism as the triumph of Thermidor and the restoration of private property, dwells entirely on the negative logic of the new class society, nowhere even mentioning its accomplishments. Similarly, in Anton Antonov-Ovseenko's account, Stalinism is made to seem as a great obstacle to social and technological progress. 'Joseph the Builder expended all of his extraordinary energy in helping to foul up the industrialization of the country. Stalin's leadership created unbelievable extra difficulties which the workers had to heroically overcome. What the Soviet people were able to build in the first five-year plan was the accomplishment exclusively of the people themselves.' (*The Time of Stalin*, New York 1981, p. 73).

[10]Francis B. Randall, *Stalin's Russia: An Historical Reconsideration*, New York 1965, p. 283.

[11]Ibid. p. 282.

[12]Maurice Dobb, *Soviet Economic Development Since 1917*, London 1966, p. 300.

[13]A preoccupation with statistics, striking as they may be—industrial production trebled from 1928 to 1940; by 1940 the USSR had more doctors per thousand people than the US, Britain, Germany or France—may lead us to distort their impact and, eventually, to ask the wrong questions. Thus Peter Berger wonders out loud whether Russia might not have industrialized equally—or perhaps even more—rapidly under a different social system (*Pyramids of Sacrifice: Political Ethics and Social Change*, New York 1976, p. 84). I agree with Berger that any assessment of Soviet (or Chinese) socialism that ignores its 'hecatombs of victims is morally contemptible' (p. 95). Yet what sort of contempt then do we heap on an assessment that denies its achievement? The point is that the basis for a new society was created in scarcely a dozen years from a painfully backward one—a highly organized, productive, literate, modern industrial society. Its physical and human size, its low level of development, and its diversity make the achievement all the more striking. The official Soviet analysis is presented in

N. A. Voznesensky, *Soviet Economy During the Second World War*, New York 1949; see also Alexander Werth, *Russia At War 1941-45*, New York 1965, pp. 569-77.

[14]Robert Conquest, *The Great Terror: Stalin's Purge of the 1930s*, New York 1968, pp. 23-4.

[15]Until Soviet sources become available, writes Alec Nove, all estimates of the human toll (Conquest, pp. 523-35) are at best highly speculative (*Soviet Studies*, vol. xx, October 1968, pp. 536-42). He and S.G. Wheatcroft (*Soviet Studies*, vol. xxxiii, April 1981, pp. 265-95) both would lower Conquest's figures, but at the moment they are the most complete and carefully researched we have.

[16]Conquest, pp. 538-9.

[17]Antonov-Ovseenko, pp. 214-15.

[18]Roy Medvedev, *Let History Judge: The Origins and Consequences of Stalinism*, New York 1973, p. 349.

[19]Antonov-Ovseenko, p. 344.

[20]Jean-Paul Sartre, 'Socialism in One Country', *New Left Review* no. 100, p. 150.

[21]Conquest, p. 479. [For a discussion of Solzhenitzyn's political evolution see Daniel Singer, *The Road to Gdansk*, New York 1981, pp. 19-60.]

[22]Issac Deutscher, *Stalin: A Political Biography*, New York 1967, p. 32.

[23]Deutscher, *The Unfinished Revolution: Russia 1917-1967*, London 1967. p. 34.

[24]Leon Trotsky, *The Revolution Betrayed*, London 1937, pp. 61-2.

[25]Ibid., p. 18.

[26]Ibid., p. 255.

[27]Ibid., p. 38.

[28]Deutscher, *The Prophet Outcast: Trotsky: 1929-1940*, London 1963, p. 95. Hereafter, PO.

[29]Ibid., p. 69.

[30]Ibid., p. 96.

[31]Ibid., pp. 67-8.

[32]Conquest, p. 26.

[33]Deutscher, *Stalin*, p. 568.

[34]Antonov-Ovseenko, p. 346.

[35]Paul Avrich, *The Russian Anarchists*, Princeton 1967, p. 228.

[36]Stephen F. Cohen, *Bukharin and the Bolshevik Revolution: A Political Biography*, 1888-1938, Oxford 1980, p. 106.

[37]Leonard Schapiro, *The Communist Party of the Soviet Union*, New York 1964, p. 204.

[38]Ibid., p. 206.

[39]See Paul Avrich ed., *The Anarchists in the Russian Revolution*, Ithaca, N. Y. 1973, pp. 158-9.

[40]Deutscher, *The Prophet Armed: Trotsky 1879-1921*, London 1954, pp. 518-19. Hereafter, PA.

[41]Deutscher, *The Prophet Unarmed: Trotsky: 1921-1929*, New York 1958, p. 5. Hereafter, PU.

[42]V. I. Lenin, 'Speech ... Dedicated to the Third Anniversary of the October Revolution, 6 November 1920', *Collected Works*, vol. 31, Moscow 1966, p. 399. David Rousset calls this outlook the 'ABC of Leninism'; see *The Legacy of the Bolshevik Revolution*, p. 90. See also E. H. Carr, *A History of Soviet Russia: Socialism in One Country 1924-1926*, vol. 1. Baltimore 1970, p. 107.

[43]Carr, Ibid., p. 115.

[44]Ibid., p. 149.

[45]Deutscher, PA, pp. 508-9.

[46]See Rousset, pp. 37-73.

[47]Moshe Lewin, *Lenin's Last Struggle*, New York 1968, p. 3.

[48]Roger Pethybridge, *The Social Prelude to Stalinism*, New York 1974, p. 8.

[49]Lewin, pp. 16–17.

[50]Ibid., p. 16.

[51]Ibid., pp. 18–19.

[52]Deutscher, *PA*, p. 516.

[53]Peter Arshinov, *History of the Makhnovist Movement 1918-1932*, Detroit 1974, p. 268.

[54]Deutscher, *PU*, p. 9.

[55]Arshinov, p. 37.

[56]Rousset, p. 37. For a balanced and detailed discussion of the rise and fall of workers' control, see Carmen Sirianni, *Workers Control and Socialist Democracy*, London 1982.

[57]V.I. Lenin, *What is to be Done, Selected Works*, vol. 1, Moscow, 1970, p. 143.

[58]Ibid., p. 213.

[59]Herbert Marcuse, *Soviet Marxism: A Critical Analysis*, New York 1961, p. 17.

[60]V. I. Lenin, *State and Revolution, Selected Works*, vol. 2, p. 376.

[61]Ibid., p. 392.

[62]*What Is to Be Done*, pp. 231–32.

[63]*State and Revolution*, p, 271.

[64]Deutscher, *PU*, pp. 14–15.

[65]Pethybridge, p. 37.

[66]Ibid., p. 35.

[67]Ibid., p. 8.

[68]Deutscher, *PU*, p. 139.

[69]Ibid., p. 14.

[70]V. I. Lenin, 'Report . . . to the Tenth Party Congress', Selected Works, vol. 3, p. 569.

[71]V. I. Lenin, 'Report . . . to the Eleventh Party Congress', Selected Works, vol. 3, p. 693

[72]Lucio Colletti, 'The Question of Stalin', Robin Blackburn ed., *Revolution and Class Struggle: A Reader in Marxist Politics*, Sussex 1978, p. 179.

[73]Sartre, 'Socialism in One Country', p. 152.

[74]Ibid., p. 160.

[75]Ibid., p. 148.

[76]Ibid., p. 161.

[77]Lewin, *Lenin's Last Struggle*, p. 136.

[78]Deutscher, *PO*, p. 271.

[79]Ibid., p. 272.

[80]Deutscher, *PU*, p. 315.

[81]David Rousset sees in the political shifts only analogues of the root economic change—restoring capitalism and severing the proletariat at work in the factory from the proletariat managing their labour. I think Rousset's approach too deductive; he does not give a proper weight to the ways in which the state became autonomous. Theda Scokpol has better appreciated this phenomenon in *States and Social Revolution*, Cambridge, 1979.

[82]Leon Trotsky, *The Real Situation in Russia*, New York 1928, p. 24.

[83]Deutscher, *PU*, pp. 274–5.

[84]*Trotsky, The Real Situation in Russia*, p. 115.

[85]Deutscher, *PA*, p. 96.

[86]Ibid., p. 132.

[87]Deutscher, *PO*, pp. 170–1.

[88]Leon Trotsky, *The Stalin School of Falsification*, New York 1938, pp. 89–99.

[89]Deutscher, *PU*, p. 303-4.

[90]R. W. Davies, *The Socialist Offensive: The Collectivization of Soviet Agriculture,* 1929-1930, London 1980, p. 382.

[91]Cohen, *Bukharin*, p. 266.

[92]Moshe Lewin, *Russian Peasants and Soviet Power: A Study of Collectivization,* Evanston, Illinois 1968, p. 462.

[93]E. H. Carr and R. W. Davies, *A History of Soviet Russia: Foundations of a Planned Economy 1926-1929*, vol. I-1, New York 1969, p. 327.

[94]Roy Medvedev, *The October Revolution*, New York 1979, pp. 177-87.

[95]Carr and Davies, I-1, p. 327.

[96]Davies, ch. 1, See p. 10.

[97]Carr and Davies, I-1, p. 218.

[98]Deutscher, *PO*, p. 96.

[99]Carr and Davies, I-1, p. 217.

[100]Lewin, *Russian Peasants*, p. 460.

[101] Lewin, 'The Social Background of Stalinism', in Robert C. Tucker ed., *Stalinism: Essays in Historical Interpretation*, New York 1977, p. 122.

[102]Davies, p. 52.

[103]E. H. Carr, *A History of Soviet Russia: Foundations of a Planned Economy* 1926-1929, vol. 2, New York 1971, p. 179.

[104]Carr and Davies, I-1, p. 264.

[105]Ibid., p. 265.

[106]Cohen, *Bukharin*, p., 296.

[107]Deutscher, *Stalin*, p. 324.

[108]Cohen, *Bukharin*, p. 303.

[109]Deutscher, *Stalin*, p. 328.

[110]Cohen, *Bukharin*, p. 248.

[111]Rousset, ch. 7-8.

[112]Bruce R. Franklin, ed., *The Essential Stalin*, Garden City, New York 1973, p. 257.

[113]Nettl, pp. 134-5.

[114]Lewin, *Russian Peasants*, p. 445

[115]See Ibid., pp. 41-80 and 'Conclusion'.

[116]Ibid., p. 460

[117]Roy Medvedev, *On Stalin and Stalinism*, Oxford 1979, pp. 73-4.

[118]Deutscher, *Stalin*, pp. 321-2.

[119]Robert C. Tucker and Stephen F. Cohen eds., *The Great Purge Trial*, New York 1965, p. 657.

[120]*The Great Purge Trial*, pp. 687-88.

[121]Antonov-Ovseenko estimates that 500,000 were involved.

[122]Ibid., pp. 272-96.

[123]Nikita Khrushchev, *The Anatomy of Terror*, Washington 1956, p. 34.

[124]Alec Nove, *Was Stalin Really Necessary?*, London 1964, p. 27.

[125]Medvedev, *Let History Judge*, p. 564.

[126]See, for example: Nove, Khrushchev, Cohen, Medvedev.

[127]Franklin presents this position in his introduction.

[128]See Adam Ulam, *The Bolsheviks: The Intellectual and Political History of The Triumph of Communism in Russia*, New York 1965.

[129]Cohen, 'Bolshevism and Stalinism', in *Stalinism*, p. 12.

[130]To be sure, David Rousset, in a *reducto ad absurdum* of Marxist derivation of politics from socio-economic structures, insists on the socio-economic source of the worst excesses of the Terror. No doubt they achieved a vital function (see his ch. 13), but were their sources entirely economic?.

[131]Jean-Paul Sartre, Critique de la raison dialectique, II (Manuscript), p. 432.

132Ibid., p. 445.

133Nove, pp. 24–5.

134Deutscher, *Stalin*, p. 328.

135Nove, p. 29.

136See his introduction to *The Great Purge Trial*.

137Medvedev, *Let History Judge*, pp. 324–5.

138Ibid., p. 326.

139Ibid., p. 313.

140Rousset traces the Soviet Union's legal structures, then and now, to the years of Terror. His point is to show that the Terror created today's structures and social relations. See his ch. 17–20.

141Medvedev, *Let History Judge*, p. 330.

142Franklin, p. 243.

143Ibid., pp. 367–8.

144Lewin, 'The Social Background of Stalinism', p. 113.

145Medvedev, *Let History Judge*, p. 356.

146Ibid., p. 351.

147Deutscher, *PO*, p. 346.

148Conquest, p. 485. Antonov-Ovseenko's estimates are even higher. See *The Time of Stalin*, pp. 205–13.

149Conquest., pp. 316–17.

150Ibid., p. 345.

151Ibid., p. 112.

152Ibid., p. 179.

153Quoted in Lewin, *Lenin's Last Struggle*, p. v.

154Deutscher, *PO*, p. 151.

155Quoted in Trotsky, *The Russian Revolution*, p. 223.

4. The Bourgeois-Democratic Holocaust: America's Vietnam

1Samuel 13:19-20, *The Prophets*, Philadelphia 1978, p. 126.

2Ibid., 17:4–8, p. 135

3Ibid., 17:24, p. 136.

4Ibid., 17:33, pp. 136–7.

5Ibid., 17:8–9, p. 135.

6Ibid., 17:40–1, p. 137.

7Ibid., 17:41–2, p. 137.

8Ibid., 17:45, p. 137.

9Ibid., 17:49–51, p. 138.

10The opposite argument is made by Norman Podhoretz, *Why We Were in Vietnam*, New York 1982; see especially the first and last chapters.

11For the history according to this analysis see James Pinckney Harrison, *The Endless War*, New York 1982.

12George C. Herring, *America's Longest War: The United States and Vietnam 1950-1975*, New York, 1979, p. 220.

13Like every aspect of the war, the estimates are debated. In his *America in Vietnam*, Gunter Lewy relies on official American sources to arrive at his estimate of slightly over one million killed (New York 1978, p. 453); James Pinckney Harrison apparently uses Vietnamese estimates of over 1.7 million. See his *Endless War*, p. 301.

14Leslie Gelb, *The Irony of Vietnam: The System Worked*, Washington 1979, see especially Introduction, ch. 13.

316   (pp. 142-147)

15Noam Chomsky and Edward S. Herman, *After the Cataclysm: Postwar Indochina and the Reconstruction of American Ideology; The Political Economy of Human Rights*, vol. II, Boston 1979, pp. 7-11.

16See for example James Fallows' review of Norman Podhoretz, *Why We Were in Vietnam*, New York Times Book Review, 28 March 1982, p. 7.

17Noam Chomsky, *Towards A New Cold War: Essays on the Current Crisis and How We Got There*, New York 1982, especially Introduction, ch. 3-4.

18See below, ch. 7.

19Major General Nguyen Duy Hinh and Brigadier General Tran Dinh Tho, *The South Vietnamese Society*, Washington 1980, p. 135.

20Ibid.

21Douglas Pike, *Viet Cong: The Organization and Techniques of The National Liberation Front of South Vietnam*, Cambridge, Mass. 1966, p. 58.

22Ibid., p. 29. See also an earlier discussion in Phillipe Devillers, 'Ngo Dinh Diem and the Struggle for Reunification in Vietnam' in Marvin E. Gettleman ed., *Vietnam: History, Documents and Opinions on a Major World Crisis*, Greenwich, Conn. 1965, p. 211.

23This dimension of the first Indochina war is made clear by Jeffrey Race, *War Comes to Long An: Revolutionary Conflict in a Vietnamese Province*, Berkeley 1972, pp. 3-43.

24The early history of this process, reaching back into the 1920s, shows how the Communist Party became the dominant nationalist forces. See Part One of Harrison, and ch. 1-7 of William J. Duiker, *The Communist Road to Power in Vietnam*, Boulder, Colo, 1981.

25Ibid. Subsequent studies discuss various aspects of the superior vitality, intelligence, courage and commitment of the Viet Cong. See for example John T. McAlister, Jr. and Paul Mus, *The Vietnamese and Their Revolution*, New York 1970, Frances FitzGerald, *Fire in the Lake* (see below), and Paul Berman, *Revolutionary Organization*, Lexington, Mass. 1974. All writers agree, in Berman's words, that '[t]he genius of the Communist Model in Vietnam was its ability to create a revolutionary organization that reflected the past even as it attempted to reshape the future. (p. 207). That is, the Communists alone were able to transform the traditional Vietnamese outlook into the pointing towards independence and modernization. See also Duiker, p. 324.

26Race, p. 189.

27Ibid., p. 20.

28Ibid., p. 32.

29Ibid., p. 47.

30Ibid., p. 68.

31Ibid., p. 19.

32Ibid., p. 41.

33Ibid., p. 5.

34Ibid., p. 42.

35Ibid.,

36Harrison estimates that they controlled up to 60 per cent of the territory and one third the population. See his discussion, pp. 98-129.

37Race details who was left and who regrouped, pp. 32-7.

38Generals Hinh and Tho address Diem's efforts to remove the French presence, pp. 34-6.

39Frances FitzGerald, *Fire In The Lake: The Vietnamese and The Americans in Vietnam*, New York 1972, ch. 3.

40Robert Scheer, 'The Genesis of United States Support For Ngo Dinh Diem, in

Gettleman, p. 251.

⁴¹See FitzGerald, ch. 1.

⁴²Norman Podhoretz is the outstanding current example. See his defence of 'containment' in ch. 2 of *Why We Were in Vietnam*.

⁴³Pike, pp. 71–3; see also Wesley Fishel, 'Vietnam's Democratic One-Man Rule', in Gettleman, pp. 195–204.

⁴⁴Pike, p. 110.

⁴⁵Devillers, p. 234.

⁴⁶Fitzgerald, p. 320.

⁴⁷See the review by Dennis Duncanson, *Pacific Affairs*, Spring 1977.

⁴⁸Nguyen Cao Ky, *Twenty Years and Twenty Days*, New York 1978, p. 27.

⁴⁹Ibid., p. 45.

⁵⁰Ibid., p. 137.

⁵¹Ibid.

⁵²Nguyen Thi Dinh, *No Other Road to Take*, Ithaca, New York 1976, pp. 44–5.

⁵³Harrison, p. 20.

⁵⁴Nguyen Thi Dinh, p. 54.

⁵⁵Ibid., p. 55.

⁵⁶McAlister and Mus, p. 160.

⁵⁷Nguyen Cao Ky, p. 225.

⁵⁸Nguyen Hi Dinh, p. 77. To be sure, the Communist outlook does more than reflect the traditional Vietnamese outlook. Paul Berman argues that the 'revolutionary would appear to have an identity quite different from that of the peasant in the village settings. Critical dimensions of the Vietnamese model personality would have had to have been transformed: rather than acceptance of nature, there is mastery over fate; rather than denial of emotion, there is hate, enthusiasm, zealotry; rather than political apathy, there is politicization; rather than self-fulfilment, there is self-sacrifice; rather than devotion to the family, there is commitment to the organization.' (p. 87). See also footnote 25 above.

⁵⁹Samuel Huntington, 'The Bases of Accommodation', *Foreign Affairs*, June 1968, quoted in Harrison, p. 195.

⁶⁰Estimated at 15,000 by the New York Times, 25,000 by its organizers.

⁶¹Herring, p. 125.

⁶²*The Pentagon Papers: The Defence Department History of US Decision making on Vietnam* (The Senator Gravel Edition); vol. III, Boston 1971, p. 153.

⁶³Ibid.

⁶⁴Ibid., p. 315.

⁶⁵Ibid., p. 689.

⁶⁶Ibid., p. 316.

⁶⁷The quote is from Taylor, Gelb, p. 119. See also Herring, pp. 126–31.

⁶⁸Herring, p. 130.

⁶⁹*Pentagon Papers*, vol. III, Boston 1971 p. 309.

⁷⁰*Pentagon Papers*, II, p. 321.

⁷¹Ibid., pp. 343–8.

⁷²*Pentagon Papers*, III, p. 311.

⁷³See William Darryl Henderson, *Why the Vietcong Fought: A Study of Motivation and Control in a Modern Army in Combat*, Westport, Conn. 1979, ch. 3.

⁷⁴See Race, p. 208.

⁷⁵Podhoretz's attempt to revive the justification for the war was based, from beginning to end, on the claim of a Northern invasion.

⁷⁶Gelb, p. 110.

⁷⁷*Pentagon Papers*, II, p. 204.

[78]*Pentagon Papers*, III, p. 314, Gelb, p. 119.

[79]See George Herring's discussion of the military and domestic political miscalculations, pp. 143-44.

[80]Wilfred Burchett quotes as Kissinger's cable to Nixon on 13 October 1972: 'We've been doublecrossed. Bomb! Bomb! Bomb!' He claims this text is 'known in well-informed journalistic circles'; *Grasshoppers and Elephants: Why Vietnam Fell*, New York 1977, p. 169.

[81]Herring, p. 249.

[82]See Harrison, p. 288.

[83]*Pentagon Papers*, IV, p. 420.

[84]Noam Chomsky, *For Reasons of State*, New York 1973, pp. 70-87.

[85]For a presentation of the concept see Harrison, pp. 159-68.

[86]FitzGerald, p. 344.

[87]Chomsky, *For Reasons of State*, p. 78.

[88]See, for example, Harrison's discussion of Operation Cedar Falls, p. 262.

[89]Quoted in Herring, p. 189.

[90]Gunther Lewy, and following him, Podhoretz, minimize the damage. See Chomsky's review of Lewy in chapter 5 of *Towards a New Cold War*.

[91]Harrison, p. 115.

[92]Quoted from the *Dictionary of US Military Terms* in Raphael Littauer and Norman Uphoff eds., *The Air War in Indochina*, revised edn, Boston 1972, p. 18.

[93]Harrison, p. 255.

[94]Ibid, p. 339.

[95]The North Vietnamese estimate was 55,000 tons, cited by Burchett, p. 167; the American estimate was 36,000 tons, cited by Herring, p. 248.

[96]Littauer and Uphoff, p. 86; Harrison, p. 301.

[97]Littauer and Uphoff, p. 95.

[98]Ibid., p. 249.

[99]Quoted in Noam Chomsky, *At War with Asia*, New York 1970, pp. 54-5.

[100]Harrison, pp. 301-4.

[101]Littauer and Uphoff, p. 63.

[102]Ibid., p. 93.

[103]Yehuda Bauer, *The Holocaust in Historical Perspective*, p. 35.

[104]Senator Fulbright's description, quoted in a striking comment by T.D. Allman, Chomsky and Herman, p. 8.

[105]Jean-Paul Sartre, 'On Genocide', John Duffet ed., *Against The Crime of Silence; Proceedings of The Russell International War Crimes Tribunal*, New York 1968, p. 617.

[106]For example, the Fallows review of Podhoretz cited above.

[107]Gunter Lewy devotes a section of *America in Vietnam* to attacking the 'War Crimes Industry' and another to refuting the charge of genocide.

[108]Robert Jay Lifton, *Home from The War: Vietnam Veterans: Neither Victims nor Executioners*, New York 1983, p. 65.

[109]Ibid., pp. 42-3.

[110]Ibid., p. 44.

[111]FitzGerald, p. 375.

[112]Lifton, p. 45.

[113]FitzGerald, p. 369.

[114]Estimates differ as to how many were killed. See Lifton, pp. 62-3; Harrison, p. 194.

[115]Lifton, p. 50.

[116]Harrison (p. 194) cites a list of some thirty massacres between 1965 and 1969.

[117]FitzGerald, p. 83.

[118]Ibid., p. 346.

[119]Ibid., p. 317.

[120]Ibid., p. 348.

[121]See Harrison, pp. 120-2, pp. 243-5.

[122]Fitzgerald, p. 384.

[123]Ibid., p. 353.

[124]Ibid., p. 349.

[125]Michael Walzer, 'Comment', *Dissent*, Spring 1965, pp. 155-6.

[126]Chomsky and Kolko both recognized it but did not draw their sense of the policy's gross irrationality into the heart of their analysis.

[127]Leon Trotsky, *The Russian Revolution*, Garden City, 1959, p. 4.

[128]Karl Marx and Frederick Engels, *Manifesto of the Communist Party, Collected Works*, vol. 6, New York 1976, pp. 487-8.

[129]Joyce and Gabriel Kolko, *The Limits of Power: The World and United States Foreign Policy, 1945-1954*, New York 1972, p. 710.

[130]Ibid., p. 11.

[131]Heilbroner, p. 44.

[132]Gelb, p. 240.

[133]Doris Kearns, *Lyndon Johnson and The American Dream*, New York 1975, p. 263.

[134]Kearns, p. 26.

[135]Herring, p. 220.

[136]Podhoretz, p. 197.

[137]Gabriel Kolko, 'Summary of a Historical Report', Duffet, p. 63.

[138]Kearns, p. 260.

[139]Ibid., p. 329.

[140]Ibid., p. 331.

[141]Kolko, 'The American Goals in Vietnam', *Pentagon Papers*, V.

[142]Druiker, p. 262.

[143]Ibid., pp. 262-3, p. 290.

[144]Ibid., pp. 303-4.

[145]Captured documents validate the central role, from a very early date, of North Vietnam, and thus decisively resolve an old argument. Having studied the documents, Druiker attempts to place the relations betweem the DRV and NLF in perspective by concluding that 'the insurgency was a genuine revolt based in the South, but it was organized and directed from the North.' (p. 198).

[146]Harrison, p. 19.

[147]See Herring, p. 224.

[148]Druiker explores the tensions felt by the Communists between a political and a military emphasis. See pp. 240-265.

[149]Truong Nhu Tang, 'The Myth of a Liberation', *The New York Review of Books*, 21 October 1982, p. 36.

[150]Truong Nhu Tang, p. 35.

[151]Harrison, p. 301.

[152]Ibid.

[153]Don Luce, 'Making Vietnam "Feel Pain"', *The Nation*, 27 March 1982, p. 363.

[154]See William Shawcross, *Side-Show: Kissinger, Nixon and the Destruction of Cambodia*, New York 1979, ch. 24.

[155]Chomsky and Herman, pp. 10-17.

[156]Harrison, p. 314.

[157]'Do the recent events in Cambodia warrant a reconsideration of our opposition to

320   (pp. 186-211)

the Vietnam War?' was the organizing question of a 1978 symposium in *Dissent*. The participants, Noam Chomsky, Hans Morgenthau, and Michael Walzer all agreed, in Morgenthau's words that 'the moral case for resistance to the Vietnam War has not been impaired, but rather strengthened, by the catastrophe that has befallen Cambodia.' (Fall 1978, p. 390).

5. Afterword to Catastrophe, Preface to Hope

[1]Jean-Paul Sartre, *Critique of Dialectical Reason*, London 1976, p. 132.
[2]*The Communist Manifesto*, p. 488.
[3]Moore, *Social Origins of Dictatorship and Democracy*, p. 30.
[4]See Shlomo Avineri, *Karl Marx on Colonialism and Modernization*, New York 1968, esp. Introduction and p. 439.
[5]Leon Trotsky, *The History of the Russian Revolution*, London 1967, vol.I, p. 23.
[6]Ibid., p. 22.
[7]See the recent re-examination of the literature by Ronald Grigor Suny, 'Toward a Social History of the October Revolution', *The American Historical Review*, vol. 88, no. 1, February 1983.
[8]Karl Marx, Preface to the First German Edition of *Captial*, Moscow 1961, pp. 8-9.
[9]Marx, *The Poverty of Philosophy*. *Collected Works*, vol. 6, p. 166.
[10]Jean-Paul Sartre, foreward to R. D. Laing and D. G. Cooper, *Reason and Violence*, London 1964, p. 7.
[11]*The Communist Manifesto*; p. 489.
[12]Lewis Mumford, *The Myth of the Machine*: vol. II. *The Pentagon of Power*, New York 1970, p.168.
[13]Ibid., pp. 171-2.
[14]Ibid., pp. 253-8.
[15]Edmund Stillman and William Pfaff, *The Politics of Hysteria*, New York 1964, p. 249.
[16]Max Horkheimer, *Eclipse of Reason*, New York 1947, pp. 108-9.
[17]The phrase is from André Glucksmann; *The Master Thinkers*, New York 1980.
[18]Horkheimer, p. 94.
[19]Ibid., p. 119.
[20]Ibid., pp. 119-120.
[21]Ibid., p. 120.
[22]Ibid., pp. 120-1.
[23]Bloch, 'Nonsynchronism and the Obligation to its Dialectics', p. 26.
[24]Once we pass beyond Hitler, we find few such examples of absolute Evil, and encounter instead the more confusing realities of good-and-evil intermingled. Which is why Stalin, even today, receives and deserves both respect and detestation; why anticommunism can be both so regressive and so accurate; why capitalism can be correctly seen as both brutally exploitative and humane and democratic; why Zionism can be treated both as the great pride of a great people and a latter-day form of colonialism. Once we pass Hitler, the path through the century becomes morally, intellectually and emotionally more complex. We strain to apply concepts and labels drawn from that struggle of light against darkness in the grey world in which we mostly live.
[25]Viktor E. Frankl, *Man's Search for Meaning: An Introduction to Logotherapy*, New York 1963, p. 132.
[26]Dawidowicz, *The War against the Jews*, p. 459.
[27]Ibid., p. 447.
[28]Frankl, p. 105.
[29]The argument is developed and criticized in my *Jean-Paul Sartre—Philosophy in*

the World, London 1981, pp. 76-7.

[30]Karl Marx. 'Theses on Feuerbach', in *Early Writings*, Harmondsworth 1977.

[31]Harold Fletcher, *Rescue in Denmark*, New York 1963.

[32]'The Revolt in the Death-Camp, Treblinka', *Dos Neie Lehen*, Lodz, 10 May 1945, p. 8; in Yuri Suhl ed., *They Fought Back: The Story of the Jewish Resistance in Nazi Europe*, New York 1975, p. 133.

[33]Samuel Rajzman, 'Uprising in Treblinka', ibid., p. 131.

[34]Jean-François Steiner, *Treblinka*, New York 1967.

6. Zionism and the Palestinians

[1]See Ephraim Kishon's 'apocalyptic appeal' for an Israeli nuclear deterrent cited in David Hirst, *The Gun and the Olive Branch: The Roots of Violence in the Middle East*, New York 1977, pp. 350-1. The case for an Israeli nuclear strategy is put by Shai Feldman, *Israeli Nuclear Deterrent: A Strategy for the 80s*, New York 1982.

[2]Herbert Marcuse, *One-Dimensional Man: Studies in the Ideology of Advanced Industrial Society*, Boston 1964, p. 220.

[3]Simha Flapan, *Zionism and the Palestinians*, London 1979, p. 13.

[4]Ian Lustick, *Arabs in the Jewish State: Israel's Control of a National Minority*, Austin, Texas 1980, p. 311.

[5]Ibid., p. 177.

[6]Ibid., p. 246.

[7]Noam Chomsky, *Towards a New Cold War: Essays on the Current Crisis and How We Got There*, New York 1982, p. 51.

[8]Maxime Rodinson, *Israel: A Colonial-Settler State?*, New York 1973.

[9]Arthur Hertzberg, *The Zionist Idea: A Historical Analysis and Reader*, New York 1970, p. 222.

[10]Ibid., p. 219.

[11]Ibid., p. 209.

[12]See for example the brilliant analysis by Nahman Syrkin in Hertzberg, pp. 337-44.

[13]Theodor Herzl, *The Jewish State*, in Hertzberg, p. 225-6.

[14]Walter Laqueur, *A History of Zionism*, New York 1972, pp. 126-9.

[15]Shlomo Avineri, *The Making of Modern Zionism: The Intellectual Origins of the Jewish State*, New York 1981, p. 13.

[16]Ibid., p. 5.

[17]Ibid., p. 9.

[18]Ibid., p. 13.

[19]David Ben-Gurion, *Memoirs*, Cleveland 1970, pp. 25-26.

[20]Avineri, p. 122.

[21]Edward Said, *The Question of Palestine*, New York 1980, p. 95.

[22]See, for example, the 1940 statement by Joseph Weitz, director of the Jewish National Fund. Ibid., pp. 99-103.

[23]Laqueur, pp. 270-337; See Aaron David Gordon's writings in Hertzberg (pp. 368-387); see also Avineri, pp. 125-54.

[24]Aharon Cohen tells the story of the struggle for an acceptable settlement between Jews and Arabs in *Israel and the Arab World*, abridged edn, Boston 1976.

[25]See Syrkin and Ber Borochov in Hertzberg, pp. 330-66.

[26]Joseph Neyer, 'The Myth of Zionist 'Original Sin': A Few Historical Notes', Irving Howe and Carl Gershman, *Israel, The Arabs and The Middle East*, New York 1972, p. 142.

[27]Marie Syrkin, 'The Palestinian Refugees: Resettlement. Repatriation, or Restora-

tion' ibid., p. 177.

[28]Avineri, pp. 204-9.
[29]A. W. Kayyali, *Palestine: A Modern History*, London n.d., p. 230.
[30]Laqueur, p. 209.
[31]Kayyali, p. 95.
[32]Laqueur, p. 246. This is confirmed by Joel Beinen's 'The Palestine Communist Party 1919-48', *Merip Reports*, No. 55.
[33]Flapan, p. 83.
[34]A. B. Yehoshua, *Between Right and Right*, Garden City, New York 1981, p. 79.
[35]Ibid., p. 84.
[36]Ibid., p. 101; emphasis in original.
[37]Flapan, p. 83.
[38]Syrkin, p. 182.
[39]Said, p. xliii.
[40]All are presented, for example, in Frank Gervasi, *The Case for Israel*, New York 1967.
[41]Even the fact of a generation of native-born Israelis living in their country is not a compelling world-historical claim. In many eyes it simply recalls the claims of many even more deeply-entrenched European settlers of Algeria, Mozambique and Angola who were physically displaced as those countries were reclaimed by their original inhabitants.
[42]Emil L. Fackenheim, *The Jewish Return into History: Reflections in the Age of Auschwitz and a New Jerusalem*, New York 1978, p. 174.
[43]Ibid., p.. 282.
[44]Laqueur, pp. 215-16.
[45]Ibid., p. 595.
[46]I. F. Stone, *Underground to Palestine*, New York 1946.
[47]Yehoshua, p. 79.
[48]See Avineri, p. 45.
[49]Ibid., p. 122.
[50]Shlomo Avineri, 'Territory and Security', *The Jerusalem Post International Edition*, 26 September—2 October 1982, p. 11.
[51]Menachem Begin, *The Revolt*, Los Angeles 1972, p. 60.
[52]Avineri, 'Territory and Security'; p. 11.
[53]Amos Kenan, 'Smothering Israel', *The New York Times*, 26 October 1982, p. 19.
[54]Lustick analyses a policy of 'segmentation', 'dependence', and 'cooptation'; see pp. 82-231.
[55]Avineri, *The Making of Modern Zionism*, p. 182.

7. Technological Madness

[1]Richard Falk, 'Political Anatomy of Nuclearism', in Robert Jay Lifton and Richard Falk, *Indefensible Weapons: The Political and Psychological Case Against Nuclearism*, New York 1982, p.212.
[2]Jonathan Schell, *The Fate of the Earth*, New York 1982, p. 182.
[3]Ibid., p. 43.
[4]Edward Thompson, 'Notes on Exterminism, The Last Stage of Civilization', In New Left Review ed., *Exterminism and Cold War*, London 1982, pp. 27-8.
[5]Schell, p. 139.
[6]Robert Jay Lifton, 'Imagining the Real', *Indefensible Weapons*, pp. 13-22.
[7]Ibid., p. 107.
[8]Herman Kahn, *Thinking about the Unthinkable*, London 1962, pp. 102-3.
[9]Ibid., p. 107.

[10]Herman Kahn, *On Thermonuclear War*, Princeton 1960, pp. 40–95.

[11]*Thinking about the Unthinkable*, p. 102.

[12]Ibid., p. 101.

[13]Eugene Rostow in Robert Scheer, *With Enough Shovels: Reagan, Bush and Nuclear War*, New York 1982, p. 101.

[14]Committee on the Present Danger, Scheer, p. 48.

[15]See interviews in Scheer with Warnke, MacNamara, Vance, York, Bethe.

[16]Lifton, p. 47.

[17]Ibid., p. 49.

[18]Ibid., p. 68.

[19]For a development of these themes see Ronald Santoni, 'Nuclear Madness', Israel Chary and Shamni Davidson, *The Book of the International Conference on the Holocaust and Genocide, Book Two: Towards Understanding, Intervention and Prevention of Genocide*, Tel Aviv 1984.

[20]E. P. Thompson, A Letter to Americans', Thompson and Dan Smith ed., *Protest and Survive*, New York 1981, p. 37.

[21]Louis René Beres, *Apocalypse: Nuclear Catastrophe in World Politics*, Chicago 1980, p. 7.

[22]Scheer, p. 121.

[23]Lifton, p. 7.

[24]Thompson, 'Notes on Exterminism', p. 20

[25]Ibid., pp. 20–21.

[26]For a discussion of the early nuclear war decisions, as well as the decisions at each stage in the development of nuclear power, see Peter Pringle and James Spigelmen, *The Nuclear Barons*, New York 1981.

[27]Alan Wolfe, *The Rise and Fall of the 'Soviet Threat': Domestic Sources of the Cold War Consensus*, Washington 1979.

[28]A striking example is the remark to Scheer by Assistant Secretary of State Richard Burt that 'SALT was a favour to the Russians' because it conceded 'their arrival as a co-equal superpower' (p. 95).

[29]Rudolf Bahro, 'A New Approach for the Peace Movement in Germany', *Exterminism and Cold War*, p. 96.

[30]Thompson, p. 20.

[31]Daniel Ellsberg, Introduction to *Protest and Survive*, p. 1.

[32]Falk, pp. 178–180.

[33]Lifton, p. 108.

[34]Dr. Lynn Campbell, 'Nuclear Madness—Causes and Effects', Lecture at Lafayette Clinic, Detroit, 6 August 1982.

[35]Lifton, p. 102.

[36]Robert Kennedy, *Thirteen Days: A Memoir of the Cuban Missile Crisis*, New York 1969, p. 38.

[37]Ibid., p. 23.

[38]Note by Theodore Sorenson at the end of ibid., p. 128.

[39]Ibid., pp. 105–6.

[40]Ibid., p. 89.

[41]Ibid., p. 95.

[42]Ibid., p. 67.

[43]Falk, p. 229.

[44]John Somerville, *The Crisis: The True Story about How the World Almost Ended*, San Diego, California 1976, p. 56.

[45]Kennedy, p. 109.

[46]Somerville, p. 62.

[47]Falk, p. 151.

[48]Thompson, p. 23.

[49]See my *Jean-Paul Sartre: Philosophy in the World*, III, ch. 4 and my 'Sartre's Turning Point: *The Unfinished Critique de la raison dialectique, Volume Two*', Paul Arthur Schilpp ed., *The Philosophy of Jean-Paul Sartre*, LaSalle, Illinois, 1981.

[50]Falk, p. 226.

[51]Thompson, p. 15.

[52]Schell, p. 195.

[53]Ibid., p. 197.

[54]Ibid., p. 201.

[55]Kahn, *Thinking about the Unthinkable*, p. 111.

[56]Schell, p. 204. See also Kahn, *On Thermonuclear War*, pp. 181-5. But for Kahn's reservations see ibid., pp. 155-9.

[57]Falk, p. 171.

[58]Ibid., p. 220.

[59]Ibid., p. 223.

[60]Ibid., pp. 183-4.

[61]Ibid., p. 219.

[62]Ibid., p. 43.

[63]Ibid., p. 185.

[64]Ibid., see also Noam Chomsky, 'Strategic Arms, the Cold War and the Third World', *Exterminism and Cold War*, p. 235.

[65]Lifton, p. 75.

[66]Ibid., p. 32.

[67]Falk, p. 167.

[68]Bahro, p. 90.

[69]Ibid., p. 87.

[70]Ibid., pp. 87-8.

[71]Ibid., pp. 88-9.

[72]David F. Noble, *America by Design: Science, Technology, and the Rise of Corporate Capitalism*, New York 1977, p. xvii.

[73]Ibid., p. 3.

[74]Ibid., p. xxv.

[75]Marcuse, *One-Dimensional Man*, p. 32.

[76]Ibid., p. 166.

[77]Noble, p. 321.

[78]Bahro, p. 89.

[79]Ibid., p. 88.

[80]Karl von Clausewitz, *On War*, Princeton 1976, p. 149.

[81]Ibid., p. 605.

[82]Ibid.

[83]Schell, pp. 188-9.

[84]Clausewitz, p. 90.

[85]See Jeremy Seabrook, *What Went Wrong?*, New York 1978.

[86]Leiss, p. 79.

[87]Ibid., p. 86.

[88]Ibid., p. 96.

[89]William Ophuls, *Ecology and the Politics of Scarcity*, San Francisco 1977, pp. 184-91.

[90]Those controls over and above those indispensable for civilized human association, arising from specific institutions of domination. Herbert Marcuse, *Eros and Civilization: A Philosophical Inquiry into Freud*, Boston 1966, p. 37.

91Ibid., p. 136.
92Ibid., p. 143.
93Leiss, p. 198.
94Raymond Williams, 'The Politics of Nuclear Disarmament', *Exterminism and Cold War*, p. 69.
95Ibid.
96*The Communist Manifesto*, p. 496.

8. Lessons of the Present: Hope and Action Today

1Marcuse, *One-Dimensional Man*, p. 257.

2Thomas Mann, *Doctor Faustus: The Life of the German Composer Adrian Leverkühn as Told by a Friend*, New York 1948, p. 491.

3See my 'Dear Herbert', George Fischer ed., *The Revival of American Socialism*, New York 1971.

4Marcuse reconsidered this conclusion, of course, in *An Essay on Liberation* (Boston 1966) and then again in *The Aesthetic Dimension* (1977).

5Plato, *The Republic*, F.M. Cornford trans., London 1941, VII: 519-21; pp. 233-6.

6Jean-Paul Sartre, *Being and Nothingness*, New York 1957, p. 554.

7'Burnout' seems to be accompanied by despair at failing to achieve anything significant. Is the problem a lack of effectiveness or of knowing how to evaluate and recognize effectiveness?

8Sartre speaks of 'the joyful surprise which all assembled demonstrators feel when, on the occasion of a demonstration which has been forbidden by the police, they see individuals and small groups converging from every direction, *more numerous than they had expected*, and representing hope to everyone.' (*Critique of Dialectical Reason*, p. 375)

9Sartre has described the revolutionary process of 'the liquidation of an inert seriality' of separated individuals and its transformation into a 'fused group' with a common praxis. See pp. 351-404.

10Daniel Cohn-Bendit, *Obsolete Communism: The Left-Wing Alternative*, New York 1969.

Index